JUDGE,
LAWYER,
VICTIM,
THIEF

NICOLE HAHN RAFTER

ELIZABETH ANNE STANKO

Judge
Lawyer
Victim
Thief

Women, Gender Roles, and Criminal Justice

NORTHEASTERN UNIVERSITY

Editors, Robilee Smith & Katherine Talmadge
Designer, Ann Schroeder

Northeastern University Press
Copyright ©1982 Nicole Rafter & Elizabeth Stanko

Library of Congress Cataloging in Publication Data

Main entry under title:

Judge, lawyer, victim, thief.

Includes bibliographical references and index.
Contents: Introduction / Nicole Hahn Rafter and
Elizabeth Ann Stanko—One hundred years of fear /
Elizabeth Anne Mills—Would you believe this
woman? / Elizabeth Ann Stanko—(etc.)
1. Sex discrimination in criminal justice
administration—United States—Addresses, essays,
lectures. 2. Women—United States—Crimes against
—Addresses, essays, lectures. 3. Female offenders
—United States—Addresses, essays, lectures.
4. Women prisoners—United States—Addresses,
essays, lectures. I. Rafter, Nicole Hahn,
1939-   II. Stanko, Elizabeth Anne, 1950-

HV6791.J83   364'.088042   82-2285
ISBN 0-930350-29-4   AACR2
ISBN 0-930350-45-6 (pap.)

Printed and bound by The Alpine Press,
Stoughton, Massachusetts. The paper is
Glatfelter Offset, an acid-free sheet.

Manufactured in the United States of America
89 88 87 86 85   6 5 4 3

Contents

Table of Contents

PART IV:
Women as Practitioners and Professionals

Preface

Our interest in the area of women and criminal justice is in large part a product of the process by which we developed professionally, though we came to explore the subject through different routes. Rafter's research on the history of the prison system alerted her to serious discrepancies between textbook assumptions about female prisoners of the past and the ways in which such women were actually treated; Stanko's work on prosecutorial screening stimulated her to question the criminal justice system's differential responses to men and women. As we each began to develop courses on women and crime, we became aware of the many gaps in the literature pertaining to women. And, as time went on, we each became more attuned to the wide spectrum of problems with which women involved in criminal justice must deal. Rafter became increasingly uncomfortable with her inability to answer questions about female criminal justice professionals brought to her by graduate students who, as workers in the field, encountered many situations not addressed in the literature. As a result of cofounding a shelter for battered women in Worcester, Massachusetts, Stanko gained first-hand knowledge about female victimization and became increasingly dissatisfied with the criminal justice response to it.

Out of these experiences grew the idea for a book that would analyze the treatment of women who come to the criminal justice system through a variety of routes—as victims, defendants, and workers in the field—and would look for commonalities among their problems. Interacting with students and searching for a way to explain similarities in the responses to female victims, offenders, and professionals, we were continually reminded that womanhood itself is the central focus of theory and practice in the field. Gender roles of women, we came to understand, powerfully affect the perception and reception of women at all levels in criminal justice. In this field as in American society as a whole, we concluded, gender stratification has far-reaching effects.

Thus, this collection of essays is a study of women as much as it is a study of criminal justice. We hope it will shed light on the situation of women in both criminal justice and American society as a whole.

viii

Preface

No project is ever completed without the assistance of others. We would like to take this opportunity to thank some of them. From the point of the book's conceptualization and throughout its development, our colleagues listened to and supported us. Among them Cynthia Enloe, Edith E. Flynn, David Greenberg, John Laub, Nicolette Parisi, and Joseph A. Zillo stand out. Charlotte Field and Lynn Olson helped immensely with the typing and many administrative chores. We benefitted greatly from our association with Robilee Smith of Northeastern University Press; her unique blend of sensitivity and professionalism taught us how to proceed through difficult moments. Kathy Talmadge, our copyeditor, helped us polish the final draft. Finally, to Robert Hahn for his help, resilience, and understanding and to Charley and Sarah Hahn for coping with this project's intrusion into their lives for so long, we owe a special debt of gratitude.

About the Contributors

PHYLLIS JO BAUNACH is a correctional research specialist at the National Institute of Justice in Washington, D.C. She received her doctorate in social psychology from the University of Minnesota; has worked in the Evaluation Unit of Minnesota's Crime Control Planning Board; and has taught criminal justice courses at the University of Minnesota, George Washington University, and the University of Maryland. During 1978 she was on sabbatical leave to the University of Maryland, conducting research on inmate mothers and their children. She has been appointed as an Executive Counselor to the Board of the American Society of Criminology for the 1981–82 year, and the American Association of University Women Educational Foundation has named her the recipient of their 1982 Young Scholar Award. She has published articles and chapters on women and crime, evaluation research, and participatory management, and recently coedited a volume on criminal justice models and findings. Her other research interests include restitution and community-based corrections.

CAROL FENSTER is a research associate for the Suburban Youth Project, Department of Sociology, University of Denver. She received her Ph.D. in 1979 from the University of Denver, where she was granted a Graduate Research Fellowship from the Law Enforcement Assistance Administration. Recent publications include "The Adjudication of Male Co-Defendants: An Application of Societal Reaction Theory," in *Courts and Diversion: Policy and Operations Studies*, edited by Patricia L. Brantingham and Thomas C. Blomberg, Sage Publications, 1979.

EDITH ELISABETH FLYNN, Ph.D., is a professor of criminal justice at Northeastern University, Boston. She is a member of Phi Beta Kappa; a National Science Foundation Fellow; Executive Counselor, American Society of Criminology; and a member of the Joint Commission on Criminology and Criminal Justice Standards. She is author of books and articles on criminology, criminal justice, and criminal justice planning, and has served as a consultant to federal, state, and local agencies throughout the country.

About the Contributors

DORIE KLEIN holds a doctorate in criminology from the University of California at Berkeley. She has been conducting research on battering, particularly on battering men and the role of alcohol, through the Alcohol Research Group, Berkeley. She has taught sociology in California, Oregon, and Washington, and has been active in women's studies. Her research on women and criminal justice has been published in *Crime and Delinquency, Crime and Social Justice,* and *Issues in Criminology.* She has also studied and worked in the field of drug abuse treatment and has long been active in radical sociology. Recently, she has become involved in the reproductive rights movement.

ANNE RANKIN MAHONEY is an associate professor in the Department of Sociology at the University of Denver with a specialty in sociology of law. She received her Ph.D. from Columbia University in 1970, where she was a Russell Sage Fellow in Law and Sociology, and her M.A. from Northwestern University. Recent publications include: "Gifted Delinquents: What Do We Know About Them?" in *Children and Youth Services Review,* 1980; "Sexism in Voir Dire: The Use of Sex Stereotypes in Jury Selection," in *Women in the Courts,* edited by W. Hepperle and L. Crites, National Center for State Courts, 1978; and "The Effects of Labeling Upon Youths in the Juvenile Justice System: A Review of the Evidence," in *Law and Society Review* 8 (Summer 1974).

ELIZABETH ANNE MILLS is a research analyst at the Crime and Justice Foundation, a private, nonprofit, criminal justice research and planning agency in Boston. She holds a Master of Science in criminal justice from Northeastern University, and her main areas of study are juvenile justice, women's rights, and other legal issues.

NICOLETTE PARISI has taught in the Department of Criminal Justice at Temple University. Prior to teaching criminal justice, she was Project Coordinator and Coeditor of the *Sourcebook of Criminal Justice Statistics* at the Criminal Justice Research Center in Albany, New York. She has also published several articles on sentencing alternatives.

NICOLE HAHN RAFTER teaches criminology at Northeastern University's College of Criminal Justice. She has published in several collections and in *The Atlantic Monthly, Crime and Delin-*

About the Contributors

quency, *Criminology*, and the *Tennessee Historical Quarterly*, among other journals. She is currently completing a history of prisons for women in the United States.

MARSHA ROSENBAUM is a research associate at the Institute for Scientific Analysis in San Francisco. She is currently principal investigator on a grant from the National Institute on Drug Abuse, entitled "Women on Methadone." Dr. Rosenbaum also teaches sociology at San Francisco State University. She has published several journal articles on women and drugs and is the author of *Women on Heroin*, published by Rutgers University Press in 1981.

CLAUDINE SCHWEBER is an assistant professor of criminal justice at the State University College at Buffalo, New York (SUC/Buffalo), teaching at the graduate and undergraduate levels. She has written extensively on women and crime, testified before the United States House of Representatives on the problems of women prisoners, and worked with the National Archives in the 1981 FBI records lawsuit. She has won several Criminal Justice Mini-Grants from SUC/ Buffalo, fellowships from the National Endowment for the Humanities, and internships with the Institute for Educational Leadership. She is a member of Phi Beta Kappa as well as several professional associations. Since 1978 Dr. SchWeber has been a consultant with the Research Office of the Federal Prison System and has recently been appointed to the FPS National Advisory Group on records retention. Her professional specialties and interests include women in prison (both historical and current), federal drug policy, and collective bargaining in the criminal justice professions.

NANCY STOLLER SHAW teaches community studies and sociology at the University of California at Santa Cruz. She is the author of *Forced Labor: Maternity Care in the United States* and has published in *Women and Health*, *Birth and the Family Journal*, *Prison Law Monitor*, and the *Journal of Prison Health*. Her videotape and slide presentations on women in prison have been shown at a variety of conferences, community meetings, and universities.

ELIZABETH ANNE STANKO is an assistant professor of sociology at Clark University, Worcester, Massachusetts. She received her Ph.D. in 1977 from the City University of New York. Her research focuses on the victimization of women, prosecutorial decision making, and the everyday practice of the criminal justice system.

MARGUERITE Q. WARREN is a professor at the School of Criminal Justice, State University of New York at Albany. She has published in numerous psychology, criminal justice, and law journals, and has served as a consultant to federal and state agencies in this country and elsewhere.

WILLIAM WILBANKS is an associate professor with the Department of Criminal Justice at Florida International University in Miami, Florida. He received the Ph.D. from the School of Criminal Justice, State University of New York at Albany, in 1975. He was a member of the Special New York State Commission on Attica in 1971. Most of his research in the past three years has been in the area of homicide. His most recent publications have been in *Victimology*, the *International Journal of Women's Studies*, and the *International Journal of Aging and Human Development*.

NANCI KOSER WILSON is an assistant professor of criminal justice in the Center for the Study of Crime, Delinquency, and Corrections, Southern Illinois University. Dr. Wilson's publications include works on women as criminals, as victims of crime, and as criminal justice workers. Recent articles appear in *The Journal of Criminal Justice* and the *LAE Journal* of the American Criminal Justice Association. Currently she is conducting research on the role of women in homicide.

1

Introduction

NICOLE HAHN RAFTER &
ELIZABETH ANNE STANKO

Too often, assumptions about women have interfered with research-ers' ability to examine behavior impartially; inquiries about female behavior have been filtered through preconceptions about women's nature and appropriate social roles. In recent years, however, as part of an overall reexamination of the role of women in society, feminist scholars have begun to identify such preconcep-tions, demonstrate their biasing effects, and study women more ob-jectively. This volume presents the work of feminist scholars in the field of criminal justice.

The task of this collection is twofold: (1) to identify assump-tions about women that have distorted criminal justice research; and (2) to analyze, without relying on traditional assumptions, the behavior of women who become involved in criminal justice through various routes — as victims, offenders, and criminal justice professionals.

Before undertaking either task, we must first address the meaning of gender in our society. Gender — the quality of being male or female — refers in part to the biological distinction between the sexes.[1] Anatomical differences, however, are but one dimension

1

Nicole Hahn Rafter & Elizabeth Anne Stanko

of gender. Closely related are the gender-based roles and role expectations that often form a foundation for social relations. For women, the typical gender roles have been those of wife, mother, and nurturer. These roles carry with them a variety of behavioral expectations. Thus, gender serves as both a primary predictor of an individual's behavior and an assessment tool by which others gauge whether that individual is acting properly.

Serving as a filtering device, gender roles have frequently obscured researchers' interpretations of women's behavior in relation to the field of criminal justice. Victimologists, for example, have sometimes referred to women's presumed physical and emotional weaknesses in their analyses of female victimization. Similarly, criminologists have relied on assumptions about female biology in their explanations of the criminality of women. And the exclusion of women from positions of authority in criminal justice has been attributed to their alleged bio-psychological instability. In each of these three areas — victimology, criminology, and the criminal justice professions — roles, images, and expectations about women have had, and continue to have, a major impact on both theory and practice.

What are the controlling images of women in criminal justice? And how have these images affected criminal justice theory and practice? By examining these issues, we can begin to separate *assumptions* about women's involvement from *facts* concerning their actual participation in all aspects of the criminal justice system.

CONTROLLING IMAGES OF WOMEN IN CRIMINAL JUSTICE

Portrayals of women involved with the criminal justice system are often based, implicitly or explicitly, on certain key images of women in general. These images, which draw upon assumptions about how women ought to behave in specific situations, frequently function to reinforce the view of women as dependent, emotional, and in need of manly support. Furthermore, they help determine how women will be perceived and treated by guards, judges, juries, police, and (too often) analysts of the criminal justice system. There are at least six of these images:

1. **Woman as the Pawn of Biology**. The image of woman that ap-

pears with perhaps greatest frequency in criminal justice literature is that of woman gripped by biological forces beyond her control. For instance, female criminal behaviors are linked to menstrual cycles. Similarly, prostitutes and other female offenders are portrayed as driven by unmanageable sexuality. In both cases, biology, not the woman herself, is in control.[2] Such imagery is compatible with the female gender roles of mother and wife, which also stress biological functions.

2. **Woman as Passive and Weak**. The image of the helpless woman also appears with frequency in the criminal justice literature. According to one version of this theme, women are easy prey for criminal types because of inherent physical and emotional weakness. Because women are followers rather than leaders, according to another variation, they tend to be accomplices to male criminals. Certainly they are incapable, according to yet a third variation, of assuming roles as leaders in the professional sphere.[3] This image of woman as passive and weak again clearly derives from traditional gender roles.

3. **Woman as Impulsive and Nonanalytic**. According to this image, women act intuitively, illogically. They seldom make rational decisions. This image implies that woman is in need of manly guidance to make logical, correct choices.[4]

4. **Woman as Impressionable and in Need of Protection**. This image portrays woman as gullible and easily led astray. Because women are childlike and vulnerable, according to this line of reasoning, they need a greater degree of protection than do men.[5]

5. **The Active Woman as Masculine**. When women break with their traditional gender roles to become involved with crime or crime control, they are sometimes portrayed as masculine — aggressive, dark, too large, hairy, "unnatural."[6] The appearance of this image in the criminal justice literature is probably a function not only of gender roles *per se*, but also of the strong association of criminal justice with masculine activities and values.

6. **The Criminal Woman as Purely Evil**. Many criminal justice commentaries depict the criminal woman as a monstrosity, beyond rehabilitation or redemption, far more deeply sunk in evil than the typical male criminal. The roots of this image probably lie in the old notion that women — or at least "true" women — are more moral than men. It is they who uphold the

Nicole Hahn Rafter & Elizabeth Anne Stanko

social morality, they who return errant men to the path of righteousness. When this virtuous woman falls, however, she falls further than any man, for her compliance with proper gender roles is a foundation of social morality. Thus when women step out of traditional gender roles, they create havoc.[7]

These images are neither mutually exclusive nor always compatible. They are cultural configurations, fragments of a broader fabric of gender-role assumptions. Despite their nonscientific (indeed, at times almost mythological) aspects, they exert a powerful influence on theories about women involved with the criminal justice system. In what follows, we explore ways in which these and other stereotypes affect attitudes toward women in the specific areas of victimology, criminology, and access to criminal justice professions.

Images of the Female Victim

Victimology, the study of why and how persons become victims of criminal offenses, focuses on the object of criminal behavior. According to this approach, certain categories of persons and property *attract victimization* because of "weakness or availability," while other kinds of individuals *precipitate criminal action*, generally by escalating social interactions into fights.[8] As might be expected, women have been identified as one special category of victims, and explanations of their victimization have often been based upon gender roles and gender expectations.

Hans von Hentig, the first to explore the role of the victim in crime, specifically listed females among his general classes of victims. He included in his typology such other categories as the intoxicated, the young, and the mentally defective, assuming that, by definition (or biology), women are akin to the enfeebled of all types. The female, according to this thinking, is both emotionally and physically weaker than the normal male. In his study of victims, von Hentig further postulated that "in a sense, the victim shapes and moulds the criminal."[9]

This "shaping and moulding" became an active process of attracting victimization in the work of Menachem Amir, who, using von Hentig's framework, formulated the notion of victim-precipitated rape.[10] Amir's concept of victim-precipitated rape is steeped in assumptions about women; it is but one example of how common images about women's behavior become cemented into a discipline's traditional thinking. The concept of victim-precipitated rape places the ultimate responsibility for victimization on the woman herself.

Thus, stereotypes about rape and battering victims are closely related to von Hentig's and Amir's explanations of victimology, for they include assumptions about a victim's weakness and desire for injury. Rape victims are often viewed as precipitating their own victimization: somehow they ask or desire to be raped and thereby entice the rapist into his act. Battering victims are similarly assumed to have elicited, even secretly desired, the attack and thus to deserve their beatings.[11]

How are the assumptions of provocation set forth by victimologists compatible with the stereotypical images about women? According to these images, females are likely to misjudge character, to be sexually uncontrolled, and to be easily duped into situations in which they are vulnerable to attack. Victimologists have seized upon these images to explain rapes (of women who are "sexually uncontrolled") and beatings (of women who are "masochistic"). Thus, stereotypical images about women have been used to provide the reason for their victimization: it flows naturally from women's supposedly typical state of weakness, vulnerability, and provocativeness.

Images of the Female Criminal

Similar imagery has been elaborated to explain female criminality. Criminologists seem to have theorized about women in general first and then to have applied these stereotypes to the study of female criminality. The somewhat contradictory images of women as biologically determined, passive, impulsive, impressionable, masculine, and evil predominate in the literature.[12]

Stereotypical images of female criminals frequently coalesce into two master images — almost stock figures. One is that of the *Evil Woman*, a hardened violent or serious property crime offender who is masculine in appearance (Lombroso emphasized her hairiness) and sexually aggressive. This figure is thought to deserve harsh punishment, for in committing crimes she has violated her very womanhood. The other stock figure is that of the *Bad Little*

Nicole Ḥahn Rafter & Elizabeth Anne Stanko

Girl—passive, impressionable, impulsive, and sexually promiscuous, easily led astray by those stronger than she. This second type of female offender traditionally has been viewed as reformable; with benign, proper training, the bad little girl can be resocialized into the good woman. While significantly different, the two images share certain features, the most notable of which is the reference to the female criminal's sexuality.

Criminal women were depicted as either evil women or bad little girls by Lombroso, the "father" of criminology. He believed that women were less likely than men to be born criminals, but that those women who were born criminals were more perverse and wicked than male counterparts. Women who did not commit serious crime, he postulated, probably had been led into the criminal act by men. While Lombroso's position was not totally accepted by later theorists, he did much to cement stereotypes of female criminality by developing them in the first major treatise on the female offender.[13]

In the late nineteenth century the images of the female offender as either evil woman or bad little girl coexisted.[14] However, in the early twentieth century, that of the bad little girl began to predominate in the criminological literature. Researchers' almost exclusive focus on the soft, errant offender between 1900 and 1930 seems to have been a function of two factors: the social purity movement of the period, which resulted in the long-term incarceration of prostitutes and other relatively young, minor offenders;[15] and the fact that researchers sought their "delinquent" subjects in institutions that held such minor offenders.[16] By conceptualizing female offenders as bad little girls, these researchers set the stage for gender-based treatment modalities that trained fallen women to be proper women.

Nearly all traditional commentaries on female offenders, whether focused on the serious or the minor criminal, have been overwhelmingly concerned with violations of gender prescriptions. Observing that women are arrested far less frequently than men, theorists have attributed these low arrest rates to the inherently law-abiding nature of women. Accordingly, they have assessed the female criminal by the fit of her crime to men's crime and the extent to which she violated her naturally law-abiding nature. Since crime was assumed to be a masculine phenomenon, women who committed crime were thought to do so either because they were too masculine (the evil woman theory) or because they had been led astray (the bad little girl theory).

Images of the Female Criminal Justice Professional

Women who broke into criminal justice professions in the late nineteenth and early twentieth centuries did so by emphasizing their womanly qualities. Their emotional and sympathetic nature, they claimed, prepared them for work with women, children, and other dependent groups. Although they carved out new categories of women's work, these early criminal justice professionals reinforced the stereotypical images about women and ultimately limited women's professional possibilities.[17]

Once women gain entry into criminal justice, they are either excluded from certain spheres or limited by occupational specialization. Frequently, their participation is restricted on the basis of familiar stereotypes concerning their "likely" behavior. Two of these images stand out. According to the first, women are fragile; therefore, they must be protected from evil and placed in positions that minimize contact with danger or the horror of crime. Once placed in such supposedly safe arenas, they are assigned subordinate positions; for, according to the second image, women are impulsive and nonanalytic, incapable of making leadership decisions.

Occupational specialization or total exclusion from certain spheres under the guise of protection is found in each of the criminal justice components. Historically, women in law enforcement were given the special status of police matrons and assigned to protect arrested women. Similarly, women in corrections were employed in separate facilities founded to handle female offenders and thus only female problems.[18] And in the courts, women were excluded from jury duty, for example, on the grounds that they needed to be protected from sordid, embarrassing matters.[19] The result of such protection, however, has been to limit women's occupational flexibility and overall participation in criminal justice.

The second image, that of women as nonanalytic, influences women's appointments to supervisory positions. With few exceptions, women occupy low-status occupations in criminal justice.[20] Women, it is assumed, need supervision and guidance. Consequently, both police and corrections matrons have historically had little opportunity for advancement. Similarly, within the hierarchy of the court structure, women are considered unlikely candidates for judgeships, positions that supposedly require a logical, definitive (male) mind. Thus, in large part, women's employment opportunities and participation in the criminal justice process are shaped by the stereotypical images about them.

EFFECTS OF IMAGES ON RESEARCH AND PRACTICE

Stereotypical images about women also find their way into the theory and practice of the criminal justice process. Whatever her position in the criminal justice system — victim, offender, or professional — a woman will confront a variety of gender images through which her behavior is likely to be judged and subsequently treated. The actual effects are influenced by the context within which the individual is assessed, the structural positions of those making the assessments, and a variety of other variables pertinent to the decision-making process.[21] This section examines how the differential treatment of women stems from a variety of stereotypes about them.

Gender and Victimology: Women as Victims

Theoretically, crime is a violation against not only an individual, but society as a whole. For instance, robbery is prosecuted publicly because it not only harms the victim, but also threatens the social fabric.[22] However, some harms against individuals are either minimized or ignored entirely by the criminal justice system. Stereotypical images of women that depict them as vulnerable and somehow deserving victims provide a context within which violations against women are defined as something other than socially threatening. Accordingly, the harm to female victims is devalued, often by the victims themselves as well as criminal justice personnel.

That the complaints of women are devalued is also a function of gender stratification itself. The victimizers of women are frequently men.[23] Thus, to report a crime, the female victim must complain about someone higher up in the hierarchy; the powerless complaining about the actions of the powerful is often no complaint at all. Furthermore, the complaints of women tend to be disregarded just because they come from women. This phenomenon has been documented by the research on wife battering.[24] Women, it seems, are still the property of men; within the context of intimate relationships, criminal behavior of men is presumed to be natural. Having absorbed the stereotypes themselves, women often are confused by battering and ask whether they somehow provoked it, an indication that they too have bought into the notion of themselves as inferiors. Women who stop questioning their own behavior and decide to file complaints for assault frequently confront criminal justice personnel who belittle their complaints; for example, such personnel frequently ask the victim how she provoked the man's behavior.[25] By defining assaultive behavior as merely a family dispute, criminal justice personnel categorize (and, therefore, treat) battering as normal and nonthreatening to society as a whole. Thus, they reinforce women's powerlessness and inferior social position.

Similarly, as research on the crime of rape shows, female victims of sexual assault face not only the initial trauma of the rape, but additional trauma when they enter the system as complainants. This trauma is frequently the result of the criminal justice actors' use of imagery about women in their handling of rape complaints. Burgess and Holmstrom, in what is perhaps the most sensitive and revealing study of rape victims, note that rape victims fear the criminal justice process as much as they fear their rapists.[26] Police officers and prosecutors often feel it is their professional duty to question a rape victim about her sexual history, her attire, and her actions in order to discover whether she contributed to the act.[27] For as any prosecutor knows, defense attorneys will rely upon imagery about women, focusing their strategies on questioning the victim about her provocative behavior. Women have learned (only too well) that being the victim places them in the precarious position of being judged according to their assumed gender behavior, particularly that which relates to sexuality; again they are reminded of the powerless position in which their gender places them.[28]

The crimes of rape and battering are glaring illustrations (though not the only ones) of the influence of gender on the ability of victims to complain and to be taken seriously. Devaluation of women's complaints about serious physical harm is an indication of women's status in this society. Essentially, female victims become "legitimate" victims. This legitimation of women's victim status is based in cultural mythology that defines a woman as "an article

Nicole Hahn Rafter & Elizabeth Anne Stanko

of male property.''[29] Thus, both images about women and social approval of victimization serve to maintain and, in some instances, to increase women's injuries.

Gender and Criminology: Women as Offenders

As we have seen, past explanations of female criminality were steeped in gender assumptions: theorists were often more concerned with women's violations of gender roles than with violations of criminal statutes. Concern about gender roles continues to dominate research into the causes of female crime. Recently, however, theorists have begun to cast aside the earlier assumptions and to examine instead the effects of gender roles *per se* on crime.[30]

There are three leading explanations of the apparent recent increases in female crime. According to Adler, these increases are mainly in violent crime and are caused by women's ''liberation.'' Adler believes that due to the women's movement, American women are becoming more like men:

> In [the] gradual but accelerating social revolution . . .
> women are closing many of the gaps, social and criminal.
> . . . The closer they get, the more alike [women and men]
> look and act.[31]

Adler's work continues to limit our understanding of criminal behavior, based as it is on the assumptions that crime is a male phenomenon and that any woman who commits crime is masculine. Her theory, moreover, reinforces the traditional stereotype of the female offender as the evil woman, for Adler depicts the female criminal as dark, aggressive, and masculine.

The second leading explanation, that put forth by Simon, denies increases in *violent* crime by women; instead, Simon claims that the increase has been in female *property* crime, and she attributes the increase to women's expanded occupational opportunities. She maintains that as women move into white-collar banking positions, there is a corresponding increase in embezzlement committed by women.[32] Simon's data indicate the effects of gender stratification on women's lives: as women's economic roles begin to change, she states, opportunities for females to commit work-related crime also change. Yet, Simon assumes that employment opportunities for women lead them into the same experiences as men. Implicitly, Simon expects a convergence of gender roles and, like Adler, believes that the convergence will not be androgynous, but male.

In the third analysis of the relationship between gender and crime, Steffensmeier argues against both "liberation" and the equalization of occupational opportunities as explanations for the increase in women's crime rates. Instead, he believes that the level of female criminality is a product of traditional gender roles in both "legal and illegal marketplaces; from shopper to shoplifter, from cashing good checks to passing bad ones, from being a welfare mother to being accused of welfare fraud," the female criminal reflects traditional stereotypes rather than new, liberated ones.[33] Increases in female arrest rates, Steffensmeier concludes, can be attributed to the changes in opportunities for committing an offense and the increased willingness of business officials — those most affected by the types of property crime women commit — to prosecute these offenses. In sum, changes in such factors as the economy or the law enforcement policy, *not* changes in gender roles, are linked to increases in female arrest rates.

Quite clearly, there is a close relationship between gender roles and criminal behavior.[34] However, conceptual ambiguity about women's roles and disagreements about the current nature of female crime interfere with understanding the nature of crime and its relationship to the offender's gender.[35] Hence the exact nature of that relationship is not known. Stereotypical images about women continue to powerfully influence theories concerning female offenders.

Gender and Criminal Justice Processing: Women as Defendants and Prisoners

Are women treated more leniently or more harshly than men by the criminal justice system? Researchers have taken a variety of positions on this issue; however, that women are treated differently than men is a consistent finding in a number of studies.[36] The issue may relate to the two dominant female images noted previously. If a woman is perceived to be a bad little girl, she may be treated chivalrously by actors in the criminal justice system. In contrast, the evil woman, assumed to deserve whatever punishment or harm comes to her, may be treated more harshly.

Nicole Hahn Rafter & Elizabeth Anne Stanko

In the first major work to hypothesize that women are treated more leniently than men, Pollak drew upon both images. He argued that although female criminals really are evil, they are treated like bad little girls because of men's chivalry. While women may well commit as much crime as men, according to Pollak, their crimes are less visible; and, moreover, when criminal women are detected, they are less likely than men to be charged, convicted, and sentenced severely:

> *Men hate to accuse women and thus indirectly to send them to their punishment, police officers dislike to arrest, district attorneys to prosecute them, judges and juries to find them guilty, and so on.*[37]

As this quotation suggests, Pollak was in fact more concerned with men's perceptions of female criminality than with female criminality itself. Therefore, his work sheds more light on our images of female criminality than on its actualities.

Chivalry is usually assumed to lead to more lenient treatment of women. As Chesney-Lind has shown, however, the opposite may in fact be the case. In the jurisdiction she studied, Chesney-Lind discovered that offenses by girls were reinterpreted in sexual terms. Moreover, juvenile women were more likely to be institutionalized for status offenses than their male counterparts. Although these juvenile women were charged with less serious offenses, they were, then, treated more harshly — evidently because they had been labeled as ''bad little girls.''[38]

In like fashion, until recently women in a number of states could receive longer sentences than men convicted of similar crimes. According to the theory on which such sentences were based, the state does women a favor by providing them with longer periods for rehabilitation. Pennsylvania's Muncy Act is but one example of legislation that was intended to protect such women, but ironically has brought them more punitive treatment. It and similar sentencing provisions show how *images* of women become a base for *treatment* of women by the criminal justice system.[39]

During incarceration differential treatment of women continues, again based on gender stereotypes. Courses in clerical work, cosmetology, and homemaking skills dominate the training programs available to them. Furthermore, incarcerated women are often forced by the inmate social structure to adopt domestic

Introduction

roles.[40] In each successive phase of the criminal justice process, then, stereotypical gender images affect the processing and treatment of women.

Gender and Occupation:
Women as Criminal Justice Professionals

Women were first granted entry into criminal justice occupations on the basis of gender stereotypes. Police matron positions were created on the grounds that men were by nature less qualified to help arrested women and juveniles. Similarly, women were granted access to positions in penal institutions for juveniles and women on the grounds that they had inherent sympathy and the ability to deal with the weak. Women themselves frequently put forth such arguments as they sought to enter criminal justice work. The problem, of course, is that such arguments have locked women into sex-stereotyped roles, and out of jobs reserved for men — jobs that are far more numerous (and often more lucrative).

To date, there has been almost no research on the structural barriers to women who wish to enter criminal justice professions. On the other hand, a number of studies have recently been made to see whether gender stereotypes are "true" — whether, for instance, policewomen are in fact more passive than policemen.[41] So great is the power of images about women that such questions continue to be asked. Of course, they need to be answered; however, it does not seem that such studies should use the term *surprising*, (as did one recently), to describe the finding that "the women's 'style' of patrol was almost indistinguishable from the men's."[42]

It is also important to move beyond research on the effects of gender roles on performance to ask questions about ways in which gender-role stereotypes block women's access to employment in criminal justice.[43] In fact, we find it difficult to think of any factor that creates a greater barrier to women who wish to enter criminal justice fields than gender stereotyping. Images of women as submissive and ineffectual, as pawns of their biology, and as primarily sexual beings work to keep women either out of these jobs entirely or isolated in those that relate to children and other women.

When women do gain access to formerly all-male preserves, they often encounter an occupational culture that negatively affects their ability to learn professional competencies. Access to the informal occupational subculture, where many practical job skills are acquired, may be closed to women by virtue of their gender.[44] Furthermore, because women are sometimes viewed as introducing a sexual element into a previously asexual (male) profession, their colleagues may react with hostility or fear, isolating them from support systems within the occupation. Or, resistance from male coworkers may take the form of bureaucratic and sexual harassment.[45] Finally, like some women who commit crime, women who enter criminal justice professions may be ostracized as "masculine," in this case for desiring the same employment opportunities and job responsibilities as their male counterparts.

Thus gender roles, which help define job categories as appropriate or inappropriate for women, restrict women's occupational choices and their ability to gain acceptance within criminal justice professions. The female judge and lawyer find, as do the female victim and thief, that gender images color the ways in which they are perceived and processed by the criminal justice system.

OVERVIEW OF THE COLLECTION

Part I: Women as Victims

Chapter 2. Elizabeth Anne Mills: "One Hundred Years of Fear: Rape and the Medical Profession"

Chapter 3. Elizabeth Anne Stanko: "Would You Believe This Woman? Prosecutorial Screening for 'Credible' Witnesses and a Problem of Justice"

Chapter 4. Dorie Klein: "The Dark Side of Marriage: Battered Wives and the Domination of Women"

The first of this book's four parts deals with women as victims of crime. The initial two chapters focus on male authorities — physicians in one case, prosecutors in the other — who have the task of identifying "true" victims. These authorities are important gatekeepers in criminal justice, for they and others in similar positions decide which victims shall be admitted past the system's threshold. Both chapters indicate — that by Mills from an historical point of view, and that by Stanko through a study of contemporary victim assessment — that stereotypes of female victims influence the judgments of these decision makers. Both suggest that assumptions about which women can be considered "true" victims are deeply entrenched on the organizational, societal, and ideological levels. This entrenchment makes it difficult to open the system to female victims who do not fit traditional victim stereotypes. The third and final chapter of this section deals more explicitly with the social reproduction of male gender dominance: in it Klein shows that the victimization of women is in fact reinforced by many aspects of society, including the criminal justice system.

In Chapter 2, Mills reviews a little-known body of literature — commentary on rape written by physicians who were responsible for collecting the evidence to convict or exonerate alleged rapists. The commentaries, which span one hundred years, reveal the physicians' preconceptions about the nature of rape and its "true" victims; as Mills shows, such preconceptions, which dominated the literature for eighty years, negatively affected the physicians' supposedly scientific and objective examinations of rape victims. Although the influence of the traditional preconceptions is weaker in the more recent articles, it lives on in a concern about false accusation and victim precipitation that is sometimes disproportionate to concern about victimization itself.

Chapter 3 examines the way in which prosecutors rely on victim stereotypes as they assess the credibility of complainants, the seriousness of alleged crimes, and the probability that complainants will persist in prosecution. Stanko suggests that female complainants do not have equal access to the criminal justice system because their gender sometimes raises questions with prosecutors about the reality of the victimizations they claim and their usefulness as witnesses: Did the rape complainant at one time have an intimate relationship with her alleged attacker? Will the wife who charges battering subsequently make up with her husband and drop charges? Is the prostitute who alleges robbery a "worthy" victim? Were any of these female victims somehow "asking for it"?

Chapter 4 deals with the social reproduction of violence against women in terms of wife battering. Klein's analysis reveals a cycle in which the helplessness and self-blame of victims and the inadequate responses of the system reinforce one another. She identifies deeply rooted cultural supports for violence against women, including aspects of marriage itself. Whereas she sees some hope for battered wives in the feminist shelter movement, she predicts that this movement will in the future be deflated by withdrawal of

Nicole Hahn Rafter & Elizabeth Anne Stanko

funds, bureaucratic co-optation, and governmental redefinitions of the problem of battering.

The three chapters of Part I address major issues in the field of victimology: how victims are identified; why victims tend to be blamed for their injuries; why victims often fail to pass their troubles on to the criminal justice system; and what remedies are available to the victims of crime. As a group, these articles indicate that the criminal justice system, influenced by gender stereotypes, fails to give female victims adequate attention and devalues their complaints. Such treatment actually perpetuates female victimization and gender stereotyping.

Part II: Women as Offenders

Chapter 5. Nicolette Parisi: "Exploring Female Crime Patterns: Problems and Prospects"

Chapter 6. Marsha Rosenbaum: "Work and the Addicted Prostitute"

Chapter 7. William Wilbanks: "Murdered Women and Women Who Murder: A Critique of the Literature"

Chapter 8. Marguerite Q. Warren: "Delinquency Causation in Female Offenders"

The chapters of Part II focus on women as criminal offenders. This area of study received little attention until recently, to the detriment of our understanding of crime in general. These chapters vary considerably in their scope, ranging from an empirical and theoretical overview (Parisi) to more specific concentrations on addict/prostitutes (Rosenbaum), female homicide victims and offenders (Wilbanks), and female delinquents (Warren).

Nicolette Parisi's chapter examines an issue that has dominated discussions of female criminality in the last five years: is female crime increasing, and if so, in what ways? Her methodological discussion explains how existing data sources both illuminate and obscure our understanding of this issue in terms of the level and incident characteristics of female crime. She then evaluates the major theoretical explanations of female criminality in light of the data, concluding with a discussion of areas in which research is most urgently needed.

Introduction

Rosenbaum's chapter examines the work of the addicted prostitute: her routes of entry into prostitution, her rationalizations and work patterns, her status in the prostitution hierarchy, and the special problems caused by her addiction. Giving particular attention to identity issues, Rosenbaum finds that the "junkie whore" identifies herself as an addict rather than a prostitute; as such, she sees her life as merely a series of odd jobs necessary for survival. This chapter is unusual for its treatment of crime as work; it also makes an important contribution to the literature on criminal subcultures.

In Chapter 7, Wilbanks points out that homicide involving women (as either victims or offenders) is often an intimate crime, a function of interactions with men. Perhaps because of this interactive aspect of female homicide, the literature has been dominated by a mythology of gender stereotypes. In particular, Wilbanks indicts the psychological literature, which has frequently depicted female homicide victims and offenders as mentally ill. As a partial corrective to this situation, he reviews current statistical data on homicide involving women; he is one of the few sociologists to give scholarly attention to this much-mythologized subject.

Marguerite Q. Warren's chapter, the last in this part, takes theories usually used to explain male criminality and tests them against a sample of female delinquents. Warren finds that social control theory fits best across subtypes of girls, and strain theory most poorly. But she concludes that the theories have differential applicability to different categories of delinquent girls. Her study indicates that just as we should not treat all males as a unit, so we must not approach females as though they automatically share common socio-psychological characteristics by virtue of their sex.

The chapters of Part II deal with key issues in criminology: levels and types of crime; the effects of sex and race on crime and victimization rates; and the social psychology of crime. As a unit, they help overcome the gap in our knowledge of crime created by the traditional lack of attention to female offenders.

Part III: Women as Defendants and Prisoners

Chapter 9. Nicolette Parisi: "Are Females Treated Differently? A Review of the Theories and Evidence on Sentencing and Parole Decisions"

Chapter 10. Anne Rankin Mahoney and Carol Fenster: "Female Delinquents in a Suburban Court"

Chapter 11. Nicole Hahn Rafter: "Hard Times: The Evolution of the Women's Prison System and the Example of the New York State Prison for Women at Auburn, 1893–1933"

Chapter 12. Nancy Stoller Shaw: "Female Patients and the Medical Profession in Jails and Prisons: A Case of Quintuple Jeopardy"

The chapters of Part III address two questions concerning women as defendants and prisoners: does gender affect the treatment of women as they pass through the criminal justice system; and, if so, does gender-based discrimination result in unfair treatment? The complexity of these issues is evident from the variety of answers given by the chapters. That gender does influence treatment is indicated by the chapters by Parisi and Shaw. Rafter's answer is more ambiguous; while she finds some influence of gender, she suggests that offense seriousness has a stronger impact on the treatment of women. Finally, Mahoney and Fenster argue that gender roles, in their contemporary incarnation, have little impact: their study examines whether courts have become harsher in their treatment of female juvenile offenders as a result of the "women's liberation" movement, and finds no effects.

The second question, whether differential treatment results in unfair treatment, also receives a variety of answers. Rafter's findings suggest that "different" and "unfair" may be practically synonymous in the treatment of women. But according to Parisi, we do not have enough evidence to tell. Further complicating the matter is the Shaw chapter; although it does not compare treatment of the sexes, it contends that gender operates (with other factors) to produce poor health care in female penal institutions. These chapters, then, address exceedingly difficult questions.

In Chapter 9, Parisi reviews the literature on differential treatment at post-adjudicative stages in the criminal justice process. She outlines the three major viewpoints (the preferential, punitive, and equality perspectives) and tests these against the available data. Concluding that females do receive differential, but not conclusively disparate, treatment, Parisi ends with the startling recommendation that sentencing should take into account differential family obligations of males and females. Parisi feels that until both sexes share equal responsibility for dependent children, separate sentencing standards should be applied in cases involving female parents in order to reduce overall social harm.

The chapter by Mahoney and Fenster poses two specific questions: has female delinquency increased in level and seriousness in recent years, and has the criminal justice system come to respond to female delinquents more harshly as a result of the "women's liberation" movement? Their answer to both questions, based on the activities of a suburban juvenile court over a recent ten-year period, is *No:* female delinquency has changed little in level or seriousness, and the juvenile court does not appear to be responding to female delinquents with more severity. Another significant finding of the Mahoney and Fenster chapter is that the "women's liberation" movement has not (at least in the jurisdiction they covered) set off a crime wave among juvenile women.

Nicole Hahn Rafter's chapter, one of the first historical studies of women's prisons, treats a type of institution ignored by nearly all research on incarceration: that of the "custodial" or "masculine" type that held female felons under high security conditions. Rafter briefly contrasts this type with the women's reformatory, which was rehabilitative in design, low in security, and often dedicated to resocializing misdemeanants. But her main thrust is to present a full-scale portrait of a custodial type of women's prison through the example of the State Prison for Women operated at Auburn, New York, from 1893 to 1933. Rafter concludes that sociologists and historians have, through their exclusive concentration on "feminine" institutions of the reformatory type, biased our understanding of the incarceration of women.

Shaw's chapter, like the earlier one by Mills, discusses ways in which sexual stereotypes influence physicians in their decisions about women involved with the criminal justice system. The health care of incarcerated women is often approached on the basis of beliefs about female intelligence and "appropriate" behaviors. According to Shaw, five factors contribute to the inadequacy of health care of imprisoned women: sexism (assumptions based on gender); racism (assumptions based on color); classism (the lack of resources of the lower-class women who are most frequently incarcerated); legal status (dependency through conviction); and social role (patienthood, another instance of dependency). Shaw concludes by reviewing programs designed to overcome these obstacles to adequate health care for imprisoned women.

Nicole Hahn Rafter & Elizabeth Anne Stanko

The chapters of Part III indicate the limitations of existing data bases: there is a great need for more research that compares the treatment of women and men and the treatment of different types of women (such as blacks and whites) at different points in the criminal justice process. The issues in this area of differential treatment are complex; allowance must be made for the possibility that the criminal justice system may operate with both leniency and severity toward women, depending on ways in which they present themselves and are perceived. Paternalism, in other words, seems to produce mixed, and sometimes contradictory, results. The possibility of differential responses to different types of women must be addressed before we can reach definitive answers to the questions posed in Part III.

Part IV: Women as Practitioners and Professionals

Chapter 13. Claudine SchWeber: " 'The Government's Unique Experiment in Salvaging Women Criminals': Cooperation and Conflict in the Administration of a Women's Prison — The Case of the Federal Industrial Institution for Women at Alderson''

Chapter 14. Edith Elisabeth Flynn: "Women as Criminal Justice Professionals: A Challenge to Change Tradition''

Chapter 15. Phyllis Jo Baunach and Nicole Hahn Rafter: "Sex-Role Operations: Strategies of Women Working in the Criminal Justice System''

Chapter 16. Nanci Koser Wilson: "Women in the Criminal Justice Professions: An Analysis of Status Conflict''

The study of women as practitioners and professionals in criminal justice is just beginning to attract scholarly attention. In this section, two key issues emerge. The first concerns the small number of women working in criminal justice areas and their concentration at the lowest bureaucratic levels: what are the structural barriers to their entry and advancement, and how might these be overcome? The second concerns coping from the inside: being a minority, and a minority based on gender, how can women who do gain criminal justice positions retain them without paying a high price in stress and loss of self-respect? Taken as a whole, the chapters of this section present a bleak picture: when women do gain entry to criminal justice positions, they face overwhelming problems.

Part IV opens with SchWeber's historical chapter on the founding and early years of the first federal prison for women at Alderson, West Virginia, and its first superintendent, Mary Belle Harris. From the opening of Alderson in 1928, there was a struggle between Harris and her female allies on the one hand and the newly established Bureau of Prisons on the other. From what was, SchWeber shows, essentially a struggle between feminine and masculine roles, flowed innumerable and heated disputes between Alderson and the Bureau of Prisons over appropriate treatment of female prisoners. SchWeber reviews Harris's political tactics; her use of support networks, especially those of women's clubs; and the (often amusing) maneuvers she and the Alderson Advisory Board executed to protect their turf against the Bureau's encroachments. Harris, interestingly enough, insisted on the validity and primacy of gender roles — perhaps because such insistence was a way she could justify her own work as a criminal justice professional.

In Chapter 14, Flynn presents a comprehensive overview of the employment of women in criminal justice. She begins by identifying patterns of sex discrimination in all areas of criminal justice employment. Flynn discusses a number of factors that work to hold employment of women at low levels: veterans' preference rules; physical requirements based on male standards; concern about safety and privacy; gender stereotyping; and the ineffectiveness of most legal remedies. However, she concludes on a note of cautious optimism. Recent legislation has laid a foundation for progress, she argues, and women have finally broken into previously closed employment areas. The presence of competent women in such jobs will begin to whittle away at stereotypes and prejudices. As women continue to make their way into the judicial and legislative branches, legal remedies will become more effective. And last, Flynn predicts that "the combined progress of women working within criminal justice at all levels will generate the momentum needed to accelerate current trends. While full equality will probably not be realized in this generation, I do expect it to be achieved in the next."

The chapter by Baunach and Rafter picks up where the Flynn chapter leaves off by identifying problems and strategies of women who do manage to find criminal justice work. This chapter is based on the transcript of what was, to our knowledge, a unique occasion:

Nicole Hahn Rafter & Elizabeth Anne Stanko

a symposium that brought together women employed in a variety of criminal justice agencies to exchange information on sex-specific difficulties they encountered at work. The symposium participants identified four major areas of concern: "preferential" treatment; their sense that more was expected of them than of men; lack of access to the "old boys" network; and sex stereotyping in their job assignments. The chapter gives a personal view of the situation presented abstractly by Flynn — a view from the inside.

In the final chapter, Wilson conceptualizes the barriers to criminal justice employment of women by developing a model of gender-role assumptions that she then compares to the organizational orientations of various criminal justice agencies. By analyzing the lack of fit between gender roles and organizational orientations, Wilson identifies major sources of resistance to employment of women. Agencies that have adopted a service (or collaborative, or rehabilitative) stance, she argues, are relatively open to women; but those oriented toward control (or custody and punishment, or adversarial) stances are apt to exclude women. Wilson's study is valuable as one of the few efforts to pinpoint organizational *gestalts* as a primary source of employment discrimination based on sex.

THERE ARE FEW FEMALE criminal justice practitioners or professionals, just as there are relatively few female criminals. Gender roles, it seems, provide the best explanation for this commonality between women on opposite sides of the law. All sections of the collection point to the centrality of gender-role effects on the treatment of women by the criminal justice system.

NOTES

1. We use *gender* rather than *sex* because it is a more neutral, descriptive term. For information on gender roles, *see* Ann Oakley, *Sex, Gender and Society* (New York: Harper and Row, 1972) and Jean Stockard and Miriam M. Johnson, *Sex Roles: Sex Inequality and Sex Role Development* (Englewood Cliffs, NJ: Prentice-Hall, 1980).

2. For examples of the works that attempt to link biology and female criminality, *see* Cesare Lombroso and William Ferrero, *The Female Offender* (New York: D. Appleton & Company, 1916); Otto Pollak, *The Criminality of Women* (Philadelphia: University of Pennsylvania Press, 1950), p. 11; and Hans von Hentig, *Crime: Causes and Conditions* (New York: McGraw-Hill, 1947), pp. 113–117. For a critical discussion of some of the "evidence" for such theories, *see* Julie Horney, "Menstrual Cycles and Criminal Responsibility," *Law and Human Behavior* 2, 1 (1978):25–36.

3. The first version of this theme, women as prey for criminal types, is stated by Hans von Hentig, *The Criminal and His Victim, Studies in the Sociology of Crime* (New Haven: Yale University Press, 1948), pp. 406-408. Mannheim articulated the second variation of the theme when he noted that women are "more likely to play the role of instigator, aider and abetter [in crime] than that of the actual doer . . ." (Hermann Mannheim, "The Sex Factor: Female Delinquency," reprinted in *The Criminology of Deviant Women*, ed. Freda Adler and Rita James Simon [Boston: Houghton Mifflin, 1979], p. 47). The third variation, according to which women are incapable of leadership, is exemplified by denial to women of promotions in law enforcement; Feinman notes that some women have had to sue even for the right to take promotional examinations (Clarice Feinman, *Women in the Criminal Justice System* [New York: Praeger, 1980], pp. 73-74).

4. *See*, for example, Sheldon Glueck and Eleanor T. Glueck, *Five Hundred Delinquent Women* (New York: Alfred A. Knopf, 1934). Kanter analyzes the alleged incompatibility between the images of manager and woman:

> A *"masculine ethic"* can be identified as part of the early image of managers. This *"masculine ethic"* elevates the traits assumed to belong to some men to necessities for effective management: . . . analytic abilities . . . ; a capacity to set aside personal, emotional considerations. . . . These characteristics supposedly belonged to men. . . .

See Rosabeth Moss Kanter, *Men and Women of the Corporation* (New York: Basic Books, 1977), p. 22.

5. Here again, Glueck and Glueck, *Five Hundred Delinquent Women*, provides a good example; *see*, in particular, pp. 299-303.

6. For examples of descriptions of masculine women, *see* Lombroso and Ferrero, *The Female Offender*, pp. 148, 151-152.

7. *See*, for example, Lombroso and Ferrero, *The Female Offender*, p. 152; Nicolas F. Hahn (Rafter), "Too Dumb to Know Better: Cacogenic Family Studies and the Criminology of Women," *Criminology* 18, 1 (May 1980):3-25. As early as 1833, Francis Lieber attributed evil to the fallen woman, remarking "I believe I am right in stating, that the injury done to society by a criminal woman, is in most cases much greater than that suffered from a male criminal" (Francis Leiber, "Translator's Preface," Gustave de Beaumont and Alexis de Tocqueville, *On the Penitentiary System in the United States and Its Application in France* [repr. Carbondale, IL: Southern Illinois University Press, 1964], p. 9). On "true" womanhood, *see* Barbara Welter, "The Cult of True Womanhood: 1820-1860," in *Our American Sisters: Women in American Life and Thought*, ed. Jean E. Friedman and William G. Shade (Boston: Allyn and Bacon, 1973), pp. 96-115. Feinman uses the whore-madonna duality to explain how women are treated in criminal justice: women who are offenders are "whores" and deserve to be punished (Feinman, *Women in the Criminal Justice System*, pp. 1, 6).

8. Walter B. Reckless, *The Crime Problem*, 4th ed. (New York: Appleton-Century-Crofts, 1961), p. 137.

9. Von Hentig, *The Criminal and His Victim*, p. 348.

10. Menachem Amir, *Patterns in Forcible Rape* (Chicago: University of Chicago Press, 1971), esp. pp. 259-278.

11. Stereotypes of rape victims are the focus of Julia R. Schwendinger and Herman Schwendinger in "Rape Myths: In Legal, Theoretical, and Everyday Practice,"

Nicole Hahn Rafter & Elizabeth Anne Stanko

Crime and Social Justice 1 (Spring–Summer 1974):18–26. *See* Del Martin, *Battered Wives* (New York: Pocket Books, 1977), pp. 6, 77–80, for an analysis of the blame imposed on battering victims. Dorie Klein, "The Dark Side of Marriage: Battered Wives and the Domination of Women," this volume, also analyzes the process of blaming battering victims for their beatings.

12. For traditional views of the female criminal, *see* Lombroso and Ferrero, *The Female Offender*; Glueck and Glueck, *Five Hundred Delinquent Women*; Mannheim, "The Sex Factor"; and Pollak, *The Criminality of Women*. Of particular interest are the descriptions of "criminal women" found in Jean Weidensall, *The Mentality of the Criminal Woman* (Baltimore, MD: Warwick and York, 1916).

13. Lombroso and Ferrero, *The Female Offender*.

14. *See* Nicole Hahn Rafter, "Hard Times: The Evolution of the Women's Prison System and the Example of the New York State Prison for Women at Auburn, 1893-1933," this volume.

15. Steven Schlossman and Stephanie Wallach, "The Crime of Precocious Sexuality: Female Juvenile Delinquency in the Progressive Era," *Harvard Educational Review* 48, 1 (February 1978):65–94; Mark Thomas Connelly, *The Response to Prostitution in the Progressive Era* (Chapel Hill: University of North Carolina Press, 1980).

16. One report described a population of women studied during the second decade of the 1900s as follows:

> It seems a far cry to designate as "criminal" the girl of sixteen or seventeen who may be convicted of "associating with vicious and dissolute persons and being in danger of becoming morally depraved," or the woman who is convicted, even for the twentieth time, of intoxication, or, in fact, even the common prostitute whose offense against the law is made possible only by the participation of men, who are not even accomplices in a criminal act in the eyes of the law.

(Mabel Ruth Fernald, Mary Holmes Stevens Hayes, and Almena Dawley, *A Study of Women Delinquents in New York State* [New York: The Century Company, 1920], p. 13.)

17. *See*, for example, Feinman, *Women in the Criminal Justice System*, pp. 39–52, 65–68; and Estelle B. Freedman, *Their Sisters' Keepers: Women's Prison Reform in America, 1830-1930* (Ann Arbor: University of Michigan Press, 1981).

18. Feinman, *Women in the Criminal Justice System*, pp. 39–52, 65–68.

19. For a discussion of women as jurors, *see* Anne Rankin Mahoney, "Sexism in Voir Dire: The Use of Sex Stereotypes in Jury Selection," in *Women in the Courts*, ed. Winifred L. Hepperle and Laura Crites (Williamsburg, VA: National Center for State Courts, 1978), pp. 114–135.

20. *See* Feinman, *Women in the Criminal Justice System*, pp. 39–52, 65–68, 88–97, 100–102.

21. Swigert and Farrell have examined the use of stereotypical imagery in processing persons accused of murder; their analysis is similar to that we use here. *See* Victoria Lynn Swigert and Ronald A. Farrell, *Murder, Inequality, and the Law* (Lexington, MA: Lexington Books, 1976).

22. We use the concept *social harm* to refer to offenses that are specified by the criminal statute as illegal. We recognize, however, that there exist a variety of occurrences that, like the spillage of nuclear waste, are socially harmful though not illegal.

Introduction

We include in the notion of social harm some responses of public officials to requests for intervention. For example, when public officials deal with domestic violence as a private, individual matter, they increase the social harm of involved individuals.

23. Bowker notes that "while others are more likely to be victimized by offenders who are demographically similar to themselves, women are more likely to be victimized by men than other women." *See* Lee H. Bowker, "Women as Victims: An Examination of the Results of L.E.A.A.'s National Crime Survey Program," in *Women and Crime in America*, ed. Lee H. Bowker (New York: Macmillan, 1981), pp. 158–179. *See* Kurt Weis and Sandra S. Borges, "Victimology and Rape: The Case of the Legitimate Victim," reprinted in *The Rape Victim*, ed. Deanna R. Nass (Dubuque, IA: Kendall/Hunt, 1977), for an analysis of how women's victimization is legitimized, particularly when men are the assailants.

24. Martin, *Battered Wives*, pp. 88–119; Dorie Klein, "Can This Marriage Be Saved?: Battering and Sheltering," *Crime and Social Justice* 12 (1979):27; Mildred Daley Pagelow, "Secondary Battering and Alternatives of Female Victims to Spouse Abuse," in *Women and Crime in America*, pp. 277–300.

25. *See* Elizabeth Anne Stanko, "Would You Believe This Woman?: Prosecutorial Screening for 'Credible' Witnesses and a Problem of Justice," this volume.

26. Lynda Lytle Holmstrom and Ann Wolbert Burgess, *The Victim of Rape: Institutional Reactions* (New York: John Wiley and Sons, 1978), pp. 157–236.

27. French vividly describes the ordeal of a rape victim who must face interrogation by criminal justice actors who question her behavior. *See* Marilyn French, *The Women's Room* (New York: Jove, 1977), pp. 607–620. *See also* Holmstrom and Burgess, *The Victim of Rape*, pp. 221–236.

28. It seems that rapists and some criminal justice personnel have parallel perceptions of the rape victim. To those parties, the individual is inconsequential except for her most important feature, gender. For the rapist, the victim's gender is the object of his aggression. For the criminal justice actor, the victim's gender may be the trigger for the stereotypes by which to judge contributory responsibility. Both victimize (obviously, to different degrees) on the basis of gender.

29. Weis and Borges, "Victimology and Rape," p. 71. This cultural mythology was perpetuated by English common law; *see* Dorie Klein, "The Dark Side of Marriage: Battered Wives and the Domination of Women," this volume.

30. *See* Dorie Klein, "The Etiology of Female Crime: A Review of the Literature," *Issues in Criminology* 8 (Fall 1973):3–30; Dorie Klein and June Kress, "Any Woman's Blues: An Overview of Women, Crime, and the Criminal Justice System," *Crime and Social Justice* 5 (Spring–Summer 1976):34–49; Carol Smart, *Women, Crime, and Criminology: A Feminist Critique* (London: Routledge & Kegan Paul, 1977), pp. 1–26; and Joseph G. Weis, "Liberation and Crime: The Invention of the New Female Criminal," *Crime and Social Justice* 17 (Fall–Winter 1976):17–27.

31. Adler, *Sisters in Crime: The Rise of the New Female Offender* (New York: McGraw-Hill, 1975), p. 30.

32. Rita James Simon, *Women and Crime* (Lexington, MA: D. C. Heath, 1975), p. 19.

33. Darrell J. Steffensmeier, "Patterns of Female Property Crime 1960–1978: A Postscript," in *Women and Crime in America*, p. 63.

34. Michael J. Hindelang, "Sex Differences in Criminal Activity," *Social Problems* 27 (December 1979):153.

35. Stephen Norland and Neal Shover, "Gender Roles and Female Criminality:

Nicole Hahn Rafter & Elizabeth Anne Stanko

Some Critical Comments," *Criminology* 15 (May 1977):100.

36. *See* Nicolette Parisi, "Are Females Treated Differently? A Review of the Theories and Evidence on Sentencing and Parole Decisions," this volume.

37. Pollak, *The Criminality of Women*, p. 151.

38. Meda Chesney-Lind, "Judicial Enforcement of the Female Sex Role: The Family Court and the Female Delinquent," *Issues in Criminology* 8 (Fall 1973):51-59. Similar findings are reported by Susan K. Datesman and Frank R. Scarpitti, "Unequal Protection for Males and Females in the Juvenile Court," in *Women, Crime, and Justice*, ed. Susan K. Datesman and Frank R. Scarpitti, (New York: Oxford University Press, 1980), pp. 300-319.

39. *See* Carolyn Engel Temin, "Discriminatory Sentencing of Women Offenders: The Argument for ERA in a Nutshell," in *Women, Crime, and Justice*, pp. 257-261, 270. Parisi argues that gender should affect sentencing decisions; however, her argument is based not on images about women, but on practical realities of women's lives today. *See* Parisi, "Are Females Treated Differently?" this volume.

40. Clarice Feinman, "Sex-Role Stereotypes and Justice for Women," in *Women and Crime in America*, pp. 387-390; Kathryn W. Burkhart, *Women in Prison* (Garden City, NY: Doubleday, 1973); Rose Giallombardo, *Society of Women: A Study of Women's Prisons* (New York: John Wiley, 1966); Ruth M. Glick and Virginia V. Neto, *National Study of Women's Correctional Programs* (Washington, DC: U.S. Government Printing Office, 1977).

41. See, for example, Peter Block and Deborah Anderson, *Policewomen on Patrol: Final Report* (Washington, DC: Police Foundation, 1974); Lawrence J. Sherman, "Evaluation of Policewomen on Patrol in a Suburban Police Department," *Journal of Police Science and Administration* 3 (December 1975):434-438; and Joyce L. Sichel, Lucy N. Friedman, Janet C. Quint, and Michael E. Smith, *Women on Patrol: A Pilot Study of Police Performance in New York City* (Washington, DC: National Institute of Law Enforcement and Criminal Justice, 1978).

42. Sichel *et al.*, *Women on Patrol*, p. xi.

43. This important step is taken by Susan Ehrlich Martin, *Breaking and Entering: Policewomen on Patrol* (Berkeley: University of California Press, 1980).

44. Nancy Koser Wilson, "Women in the Criminal Justice Professions: An Analysis of Status Conflict," this volume.

45. Lin Farley, *Sexual Shakedown: The Sexual Harassment of Working Women on the Job* (New York: McGraw-Hill, 1978), pp. 54-60; Feinman, *Women in the Criminal Justice System*, p. 79.

PART I

Women as Victims

2

One Hundred Years of Fear
Rape and the Medical Profession

ELIZABETH ANNE MILLS

There are girls, for instance, and some who consider themselves strictly respectable, too, who have no hesitation in allowing a man, in many cases their sweetheart, to indulge in any sort of sexual play, but stop short only at intromission or sexual intercourse. They themselves are very often the aggressors, and will inflame a man's sexual passion to the most intense point, will go past the most extreme bounds of propriety, will sometimes even give hints that sexual advances would not be resisted, but will stop short at the actual performance, or anything that might rob them of their virginity. They will, in some cases, place themselves in the posture to make sexual congress very easy for the male, but will, with words, deny their consent. It sometimes happens that the man's passion has been inflamed in this way beyond the point of control, or perhaps he thinks that she is only acting the part of Byron's heroine, who 'saying she would not consent, consented,' and allows his passion to get the better

Elizabeth Anne Mills

of him, going the one slight step further, which converts spooning into the criminal act. Legally he has committed rape, that is, he has had carnal knowledge against the will of the female, yet when we consider that no passionate married man would have been able to desist if his passion were sexually aroused by his wife in a similar manner, it must be admitted that scientifically and morally we can hardly consider the foregoing a case of rape, and we are almost tempted to say that the female got about what she deserved. (Max Huhner, Medical Times, 1918)[1]

The recent move to reform rape laws stems from an increased awareness among legal scholars, women's groups, and society in general that rape victims have been traumatized by the criminal justice system for long enough. Like the criminal justice system, the medical profession has also been accused in recent years of insensitive treatment of physically and emotionally distraught victims. This chapter, through a review of medical literature on rape produced over the last century, finds that modern physicians' attitudes toward rape victims are deeply rooted in history.

During the first eighty years of medical rape literature reviewed (1880-1960), statements such as the one at the beginning of the chapter were not uncommon. In fact, they were more the rule than the exception. Until recently, medical writers simply did not consider the needs of rape victims. Their tone clearly suggested that victims often were not innocent parties to the crime; assumptions of woman as "liar" or seductress permeated many of the articles. Out of this mistrust stemmed an almost obsessive preoccupation with data collection and corroboration of the woman's testimony. By paying close attention to medico-legal evidence when examining alleged rape victims, physicians made certain that they did not bear the responsibility for convicting innocent men.

Although attitudes about women in general and rape victims in particular have changed significantly over the past twenty years, much of the literature on rape written by physicians during this period is still more concerned with proper techniques for gathering medico-legal evidence than with providing emotional support to the rape victim. Just as the criminal justice system has been slow to provide legal support to such victims, so has the medical profession failed to respond adequately to the physical and emotional needs of severely traumatized women. A better understanding of the underlying and historical precedent for these attitudes may provide impetus and guidance for change.

METHODOLOGY

The articles in this study were chosen after a complete review of all medical indexes from 1880 through 1980: *Index Medicus* (1879–1926); *Quarterly Cumulated Index Medicus* (1916–1956); *Current List of Medical Literature* (1941–1959); *Cumulated Index Medicus* (1960–1980); and *Index Catalogue of the Library of the Surgeon General's Office, United States Army*.[2] All English titles under the heading of "rape" were reviewed. Because this chapter focuses mainly on the medical and evidentiary aspects of rape, however, several indexed articles dealing more specifically with psychiatric implications of rape were excluded from the survey. Also excluded were titles representing letters to the editor, editorial comments, and articles written by nonmedical persons or medical personnel other than physicians.[3] Of the fifty-nine articles indexed for the years 1880–1960, forty-one were used as sources for this study.

Choosing articles for the years 1960–1980 presented a special problem, as there was a tremendous amount of literature indexed for those years. To keep the sample for the later period proportionate to the 41 articles reviewed for the first eighty years, 10 articles were chosen from the later years. After the exclusion of some articles from a total of 235,[4] 144 were assigned consecutive numbers and 10 were then chosen by means of a random number table.

1880–1960

Placing medical rape literature within an historical framework should provide some clues as to possible reasons for physicians' current attitudes toward rape victims. Particularly important to this understanding is background information on the period of 1880–1960 concerning status of women, composition of the medical profession, and physicians' attitudes toward women.

From 1880 to 1920, the early American feminist movement enjoyed its finest period; after nearly one hundred years of struggle, women achieved the right to vote, thus gaining a measure of "equality" with men.[5] Nevertheless, although they occasionally advocated radical causes, the movement — largely comprised of educated, middle-class women — rarely strayed far from "a strictly mainstream, Christian, Victorian approach toward marriage and morality."[6] In other words, "equality" seldom reached into the home. There, female sexuality was still largely regulated by men and any sexual response was considered "unwomanly." If a woman showed signs of the "disease" of sexuality, medical treatment might be sought to effectuate her cure.[7]

After 1920, in part due to American's preoccupation with two world wars and the Great Depression, the feminist movement lost momentum. The issue of equality diminished in importance as both sexes struggled with economic survival.[8] War economy created new job opportunities for women; it was not until after World War II that many women were "displaced" by returning veterans. As millions of women voluntarily turned back to homes and families in the late 1940s and 1950s, "domestic feminism" embraced the ideal of "full womb and selfless devotion to husband and children."[9]

During this same period of 1880–1960, medicine experienced reforms that in effect excluded most women from the profession. Beginning early in the twentieth century, rapid professionalization thoroughly reformed medical education in the United States. "Irregular" and "nonscientific" medical schools were forced to reform or close, admission standards were raised to require college training, and licensing boards were created.[10]

In the process, this sweeping reform movement established medicine as a predominantly white, upper-class, male profession.[11] Although the nineteenth-century feminist movement aided women's struggle to enter medical school, the fight was largely unsuccessful; at no point during the eighty-year period did women make up more than 6 percent of the total number of American physicians.[12] Those few who did practice were generally viewed with disfavor by male physicians, often because they advocated "unpopular" sexual reforms.[13]

As this brief historical overview indicates, America was predominantly a male-oriented society during this period. Societal attitudes and beliefs about women, and particularly about their sexuality, were largely dictated by men. And, as members of a highly respected profession, medical men were in an even stronger position to offer opinion as "fact" on such issues as rape, female neurosis, and nymphomania. As "scientific experts," male doctors "decided what constituted normal female sexuality"[14] and helped shape social beliefs about the physiology and psychology of American women.[15]

Some physicians specialized in the more specific area of rape. The majority of physicians treating and writing articles about rape victims were elite, white males. As "scientific experts," their views on sexuality and rape were highly regarded and frequently accepted by the general public. Medical rape literature during this period reflected and shaped society's perception of rape victims. The following sections review and analyze common themes and preoccupations in this literature: woman as liar; assaults on children; and common law and the medico-legal elements of rape.

Woman as Liar

> *It is true that rape is a most detestable crime and therefore ought severely and impartially to be punished with death; but it must be remembered that it is an accusation easily to be made and hard to be proved, and harder to be defended by the party accused though never so innocent.*[16]

This seventeenth-century statement by Justice Matthew Hale of England expressed the common belief in, and fear of, fabricated rape charges. That this belief was held by those in other than the legal profession is evidenced by its appearance in much of the medical literature, even as recently as the 1950s.[17] The general consensus among medical writers was that large numbers of cases brought to court were unfounded; one source stated that there were as many as twelve false accusations for every one true charge.[18]

Not only were men falsely accused, these authors contended, but they were also wrongly convicted and hanged or imprisoned.[19] Thus:

> *[F]or a man to have the finger of a woman pointed at him with a charge of a sexual offense is . . . to secure that man's extinction, no matter what the verdict of the jury may be, and that is . . . almost certain to be against him, no matter what the evidence may be.*[20]

Elizabeth Anne Mills

One reason that medical writers stressed false accusations was professional — to remind physicians of their vital role in determining the authenticity of physical rape evidence. Additionally, the fear of being wrongly accused of the crime probably also affected even the elite (and predominantly male) members of the medical profession.

To explain what they perceived as a high incidence of false accusations, physicians pointed to many motives, including revenge,[21] blackmail,[22] hallucinatory or delusional ideas,[23] a desire to inflict punishment or suffering,[24] an attempt to preserve a "chaste" reputation,[25] and an attempt to force marriage.[26] Discussions of these motives provide valuable insight into medical thinking about women and rape during the period under discussion.

Some physicians hypothesized that a woman sought revenge because she had sex with a man who then spurned her, and "[m]addened at the thought that she yielded to him perhaps too readily, unable to view with equanimity his lack of interest for her, the woman [would decide] to make him suffer."[27] Bronson, an early twentieth-century physician, maintained that upper-class women sometimes attempted extortion or blackmail in the hope of gaining out-of-court settlements. Such accusations, it was thought, were usually made with the support of the woman's husband or family, and often the family name itself added credence to the accusation.[28]

In earlier years, it was said, fear of blackmail had kept some men from traveling alone in railway carriages with single, unknown "female companions."[29] Bronson related a tale of an English judge who responded to a series of sexual assaults on women in railway trains by saying that "in his opinion men traveling on the railways were in greater danger from women's attempts at blackmail than were women from men's attempts at rape."[30]

Bronson's entire article focused on the subject of false rape accusations. In his opinion, many would-be rape victims were "hysterical": "We have to deal here with instances of enormous craving for public notice, a desire to attract attention as well as pity, in other words a manifestation of hysteria."[31] He stressed that these women were often convinced that the act had actually occurred, and sometimes even developed "hysterical stigmata" on their bodies showing "evidence" of a struggle. Bronson pointed out that the presence of such "injuries" would prove difficult for the accused to overcome in court.[32]

One of the reasons most commonly used to explain why women cried rape was their concern over reputation: "Not only innocent men but those who have been actually seduced have 'danced at the rope's end' on account of the woman's swearing away the life of the man in order to shield her priceless reputation!''[33] Bronson maintained that rape charges were usually brought against a friend, fiancé, or lover rather than a stranger. The following illustrates his interpretation of such an incident:

> [T]he relations between [them] . . . prior to the offense were by no means on a purely platonic plane. From secret loving glances to . . . intimate amorous caress, they have, to their mutual satisfaction traversed the whole via voluptatis. At length . . . [t]he man's erotic sensualism has attained its extremest tension, and he has therefore "suddenly" demanded complete possession — in other words he has arrived at the natural conclusion of all that has gone before. But at this point [she] . . . hesitates. . . . Although . . . she fails to understand . . . the sudden uprush of sexual need in the male . . . and although, owing to the comparatively undeveloped state of her own sexual sensibilities, she has but a hazy idea of . . . the sexual act, . . . she also yearns for the culmination of voluptuous ecstasy and for complete self-surrender. . . . [I]n most cases . . . the girl is a fully consenting party to what follows. [Sometimes], however, . . . [she] refuses [that which] . . . appears, of a sudden, insolent, and even criminal. But this revolt often comes too late. The man is now, in part owing to to [sic] the woman's own actions, in a state of sexual hyperexcitability which has . . . [deprived] him of the power of free rational self-determination. . . . [H]er sudden return to virtue is . . . regarded by him as merely an incomprehensible mood or as an underhand trick. Thus the amorous sport ends in an act of "rape," for which both parties are equally responsible, in the moral sense, but for which legally the man alone has to pay the hard and disgraceful penalty of imprisonment.[34]

According to the literature, certain community figures were more vulnerable than others to false accusations. Unfounded charges were likely to be made against teachers, for example, ''by hysterical girls who have a secret attachment for them.''[35] Physi-

Elizabeth Anne Mills

cians and dentists were often accused of raping patients who were under anesthesia.[36] To avoid unfair accusations, physicians were warned never to administer anesthetics to a woman without witnesses:

> *Women are peculiar and unreliable, and there is no ac-*
> *counting for the queer notions they may sometimes get*
> *into their heads; so that no physician is surely safe from*
> *trouble who has passed a period alone with a woman who*
> *has been made unconscious by an agent administered to*
> *her by him.*[37]

Alleged incidents of rape taking place during states of unconsciousness were to be carefully scrutinized, medical writers warned, because drugs may have caused dreamy "remembrances" or hallucinations. These in turn could have precipitated charges that were untrue. There also might have been other "collateral circumstances (such as the conduct and reputation of each party regarding the alleged crime and in general) that should be investigated.[38]

Medical authorities claimed that some women in these cases were so shrewd and devious that they would go to any lengths, even to smearing semen on themselves as a ruse[39] or placing blood-saturated sponges within the vagina to simulate the hemorrhaging that often follows first coitus.[40] They even inflicted injuries on their own bodies as "counterfeit signs of violence" to corroborate their testimony.[41] Chaddock warned physicians that:

> *[S]uch injuries are usually trivial in nature, and are*
> *situated on parts of the body easily accessible to her*
> *hands — i.e., the limbs and genitals . . . [and] are more*
> *likely to be present as abrasions and scratches than as*
> *bruises.*[42]

Physicians stated that the best way to combat these false accusations was to be extremely careful and methodical in the physical examination for injuries and presence of semen. Also, "[t]he victim should be encouraged to elaborate upon her account in order that any important discrepancies in her story may be brought to light."[43] According to Bronson, "[m]ore than half of all accusations of rape break down on close enquiry and are dismissed as false," either because the woman consented or because the act "could not possibly have taken place."[44] This placed tremendous responsibility on a physician and the subsequent medical report:

> *The . . . physician engaged for the preparation of testimony in an alleged case of rape has a massive burden of responsibility heaped upon him. There are so many factors which play a part in altering the physical evidence, that he must ever be on his guard lest some of his findings are misinterpreted or some fraud has been so subtly practiced that he may be led to a misinterpretation of his actual findings. The fact that the liberty, perhaps even the life, of the accused is in jeopardy renders the correct interpretation of the physical findings noted by the physician of the utmost importance.*[45]

Clearly, physicians of this period agreed with Hale's assertion that rape was "an accusation easily to be made," and they took upon themselves the task of interpreting the "facts" in cases of alleged rape. As the next section illustrates, their sense of responsibility for "weeding out" mistruth and "saving" innocent men from conviction extended even to cases involving children.

Assaults on Children

Sexual assaults on children were considered more prevalent than those on adult females. According to Anthony (1895), for example, the incidence was three to five times higher for children;[46] Mapes (1906) stated that of 22,017 cases of rape studied by Tardieu in France, 17,657 were on children, with 75 percent of the victims under the age of twelve.[47] Explanations for such figures included the common belief that intercourse with a virgin would cure gonorrhea; the opinion that the age of consent for statutory rape was too high; and, to a lesser degree, the hope or knowledge among perpetrators that childish weakness and innocence would render them easy prey.

In Europe, it was said, many cases of juvenile rape were motivated by the superstitious idea that venereal disease could be cured by intercourse with a virgin;[48] such cures were reportedly often suggested to men by "old women doctresses."[49] Although a virgin of any age would do, the younger the child, the more certain she was "uncontaminated" and would offer little or no resistance to the assault.[50]

Elizabeth Anne Mills

According to the medical literature, another factor having significant impact on the high number of juvenile assaults was the "age of consent." In the medico-legal context, this referred to the age at which a young woman could legally consent to sexual intercourse. Under common law, children below the age of ten were presumed incapable of giving such consent;[51] certain jurisdictions in Europe and the United States, however, established higher statutory limits.[52] Clearly, the higher the age limit, the greater the number of girls legally able to charge statutory rape. Some authors maintained that raising the age too high could result in a familiar problem — lies and false accusations. Mapes, for example, stated that:

> With the age of consent raised to eighteen years, it would, when placed within reach of the licentious, designing demi mondaine, many of whom are under the age of eighteen years, constitute a means for working evil that must not be underestimated; it would then be within her power to entice an innocent, ignorant schoolboy to her bagnio, and, after seducing him, institute criminal proceedings under protection of the law.[53]

Documenting cases of sexual assault would seem to be easier with children than with adults, simply because of the more severe injuries one would expect in instances of violent attempts at intercourse with young girls. However, medical authorities in the period under consideration would not have agreed with this supposition; they implied instead that many such cases were entirely unfounded. In some cases, they contended, adults coached girls for purposes of blackmail, and not only induced the child to tell a "rape story" but went so far as to injure her genitals to corroborate the story.[54] In other cases, the parents were said to have been innocently misled into filing charges by such symptoms as vaginal discharge.[55] In still other cases, the children were said to have had active "imaginations," to have made up stories for no apparent reason, or to have lied about their previous sexual experience.[56]

This attitude of disbelief toward juvenile assault victims made the physician's examination crucial. The presence of lacerations to the vagina or hymen, general body bruises, or profuse vaginal discharge were considered convincing evidence in some cases. Proof that the child as well as the alleged assailant had gonorrhea was also sometimes taken to indicate that the assault had actually occurred — in other words, that the child was telling the truth.[57]

In many cases, however, even the presence of such evidence led to debate. For example, physicians held that in most cases of alleged attempted penetration, there should be evidence of trauma to the child's genital organs. But on the other hand, some held that complete "defloration" (rupture of the hymen) was rare except in cases of extremely violent assault; supposedly, this was due to the improbability of achieving full penetration of an infantile vagina.[58] Further, it was claimed that some children showed little evidence of genital trauma either because they were bribed and did not resist the assault or because the assailant attempted only vulvar penetration or manual dilitation.[59] Because small children would be generally unable to resist attack, it was also pointed out that there might be no evidence of general resistance such as body bruises, cuts, or torn clothing.[60] Some of the literature on sexual assault of children, in other words, suggests a deep confusion on the part of medical men as they attempted to deal simultaneously with their suspicion of false accusation on the one hand and special consideration for children on the other.

Evidence of vaginal discharge created even greater confusion. According to medical authorities, profuse vaginal discharge often indicated the existence of venereal disease, generally gonorrhea, and the probability that sexual assault had occurred. The problem, they said, was that in many cases it was difficult to distinguish between venereal discharge and vaginal leukorrhea, an infection often resulting from worms or uncleanliness. When examining children who lived in unsanitary conditions, physicians frequently had difficulty ascertaining whether the infection was venereal (and therefore evidentiary) or of the more common leukorrheal type.[61]

In 1886, Dr. Jerome Walker described in detail the physician's role in juvenile assault cases. His article, describing twenty-one cases of alleged assault, suggested guidelines for physicians to follow. Although Walker stated that any sexual penetration of a child was rape, and that even the feeling of a child's legs was indecent assault, he also stressed that doctors had to be very careful not to "wrongfully swear away a fellow being's liberty" or bring "disgrace and damage [on] both the man and his family" by presenting "carelessly-arrived-at conclusions" to the court.[62] Walker sug-

Elizabeth Anne Mills

gested that physicians involved in juvenile assault cases routinely ask themselves the following questions in the course of examination:

1. *Is the child's story probable, possible? What motive is there, if any, for her falsifying?*
2. *What motive, if any, is there for one or both parents, or any relation or friend, abetting the child in her statements?*
3. *What was the motive that induced the alleged assailant to attempt connection? Is his story probable?*
4. *What physical evidence is there that the child has been injured or penetrated?*
5. *Has the injury found resulted from attempted connection or . . . some other [action]? Is the discharge leucorrhea [sic] or gonorrhea?*[63]

Walker used the twenty-one cases of "alleged" juvenile assault and rape to illustrate the types of difficult cases that a physician might encounter. All twenty-one cases involved children between the ages of two and fourteen years; eleven were incest cases involving a father, stepfather, foster father, brother, or uncle. In eight of the twenty-one cases, over one-third of the total, the child's story was looked upon with disbelief and charges were made but never pursued. Even cases showing evidence of genital trauma remained suspect. Essentially, the physician and others felt that the child was making up the story or that the mother was inducing her to tell it because of her own ulterior motives.[64] Although these particular cases are perhaps not representative of all juvenile assault cases, it is interesting to note the outcomes: seven were dismissed for lack of evidence, two were still pending at the time of publication, and the defendants in the rest were sentenced as follows: twenty years (1); ten years (4); five years (2); four years, six months (1); eighteen months (1); one year (1); and six months (2).[65]

Walker's data are too extensive to present here in their entirety. However, two cases that illustrate the general attitude of physicians toward juvenile assault victims are summarized below. One case involved possible evidence of genital trauma and venereal disease; the other lacked specific findings, relying instead on the child's testimony.

One Hundred Years of Fear

The first case was that of a two-year-old girl whose genitals were reported to be "quite red" and to show evidence of pus and "healing excoriations." Walker's examination of her father indicated that he might have gonorrhea, which he admitted having had several weeks earlier. He also said he had had the disease before, at the same time his older daughter had it. Walker examined the child's mother and found that she showed large amounts of leukorrhea. She told Walker that both her daughters had "slept with the father when he had 'the disease.' "[66]

It would seem that Walker had found good evidence of sexual assault in this case: genital injury to a very young child and evidence of venereal disease in both father and child. The result, then, was surprising: the child's parents were each sentenced to six months on a vagrancy charge, and assault charges were never even proffered. Dr. Walker noted: "character of both parents was bad, but there was no evidence of any indecent assault on [the] child. Still if I had been positive that [the] child had gonorrhea, punishment would have been different."[67]

In the second case, Walker examined a seven-year-old girl and found no inflammation or injury to her genitals. The child's foster mother told him she woke up one night and saw her husband in bed with the child. The next day, she said, the girl walked lamely, did not feel well, and had swollen "privates." She said the girl told her that the man had "peed all over her . . . when he slept with her," that he put his hand on her "but didn't touch her otherwise," and that she was wet on her legs when she woke and saw him "turning away from her." She also said the moisture was not "white or sticky."[68]

This case resulted in the child's removal from the foster home. Walker's conclusion, however, indicated that he felt the child was lying:

> The questions [that] arise in this case [are:] did the child concoct this story in dread of the mother; did the child wet herself by urination; did the father urinate on or near her; did he handle her. It is fair to presume that the child's story is not true, and that the mother made the child lie. Yet in this case if a doctor had testified as to the slightest abrasion within the privates, the father's chances for a term in prison were good.[69]

The lack of visible evidence in this case apparently led Walker to conclude that both women — mother and child — had lied. Each case illustrates Walker's reluctance to testify against alleged rapists, even when clinical evidence seemed to exist.

Clearly, a juvenile rape victim's age did not make her any more "believable" in the eyes of physicians. As in adult rape cases, physicians were primarily concerned not with the victim's feelings, but with the search for evidence to prove, or more likely *disprove*, the allegations. Examination of the medico-legal requirements of rape, as described in the medical literature, provides further evidence of this pattern.

Common Law and the Medico-Legal Elements of Rape

The word *rape* probably originated from a number of other words generally interpreted to mean "violently or forcibly snatch, seize, attack, plunder, steal, or carry away."[70] Expansion of this definition by medico-legal writers produced the common law definition of rape as "the carnal knowledge of a woman forcibly and against her will. . . ."[71] This definition was not all-inclusive, as many jurisdictions operated under statutory laws slightly different from common law; case law also created a number of definitional problems.[72] This section, however, is limited to an examination of common law elements of rape as they were dicussed in the surveyed literature.

At one time, carnal knowledge by legal definition required both full penetration of the penis into the victim's vagina and seminal emission.[73] By the late 1880s, however, even the slightest degree of penetration of the female genitals by the male organ legally constituted carnal knowledge.[74] Although most of the literature dealt with vaginal rape of females, there was some mention of females raping male children[75] and of anal assaults and assaults utilizing foreign objects.[76]

What were physicians to look for as evidence of "carnal knowledge?" According to several authors, there were three good indicators: (1) genital lacerations or bruising, especially tearing of the hymen in virgins; (2) presence of semen and/or spermatozoa in the vagina or in/around the genitalia; and (3) presence of venereal disease.

Medical literature, especially that written for forensic physicians, described female genitalia in great detail — how they appeared in the normal state and what changes were to alert a physician that "carnal knowledge" had taken place.[77] According to the literature, the easiest and most obvious cases to document involved virgins in whom the hymen had been ruptured. However, in other cases:

> [I]t is . . . sometimes difficult, and often absolutely impossible, to say whether the penis has . . . merely impinged upon, or has . . . penetrated just inside, the vulva, unless the amount of violence used in its introduction has . . . been sufficient to cause abrasion or laceration.[78]

In yet other cases in which the victim was not a virgin, had borne children, and/or was accustomed to intercourse, genital trauma was not as likely to have occurred except in cases of extreme violence.[79]

Several articles discussed the hymen, particularly in relation to virginity and evidence of carnal knowledge in sexual assault victims. Detailed descriptions of the types and characteristics of hymens acknowledged tremendous variation from woman to woman. In fact, cases were cited of women who had intact hymens after many years of intercourse or even after bearing children.[80] Thus, although popularly regarded as "absolute proof" in rape cases, the presence or absence of hymenal injury was not in itself considered conclusive evidence for or against rape.[81]

According to many authors, the presence of semen and/or spermatozoa on the victim's genitalia or upon clothing or bedclothing also indicated that sexual activity had taken place.[82] Gathering evidence of this type required special techniques when suspicious stains on clothing were involved. There were two methods of determining whether stains were of seminal origin. The first and most reliable, isolating intact spermatozoa from cloth, involved careful observation (often with the aid of ultraviolet light), painstaking dissolution, and microscopic inspection for the presence of intact sperm.[83] This process was extremely difficult, tedious, and far from foolproof, especially because the only clearly distinguishing feature between sperm and other *Trichomonas vaginae* was the "tail" commonly found on intact spermatozoa.[84]

If spermatozoa could not be isolated, or if additional evidence was sought, a second method, performing chemical tests to detect the presence of seminal fluid, was utilized. The first chemical test for semen was described in 1896.[85] By the 1940s, these tests had become more specific and useful to physicians, and blood groups of individuals could be determined from seminal stains.[86] The tests enabled forensic physicians to isolate evidence that matched up alleged assailants with their victims.[87]

A third type of evidence important to proving sexual contact or carnal knowledge was the existence of gonorrhea or syphilis. When the alleged rapist as well as the victim evidenced venereal infection, the woman's testimony was corroborated.[88] Physicians were urged to be cautious, however, to be sure that incubation periods of the disease were taken into consideration. This meant that tests had to be made immediately after the alleged rape to rule out the possibility that the woman had venereal disease at the time of the assault.[89] The point was also made that gonorrhea, in particular, was difficult to diagnose in women because its symptoms resembled those of other vaginal infections.[90]

Force and Absence of Consent

Other issues raised by the legal definition of rape involved questions of force, resistance, and consent. Often, physicians' interpretations of the law differed significantly from those of legal professionals. A 1923 law review note, for example, argued that although force was one way of having intercourse against a woman's will, other means such as "taking advantage of the victim while she is asleep or unconscious" were also used by rapists. The legal point of view here was that "[t]he crime . . . consists in the outrage to the modesty and feelings of the female by carnal knowledge effected without or against her consent," and that actual force did not have to be proved.[91] The philosophy endorsed by this member of the legal profession was not generally shared by medical writers of the same period or even later. Rather, they stated that a sexual assault committed while a woman was asleep or in a state of drug- or alcohol-induced unconsciousness raised legal questions of consent and absence of resistance. Cases of fraud — for example, pretending to be a woman's husband to obtain consent to intercourse — were generally thought to be invalid.[92] Chaddock (1948) flatly stated, for instance, that "[i]ntercourse accomplished by means of deception, where there has been neither threat nor purpose to use violence or force of any kind, is not rape in the eyes of the law."[93]

Issues of force, resistance, and consent were all intertwined. The resistance standard was used to measure not only the amount and extent of force used, but also whether or not the victim consented to the rape: "Resistance is the most immediate expression of the act being against the will of the female."[94] To physicians, then, physical evidence of force — severe injuries resulting from beating, choking, and other brutal physical violence — was "tangible proof" not only that rape had occurred, but that it had occurred with force and without consent.[95]

The law dictated that women were to resist rape with all their strength, and that force had to be of sufficient intensity to accomplish its purpose.[96] However, "moral force" — threats of violence, of injury to a relative, of weapons, or of several assailants — was recognized to be as powerful as physical force in terms of lowering resistance.[97] Nevertheless, many authors insisted that few rapes occurred without a victim's consent if she was healthy and truly unwilling. Mapes (1917) provided a good example of this philosophy:

> [E]very physician knows that so long as consciousness and consequent physical ability to resist remain, no adult female can be forcibly compelled to acquiesce, since for anatomic and physiologic reasons the male is incapable of successfully "fighting and copulating" at the same time; moreover, regardless of what may be the relative strength of the male compared to the female, so long as she remains conscious and retains the ability to preserve intimate contact of her thighs, vaginal phallic intromission is a physical impossibility. . . . "The man who enters into so hard a task will find that his penis will drop inevitably; because the excitement of all his muscles to action in order to accomplish his designs drains the tide of blood necessary to sustain erection away from the penis and it will irrevocably fall."[98]

By 1948, however, another author expressed a more enlightened point of view:

> Absence of such evidence of resistance must not be construed as conclusive proof that the woman has not offered all the resistance of which she was capable. . . . It should be remembered that nothing is so likely to cause temporary psychic paralysis in a woman as a violent and

unexpected sexual approach. Fear of intent or threat to inflict bodily injury is a potent source of failure to use strenuous physical resistance. Attempts to gain help by outcry are means of resistance, but . . . fear or psychic paralysis intervenes to prevent the cry of alarm.[99]

The literature represented above illustrates a singular lack of concern for the emotional needs of rape victims. A pervasive attitude of "all women are liars" formed the basis for many articles. Beyond this assumption was an overriding concern with the medico-legal protection of the examining physician.

Admittedly, it was the legal profession (also male-dominated) that was responsible for establishing complex rules for rape prosecutions that required corroborative proof of the victim's testimony:

[M]an's law has sought to measure such relative, qualitative and interrelated concepts as moral character, force, fear, consent, will and resistance to satisfy the overriding male concern that beyond the female's oath, her word, her testimony, there was not mutual intercourse and subsequent vindictiveness and wrath, but an objective, tangible crime.[100]

However, it seems clear that the predominantly male composition of the medical profession had some bearing on the demonstrated fear of false accusations and resultant anxiety over being responsible for wrongful convictions. As men, they undoubtedly believed that many women lied in these cases; as physicians, they were only too willing to comply with the "protective" legalities created by the criminal justice system.

1960–1980

The period of 1960 to 1980 has witnessed a rebirth of feminism. Since the late 1960s, feminists have sought to unite American women in the fight for the Equal Rights Amendment, child-care centers and equal pay, and sexual autonomy. Several goals have been achieved: mass entry of women into many levels of the work force, decline in sexual double standards, access to abortion and birth control, and reform in rape law and its evidentiary requirements.[101] Even the historically sexist medical profession has

One Hundred Years of Fear

lowered its barriers to women.[102] The physician's reputation as "scientific expert" has been disputed, as women now "question their doctor's opinion on their cervix, not to mention his ideas about sexuality, marriage or femininity."[103]

Despite recent major advancements by women, however, deeply imbedded societal and medical attitudes have been slow to recede. Review of medical rape literature written during the past two decades reveals that some striking similarities in philosophy have spanned one hundred years of medical writing. In spite of changing attitudes toward women, medical writers of the 1960s and 1970s share many attitudes and misconceptions with their colleagues of earlier years.

For example, a recent article by Woodling, Evans, and Bradbury begins by acknowledging that rape is no more falsely reported than other offenses, but then proceeds to discuss the fantasies, hysterical personalities, and other "unconscious factors" that could lead to false rape reports: "[R]epressed erotic wishes or masturbational fantasies may be changed into beliefs that are so structured that the woman may be convinced of her claim of rape despite convincing contrary evidence."[104] Other authors also address the problem of false accusations, citing such motives as revenge,[105] blackmail,[106] and protection of reputation.[107]

As was the case in earlier literature, modern physicians are urged to be extremely careful in their examinations of alleged rape victims because rape is a serious crime that is difficult to prove. Graves and Francisco echo Justice Hale and other early writers on this point:

> Medical evidence usually determines whether the complaint of a rape was alleged or real. Since this is true, a doctor is usually the key witness, and in addition may need to double as an "expert." Thus, the attending physician has a legal responsibility he cannot avoid. The need for careful examination and meticulous records is obvious. . . . It is always well to bear in mind that there is no charge which is more easily made than that of the crime of rape and there is no crime in which the innocence of the accused may be so difficult to prove.[108]

Physicians continue to point out that a physical examination and a complete history of the attack may reveal subtle motives on the part

Elizabeth Anne Mills

of the alleged victim and/or self-inflicted injuries.[109] Further, the medical report is still viewed as so important that "the life of a man may depend upon the examiner's competence and skill."[110]

Despite recent attention focused on medical responses of both physicians and hospital staff to rape victims, many problems persist. One problem raised recently concerns the reluctance of many private physicians to appear in court to testify in rape cases. Reasons range from uneasiness about their expertise and fear of how they will appear before a defense attorney to, most commonly, resentment of the time and money lost by court appearances.[111] Increasingly, this problem has led to an upswing of treatment in hospital emergency rooms. But, in many cases, even emergency rooms will send these patients to city hospitals, which cannot turn anyone away. In Philadelphia, for example, all rape victims are routinely taken to Philadelphia General Hospital for treatment unless there is a medical or surgical injury.[112]

Although many emergency rooms are developing strong rape crisis and response units,[113] not all hospital personnel are objective in their response to victims. Said one male gynecologist: " 'There is one type of woman I would have a hard time believing was raped: a woman between 16 and 25, on the pill and no longer a virgin.' "[114] In another instance, physicians reportedly told patients before or during examination that there was "no such thing as rape."[115]

Attitudes like these serve only to undermine efforts to respond more fairly and humanely in cases of rape. But fortunately, as the next section illustrates, medical attitudes toward *juvenile* assault victims have shifted significantly in the past twenty years.

Assaults on Children

Recent literature, like that of the past, reports a high incidence of sexual assault on female children. One study found that an estimated two hundred thousand to five hundred thousand assaults occur annually in the United States, with five thousand of them being incestuous.[116] Other studies report 24 percent of all rape victims to be in the pediatric age group (fourteen years and under), with 53 percent of these cases involving incest.[117] Like those from earlier years, these rates are attributed, in part, to the accessibility and manageability of young girls. Another reason advanced is the persistence, in some parts of the world, of the superstitious belief that venereal disease is cured only by intercourse with a virgin.[118]

Like their earlier counterparts, modern physicians consider the physical examination to be crucial in these cases. They agree that general bodily injuries are rare, as children do not know how to resist, but state that trauma to the genitals often occurs during violent attacks.[119] Other recommended tests parallel those in adult examinations: presence of spermatozoa, gonorrhea, and/or pregnancy.[120]

Unlike the earlier literature, however, recent articles make no reference to the likelihood of false accusations by children. Rather, they assert that juvenile sexual assault cases are more likely to be believed and reported than adult cases.[121] There is also an emphasis in recent literature on the importance of being gentle with children during examination and counseling them when necessary, something unheard of in the past.[122]

Medico-Legal Elements of Rape

The common law requirements of rape — carnal knowledge, force, and lack of consent — must be met today as in the past,[123] and medico-legal corroboration of these elements is still a determining factor in the courtroom. In recent years, clinical techniques have grown more sophisticated; laboratory testing is now more precise and therefore more valuable in rape cases, especially to corroborate carnal knowledge. As a result, modern physicians are able to present more accurate data to judges and jurors who may then decide for themselves whether the alleged rapist is guilty or innocent. This is a significant change from the past, when judicial decisions were often based on the opinions of medical rape "experts."

Although any degree of vulvar penetration by the penis constitutes rape, and there need not be trauma to the hymen or its appendages for rape to have occurred,[124] the absence of any finding concerning penetration is often used legally to deny that carnal knowledge occurred.[125] Thus, findings of genital injury or evidence of seminal emission or venereal disease still help corroborate this element of the crime.

Today, the technology of forensic chemistry has simplified detection of spermatozoa or seminal fluid. No longer is laboratory examination of clothing subject to the painstaking and inexact process of dissolution described by earlier writers. Now there are such chemical tests as acid phosphatase, which can detect the slightest amount of seminal fluid present. Most writers advise taking immediate smears, swabbings, and wet mounts from rectal, vaginal, perianal, and oral zones; examining wet mounts immediately for motile sperm; and sending any suspiciously stained clothing to the laboratory.[126] Even with the perfection of these techniques, however, writers still observe that positive visualization of spermatozoa is the only reliable proof of the presence of semen.[127]

Forensic chemistry may also be a valuable tool in establishing links between victim and suspect. Pubic hairs may be admissible evidence on the issue of identity, and specimens of blood and/or saliva collected from both suspect and victim may help establish linkages by seminal fluid grouping and blood grouping.[128]

Force and Absence of Consent

As noted earlier, the issues of force and lack of consent are closely intertwined. Common legal definitions, according to two recent articles, often require victims to resist sexual assault to the end, giving up only if unconscious, paralyzed by fear of death or severe bodily harm, or overcome by brute force.[129] Modern physicians maintain that proof of such resistance may often be established on the basis of a medical history, evaluation, and physical examination. For example, Woodling, Evans, and Bradbury note that:

> The issue of consent may be clarified by the physician's comments regarding (1) the presence or absence of physical injuries; (2) the victim's emotional responses; (3) the victim's clothing, e.g., tears, debris, soiling; (4) the serum alcohol or drug levels of the victim or the accused or both; (5) the promptness of the victim's crime report as confirmed by the physician's examination.[130]

The literature offers many suggestions for interviewing and examining rape victims; the physician is again reminded that his/her report is "a strong piece of courtroom evidence that cannot be prepared hastily."[131] Initial observation of the victim is urged in terms of dress, apparent intelligence, hysteria, and (particularly) demeanor. Also, physicians are advised to note the approximate time of assault, time of arrival at the hospital, and the victim's actions between the alleged rape and presentation for examination.[132]

The physical examination is key in determining "forcible rape." The physician is directed to pay careful attention to such signs of violence as contusions, abrasions, scratches, lacerations, grip marks on arms and neck, bite marks, and so on. Examination of the head and throat is especially important because choking or a blow to the head could impair the ability to resist.[133] As Woodling, Evans, and Bradbury note:

> *Many times the precise documentation of these signs can be as persuasive in the minds of jurors as laboratory tests. In fact, the absence of these physical findings frequently detracts from the credibility of the victim's story at the trial.*[134]

Thus, it is recommended that the physician be as thorough as possible in examining the genitals, face, mouth, breasts, and rectum. Any bruises, lacerations, or signs of fondling or trauma are to be "described with meticulous detail as to size, coloration, and body location."[135]

New Topics: Treatment and Counseling

Recent medical literature addresses two topics neglected by earlier writers, both of them dealing with the physician's management and treatment of rape victims. The first involves the chance of a victim becoming pregnant or getting venereal disease. Possible ways of protecting victims against each are discussed.[136] The second topic reflects the importance of counseling for rape victims.[137] Both areas are discussed in terms of suggested protocol for hospitals in the emergency care of rape and sexual assault victims.[138]

Although there has clearly been a significant attitudinal change in medical rape literature during the last twenty years, many prejudicial attitudes are still evident. For example, although there are some entirely new foci on rape counseling and protection of victims from pregnancy and venereal disease, some physicians still believe there is "no such thing as rape." Physicians' attitudes, like those of the criminal justice system and society in general, are steeped in tradition; as such, they are in need of extensive change. A better understanding of the origins of such attitudes may prove to be the impetus necessary for that change.

Elizabeth Anne Mills

CONCLUSION

Over the past twenty years, feminists and other concerned citizens have deplored the shoddy treatment rape victims receive from the criminal justice system — judges, jurors, police, and prosecutors. From the initial interview of the victim by leering police officers to the courtroom scenario where the victim, not the alleged rapist, is "on trial," the criminal justice system's method and attitude seem guided more by the fear of wrongfully convicting a man of the crime than by the principles of justice and due process.

As this chapter has illustrated, medical treatment of rape victims during the past one hundred years has often also reflected that fear. Between 1880 and 1960, a predominantly male group of physicians "enlightened" their colleagues and the rest of society about the most important thing to remember in rape cases: be extremely meticulous in your examination and history, as many women and girls falsely accuse men of sexual assault; if you make erroneous, hasty conclusions, you may be responsible for sending an innocent man to his death. Although early medical articles provided superb testimonials to the science of gynecology and rape forensics of the day, they simply ignored the victim herself except in terms of medico-legal relevance. Perhaps this disproportionate concern for the accused was based upon cases in the physicians' experience; more likely, it reflected the ideology of "women as liar" that has long pervaded male attitudes toward rape victims.

Recently, physicians and hospitals have attempted to respond more adequately to what has been termed the "rape trauma syndrome"; to an extent, current literature recognizes the importance of treatment and counseling for victims. Further, there has recently been a major shift in legal philosophy: modern physicians recognize that they are responsible only for gathering evidence and submitting a medical finding, and that the question of whether rape occurred is a legal issue for the courts to decide. In the past, many courts allowed "expert" medical witnesses to testify to the authenticity of the assault. Despite these changes, a tone of caution is evident with regard to victim credibility; discussions of evidentiary requirements and physician responsibility fill page after page of recent articles by physicians.[139]

Clearly, legal processes established by the criminal justice system and physicians' reactions to rape victims have reinforced each other throughout the past one hundred years. Existence of any cause/effect relationship is a matter of speculation. It is probably safe to say, however, that it was male control over both professions that formed the basis for prejudicial attitudes persisting today — both within these professions and among the general public. Attempts to reverse these attitudes have been fraught with frustration. Rape continues to result in quadruple victimization, as the actual assault is followed by psychological assaults from police, medical personnel, and the judicial system.

NOTES

1. Max Huhner, "Is Rape Always a Crime?" *Medical Times* 96, 2 (February 1918):34.

2. Using medical indexes proved to be a formidable task. Many of the early ones were poorly indexed and catalogued, making the process of review both tedious and confusing. For instance, some indexes recorded only the authors' names and the page number where the citations could be found under the index heading ("rape"). It was then necessary to go to each page number, look for the author's name, and find out whether the article was in English. Often, the title was in English while the article itself was not; the only way to determine this was to look up the full title of the journal in question and determine its place of publication. An additional problem was the overlap among various indexes. Several covered some of the same years, yet all had to be reviewed due to the possibility of different selection criteria within each indexing body.

3. Early medical authors were all physicians; therefore, for consistency, later articles written by nonphysicians were excluded. Additionally, articles dealing with purely legal aspects of specific rape cases were not included.

4. *See* note 3 and accompanying text *supra*.

5. For an example of a more detailed history of women during this period, *see* Lois W. Banner, *Women in Modern America* (New York: Harcourt Brace Jovanovich, 1974), pp. 1–26.

6. Gerda Lerner, *The Majority Finds Its Past* (New York: Oxford University Press, 1979), p. 33.

7. *See* Gena Corea, *The Hidden Malpractice: How American Medicine Treats Women as Patients and Professionals* (New York: William Morrow, 1977), pp. 86–92. In particular, women who demonstrated "the illness of sexuality" (nymphomania) were often handled by simply cutting out their sexual organs — clitorises, ovaries, and uteri (ibid., pp. 94–96).

8. *See*, for example, Banner, *Women in Modern America*, pp. 191–96; and Lerner, *The Majority Finds Its Past*, p. 35.

9. Marlene Dixon, "The Rise of Women's Liberation," in *Masculine/Feminine*, ed. Betty Roszak and Theodore Roszak (New York: Harper and Row, 1969), pp. 188–89. *See also* Lerner, *The Majority Finds Its Past*, p. 35; Banner, *Women in Modern America*, pp. 216–23; and Barbara Ehrenreich and Deirdre English, *For Her Own Good: 150 Years of the Experts' Advice to Women* (New York: Anchor, 1978), pp. 160–64. Female sexuality remained a dormant issue until the

Kinsey Report in the mid-1950s; *see* A. C. Kinsey et al., *Sexual Behavior in the Human Female* (Philadelphia: W. B. Saunders, 1953).

10. Nineteenth-century medicine was far from "professional," as hundreds of ill-trained doctors joined the ranks each year. No formal educational requirements existed, and licensing boards were still a thing of the future. Realizing the futility of trying to change the "rank and file," medical reformers and the American Medical Association fought to reform medical education instead. For a detailed description of the medical reform movement and the professionalization of medicine, *see* James G. Burrow, *Organized Medicine in the Progressive Era* (Baltimore: Johns Hopkins University Press, 1977), pp. 14–104; and Eliot Friedson, *The Profession of Medicine* (New York: Dodd, Mead, 1970).

11. Ehrenreich and English, *For Her Own Good*, pp. 79–80. Many of the so-called irregular or nonscientific medical schools forced to close were among the few progressive enough to admit women and minorities. Also, the establishment of college training as a requirement for medical school was highly restrictive in a nation where only 5 percent of the population attended college. For more detailed descriptions of women's fight to enter medicine, *see* Mary Roth Walsh, *"Doctors Wanted: No Women Need Apply"* (New Haven: Yale University Press, 1977); and Corea, *The Hidden Malpractice*, pp. 22–73.

12. Walsh, *"Doctors Wanted,"* pp. 185–86.

13. Ehrenreich and English, *For Her Own Good*, p. 60.

14. Corea, *The Hidden Malpractice*, p. 94.

15. *See generally* Corea, *The Hidden Malpractice*, and Ehrenreich and English, *For Her Own Good*, for discussions of how women have been (and continue to be) treated by male physicians, particularly gynecologists.

16. Justice Matthew Hale, as quoted in Susan Brownmiller, *Against Our Will: Men, Women and Rape* (New York: Simon and Schuster, 1975), p. 413.

17. *See*, for example, Sidney Smith, "Alleged Rape," *British Medical Journal* 2 (15 December 1951):1454.

18. Charles C. Mapes, "A Practical Consideration of Sexual Assault," *The Medical Age* 24 (1906):937.

19. For example, Mapes (ibid., p. 936) wrote:
[It] is safe to state that Jackson State Prison (Michigan) contains more innocent men convicted of rape (sexual assault) than all other innocents there multiplied together, for the reason that in such cases there are usually but two witnesses to the crime, and the man's evidence counts for nothing as a rule, while the woman's testimony is accepted verbatim. . . . Judge Lynch has executed more innocent men for this crime than for all others combined.

It should be noted, however, that not all authors believed that too many men were wrongfully punished. One extremely racist article written in 1904, for instance, argued for the use of penile amputation as punishment for rape; however, the author confined himself to a savage attack on blacks as perpetrators of "lust crimes." He insisted that this was due to "brute instinct" and that the way to prevent further criminal assault was through total asexualization. *See* F. D. Daniel, "The Cause and Prevention of Rape," *Texas Medical Journal* 19, 11 (1904):451–62; cf. J. A. deArmand, "Asexualization as a Punishment for Rape," *The Medical Bulletin* 20 (1898):55–56.

One Hundred Years of Fear

20. Lawson Tait, "An Analysis of the Evidence in Seventy Consecutive Cases of Charges Made Under the New Criminal Law Amendment Act," *The Provincial Medical Journal* 13 (1 May 1894):226.

21. Ibid., p. 232; J. P. Gonzales, "Virginity: Rape and Other Sexual Assaults: Examination of Semen," in *Legal Medicine, Pathology and Toxicology*, ed. A. Gonzales (New York: Appleton-Century, 1937), p. 605; F. R. Bronson, "False Accusations of Rape," *The American Journal of Urology and Sexology* 14 (December 1918):540; Charles G. Chaddock, "Rape," in *Textbook of Legal Medicine and Toxicology*, ed. Frederick Peterson and Walter S. Haines (Philadelphia: W. B. Saunders, 1904), p. 137.

22. Tait, "An Analysis of the Evidence," pp. 228-29, 232; Gonzales, "Virginity," p. 605; W. D. Sutherland, "Charges of Rape," *The Indian Medical Gazette* 50 (May 1915):171; Francis W. Anthony, "Rape," *Boston Medical and Surgical Journal* 132, 2 (17 January 1895):31; Bronson, "False Accusations," p. 540; Charles C. Mapes, "Higher Enlightenment Versus 'Age of Consent,'" *The Medical Age* 14(1896):106.

23. Bronson, "False Accusations," pp. 540–42; Chaddock, "Rape" (1904), p. 137.

24. Bronson, "False Accusations," p. 450.

25. One author illustrated this with the case of an old woman who accused some young boys of a sexual offense because they owed her money; she wanted "merely to get the young men into trouble, as they had not repaid the loan" (Sutherland, "Charges of Rape," p. 171). *See also* Tait, "An Analysis of the Evidence," pp. 226, 230; and Bronson, "False Accusations," p. 540.

26. Tait, "An Analysis of the Evidence," p. 229; Bronson, "False Accusations," p. 540.

27. Bronson, "False Accusations," p. 540.

28. Ibid.

29. Tait, "An Analysis of the Evidence," p. 226.

30. Bronson, "False Accusations," p. 551.

31. Ibid., p. 541.

32. Ibid., pp. 541–42.

33. Mapes, "A Practical Consideration," p. 937.

34. Bronson, "False Accusations," pp. 551–52.

35. Ibid., p. 545.

36. *See* "Unconscious Impregnation," *Lancet* 1 (20 February 1886):361; Chaddock, "Rape" (1904), p. 138; and Mapes, "A Practical Consideration," p. 937. Cf. Henry A. Riley, "A Crime Peculiar to a Physician," *The Medical Record* 27 (10 January 1885):34–35. Riley discussed several cases involving physicians who induced female patients to have "sexual connection" with them by force or fraud; often they told the women that sex was part of their medical "treatment."

37. "The Danger of Administering Anesthetics Without Witnesses," *The Medical and Surgical Reporter* 46 (18 February 1882):185.

38. Chaddock, "Rape" (1904), pp. 138-39; Bronson, "False Accusations," p. 544; "Unconscious Impregnation," p. 361.

39. J. R. Garner, "Detailed Examination Required to Determine Whether Rape Has Been Committed," *American Journal of Medical Jurisprudence* 1, 1 (September 1938): 30.

40. Mapes, "A Practical Consideration," p. 934.

41. Chaddock, "Rape" (1904), p. 137; Bronson, "False Accusations," pp. 540-41.

42. Chaddock, "Rape" (1904), p. 137.

43. Gonzales, "Virginity," p. 606. *See also* Garner, "Detailed Examination," pp. 29-31; Chaddock, "Rape" (1904), pp. 127-40; Anthony, "Rape," pp. 30-32; Smith, "Alleged Rape," pp. 171-72; and "Rape," *The Medical Press and Circular* (23 July 1890):87.

44. Bronson, "False Accusations," pp. 550-51.

45. Garner, "Detailed Examination," p. 29. *See also* articles cited in note 43 *supra*.

46. Anthony, "Rape," p. 31.

47. Mapes, "A Practical Consideration," pp. 933-34. The period of study was not specified.

48. *See,* for example, Frederick W. Lowndes, "Syphilis in a Girl, Aged 14, The Result of an Alleged Criminal Assault: with Remarks on Some of the Medico-Legal Aspects of Such Cases," *Liverpool Medico-Chirurgical Journal* 4, 7 (July 1883):299-304; Gurney Williams, "Rape in Children and in Young Girls," part II, *International Clinics* III (23rd Series, 1913):252-53.

49. Lowndes, "Syphilis in a Girl," p. 301; idem, "Criminal Assaults on Children Resulting in Infection with Disease," *The Medical Press and Circular* (26 November 1884):455.

50. Chaddock, "Rape" (1904), p. 139; *See also* Lowndes, "Syphilis in a Girl," pp. 300-304; and idem, "Criminal Assaults," pp. 455-56, in which the author reviewed recent literature pertaining to this superstition.

51. Mapes, "A Practical Consideration," p. 932.

52. *See* Mapes, ibid., for a scattered listing of ages of consent in various states.

53. Mapes, "Higher Enlightenment," p. 106. Mapes did not favor raising the age of consent to "legislate morality"; rather, he advocated encouraging parents to try harder to instill knowledge of sexuality and sexual morality in their children at an early age. He believed (ibid., p. 107) that higher age-of-consent laws were unfair to males by punishing only the boy involved in statutory rape, and that there should be "the same degree of enlightenment on the part of both [as] each is equally guilty if the law be transgressed." *See also* Tait, ("An Analysis of the Evidence," p. 229), who suggested that raising the age of consent created a "fertile source of blackmail" because a young woman might seduce a man, blackmail him, and then if he "paid up," arrange for a defense that included making her look much older. If he would not pay, she would be made to look much younger.

54. Jerome Walker, "Reports, with Comments, of Twenty-One Cases of Indecent Assault and Rape Upon Children," *Archives of Pediatrics* 3, 6 (June 1886):332-33; Gurney Williams, "Rape in Children and in Young Girls," part I, *International Clinics* II (23rd Series, 1913):248-49; Chaddock, "Rape" (1904), p. 137; Gonzales, "Virginity," p. 607; Bronson, "False Accusations," pp. 226-33. Bronson (p. 545) related this story:

> A woman accused several individuals of having raped her child, aged nine and a half years. The expert showed that this accusation had no foundation. The genital organs of the child were healthy; but there was noticed on the superior portion of the vulva a red circle, of recent origin, as large as a silver half dollar. The woman herself had bruised her child to form a ground for her accusation, the motive being blackmail.

55. Chaddock (*"Rape"* [1904], p.137.) stated:

Ignorance of the fact that young children are often subject to acute genital catarrh [discharge] of an innocent nature has often led to trials for rape, on the assumption that a child was suffering with specific venereal disease. Men who have been innocently associated with such a child are the easy victims of such a combination of accidental disease and common ignorance and suspicion.
See also Anthony, "Rape," p. 31; and Williams, "Rape in Children," p. 255.

56. F. R. Bronson described what he considered to be a totally fabricated story by a thirteen-year-old girl who was "acting out" a story told her by an older friend. *See* F. R. Bronson, "A Case of Rape on a Young Girl," *The American Journal of Urology and Sexology* 14 (1918):490–94. *See also* Tait, "An Analysis of the Evidence," and Bronson, "False Accusations," for general discussions of several cases of children fabricating stories simply for excitement or to harm someone for a real or imagined wrong. Tait (p. 231) took a cynical view of the many young girls, generally from the lower class, who, when reporting alleged assaults, were capable of including sexual descriptions that "would outrun the curiosities of pornographic literature." *See also* Williams, "Rape in Children" (part I), pp. 247–50.

57. Chaddock, "Rape" (1904), p. 139; Anthony, "Rape," p. 31; Mapes, "A Practical Consideration," pp. 934–35; Gonzales, "Virginity," pp. 606–07; Walker, "Reports, with Comments" (June 1886), pp. 330–41; Williams, "Rape in Children" (part I), pp. 253–58; W. Constantine Goodell, "The Anatomy of Rape," *University Medical Magazine* 8 (1895–1896):767.

58. Goodell, "The Anatomy of Rape," p. 767; Mapes, "A Practical Consideration," pp. 934–35; Williams, "Rape in Children" (part I), pp. 256–57.

59. Gonzales, "Virginity," p. 607; Mapes, "A Practical Consideration," pp. 934–35; Goodell, "The Anatomy of Rape," p. 767; Chaddock, "Rape" (1904), p. 139.

60. Williams, "Rape in Children" (part I), p. 257.

61. *See* Walker, "Reports, with Comments" (June 1886), pp. 339–41, for a discussion of the differences between leukorrhea and gonorrhea. *See also* Gonzales, "Virginity," p. 607.

62. Walker, "Reports, with Comments of Twenty-One Cases of Indecent Assault and Rape Upon Children," *Archives of Pediatrics* 3, 5 (May 1886):270–71.

63. Ibid., p. 272. *See also* Williams, "Rape in Children" (part I), pp. 252–53, for another physician's suggestions on techniques for interviewing children.

64. Walker, "Reports, with Comments" (May 1886), pp. 274–86; idem (June 1886), pp. 321–29, cases II, IV, V, VIII, IX, XII, XVIII, XXI.

65. Ibid., cases I–XXI.

66. Walker, "Reports, with Comments" (May 1886), case VI, p. 279.

67. Ibid.

68. Ibid., case IX, pp. 281–82.

69. Ibid.

70. Charles C. Mapes, "Sexual Assault," *The Urologic and Cutaneous Review* 21, 8 (August 1917):430.

71. Smith, "Alleged Rape," p. 1454.

72. Mapes, "A Practical Consideration," pp. 931–32; Mapes, "Sexual Assault," pp. 430–31; Smith, "Alleged Rape," pp. 1454–55; Chaddock, "Rape" (1904), p. 127; Goodell, "The Anatomy of Rape," p. 766; Gonzales, "Virginity," p. 605; Garner, "Detailed Examination," p. 29; Anthony, "Rape," pp. 29–30; Jacob F.

Miller, "The Law of Rape," *Papers of the Medico-Legal Society of New York*, Second series (1882):524-28.

Although this chapter excludes purely legal articles, an article in *The Woman's Medical Journal* (1905) deserves some mention. Written by a female physician, the article described a "Proposed Law on Rape" in Colorado that advocated an early version of "staircasing" of rape charges. Three degrees of guilt were proposed along with graded punishments. Also proposed were prosecutions for accessory to rape and for rapes of young men by women. *See* Mary E. Bates, "The Law on Rape in Colorado," *The Woman's Medical Journal* 15, 1 (January 1905):9-12.

73. Miller, "The Law of Rape," p. 525.

74. Mapes, "Sexual Assault," p. 432; Chaddock, "Rape" (1904), p. 127; Williams, "Rape in Children" (part I), p. 260; Gonzales, "Virginity," p. 605; Smith, "Alleged Rape," p. 1454; Goodell, "The Anatomy of Rape," p. 766; Miller, "The Law of Rape," p. 525.

75. Anthony, "Rape," p. 58.

76. *See*, for example, J. P. Gonzales, "Sexual Perversions," in *Legal Medicine, Pathology and Toxicology*, pp. 608-11, esp. p. 609.

77. *See* Gonzales, "Virginity," p. 603; Smith, "Alleged Rape," p. 1456; Garner, "Detailed Examination," p. 30; Chaddock, "Rape (1904), pp. 128-33; Williams, "Rape in Children" (part I), pp. 260-62; and Goodell, "The Anatomy of Rape," pp. 767-68.

78. Goodell, "The Anatomy of Rape," pp. 766-67. Goodell (p. 769) felt that the location of abrasions was critical to the case:

> *Marks of violence just* inside *the vulvar orifice could then be taken into account but nothing outside the line of mucous membrane should be medico-legally considered. We can thus see that the expert's duty is one requiring the greatest amount of care and judgment, as well as anatomical experience and an accurate knowledge of the external organs of generation (in original).*

79. Gonzales, "Virginity," p. 607; Goodell, "The Anatomy of Rape," p. 767; Smith, "Alleged Rape," p. 1456.

80. Gonzales, "Virginity," p. 603; Chaddock, "Rape" (1904), pp. 128-33; Smith, "Alleged Rape," p. 1456; Garner, "Detailed Examination," p. 30.

81. Smith, "Alleged Rape," p. 1456; Garner, "Detailed Examination," p. 30; Mapes, "A Practical Consideration," pp. 935-36; Chaddock, "Rape" (1904), p. 133; Goodell, "The Anatomy of Rape," pp. 767-69; Anthony, "Rape," p. 56.

82. Chaddock, "Rape" (1904), p. 133; Anthony, "Rape," p. 57.

83. Anthony, "Rape," pp. 56-57; Smith, "Alleged Rape," p. 1457; O. J. Pollack, "Post-Mortem Examinations in Cases of Suspected Rape," *American Journal of Clinical Pathology* 13, 6 (June 1943):311-13.

84. Anthony, "Rape," pp. 56-57.

85. Sidney Kay, "Acid Phosphatase Test for Identification of Seminal Stains," *Journal of Laboratory and Clinical Medicine* 34 (June-December 1949):728.

86. *See* Kaye, "Acid Phosphatase Test," pp. 728-31; and J. Steven Faulds, "Phosphatase in Dried Seminal Stains," *Edinburg Medical Journal*, New series, 58 (January-December 1951):94-98, for discussion of acid phosphatase testing to identify seminal stains. *See also* Garner, "Detailed Examination," p. 31; Gonzales,

"Virginity," p. 606; and Smith, "Alleged Rape," p. 1457.

87. Smith, "Alleged Rape," p. 1457.

88. Chaddock, "Rape" (1904), p. 134; Goodell, "The Anatomy of Rape," p. 769; Garner, "Detailed Examination," p. 31; Gonzales, "Virginity," pp. 606-7.

89. Garner, "Detailed Examination," p. 31; Chaddock, "Rape" (1904), p. 134; Williams, "Rape in Children" (part II), pp. 250-55.

90. Goodell, "The Anatomy of Rape," p. 769.

91. "Rape—Allegations of Force," *Michigan Law Review* 21 (1923):803.

92. *See generally* Mapes, "A Practical Consideration," and Mapes, "Sexual Assault," for extensive discussion of medico-legal considerations in this area, examples of variation in state law, and judicial decisions governing alleged rapes in different situations. *See also* Miller, "The Law of Rape," pp. 525-26; Chaddock, "Rape" (1904), pp. 136-38; Goodell, "The Anatomy of Rape," pp. 766-69; Anthony, "Rape," pp. 30-31; and Gonzales, "Virginity," p. 605.

93. Charles G. Chaddock, "Rape," in *Legal Medicine and Toxicology*, ed. M. Peterson et al., vol. I (Philadelphia: W. B. Saunders, 1948), p. 1033.

94. Ibid. *See also* Garner, "Detailed Examination," p. 29.

95. Anthony, "Rape," p. 31; Chaddock, "Rape" (1948), p. 1041; Garner, "Detailed Examination," p. 30; Mapes, "A Practical Consideration," p. 934; Smith, "Alleged Rape," pp. 1455-56; Gonzales, "Virginity," p. 605.

96. Garner, "Detailed Examination," p. 29; Anthony, "Rape," p. 30; Chaddock, "Rape" (1948), pp. 1033-41; Mapes, "Sexual Assault," p. 432; Mapes, "A Practical Consideration," pp. 931, 933-34.

97. Mapes, "Sexual Assault," pp. 430, 432; Miller, "The Law of Rape," p. 525; Smith, "Alleged Rape," p. 1455; Anthony, "Rape," p. 30; Chaddock, "Rape" (1904), pp. 135-36; Chaddock, "Rape" (1948), pp. 1041-42.

98. Mapes, "Sexual Assault," p. 434. The portions of this quotation appearing in quotation marks were expressed by another author, cited only as "Palmer" by Mapes. *See also* Williams, "Rape in Children" (part I), p. 259; Tait, "An Analysis of the Evidence," p. 227; and Anthony, "Rape," pp. 30-31. It is equally interesting to note that at least three authors remarked that the law did not permit "forcing" of prostitutes. *See* Miller, "The Law of Rape," p. 526; Gonzales, "Virginity," p. 605; and Anthony, "Rape," p. 29. Cf. Mapes, "A Practical Consideration," p. 937; and idem, "Sexual Assault," p. 431.

99. Chaddock, "Rape" (1948), pp. 1041-42.

100. Brownmiller, *Against Our Will*, p. 413.

101. Judith Hole and Ellen Levine, *Rebirth of Feminism* (New York: Quadrangle, 1971); Banner, *Women in Modern America*, pp. 242-51; Ehrenreich and English, *For Her Own Good*, pp. 282-84; Lerner, *The Majority Finds Its Past*, pp. 31-62. The recent move to reform rape laws has suggested making laws "sex neutral," permitting marital rape charges, changing the term *rape* to the words *sexual assault*, and staircasing degress of rape charges. *See*, for example, Martin D. Schwartz and Todd R. Clear, "Toward a New Law on Rape," *Crime and Delinquency* 26, 2 (April 1980):129-51.

102. For a discussion of women and medicine during the last ten years, *see* Walsh, "Doctors Wanted," pp. 268-83.

103. Ehrenreich and English, *For Her Own Good*, pp. 285, 282-92.

Elizabeth Anne Mills

104. Bruce A. Woodling, Jerome Evans, and Michael D. Bradbury, "Sexual Assault: Rape and Molestation," *Clinical Obstetrics and Gynecology* 20, 3 (September 1977):521.

105. "One teenager, seeking revenge on a boy who had spurned her for another girl, enticed him into sexual intercourse in a schoolyard, then cried 'Rape'" (Arthur Frederick Schiff, "Statistical Features of Rape," *Journal of Forensic Sciences* (14, 1 [January 1969]:108. Copyright ASTM, 1916 Race Street, Phila., PA 19103. Reprinted with permission, as are all Schiff quotations cited in notes 106, 109, 110, 111, 134.) *See also* Woodling, Evans, and Bradbury, "Sexual Assault," p. 521; and Lester R. Graves and J. T. Francisco, "A Clinical and Laboratory Evaluation of Rape," *Journal of the Tennessee State Medical Association* 55, 10 (October 1962):390. Graves and Francisco note:

> [T]hroughout this report reference is made to the incident as the "alleged" assault and so it should be until the court makes the decision. This may appear unduly suspicious but it is so easy for some designing woman, for the purpose of spite or revenge, to deceive the physician.

106. Schiff, "Statistical Features of Rape," pp. 108–9; Woodling, Evans, and Bradbury, "Sexual Assault," p. 521.

107. Ibid.

108. Graves and Francisco, "A Clinical and Laboratory Evaluation of Rape," p. 389. *See also* Woodling, Evans, and Bradbury, "Sexual Assault," p. 519.

109. Schiff, "Statistical Features of Rape," pp. 107–8; Graves and Francisco, "A Clinical and Laboratory Evaluation of Rape," p. 391.

110. Schiff, "Statistical Features of Rape," p. 108.

111. Consider, for instance, Schiff's warning (ibid.) to have an organized protocol for examination:

> How embarrassing it would be not to be able to answer questions requiring medical knowledge, how more embarrassing not to have gathered this obvious necessary information when it was available.

E. LeBourdais reports that in one hospital, physicians are not even aware of which forensic tests should be done. *See* E. LeBourdais, "Rape Victims: The Unpopular Patients," *Dimensions in Health Services* 53, 3 (1976):12–14. *See also* Joe B. Massey, Celso-Ramon Garcia, and John P. Emich, "Management of Sexually Assaulted Females," *Obstetrics and Gynecology* 38, 1 (July 1971):30; and Joseph J. Peters, "Social, Legal and Psychological Effects of Rape on the Victim," *Pennsylvania Medicine* 78, 2 (February 1975):34.

112. Peters, "Social, Legal and Psychological Effects," pp. 34–36.

113. *See* articles cited in notes 136–138 *infra*.

114. LeBourdais, "Rape Victims," p. 12.

115. Ibid. *See also*, generally, Peters, "Social, Legal and Psychological Effects," pp. 34–36.

116. L. Schultz, "The Child Rape Victim: Social, Psychological and Legal Perspectives," *Child Welfare* 52 (1973):148, reported in Woodling, Evans, and Bradbury, "Sexual Assaults," p. 511.

117. Massey, Garcia, and Emich, "Management of Sexually Assaulted Females," pp. 31–32. *See also* Schiff, "Statistical Features of Rape," pp. 104–5.

118. Gladys M. Sandes, "Sexual Assaults on Children," *The British Journal of Clinical Practice* 17, 3 (1963):143. *See* notes 48–50 and accompanying text *supra*.

119. *See* Schiff, "Statistical Features of Rape," p. 106; Graves and Francisco,

"A Clinical and Laboratory Evaluation of Rape," p. 391; and Sandes, "Sexual Assaults on Children," p. 144.

120 *See* Sandes, "Sexual Assaults on Children," pp. 143–46.

121. Peters, "Social, Legal and Psychological Effects," p. 34. Cf. Sandes ("Sexual Assaults on Children," p. 144): "It is known that children at times live a life of fantasy and may attribute episodes accounted by others to their own experience." It is generally recognized that children, especially incest victims, suffer great psychological trauma.

122. Graves and Francisco, "A Clinical and Laboratory Evaluation of Rape," p. 391; Massey, Garcia, and Emich, "Management of Sexually Assaulted Females," pp. 30, 32–34; Sandes, "Sexual Assaults on Children," pp. 143–44.

123. Frances Pepitone-Rockwell, "Patterns of Rape and Approaches to Care," *The Journal of Family Practice* 6, 3 (1978):522; Woodling, Evans, and Bradbury, "Sexual Assault," p. 519; Peters, "Social, Legal and Psychological Effects," pp. 35–36; Schiff, "Statistical Features of Rape," pp. 102–3.

124. It is interesting to note that one author reports intact hymens in women after frequent intercourse or even after delivery. *See* Graves and Francisco, "A Clinical and Laboratory Evaluation of Rape," pp. 390–91.

125. Woodling, Evans, and Bradbury, "Sexual Assault," p. 519.

126. Forensic chemistry, particularly the testing for sperm, semen, and so on, is a complex process, as mentioned by several authors. For a discussion of the discovery and importance of spermatozoa in victims of rape, *see* Noble Sharpe, "The Significance of Spermatozoa in Victims of Sexual Offenses," *Canadian Medical Association Journal* 89 (7 September 1963):513–14. For additional discussion of methods for obtaining specimens, testing, and preserving chains of evidence, *see* Massey, Garcia, and Emich, "Management of Sexually Assaulted Females," pp. 30–31, 34; Graves and Francisco, "A Clinical and Laboratory Evaluation of Rape," pp. 390–93; Judith S. Daniels, "Emergency Department Management of Rape," *Ohio State Medical Journal* 75, 6 (June 1979):352; and Peters, "Social, Legal and Psychological Effects," p. 35.

127. Graves and Francisco, "A Clinical and Laboratory Evaluation of Rape," p. 391.

128. Massey, Garcia, and Emich, "Management of Sexually Assaulted Females," p. 31; Woodling, Evans, and Bradbury, "Sexual Assault," p. 527; Graves and Francisco, "A Clinical and Laboratory Evaluation of Rape," pp. 392–93; Daniels, "Emergency Department Management of Rape," p. 352; Sharpe, "The Significance of Spermatozoa," p. 513; Peters, "Social, Legal and Psychological Effects," p. 35.

129. Woodling, Evans, and Bradbury, "Sexual Assault," p. 520; Schiff, "Statistical Features of Rape," pp. 102–3; Pepitone-Rockwell, "Patterns of Rape," pp. 526–27. The idea of "moral force" raised by earlier writers (*see* note 97 and accompanying text *supra*) is still considered a valid argument on the questions of resistance and consent. *See*, for example, Peters, "Social, Legal and Psychological Effects," p. 35; and Schiff, "Statistical Features of Rape," p. 103.

130. Woodling, Evans, and Bradbury, "Sexual Assault," p. 520.

131. Ibid., p. 523.

132. In most cases, it is suggested that case histories be extremely thorough. Recommended question areas include: victim/suspect relationship; threats of force and/or presence of weapons; use of physical restraints; number of assailants; type of coitus; use of foreign objects or forced engagement in oral sex; presence or history of

Elizabeth Anne Mills

venereal disease; most recent consensual intercourse; last menstrual period; and presence of IUD or use of oral contraceptives (ibid., pp. 523–24.). *See also* Graves and Francisco, "A Clinical and Laboratory Evaluation of Rape," pp. 390–91; Massey, Garcia, and Emich, "Management of Sexually Assaulted Females," p. 30; Daniels, "Emergency Department Management of Rape," p. 352; Pepitone-Rockwell, "Patterns of Rape," p. 527; and Schiff, "Statistical Features of Rape," pp. 107–8.

133. Graves and Francisco, "A Clinical and Laboratory Evaluation of Rape," p. 390.

134. Woodling, Evans, and Bradbury, "Sexual Assault," p. 524. Schiff ("Statistical Features of Rape," p. 106) writes that although rape on nonvirgins is less likely to cause damage, "[n]evertheless, if a woman is held to the ground, kicking, screaming, struggling, and making every effort to keep her thighs together, an examiner may reasonably expect to find some marks of violence."

135. Woodling, Evans, and Bradbury, "Sexual Assault," p. 524. *See also* Graves and Francisco, "A Clinical and Laboratory Evaluation of Rape," pp. 390–91; Massey, Garcia, and Emich, "Management of Sexually Assaulted Females," p. 30; Pepitone-Rockwell, "Patterns of Rape," pp. 526–27; and Daniels, "Emergency Department Management of Rape," p. 352.

136. *See* Daniels, "Emergency Department Management of Rape," p. 352; Pepitone-Rockwell, "Patterns of Rape," pp. 526–27; and Massey, Garcia, and Emich, "Management of Sexually Assaulted Females," pp. 29–32. Cf. John R. Connery, "Emergency Treatment of Rape Cases," *Hospital Progress* 39 (1958):64–65; which discusses the moral issues involved in contraception and abortion for rape victims.

137. *See* Daniels, "Emergency Department Management of Rape," pp. 351–52; Pepitone-Rockwell, "Patterns of Rape," pp. 524–25, 528; and Massey, Garcia, and Emich, "Management of Sexually Assaulted Females," pp. 29–30, 33–34.

138. *See* Daniels, "Emergency Department Management of Rape," pp. 351–52; Pepitone-Rockwell, "Patterns of Rape," pp. 526–27; and Massey, Garcia, and Emich, "Management of Sexually Assaulted Females," pp. 29–35.

139. It should be noted here that this holds true only for the surveyed literature written by physicians. Much of the recent medical literature written by other health professionals not only supports victim credibility, but deals extensively with her welfare and emotional needs as well. That literature, however, was not reviewed in this study. *See* note 3 *supra*.

3

Would You Believe This Woman?

Prosecutorial Screening for
"Credible" Witnesses
And a Problem of Justice

ELIZABETH ANNE STANKO

The prosecutor, as the individual who represents the state in the criminal justice process, determines how any instance of victimization will be adjudicated in court.[1] During the review of each criminal incident, the prosecutor weighs a variety of factors that contribute to the successful prosecution of a case in court. All too often such constraints as the volume of serious offenses, policy priorities, or staff shortages greatly influence a prosecutor's decisions. These decisions include whether to charge a suspect with a crime, the nature of the offense at charging, and how the case will be processed throughout the criminal justice system.[2] Prosecutors tend to accept for adjudication cases that are likely to result in the conviction of the defendant.[3] As public officials, they strive to achieve high conviction records, maintaining their image as the community's legal protector.[4] Given these constraints, prosecutors will consider the organizational context in deciding how a particular criminal incident is adjudicated.

This chapter focuses on prosecutorial decision making concerning serious criminal offenses against women and the impact of this decision making upon the female victim. Female victims report a "secondary victimization" by criminal justice personnel to whom they turn for assistance. Directly or indirectly throughout the process of legal fact finding, these victims may be made to feel that they provoked or deserved whatever happened to them.[5] Equally pertinent, these accounts of secondary victimization reflect prosecutors' use of gender stereotypes in the handling of women's personal victimization.

Exploring prosecutors' use of gender stereotypes is useful for understanding one aspect of secondary victimization felt by women. The practice of prosecutorial discretion is oriented to predicting a successfully prosecutable case, not to addressing the needs of an aggrieved victim. Together with this organizational orientation, prosecutors rely on gender stereotypes about women as a filter through which they view female victims. This filter of stereotypical imagery about women colors their assessments of female victims and, ultimately, their predictions of prosecutable cases. Through an examination of ethnographic data on prosecutorial screening activity, this chapter will illustrate prosecutors' use of imagery about women during this screening process.

PROSECUTORS' WORK: THE ORGANIZATIONAL CONTEXT OF CRIMINAL JUSTICE DECISION MAKING

The bulk of the prosecutor's workload is dependent upon the activities of others. The victim's decision to report the crime and the police officer's decision to arrest are pivotal determinations: they shape the kinds of criminal incidents that are brought to the attention of the prosecutor. Victimization surveys indicate that less than half of all serious crimes are ever reported to the police.[6] Of the crimes reported to the police, approximately 20 percent of the more serious crimes result in suspect apprehension.[7] Only after a suspect is arrested can the prosecutor make the most powerful decision in the criminal justice process: whether to charge the suspect with an offense.[8]

Prosecutors' decisions to charge a suspect with a crime are affected in many respects by their routine work processes. As they go about their organizational tasks, prosecutors develop practical skills that enable them to apply the penal code to actual criminal activity.[9] For the purpose of this discussion, a practical skill is one that is not related to personal or individual judgments. Rather, it is one that arises within the organizational context and is useful for the assessment of actions that appear to be criminal offenses. In practice, prosecutors regard the penal law as merely one element of information that helps to define a criminal offense.

Studies examining the practical skills of criminal justice actors—police officers, public defenders, juvenile probation officers, as well as prosecutors—note that each actor develops an organizationally based process to standardize the handling of criminal offenses.[10] To do so, each classifies individual events into categories of events. The event is then routinely processed as a member of a category. While it is not always possible to process all events in a routine fashion, there is clearly a preference to do so. (Routine processing simply does not work in some, hopefully few, cases.) In each setting, practicality plays a considerably more important role than legal rules.

For instance, police officers respond to an incident and make determinations about that incident on the basis of particular demand conditions. The incident's visibility, the type of individuals involved, the location of the incident, and so forth all play an important role in the decision to arrest.[11] Through another process, public defenders categorize cases to determine how a defendant will be represented. They do so in the course of defending a variety of clients. In time, public defenders acquire a working knowledge of the common features of particular types of crime. These features include the "typical manner in which offenses of given classes are committed, the social characteristics of the persons who regularly commit them, the features of the settings in which they occur, the types of victims often involved, and the like."[12] Similarly, juvenile probation officers produce rules and theories about delinquency and its occurrence within the everyday practice of processing juvenile offenses.[13] Prosecutors develop categories for cases on the basis of knowledge acquired from their organizational decision making, which is geared to the successful prosecution of the defendant. As they make their screening decisions, prosecutors are greatly influenced by the character and credibility of the complaining witness.[14]

For these actors, accusations, legal representation, adjudication, and prognostication are organizationally relevant activities subject to routine, normative construction.[15] Thus, what passes as legal decision making is, in large part, the result of social processes through which *a* reality of organizational considerations becomes *the* reality of legal decisions.

THE VICTIM'S ROLE IN EARLY CASE SCREENING: AN ORGANIZATIONAL CONSIDERATION OF A SOLID CASE

The setting for this study is a bureau within a prosecutor's office devoted to the screening of felony complaints.[16] Located in a major East Coast city, this particular office screens cases 365 days a year. Establishment of an Early Case Assessment Bureau (ECAB) has enabled the prosecutor's office to scrutinize all incoming felony cases carefully, to determine which can be prosecuted quickly because the chances of conviction seem high. Prior to ECAB, many convictable cases were either lost in the shuffle or merely continued through the criminal justice process as felony cases for subsequent filtering.

Assistant prosecutors assigned to this bureau review arrest circumstances; assess the evidence against the arrested individual; interview the complainant; and draw up an affidavit that, according to criminal statute, reflects the actions of that individual.[17] Next, focusing upon only "true" felony matters, assistant prosecutors select from among the arrests those felony cases that are to be expeditiously adjudicated in the superior court. In this way, ECAB weeds out those felony arrest charges that are likely to be reduced below the felony level during plea negotiations; as weeded cases, these arrests become ones that are handled in the lower court.

As a standard for deciding which cases to forward to the superior court, the ECAB assistant prosecutors use the concept of the "solid case."[18] A solid case is one that the assistant prosecutors recognize as having evidence strong enough to persuade a superior court jury. Put somewhat differently, prosecutors' screening activity is meant to ferret out those valued solid cases that result in convictions.

However, the assistant prosecutors are unable to define a solid case without the particulars of the offense. Such crime categories as robbery, for instance, provide a statutory framework. The dynamics of the offense—who commits it, how it is committed, who the victim is, how the arrest is made, and so forth—provide the actual substance for the statutory interpretation. Thus, in many respects, a solid case cannot be defined in general, abstract terms. Its existence can be recognized only in particular cases and on an ad hoc, immediate basis.

With selection of a solid case in mind, assistant prosecutors assess and anticipate problems that might arise during a trial, such as problems with the evidence, the arrest procedures, or the complaining witness. Potential problems with the witness are of great concern to assistant prosecutors; they may decline to prosecute or to prosecute fully if such problems are anticipated.[19] Moreover, prosecutors' perceptions about a victim's willingness to cooperate are often based upon their *assumptions* about whether the victim will pursue the complaint throughout the entire legal process and whether the victim, who is at times the sole witness, will strike a potential judge or jury as "credible."[20] For the successful prosecution of a solid case, the victim and her[21] testimony essentially become the trial prosecutor's evidence.

The assistant prosecutors speak of complainants in terms of their "stand-up" qualities, using the term *stand-up* to describe a victim who will present herself to judge and jury as articulate and credible. The only way prosecutors formulate such an assessment is to base it on what they know or feel the jurors will believe about an individual complainant's credibility.

Victim assessment is integrally linked to the prosecutor's future action on a felony incident.[22] Prosecutors are reluctant to pursue a case if they know the victim's character is questionable. For prosecutors, then, development of their practical, organizational skills means sharpening their awareness of how jurors will react to, respond to, and predict the actions of victims. When it comes to female victims, this process involves reliance on stereotypical images about women. Myths about women—about the patterns of their victimization—are interwoven throughout prosecutors' treatment and assessment of serious crimes against women.

Elizabeth Anne Stanko

FEMALE VICTIMS:
GENDER EXPECTATIONS AND
THE STAND-UP WITNESS

In the screening of cases involving violent crimes against women, prosecutors focus on victims during their overall analysis of prosecutability. If victims are to appear as witnesses during the trial, prosecutors evaluate their characters, injuries, and possible responsibility in the offense; the victim of a violent crime becomes a central feature in the case's prosecutability. The prosecutor's evaluation of a victim of serious, violent crime, then, is an organizationally relevant task and, as previously noted, is guided by the images of both the stand-up witness and (for women) gender stereotypes.[23]

Images of stand-up witnesses and of women in general are not necessarily compatible. One essential quality of the stand-up witness is "good" character, measured in large part by neat appearance, consistency in testimony, credibility, articulatory skills, and overall presence. According to stereotypical images, on the other hand, women are passive, impulsive, hysterical, and sexually unmanageable (and thus, of questionable character). As we will see, such alleged gender qualities also provide prosecutors with clues to contributory responsibility of female victims.

Screening prosecutors have three primary concerns in connection with female stand-up witnesses: (1) the victim's character; (2) the relationship between the victim and the offender; and (3) the victim's determination to prosecute.

"Good" Character

A victim's "good" character is, for prosecutors, an indication of her potential credibility as a witness. When assessing the character of a female victim, they often rely upon assumptions about "proper" female behavior and the degree of resistance a "proper" woman should put forth against her attacker. If she seems to them to have provoked the attack or to have otherwise participated in the offense, their decision to prosecute is adversely affected. In other words, the prosecutors' characterization of women who allege personal victimization draw upon common stereotypes about women "asking for" or "precipitating" their own victimization.

Relationship between Victim and Offender

The circumstances surrounding such violent crimes as rape, assault, and robbery create many problems for the screening prosecutor. As statistics reflect, often the circumstances of the offense do not fit with popular stereotypes about how these crimes occur. Such stereotypes involve images of shadowy strangers, stalking unknowing, helpless victims; however, an acquaintance, a family member, or a friend is almost as likely as a stranger to commit a violent crime against a female victim. Moreover, the likelihood of a woman knowing her assailant is considerably higher than that of a man.[24] Particularly for crimes of violence involving *women as victims* and *men as assailants*, questions about victim–offender relationships arise from assumptions about how women typically interact with men. During the screening of felony arrests, prosecutors call upon these assumptions about women: what did occur between female victim and male assailant, they ask, and was it actually a criminal offense? Hence, the victimization of women mirrors women's place in society; prosecutors (and society as a whole) consider victimization of women to be an aspect of the way in which men and women relate to one another.

The relationship between complainant and defendant is a difficult one for prosecutors, according to my study. The requirements for a solid case demand that stand-up witnesses are in no way responsible for the crime. The presence of some history between the victim and the defendant appears to create unanswerable questions about provocation or participation. Contributory responsibility is troublesome to sort out; therefore, prosecutors do not try very often. The standards they set for solid cases are so restrictive, for instance, that wife-abuse cases rarely qualify. Similarly, a major obstacle for rape victims is convincing prosecutors that they did not in any way provoke the attack or consent to the rape.[25]

Victim's Determination to Prosecute

For a solid case, prosecutors must be assured that victims will pursue the complaint throughout the entire criminal justice process. If there is a relationship between a victim and a defendant, however, prosecutors assume that the relationship, not the prosecution of a criminal offense, is the victim's priority. Further complicating this matter are the circumstances surrounding victimization against women. Often, as noted earlier, an acquaintance, friend, or family member is the assailant. Through fear of retaliation, embarrassment, or emotional attachment to the assailant, victims do drop charges. (Women, too, respond to their own socialization.) Accordingly, any victim who chooses to prosecute has to convince the screening prosecutor, acting according to organizational mandates by forwarding only solid cases to superior court, that she will pursue the matter fully. To do so, she has to combat prosecutors' categorical treatment of women's complaints. However, to avoid taking chances, a prosecutor will often assume that a woman, when prosecuting crimes against those known to her, will not follow through.

In an effort to serve the need for *organizational* predictability effectively, prosecutors view female victims through basic stereotypes concerning their behavior, stereotypes that define how women should act when they are victimized, how they are likely to behave if they file a complaint, and how far they are likely to prosecute. The organizational constraints under which prosecutors work reinforce their reliance on stereotypical stand-up witness criteria. Additionally, screening prosecutors review cases within a short period of time; in most instances, the prosecutors I studied took less than fifteen minutes to select successful cases to forward to superior court. Thus, many female complainants automatically flash to the screening prosecutors "stand-up witness problem" warning signals as they enter the criminal justice system.[26]

CASEWORK: THE PROSECUTOR'S SCREENING ACTIVITY

The following six examples of casework illustrate prosecutors' explorations of the potential problems in cases involving serious, violent crimes against women. They relate to the three previously noted areas of prosecutorial concern: (1) the victim's character; (2) the relationship between victim and offender; and (3) the victim's determination to prosecute. Each example is an excerpt from an actual screening discussion. In these excerpts, the screening prosecutor (D.A.) discusses the case with the police officer (A.O.) who arrested the suspect and interviewed the victim.

Would You Believe This Woman?

Moral Character as an Indication of Witness Credibility

Example 1: Impugning the Moral Character of a Witness; Arrest Charge: Robbery in the First Degree.

D.A. Did she see the gun?

A.O. No, they told her they had one.

D.A. What do the defendants say?

A.O. They say they picked her up and she robbed them. But I found in the one defendant's right front pocket $80, four $20s. She said that they took four $20s. There have been a series of robberies of pros[titutes] in the neighborhood. I think these are the guys. [But] I wondered to myself if it was a robbery at all.

D.A. Gun recovered?

A.O. It was in the backseat. They say they don't know how the gun got there.

D.A. The problem with the robbery is that all the complaining witnesses are pros[titutes].

During the assessment of this case, the prosecutor clearly recognized the liability of having a prostitute as a witness in a felony case. Indeed, the prosecutor concluded by washing his hands of the robbery incident. The fact that the victims were prostitutes provides important information to the prosecutor: prostitutes themselves participate in illegal activities. Such character blemishes as a record of imprisonment, prostitution, addiction, or homosexuality stigmatize an individual by implying further negative qualities. Thus, a prostitute is assumed to be dishonest or weak-willed. The prosecutors know that victims whose identities are somehow soiled are not likely to be believed by judge or jury.[27]

Note, too, that the arresting officer initially doubted the occurrence of the robbery. This example is but one of many robbery-arrest screenings I observed. Overall, these screening decisions illustrate a process whereby prosecutors sort robbery cases into two general categories: "true" ones and "phony" ones. "True" robbery cases involve credible complainants. Relying on assessments of these victims' characters, prosecutors predict the successful outcome of prosecution. Credible female victims of robbery offenses are assumed by prosecutors to be upstanding citizens who in no way either contribute to or deserve their victimization. "Phony" robbery cases involve complainants with "flaws." Treatment by screening prosecutors is often affected by the expectations for a stand-up witness as well as the model of a "proper," moral woman.[28]

Elizabeth Anne Stanko

Example 2: The Unimpeachable Witness; Arrest Charge: Robbery in the Third Degree. The complainant was an elderly woman. The incident involved a purse-snatching by a sixteen-year-old male. The complainant had chased the defendant through a park after her purse was taken. The prosecutor admired the complainant as an individual least deserving of harassment. After the complainant reported the incident, she was excused from ECAB and the prosecutor became excited about the potential case:

> *I'm going to write it up as a robbery 1 [first degree] with a tree branch [as the dangerous weapon]. I only wrote up one rob[bery] before with a tree branch [as a weapon] and that was because the victim was John F. Kennedy, Jr. These are the cases that try themselves. Any case that has a stand-up complainant should be indicted. You put her on the stand . . . the judge loves her, the jury loves her. . . . Dynamite complainant!*

The screening prosecutors I observed appreciated their daily work routines when a stand-up witness appeared. Obviously, this particular case was "true" robbery: the crime occurred between strangers, and the victim was a credible, stand-up witness. The prosecutor was surprised and excited to discover the key to convictions, the stand-up witness. In fact, he increased the degree of the crime's severity because of who the complainant was; the arrest charge was robbery in the third degree, but the affidavit charge became robbery in the first degree. Convinced of the strength of the case, the prosecutor easily predicted the reaction of judge or jury.

This complainant had several qualities that were readily recognized by the prosecutor as those belonging to an ideal victim. She was elderly, articulate, and spunky. Her age precluded the prosecutor from viewing her through gender expectations about women, particularly those involving moral standards; she did not seem to invite being victimized. This elderly woman, the prosecutor stated later, was beyond reproach. Conviction of the defendant was assured by her entire presentation. Any trial prosecutor would easily win this case. It was recommended for full prosecution through the superior court. After all, the case could have tried itself.

As we can see from the above excerpts, the moral character of complainants is an important factor in screening prosecutors' decision making. Both of the above victims are female. And that femaleness is contextually based: age, occupation, social status, and so forth are additional filters through which stereotypes about women are drawn. These images of the victims provide prosecutors with additional information that they use to infer the victim's credibility. Credibility, then, is a socially based resource from which prosecutors draw legally relevant information. At least within the screening room, a female victim's alleged moral character is tied to gender expectations and images, and thus is linked to the decisions of screening prosecutors.

Relationships between Female Victim and Male Offender

Example 3: Acquaintance Relationship and Force; Arrest Charge: Rape in the First Degree. The prosecutor interviewed the victim for approximately fifteen minutes. She told her story slowly, timidly. She had met the defendant twice before, through friends. The prosecutor then asked her to leave the room while he talked to the arresting officer from the sex crime unit.

D.A. Did you respond to the call?

A.O. Uniformed officers did. [Gives names of the officers.] The call was "person being held against their will." The owner of the apartment answered the door; the girl ran out. Apparently what she said is the ordeal that transpired.

D.A. Did you extract the story from her?

A.O. No.

D.A. What is the defendant like?

A.O. Slightly intox. He wasn't saying nothin'. Just got out of prison.

D.A. Which hospital did she go to?

A.O. Does have exam. Metropolitan Hospital. Took a semen smear. She was afraid of the guy, knowing his criminal record. He was violent.

D.A. It isn't sufficient for us, at least [for] provable force.

A.O. This guy is on the bridge of paranoia.

Supposedly, the prosecutor based his assessment on the issue of provable force. Yet, it is probable that the concern was that the complainant and the defendant were acquainted; such relationship apparently raised questions about how the victim should have behaved. Perhaps the prosecutor believed that the victim would not have been with the defendant in the first place if she were truly afraid of him. Or the prosecutor might have thought that the complainant and the defendant were better acquainted than the complainant revealed. In either case, he determined that the victim's resistance was suspect.

Rape is an offense that is particularly difficult to prosecute; the major issue during a trial is the victim's consent. If appropriate resistance cannot be established, the implication is that the victim consented and the accused is innocent. Trial prosecutors are wary of rape cases from the start because they involve so many witness problems and the well-known tactic of defense attorneys—attacking the victim's reputation. (Furthermore, if a rape case ends in an acquittal, there is a tendency for the prosecutor to blame the victim for the outcome.)[29] By focusing on the victim, the prosecutor relies upon common-sense notions about the crime of rape and how men and women interact. In my observations, this reliance by prosecutors on cultural stereotypes about women prevented some cases of rape from being fully prosecuted.

Example 4: Knowing the Defendant Too Well; Arrest Charge: Robbery in the Third Degree; Assault in the Third Degree.

> **D.A.** Could I have the D.A.'s papers? Prior relationship, eh?
> **A.O.** She kicked him out about two weeks ago.
> **D.A.** What does she claim he did?
> **A.O.** Pounded on the door; her daughter opened the door. He came into the apartment, beat her up, and took $60.
> **D.A.** How did you make the arrest?
> **A.O.** She reported it about 7 [p.m.]; then about eight she called and said that he was back. By the time we got there he was gone. About ten, we were cruising by and he was standing outside the place of occurrence. I asked him his name, took him up to her apartment, and she I.D.'d [identified] him.
> **D.A.** Say anything?
> **A.O.** He didn't say much. Don't know if he was high or drunk. Said they were living together about ten years.
> **D.A.** How long does she say he was living with her?
> **A.O.** Three years.
> **D.A.** Who let the defendant in?

A.O. Her daughter.
D.A. Couldn't smell booze on him?
A.O. [Shakes his head "no."]

The screening prosecutor categorized this offense as not a "true" robbery but "just another family dispute." Because the complaint involved individuals who were well known to each other, the prosecutor felt he could not assess this case on its own merits. Within family disputes, it is thought that interaction occurs that cannot be understood by itself, separate from the entire context of the relationship. The criminal nature of the behavior in this case, prosecutors felt, was somehow secondary to how these people interacted "normally."

Such offenses are not considered candidates for solid felony cases. In many instances during my observations, screening prosecutors automatically reduced the charges from a felony to a misdemeanor when they found prior relationships between complainants and defendants. In a sense, the category "family dispute" allows the prosecutor to eliminate such cases from solid-case prosecutions routinely. If the complainant knows the assailant, prosecutors assume that a history exists between the two parties that is relevant to, but outside of, issues raised by prosecuting this particular offense. And since prosecutors are organizationally bound to forward successful cases, the entire category of family disputes is defined by the prosecutors as an organizational problem. In this way, violence against women, especially that against intimates, is inadvertently legitimized; in their role as predictors of judge and jury reactions, screening prosecutors are reluctant to consider as solid felony cases instances of female victimization involving complainants and defendants who know each other.

The Victim's Determination to Prosecute

Example 5: She Dropped Charges Before, She'll Do It Again; Arrest Charge: Assault in the Second Degree.

D.A. Rico and Marcia are lovers?
A.O. They are.
D.A. They can't make it anymore so he takes a bottle and hits her over the head.
A.O. Her face was swollen; she had him arrested before. He

was issued a D.A.T. [desk appearance ticket, misdemeanor charge].

D.A. On the last occasion, I am willing to bet they kissed and made up before the case was decided. Tell me about your involvement.

A.O. A 1034 over the radio, assault in progress. Her mother was outside the building when we got there. This guy came up, pounded on the apartment, got into the apartment. When we got there, there was the complainant lying on the bed, bleeding; and the defendant was standing there with a bottle in his hands and no clothes on. The assault began in the street, then ended in the apartment.

D.A. Any lacerations made by the broken bottle?

A.O. No, just cuts.

D.A. Did you ask him why he had no clothes on? Did she have her clothes on?

A.O. Didn't ask him why, and she had her clothes on.

D.A. She was admitted to the hospital?

A.O. I called there. They were awaiting X rays. She was badly bruised.

D.A. He intox?

A.O. He was intox.

D.A. We see millions of these.

In cases of domestic violence, prosecutors frequently predict that victims will not follow through on prosecution. The categorical determinations seem to work in two stages. As noted earlier, women's relationships with men raise questions about the ongoing nature of the interaction. Prosecutors feel that the ongoing nature of the relationship affects the victim's determination to prosecute. Prosecutors' assumptions about victims' willingness eliminate most female family assault victims from the category of stand-up witnesses, even in cases in which the complainants finally have reached the end of their tolerance for the abuse and are determined to prosecute.

Example 6: Crime Consequences and Victim Determination; Arrest Charge: Assault in the First Degree. An off-duty corrections officer was arrested and charged with assault in the first degree. He had visited his girlfriend, an argument ensued, and the woman was shot in the head. The defendant stated that the gun discharged unintentionally. The complainant could not be interviewed, for she was in surgery with a bullet lodged in her head. The D.A. who reviewed the case summarized its chances:

> *If she dies, we have manslaughter. If she recovers and re-mains a vegetable, we have an assault 1 [first degree]. If she recovers with minor complications, we barely have a case. If she fully recovers, she will probably drop the charges.*

This case clearly illustrates the contextual nature of definitions of criminal actions. Part of the context in this instance was the complainant's determination to prosecute. The screening prosecutor reviewed organizational responses to a particular social action that were dependent on the degree to which the victim recovered. The prosecutor's office would be obligated to charge the defendant with a serious crime if the complainant were irreparably harmed. However, the prosecutor speculated on the victim's response to a full recovery and predicted the organizational response as well.

Throughout casework in the ECAB office, prosecutors remain attuned to complainants' qualifications as stand-up witnesses. An important part of their work consists of speculating, on the basis of preconceptions about women, how female victims will respond during the criminal justice process. Moreover, the prosecutors try to predict responses of judge and jury to female witnesses. The organizationally bound nature of prosecutorial screening activity—to forward only assured convictions—places female victims at a disadvantage; thus, female victims' complaints often fall on deaf ears, for it is organizationally inexpedient to take chances. Through their organizational mandates, then, prosecutors are partially responsible for any "secondary victimization" female complainants feel during the screening process.

GENDER STEREOTYPES: THE PROSECUTORS' HIDDEN APPRENTICE

In order to screen felony arrests properly and efficiently prosecutors develop a set of practical skills that enable them to ferret out solid cases for adjudication in superior court. And for prediction, prosecutors regard the penal law as merely one element of information that contributes to the definition of a solid felony case. Another,

Elizabeth Anne Stanko

more subjective element is the prosecutors' presumptions concerning the victim's character and/or behavior. To assess victim credibility, prosecutors may turn to their hidden apprentice, gender stereotypes.

The routine process of screening felony arrests demands that ECAB prosecutors predict the outcome of each arrest, taking into consideration its circumstances and its complainant. Such potential problems as a bad witness lessen the chances of a successful conviction of a felony case. With prediction in mind, ECAB prosecutors rely upon categorical assessments about types of individual complainants to aid them in their determinations. For some victims (particularly women) the prosecutors' assumptions about categories of individuals color their treatment of complainants.

Stereotypical assumptions about women in general and about their behavior as victims and complainants play a considerable role in the screening of felony arrests. Female victims of violent, personal crimes confront gender stereotypes, either directly or indirectly, in the screening process. Questions about a particular victim's provocation or consent are influenced by assumptions about the "proper" woman's probable behavior in that situation.

Within the last ten years, research examining the problems of rape victims and battered women has addressed both the trauma victims experience as a result of attack and the institutional obstacles they encounter when they turn to the criminal justice process for redress.[30] Although greater knowledge about these crimes has assisted in establishing mechanisms to facilitate a victim's physical and emotional recovery, present prosecutorial practice remains rooted in the routine organizational demands of successfully convicting a defendant. With an eye toward solid cases, screening prosecutors (who work under strict deadlines and organizational constraints) sometimes, because of perceived witness "problems," choose not to devote prosecutorial resources to a criminal complaint. In this way, cultural stereotypes based on gender (the prosecutors' hidden apprentice), and the organizational demands for a high conviction rate intervene in the decision-making process. Unfortunately, then, for some female victims, prosecutors' organizational considerations separate the problem of handling a criminal complaint from the problem of meting out justice; all too often, the organization's needs prevail over the victim's complaint.

Would You Believe This Woman?

NOTES

I WOULD LIKE TO THANK David Greenberg for his observation about female victims from my dissertation; and Lois Brynes, Lindsey Churchill, Cynthia Enloe, Gaye Tuchman, Nicolette Parisi, and Nicole Rafter for insisting on clarity in this chapter.

1. The prosecutor is the most powerful of criminal justice actors. As Davis notes, "Viewed in broad perspective, the American legal system seems to be shot through with many excessive and uncontrolled discretionary powers but the one that stands out above all others is the power to prosecute or not to prosecute." Kenneth Culp Davis, *Discretionary Justice: A Preliminary Inquiry* (Urbana, IL: University of Illinois Press, 1971), p. 188.

2. Studies of prosecutorial decision making note the relevance of significant variables for the successful prosecution of a case. The nature of the legal evidence is one such variable. *See* Frank Miller, *Prosecution: The Decision to Charge a Suspect With a Crime* (Boston: Little, Brown, 1970), pp. 28, 154; Lynn Mather, *Plea Bargaining or Trial?* (Lexington, MA: D. C. Heath, 1979), pp. 45–48; and David Neubauer, *Criminal Justice in Middle America* (Morristown, NJ: General Learning Press, 1974), pp. 117–119. Generally, the overall assessment of the whole case determines the prosecutor's actions. *See* Abraham Blumberg, *Criminal Justice: Issues and Ironies* (New York: New Viewpoints, 1979), p. 126.

3. Miller, *Prosecution: The Decision to Charge*, p. 27; Neubauer, *Criminal Justice*, p. 118; Jerome H. Skolnick, *Justice Without Trial* (New York: John Wiley, 1966), pp. 199–201.

4. Miller, *Prosecution: The Decision to Charge*, pp. 342–344.

5. Rape victims have reported the trauma of undergoing a personal as well as public trial. *See*, for example, Lynda Lytle Holmstrom and Ann Wolbert Burgess, *The Victim of Rape: Institutional Reactions* (New York: John Wiley, 1978), pp. 229–236. Battered women, too, are often not believed or taken seriously by criminal justice personnel. *See* Del Martin, *Battered Wives* (New York: Pocket Books, 1976), pp. 110–115.

6. United States Law Enforcement Assistance Administration, *Criminal Victimization in the United States, 1976* (Washington, DC: U.S. Government Printing Office, 1979).

7. Federal Bureau of Investigation, *Uniform Crime Reports—1976* (Washington, DC: U.S. Government Printing Office, 1977); Blumberg, *Criminal Justice*, pp. 11–12.

8. Blumberg, *Criminal Justice*, p. 122; Miller, *Prosecution: The Decision to Charge*, p. 11.

9. For a more thorough discussion of practical skills, *see* Egon Bittner, "The Police on Skid Row: A Study of Peace Keeping," *American Sociological Review* 32 (October 1967):701.

10. For an illustration of police officers' practical skills, *see* Bittner, "The Police on Skid Row," pp. 699–715; Skolnick, *Justice Without Trial*; Peter K. Manning, "Rules, Colleagues and Situationally Justified Actions," in *Policing: A View From the Street*, ed. Peter Manning and John Van Maanen (Santa Monica, CA: Goodyear,

80

Elizabeth Anne Stanko

1978), pp. 71–89; John Van Maanen, "Observations on the Making of Policemen," ibid., pp. 292–308; Harvey Sachs, "Notes on Police Assessment of Moral Character," ibid., pp. 187–201; and Jonathan Rubenstein, *City Police* (New York: Farrar, Straus & Giroux, 1972). David Sudnow, "Normal Crimes: Sociological Features of the Penal Code," *Social Problems* 12 (Winter 1965):255-270, discusses the routine work of public defenders. Aaron Cicourel, *The Social Organization of Juvenile Justice* (New York: John Wiley, 1968), discusses probation officers. Prosecutors' everyday decision making is explored by Elizabeth A. Stanko, "These Are the Cases That Try Themselves" (Ph.D. diss., City University of New York, 1977).

11. Bittner, "The Police on Skid Row," pp. 702–704.

12. Sudnow, "Normal Crimes," p. 259.

13. Cicourel, *The Social Organization of Juvenile Justice*, pp. 112–121.

14. *See* Elizabeth A. Stanko, "These Are the Cases That Try Themselves"; and idem, "Characteristics of Victims as a Factor in Prosecutors' Determinations About 'Real' and 'Phony' Robbery Cases" (Paper delivered at the Annual Meeting of the Academy of Criminal Justice Sciences, Philadelphia, 1981).

15. Sudnow ("Normal Crimes") suggests that the work of accusation, legal representation, adjudication, and prognostication should be examined as one would any social activity. In essence, official classification systems used by actually employed administrative personnel include the penal code as data. Examination of these classification schemes reveals the process of how categories of criminal incidents arise and form the basis for organizational action.

16. For approximately thirteen months (March 1975 through March 1976), I observed felony-arrest screening. Over that time, I recorded descriptive accounts of the interactions among the assistant prosecutor, arresting police officer, and complaining witness(es). During the last five months of observation, I was able to transcribe the dialogue among these actors. I witnessed over one thousand felony screenings and transcribed over one hundred conversational exchanges of felony case-assessment, limiting my transcription to assault, rape, and robbery cases. Additionally, I conducted extensive interviews with the assistant prosecutors of ECAB and some administrative prosecutors.

17. At the time of this study, in fact, only nine assistant prosecutors were assigned to this bureau.

18. The "solid" case is akin to the "prosecutable" case. Others have noted the strong standard of convictability prosecutors use. *See* Miller, *Prosecution: The Decision to Charge*, p. 27; Martha A. Myers and John Hagan, "Private and Public Trouble: Prosecutors and the Allocation of Court Resources," *Social Problems* 26 (April 1979):440-441; and Neubauer, *Criminal Justice*, pp. 117–119.

19. Miller, *Prosecution: The Decision to Charge*, pp. 34, 267, 341–342; Stanko, "These Are the Cases That Try Themselves," pp. 88–96. Further, Cannavale and Falcon examined 7,849 cases both of felony and misdemeanor, cases open and closed during a six-month period. Of those 7,849 cases, 6,266 (80 percent) involved at least one victim/witness. Over one-half of the total cases were not prosecuted, with victim/witness noncooperation cited to account for 38 percent of those *nolle prosequi* actions. *See* Frank J. Cannavale, Jr., and William D. Falcon, *Witness Cooperation* (Lexington, MA: D. C. Heath, 1976), pp. 24–26.

20. Holmstrom and Burgess note a similar desire of prosecutors for good witnesses, and the focus of this concern is on the victim's credibility. *See* Holmstrom and Burgess, *The Victim of Rape*, pp. 142, 143–145.

21. Due to the special emphasis placed on female victims throughout this chapter, I utilize *she* and *her* as the pronouns that refer to victims.

22. Evidence that victims are an integral part of prosecutorial decision making is noted by Stanko, "These Are the Cases That Try Themselves"; Kirsten M. Williams, "The Effects of Victim Characteristics on the Disposition of Violent Crimes," in *Criminal Justice and the Victim*, ed. William F. McDonald (Beverly Hills, CA: Sage, 1976), p. 204; Myers and Hagan, "Private and Public Trouble"; and Holmstrom and Burgess, *The Victim of Rape*, pp. 142-145.

23. My analysis is related to Swigert and Farrell's analysis of the use of the image of the "normal primitive" in the processing of homicide offenders. Swigert and Farrell illustrate how this stereotype is incorporated into the manner in which homicide offenders are perceived and subsequently treated by the criminal justice process. Furthermore, they express concern for the use of this imagery in criminal justice decision making. They note that although overt discrimination against persons for reasons of class and race is illegal, "the operation of a legally relevant stereotype of offenders in decisions concerning their adjudication is by far the more insidious process [of discrimination]." *See* Victoria Lynn Swigert and Ronald A. Farrell, *Murder, Inequality, and the Law* (Lexington, MA: Lexington Books, 1976), pp. 3, 1-11. Studies other than mine indicate that gender, as a significant individual characteristic, affects prosecutorial decision making. The "troubles" of white, older, and employed males have a better chance of being prosecuted. *See* Myers and Hagan, "Private and Public Trouble," p. 448; and Williams, "The Effects of Victim Characteristics," p. 203.

24. For a statistical presentation about women's victimization, *see* Lee H. Bowker, "Women as Victims: An Examination of the Results of L.E.A.A.'s National Crime Survey Program," in *Women and Crime in America*, ed. Lee H. Bowker (New York: Macmillan, 1981), pp. 158-179. Stereotypes about the crime of rape are addressed by Julia R. Schwendinger and Herman Schwendinger, "Rape Myths: In Legal, Theoretical, and Everyday Practice," *Crime and Social Justice* 1 (Spring–Summer 1974):18-26. *See* Dorie Klein, "Can This Marriage Be Saved? Battering and Sheltering," *Crime and Social Justice* 12 (1979):19-33, for a discussion of the myths about the crime of battering (including assault, rape, and murder) of women.

25. In my dissertation, I found that none of the felony arrests screened involving complainants and defendants known to each other were selected as felony cases because prosecutors were suspicious of the victim's responsibility for the offense. *See* "These Are the Cases That Try Themselves," pp. 67-72. Others note prosecutors' attitudes toward domestic violence incidents. *See* Neubauer, *Criminal Justice*, pp. 129-131; and Williams, "The Effects of Victim Characteristics," pp. 198-201, 204, 206. And for rape victims, Holmstrom and Burgess speak of victims' confrontations with prosecutors' assumptions of provoking behavior. *See* Holmstrom and Burgess, *The Victim of Rape*, pp. 157-200.

26. Goffman notes that "the routines of social intercourse in established settings allow us to deal with anticipated others without special attention or thought." I am arguing that prosecutors, when screening violent felony cases with female victims, similarly deal with female victims stereotypically without special attention or thought. *See* Erving Goffman, *Stigma: Notes on the Management of Spoiled Identity* (Englewood Cliffs, NJ: Prentice-Hall, 1963), p. 2.

27. Goffman speaks of reactions to people's "social identity," particularly those with spoiled identities. Along with social identity, Goffman notes, "personal

Elizabeth Anne Stanko

attributes such as 'honesty' are involved, as well as structural ones, like 'occupation.' " *See* Goffman, *Stigma*, pp. 1-40. Example 1 illustrates Goffman's point. The robbery charge was dropped and the defendents were indicted for possession of the illegal gun. This indictment charge eliminated the need for a civilian witness. In fact, the only evidence a trial prosecutor would need to convict these defendants was the testimony of the police officer about the proper search of the car and the presentation of the actual gun itself as the discovered illegal item. The prostitutes, the actual victims in the robbery, were not included as elements of this particular case.

28. "Proper" women, according to stereotypes about them, do not place themselves in situations in which they might be robbed. Discrediting the witness is a defense attorney's favorite technique. In their study of rape victims, Holmstrom and Burgess note that women's sexuality became a focus during the processing of a rape complaint. For female robbery victims, too, a process of discrediting them affected their alleged credibility and lessened their chances of being considered stand-up witnesses. *See* Holmstrom and Burgess, *The Victim of Rape*, pp. 177–183; and Stanko, "Characteristics of Victims," p. 5.

29. In their study of rape victims, Holmstrom and Burgess note similar reactions of prosecutors to victims when they lose a case. *See* Holmstrom and Burgess, *The Victim of Rape*, pp. 142–148.

30. Holmstrom and Burgess (*The Victim of Rape*) present a sensitive analysis of the problems encountered by rape victims entering the criminal justice system. Martin (*Battered Wives*) establishes the typical treatment of battered women by criminal justice personnel as well as other social service personnel. Both accounts point to an institutional secondary victimization faced by these victims.

4

The Dark Side of Marriage

Battered Wives and the Domination of Women

DORIE KLEIN

This chapter focuses on the battering of wives: the violent victimization of women by the men to whom they are married or with whom they share a marriagelike relationship.[1] Both the phenomenon of battering and the societal response to it require the development of a theoretical framework of analysis. Like most topics in the study of crime and social problems, battering is not a naturally discrete occurrence, but rather an artificially carved subject. How one chooses to define and delimit the behavior in question affects conclusions as to its etiology and the appropriate policy. For example, martial violence against women is often—and erroneously—considered apart from issues of marital power. The approach here is to analyze battering as the extreme end of a continuum of institutionalized asymmetry in marriage. This relation, in its changing manifestations, lies at the heart of patriarchy, as shaped by capitalism as the dominant mode of production.[2]

Recently, battering has been "discovered" as a social problem. It is now becoming publicly illegitimate to batter one's wife, and victims are now seen as requiring advocacy and redress. This

Dorie Klein

recognition emerges out of an ongoing political process that, like the preceding years of official silence on the subject, cannot be taken for granted; it must be examined. The definition of the problem and the emerging movements and policies to deal with it are the objects of intense conflict. It is not simply a matter of criminologists or feminists randomly and naively discovering a hitherto-hidden crime. It is a question of the social construction and reconstruction of crime, a process that is carried on within the parameters of the relations of production and reproduction in the social order. An understanding of the emergence of battering as a social problem, then, requires in turn an analysis of the relationships among the family, the status of women, the feminist movement, and the state. This chapter sketches some of the most relevant points.

THE NOT-SO-PRIVATE PRACTICES
OF PATRIARCHY

Violence against wives erupts at the intersection of social forces and individual choices, the dynamic between what C. Wright Mills called public issues and private troubles.[3] The prevalence of battering, the patterns of outsiders' responses that allow battering to persist, and the complex (yet common and recognizable) constellation of behaviors in many violent relationships all indicate that this is not a case of individual pathology or private aberration. Nor is it the random outbursts of a "sick," violent society. It is rather a behavior that emerges out of the social relations of domination. The following points illustrate the roots of battering in culture, law, economics, and the common experiences of everyday life.

1. Wife Battering: Common and Condoned
in the United States and Other Advanced
Western Countries

The shelters begun for women in Northern Europe and North America in the 1970s have from the beginning been deluged with wives seeking refuge for themselves and their children from violent husbands. A national inquiry by Lenore Walker and associates indicates that over 50,000 women were seen by queried agencies in

1977, and this figure is by no means comprehensive.[4] Despite the recent blossoming of shelters, crisis centers, and criminal justice services, demand for help has continuously outrun supply.

Police records of domestic disturbance calls, assaults, and homicides also suggest the broad scope of battering, even though most family incidents are not reported to the police.[5] It is known that nationally up to half of all police calls are for family disputes and that a large proportion of assaults are intrafamilial.[6] Marvin Wolfgang's work on homicide patterns indicates that more than one-sixth of all murders in Philadelphia from 1948 to 1952 were of spouses. Further, more than half the male spouses killed (as compared to less than one-tenth of the female spouses killed) were murdered in "victim-precipitated" incidents, suggesting histories of male conjugal violence. Other studies show that many wife killings are the culmination of years of battering and many husband killings are committed in self-defense, after long histories of abuse.[7]

There are recent national surveys based on probability samples that suggest, however tentatively, the prevalence of wife battering within the general population. A study of some 2,000 women and men by Murray Straus, Richard Gelles, and Suzanne Steinmetz found that 4 percent admitted to having experienced serious violence in their marriage during the year. This figure, which includes mutual fighting and female-initiated attacks, and which was obtained without inquiring into the context or consequences of the incidents, probably underestimates serious wife battering. The federal National Crime Survey on victimization among the public has produced the estimate of 3.8 million episodes of intimate violence (gender and age undifferentiated) over a four-year period, of which no more than half were reported to the police.[8]

Battering, and violence against women in general, takes place within a culture that supports such behavior. Pervasive abuse is reflected in media images of sexually vulnerable females and in everyday social life, with its repertoire of jokes about nagging wives inviting their just desserts. In the fantasies displayed in pornography, for example, the tenor can shift abruptly from good-natured intimidation of women to hate-filled sexual attack. More commonly, women's sexuality is used as a commodity to sell products. It is not being proposed that images of sexual objectification "cause" wife abuse, although evidence suggests that routine exposure to violent pornography encourages men's acceptance of actual violence against women.[9] But the ubiquity of these images leads us to ask what kind of social order can systematically grind out women who are displayed, bought and sold, abused and discarded? These images are not merely physical; they project female nurturance, submission, and self-sacrifice. The reverse male image is one of being catered to and taken care of, an image that radiates authority. These hegemonic standards of appropriate male and female behavior incorporate misogyny into "normal" roles for men. (The source of this culture of abuse is explored later in this chapter.)

2. Historical Permission to Batter in Marriage

Regardless of personal inclination, couples do not define their relationships in a vacuum, but inherit gender-differentiated legal, economic, social, and psychological restrictions.[10]

Under the rule of traditional patriarchy that characterized Western feudal society, the labor and possessions of the wife, children, and other subordinates were at the man's disposal. A wife's duties revolved around physical and psychological reproduction, involving household and field chores, sexual services, and the nurturance of others. Religious doctrine confirmed that the man was head of the house; the growing body of civil law affirmed that man and woman were one, and that *one* was the man. Obligations of the genders, separate and unequal as they were, were mutual:

> *The right of the husband to exercise control over the person of the wife took the form of the right to domestic services, the right to marital companionship, and the right to marital fidelity. Correlative to the husband's rights to the wife's domestic services is the wife's right to support under the doctrine of necessaries.*[11]

The husband was consequently responsible for the wife's conduct. William Blackstone noted in his *Commentaries* on the common law of England that:

> *The husband also (by the old law) might give his wife moderate correction. For, as he is to answer for her misbehaviour, the law thought it reasonable to entrust him with this power of restraining her by domestic chastisement, in the same moderation that a man is allowed to correct his apprentices or children.*[12]

The Dark Side of Marriage

Within limits, wife beating was permitted. The "rule of thumb" in English common law refers to the husband's traditional right to hit his wife with a stick no thicker than his thumb. Early mercantile capitalism did not substantively improve wives' legal position; if anything, the notion of their separate and subordinate domestic sphere—increasingly isolated from the growing public commerce and industry—was strengthened. Nor did the individual rights demanded by the rising bourgeoisie against the old regime shift the balance of marital power. Not until the development of industrial capitalism in the late 1800s were there to be significant challenges to the husband's rights of discipline.

3. Battering Becomes Private and Invisible

Beginning in the nineteenth century, husbands were gradually deprived of their legal right of chastisement. This reflected the enormous shift in the West from the family-centered mode of production toward a factory-centered mode of production, in which individuals would go out singly to sell their labor for wages, sundering the former unity of work and family. The legal system of individual, state-guaranteed liberties and contractual rights of property and labor developed in conjunction. The nineteenth-century feminists, socialists, and libertarians who attacked discretionary male power envisioned a more egalitarian form of marriage. Yet their efforts, which seemingly had history on their side, ran up against the ability of capitalism to adapt patriarchy to new conditions and force people to adapt themselves. In the United States, despite the steady growth of working-class women's participation in the wage labor force and many women's traditional involvement in agriculture and small business, the ideology of the "lady at home" reigned supreme. Political, intellectual, and civic leaders fought tooth and nail against the political and cultural challenges mounted by women in the late 1800s and early 1900s, and made every effort to strengthen the ideal of the home as haven. The nature of women's work continued to be restricted, ill-paid, or unpaid. The housewife was being fashioned to coordinate the consumption of newly marketed and heavily promoted mass goods within her family, goods that would neither lighten her load nor end her isolation.

Simultaneous with this commodification of domesticity came the growing involvement of the state. Poor families in particular became the targets of increasingly powerful public institutions of health, education, welfare, and justice. Wives and mothers were the focus for new intervention by elites, as Jacques Donzelot has noted.[13] The liberalization of certain aspects of the wife's position, exemplified by the courts' rejection of the ancient "rule of thumb," reordered rather than revolutionized marriage. Wives, still bound in economic dependence, would be reconnected to new lines of hierarchy through these state institutions of reproduction—with the assistance of new scientific theories of female inferiority, maternal instinct, and so forth.[14] And alongside the loss of autonomy experienced by most men in the workplace came the official enshrinement of the home as each man's castle and fortress against the world. This left the abuse of wives formally unmentionable and publicly invisible.

As might be expected, despite the revocation of the "rule of thumb," the law has continued to be unresponsive to battered wives. Intervention that has occurred has been oriented toward underplaying or justifying the violence and toward bolstering family unity and male authority. Although wife battering is now technically no different than any other assault or battery, it has always been treated differently. Police have often ignored family violence calls or have refused to make arrests. Prosecutors have been reluctant to press charges. The few cases that have been processed have mostly gone to such civil courts as family court, where the penalties and machinery for adjudication and enforcement are minimal, non-punitive, and geared toward family reconciliation. Judges have been prone to acquit, to accept minor pleas of guilt for serious offenses, and to hand down unusually lenient sentences for violent acts.[15] Rarely have batterers served time in jail or prison or faced any penalties for violating court restraining orders. Although public officials publicly condemn individual acts of personal violence, and despite the overwhelming prevalence and seriousness of wife battering, the reality is that battering has not been seen as illegitimate violence. Law enforcement and court officers have professed themselves unwilling to become involved in what are labeled "private affairs." This veil of privacy mystifies the fact that marital relations, far from being left to individuals, are spelled out in law. And written and practiced law has always overlooked a husband's use of force.

4. The Playing Out of Conflicts over Domination

While culture, law, and economics may promote, normalize, and perpetuate battering, personal experiences in marriage actually create it. Individual needs and tensions painfully unfold in all heterosexual relationships. The characteristic patterns of particularly violent relationships are quantitatively rather than qualitatively different from nonviolent ones; such relationships are an exaggeration of, rather than a departure from, the norm.[16] It would be misleading to search for either a "profile" of a batterer or predictive variables associated with battering relationships, as clinicians and researchers are prone to do. This would be to adopt an implicit model of the problem as a disease that one either has or does not have, to differentiate the "sick" from the "normal." (The implications of the disease model are explored later in this chapter.)

Battering, itself open to varying definitions, is not an absolute quality in an individual or marriage; instead, it is part of an overall dynamic between gender conflict and the use of force. It is during crisis that conflicts are most sharply revealed, but the extreme responses of a few tell us about the common problems and feelings of all in a gender-divided society. Marital conflicts are shaped by the specific experiences and outlooks of class and ethnicity. Research on the relationship of class to battering is inconclusive; however, it would not be unexpected to find that many of those men with the fewest coping resources and fewest outlets for socially approved force batter more. Nor would it be surprising to find that many of those women with the fewest independent resources and alternatives more frequently remain in abusive situations. However, while most studies do show a higher incidence of violence among working- and lower-class families than among middle- and upper-class ones, few studies have equal access to the latter groups. Their problems seldom surface in surveys, police records, or agency caseloads. And all studies do indicate that battering occurs in all classes, albeit with varying consequences.

To date, our knowledge in this area comes mostly from women who have been in relationships that are seriously violent over relatively long periods of time; who have been largely unable to stop the abuse on their own; and who have finally turned to shelters, therapists, police, or social services.[17] In one sense, this sample is

Dorie Klein

not representative of all wives who have been assaulted. Others are abused only briefly or less seriously, many successfully cope with it verbally or by physically defending themselves, a few fight back, some get outside assistance from family or friends, and a great many—perhaps most—quickly leave the man.[18] These coping women rarely come to the attention of agencies or researchers, who are likely to see only the women, and a few battering men, with the least material and psychological resources. Despite these limitations, stories of the latter group nonetheless reveal patterns that illuminate not only battering, but also the dynamics and uncertain patriarchal foundation of contemporary marriage. Two predominant themes emerge: (1) the tendency to blame the victim; and (2) the structural dependency of, and divisions between, the batterer and the victim.

Tendency to Blame the Victim. Husbands, police, researchers, and therapists often look for provocation or justification of battering in the woman's own behavior; they do so out of their own fear, guilt, or professional training. Traditional expectations of a wife can play an enormous role. Her failure to nurture may be central: she may be a rotten cook, a lousy housekeeper. She may be sexually unresponsive or too sexually independent—or fantasized as such. She may be unbecomingly self-reliant or a nagging harpy who would try anyone's patience. The consistency and specifics of the expectations are less crucial than the fact of blame; the power to impose the expectations matters more than the expectations themselves. The result is that the victim herself often feels at fault. She may believe not that her shortcomings warrant the beatings, but that she would not have such a dissatisfied, abusive man if she were a better woman. More pragmatically, she may not be able to help feeling that if she had been quieter, cleverer, and more docile, the violence would never have happened.

Understandably, the tendency to blame the victim is most frequently found in the battering husband, usually with the backing of the law and (as we shall later note) the social services. Often the husband will directly blame the episode on his wife's failures or provocations. However, he also may rationalize or neutralize it through a variety of techniques.[19] Injuries may be minimized or chalked off as accidentally inflicted. Deliberate beating may be reinterpreted, for example, as a necessary effort to calm an hysterical woman. He may offer the excuse of being drunk, diverting attention away from the marital relationship to the presumed effects of the alcohol. Or he may transfer to his wife guilt for outside frustrations; for example, she might be made into a scapegoat for all sorts of difficulties he has at work.

The process of blaming the victim is not limited to the intimates involved. Lack of support for victims, as we have noted, is common among criminal justice practitioners and equally prevalent among mental health and social welfare service staff. The argument is often made that violence is the interaction of two equally responsible individuals. In reality it is the wife, who is usually more receptive to counseling and to being made to feel emotionally responsible, who is blamed. Like the suspect victims of poverty whom William Ryan described in his original work on blaming the victim, battering victims are unconsciously seen by professionals as victims of their own faulty attitudes and destructive lifestyles.[20]

Victim blaming is essential for a social order in which women are valued chiefly as wives and mothers. Tragically underscoring this is the fact that a beaten woman often gathers the personal strength and social support to get help or get out only when her children are also threatened by the man. At this point, in fact, social sanction swings against the woman who stays: she is no longer expected to stand by her husband, but to protect her children. In neither case is her own welfare considered primary. This denial of battering represents de facto support, which reinforces wives' nurturing, submissive, and sacrificing roles. Victim blaming becomes a weapon in the intense conflict over a woman's place that goes on at both the individual and impersonal levels. It is used not only against traditional wives, but also against those in conscious or unconscious revolt.

Many social theorists have argued that one must view the violence as mutual interaction, without exculpating either side.[21] But if one truly examines violence as the product of interaction (as many researchers claim to do), then this interaction itself must be put in the context of marriage as an institution of gender domination. R. E. Dobash has pointed out that if one sees a wife's "nagging" as provoking a husband's hitting, for example, then that "nagging" itself should be seen as being provoked by the restrictions on a woman's autonomy that force her into economic and emotional dependence; it should also be viewed as a product of the

Dorie Klein

daily negotiations between spouses to apportion resources and support, negotiations that are played out in gender-determined ways.[22]
It is not that "marriage is a hitting license," Straus has observed;[23]
it is a set-up for women to be beaten, blamed, and kept in their
place.

Gender-based Dependency and Division. Women and men
sometimes seem to inhabit separate spheres, although the specific
character of the spheres differs by class and ethnicity.[24] The
historical origins of this separation reflect biological as well as
cultural distinctions, but it is reinforced by the division of labor inherent in the separation of work and home and by the gender-
segmented labor market. Not only are the genders brought up to
interpret the world and to behave differently, but they experience
different worlds. When a man and woman live together in a conjugal
situation, their differences stand out and can become especially
problematic—even volatile and lethal—under conditions of relative
isolation, high external pressure, and high internal expectations.

Social isolation is one element that reinforces battering. Wives
and mothers are often isolated in the home. No one and nothing can
come before their families. Men may also feel cut off, but they are
freer to go out with friends after work, go drinking, engage in sports,
and so forth. Wives thus become socially dependent on their
husbands, and husbands may resent their wives. Yet a husband may
curtail his wife's freedom even as she attacks his own. Many violent
episodes revolve around a husband's suspicions if a wife goes out or
a wife's resentment when a husband does. Sexual jealousy is only
one factor: possessiveness over a spouse's time and attention is
equally strong. Some violent husbands telephone constantly and insist upon an hourly accounting of their wives' whereabouts. Others
follow their wives to work. Because this is an exaggeration of the
"normal" husband's protectiveness and concern, many wives accept (or are even flattered by) the behavior until they see the violen
side of it.

Emotional distance also contributes to battering. The division
of emotions between the genders, "instrumental" male behavior
versus "expressive" female behavior, turns out to be quite dysfunctional—in fact, not "functional" at all—for the individuals and the
marriage.[25] Masculine standards emphasize egoism, devalue femininity, objectify other people, and create a fear of dependence on
them. The contemporary crisis in these standards, although it may

open up possible alternative models in the long run, sharpens anxiety. When men feel disillusioned with the world of work and family life and perceive that their masculine standards have not worked for them, they often erupt into violence toward the woman of the house. Battering men tend to interpret all their negative emotions—fear, hurt, guilt, disappointment—as anger, which, along with sexual desire, is one of the few feelings that they (unlike women) are permitted to express.

Violence in general has recently emerged as a much-discussed social problem, and it has been linked to male roles.[26] It is misleading to conceive of violence as a purely individual act, given institutional capacities for far greater violence, and equally misleading to see violence as "masculine" in character; however, there is an element of truth to the concept of individual violence as a masculine mode of expressing pain or frustration. But the outlets for expressing this frustration are differentially accessible by class, gender, and ethnicity. Although many battering husbands and beaten wives (as well as clinicians and researchers) point to the sources of frustration—loss of a job, a hard day at work, money troubles—as explanations for battering, such explanations omit crucial intervening steps: Why should structural obstacles result in personal frustration? Why should frustration then turn into violence? And why should violence be directed against a specific scapegoat? The dynamics of this process reflect patterns of subordination.

Given their limited options, battering men are dependent. The threatened failure of a marriage can mean injured pride, guilt, loneliness, inconvenience, and sense of failure. Many battering men have low self-esteem and are emotionally inarticulate, which is not surprising in an individualistic and impersonal male world, and their marriages may be their only source of warmth and nurturing.[27] Then, too, men who attempt to change their behavior may be stigmatized as "unmanly." And men who attempt to vent their anger where the blame rests may find themselves out of a job.

Dependency arising out of women's restrictions permits the abuse to continue. Feminine standards of "expressiveness"—empathy, submissiveness, self-sacrifice—allow women to cushion the shocks and nurture their families. If they fail to conform—and women not only rebel, but also manipulate and subvert these roles—they face both external opposition and internal conflict. Further, the contemporary crisis in these standards also creates anxiety, even as it opens up possible options. Women will frequently endure a good deal in order to remain in a relationship. The pressures on them, like all aspects of gender roles, do not merely exist in their consciousness, but are structurally reinforced. A woman who attempts to leave an abusive relationship faces the enormous difficulties of being on her own in a gender-segmented labor market and misogynic social order. Mildred Daley Pagelow has argued that many of the battering relationships she has studied were characterized by what she terms "traditional ideology": the woman's deep commitment to marriage and the man's belief in patriarchy.[28] Walker has described a "cycle of violence" wherein both partners minimize or deny the violence, hope unrealistically for future improvement, and are enormously dependent on each other during the nonviolent phases of the cycle.[29]

It would be a mistake, however, to attribute contemporary battering, and its breeding ground of asymmetrical dependency and scapegoating, solely to the traditional and accepted patriarchal power of the husband over the wife, as many feminist researchers tend to do.[30] Violence against wives may actually be exacerbated by threats to patriarchy, and even by lessening female dependence and submission, which some men combat with their traditional prerogative of force. Images of violent male abuse of women may actually become more common as gender conflicts intensify. The gaps between one's expectations and one's experiences of everyday life reflect changes in the reality of women's and men's structural positions in the world. Thus, in a dialectical fashion, it may be that male authority and violence and female dependency and victimization are thrown into relief at a time when their contradictions are sharpest, and their legitimacy and unquestioned continuation most in doubt.

We have now seen how battering privately thrives inside externally defined relations of marriage in a gender-divided society, and how that society has condoned the violence. Let us turn next to the recent "discovery" of battering as a public issue and to its emerging definition within the parameters set by both domination and resistance.

THE CHANGING OF THE GUARD: WOMEN, FAMILY, AND THE STATE

The "discovery" of battering as a social problem has involved dragging into the open what has long been hidden away as a private prac-

The Dark Side of Marriage

tice. The physical facts are real and common enough, but their recognition and interpretation as a phenomenon termed *battering* are a recent and complex development. As I have observed elsewhere:

> *A man's laying of hands on a woman can be seen as necessary discipline, proof of manhood, a felony, or hideous sin, depending on the relationship (wife, slave, stranger) which itself is socially structured.*[31]

It is the changing pattern of class, race, and gender relations, rather than universal notions of intrinsic harm, that determines which behaviors are seen as illegitimate. This leads us to understand:

> *The criminal law and its enforcement is a complex phenomenon which reflects dominant economic exigencies and their ideological supports, as well as ongoing concessions to political demands and expedient interests. Wife beating illustrates this: a traditional male marital right of patriarchy is now being challenged behaviorally and redefined as illegal in the face of women's wage labor, changing family relations, and feminist activity.*[32]

The tentative emergence of battering as a crime at this moment in history can therefore be understood only by reflexively analyzing the feminist movement, state strategies of intervention, and the continuing public struggle over problem definition and policy. The first task is to place these events in context.

1. The Family Crisis as Contradiction in Patriarchy and Capitalism

The organization of production and level of technology today in advanced capitalist areas would seem no longer to require the gender-based division of labor. Yet its persistence, transcending biology, is deeply intertwined with the private accumulation of wealth and the institutions of the contemporary state. Women remain economically disadvantaged, bound to the management of family life. At home and outside, their work continues to be child rearing, food and clothing preparing, "people handling," assisting, and being decorative objects. It appears, then, that the *social relations* of patriarchal reproduction and capitalist production impede the liberation of women that is now possible due to advances in the forces of reproduction and production. And so major contradictions in this dual system of oppression come to the fore, manifested as a crisis in the family and in women's place.

In recent years women have begun moving into the wage labor force in unprecedented numbers around the world, concentrated in low-paying service occupations and positions in offices and labor-intensive industry. Simultaneously, household work is being commodified (fast food, professional therapy, care for children and the sick) at an increasing rate, and the need for family income consequently grows. These developments speed the disintegration of the nuclear family, which relies on housewives' constant labor at home and on *male* breadwinners in the workplace. Marital ties assume tenuous contractual forms. Indeed, sexuality (and potential parenthood) becomes a commodity itself: personal life, like work life, is experienced as a marketing of oneself and others. The economic and psychic burdens of this fall primarily on women.

Attempts to experiment with fluid short-term marriage and single motherhood simultaneously embody new freedom and new hardship for women. Such trends put women under greater pressure to reproduce the labor force with their own (dwindling) private resources. Their inability or refusal to do so contributes to heightened demands on state health, education, and welfare services. Feminism, both as an organized movement and as an inchoate ideology, grows in response to these trends, further catalyzing them. Eliminating wife battering resurfaces as an elementary demand at a time when the private domination of a wife seems no longer tenable. But it is a demand that questions the entire character of marriage and thus, implicitly, the entire fabric of gender domination.

2. The Success and Cost of the Shelter Movement

Physical violence against wives, once taken seriously by an earlier generation of feminists and then buried, was rediscovered by contemporary activists in the women's movement in England.[33] Great numbers of beaten wives began responding to new refuge and crisis services; in North America and in Europe, the developing awareness of the hidden prevalence of rape was rapidly extending to cover battering and rape in marriage.[34] Grass-roots response took the form of

The Dark Side of Marriage

shelters organized on shoestring budgets by local women, many with experience in community feminist activity. The emphasis was explicitly political in the early days, with services planned along egalitarian lines under the principles of "sisterhood." The model was to integrate individual transformation with social change through mutual support, consciousness raising, and collective outreach. In its most radical phase, the analysis of battering focused on the domination of women within marriage and on the economic and political subordination that keeps them victims.[35]

The practical priorities of the sheltering effort have influenced its political direction in ways that are visible even after a short period. The hesitancy of victims to leave their batterers, and the necessity of confronting a criminal justice system that is stubbornly unresponsive in life-threatening situations, were foremost concerns. Difficulties with scant and tenuous finances, lack of security against angry husbands, staff exhaustion and "burn out," and resident-staff conflicts over lifestyle and orientation have been some of the central preoccupations. Coping with individual behavior, and the personal consequences of social inadequacies and injustices, has consumed most of the energy.

Consequently, many shelter feminists tend to view "socialization" as the primary cause of battering. Many see only a surface "macho" culture, a collection of men who have individually learned certain gender roles and are allowed to be violent; they advocate educating men and lobbying for strict legislation. Thus, they see reeducation of individuals as sufficient to prevent battering; structural change — the elimination of patriarchy — is not emphasized. Or, alternatively, they view reeducation of individuals as sufficient to effect structural change; to them, patriarchy itself consists of bad men and/or bad laws, easily reformed by reeducating or reshuffling individuals at the top, rewriting a few criminal laws, and encouraging general goodwill. This ideological world-view appears to explain daily events to shelter feminists, who, lacking a structural and wholistic understanding, see only the manifestations: bad child-rearing practices, insensitive men, inadequate laws, and so forth. Further, everyday necessity forces them to concentrate on the tasks of consciousness raising, lobbying, and therapy; the larger background becomes imperceptible despite the fact (or because of the fact) that it is pervasive. Finally, psychological and educational orientations toward social problems are heavily promoted in popular discussions of the issue and in academic disciplines providing tools of analysis. This becomes a key problem for feminist activists when the state responds with its own set of priorities and paradigms.

Shelters have enjoyed some success in attracting public interest: newspapers have reported painful beatings, miscarriages of justice, and service options; shelters and hotlines have sprung up in cities all over North America and Europe; "battered women" has become a commonly used phrase. Shelters have established links to wings of the women's movement opposing pornography and providing services to rape victims; groups have begun to coordinate education and lobbying for stricter law enforcement regarding battering, rape, marital rape, and pornography. But the state has overrun these initial efforts by intervening with its own definitions of the problem and its own approaches. Therefore, thanks to state intervention, the price of even limited success of the shelter movement has been that it has undergone a sea change, a major shift.

3. State Intervention to "Guard" Women

In the past few years the state has come under pressure from a variety of sources to develop new policies on wife battering.[36] The role of government in developing services, supporting research, and seizing the initiative in the field has quickly become central.

Criminal Justice Response: Reluctant Arrests. Police departments were first to take up the issue. Even before police policies were publicly challenged by feminists, the questionable use of police resources and the high incidence of police injury and death on domestic disturbance calls were noted by officials. Morton Bard developed a pilot project in New York in the mid-1960s to train police to intervene more effectively in conjugal disputes, using psychologists and social workers who would emphasize mediation, counseling, and avoiding arrest.[37] The project was funded by the federal Law Enforcement Assistance Administration, which, along with the National Institute of Mental Health and the National Institute on Alcohol Abuse and Alcoholism, later became active in supporting family violence services. Programs to train police, refer calls to social service agencies, and improve response procedures have been instituted in a number of cities. Efficiency and safety of the police were primary concerns.

A series of feminist court challenges and statutory revisions in many states and localities have made the mediation policy no longer feasible, however. Growing pressure to arrest and charge battering husbands, including stricter new laws in many states, has brought criminal justice agencies additional problems and forced them to attempt new policies. In New York, for example, suits by Brooklyn Legal Services forced abandonment of the Bard arrest-avoidance policy; in 1980, jurisdiction over battering cases was removed from family court to criminal court to encourage prosecution. During the same year, California state codes were revised to ease access to citizens' arrest of batterers, court restraining orders, and victim/ witness assistance projects.[38]

But courtroom time and jail space, even if seen as appropriate tools for deterrence or punishment, remain unavailable. Channeling of batterers out of the criminal justice system to "treatment" consequently becomes more of a practical necessity than a matter of rehabilitative conviction. However, while just the threat of prosecution or incarceration appears to act as an adequate immediate deterrent to many battering men who would otherwise have nothing to do with the criminal law, others, particularly working- and lower-class men who may already have police records, are processed through.

The new domestic violence diversion programs, in fact, have found ready-made models left over from the wars on crime and drugs of the 1970s. It has already been observed by many therapists working with batterers that the latter make unwilling clients, particularly when court-ordered. The coercive aspects and rehabilitative failures of drug and alcohol diversion programs are now being reproduced in battering projects. And in the context of criminal justice paradigms, given the absence or weakness of feminist perspectives, the individual counseling of batterers reinforces a view of wife battering as a problem of personal abnormality and psychopathology.

These emerging social-control and problem-redefinition features in state intervention in wife battering are inherent in the character of criminal justice. Class and race play overwhelming roles in determining who is arrested, prosecuted, and convicted. Like gender discrimination, race and class bias are not merely the result of personal prejudice among officials, but are structured into formal and operational definitions of crime, administrative discretion, criteria for probation, and so on. The attempt to transform wife battering from an unpalatable women's political issue into yet

Dorie Klein

another comfortable and manageable instance of lower-class violence reflects fundamental state interests in simultaneously quieting feminist criticism and encouraging endless campaigns against crime. It remains doubtful that fighting gender domination is to become a police priority. Arrests and prosecutions are conducted with reluctance. As Dobash and Dobash observe, legal action is taken only when abuse exceeds certain tacit limits or when a behavior becomes a public nuisance, forcing the police to act as mediators.[39]

Shelters: (Under) Funded and Outmaneuvered. State intervention in wife battering has been most significant not in the criminal justice area, but in social and mental health services for women. Shelters are being forced to rely on government funding as inflation, recession, growing demand for services, and exhaustion among volunteers feed the tendency to bureaucratize, expand, and professionalize. Shelters are under internal pressure from staff to regularize their individual and collective futures. More important, however, in order to obtain city, county, state, or federal money, shelters are required to conform to funding guidelines. Their problems are many. They must be concerned with licensing and accreditation; they must report and write grants; they must form networks to forge links to funding sources, train workers, monitor legislation, and interface with other agencies. Upper-level staff who become involved in administration soon discover that they have less time for the battered women. The early model of independent grass-roots support, collective action, and working with battered women as "sisters" rapidly gives way to hierarchies of funding and administration based on state power and requirements for academic degrees (i.e., social class). Battered women come to be handled as clients. Often out of legitimate needs for self-protection, shelters adopt the same suspicious and stigmatizing policies toward clients as do traditional professional social services. These divisions, inherent in a class-divided movement, are exacerbated by shelters' links to state agencies. At stake is the possible early demise of wife battering as a political issue of gender domination.

Therapy for victims, if appropriate, is not necessarily regressive; but, in the absence of collective movement for social change, even "assertiveness training" and other "feminist" forms of therapy promote the individualization of the problem. In an extreme form, they encourage a new form of victim blaming; a

The Dark Side of Marriage

woman's economic or emotional dependence is seen as the product of her own socialization, which she must overcome. With the current historical trend to individualize social problems, there is pressure to reject structural models requiring collective reorganization of the social order in favor of ones stressing individual achievement. This "mobility" model, however, is of purely ideological relevance for the majority of battered women in shelters and service agencies, who are working-class persons with few career options and many family responsibilities.

Even when shelter feminists take a critical stance toward this tendency to individualize problems, they no longer have control over the societal response to wife battering. Alcohol treatment programs, mental health centers, criminal diversion projects, prosecutors, child welfare services, and family agencies are becoming eager to incorporate a new area of potential funding into their domains. They have considerable financial, organizational, and professional advantages over feminist shelters in maneuvering for scarce money, sponsoring research, and commanding media attention and public legitimacy. Alcoholism treatment programs, for example, have attempted to redefine battering as an alcoholism problem by diverting batterers who drink to alcoholism treatment. They have also promoted paradigms of the pathology of the alcohol family, including the concept of the drinker's wife as a "coalcoholic" whose neurotic needs lead her to encourage her husband's drinking (and, presumably, his battering). Thus battering and victim blaming are incorporated into new interactive theories of family therapy.

State-funded Research: Domination as Pathology. The contribution of state-funded research must also be noted. In regard to research on alcoholism and battering paradigms, Patricia Morgan observes:

> This research examines wife battery through a medical-social, individualistic framework which searches for a "cause" through narrowly defined associations and correlations. . . . By merely positing a "relationship" (causal or not) between alcohol and family violence, a causal image is in fact created, the need for further research of this type is validated, and the promotion of service/treatment models are legitimized. . . . These narrow theories enjoy support because they are easy to understand, they are created with built-in solutions and

*programs, and they turn away from larger, more uncom-
fortable questions of power, structural inequality, social
control, and the shifting values and norms which
permeate contemporary society.*[40]

Agencies within the federal Department of Health and Human Services, such as the National Institute of Mental Health and the National Institute on Alcohol Abuse and Alcoholism, support both treatment and research on wife battering. The problem has largely been defined as "family violence," whether at the level of clinical case studies of violent individuals, surveys to uncover variables associated with individual violence, or studies of violence as a general cultural phenomenon.[41] On either the microsocial or macrosocial level, defining the problem as one of violence is both too narrow and too broad; it glosses over the specific character of wife battering as linked to gender domination within and without the family. The clinical literature, for example, often attributes battering to inadequate socialization or poor interaction. Surveys focus on psychosocial variables that can be correlated with battering incidents. General studies focus on domestic violence as part of an overall violent or "sick" society.

Most academic and professional researchers, like their colleagues in service delivery, have had few ties to feminist groups and little interest in studying the problem of battering until the money became available. More important, institutionally funded and individually produced research relieves researchers from accountability to community interests ("politics"), although it forces them to accommodate to funding agencies and "peer review" ("objectivity").

4. Opposition to Sheltering and the Conflict over "Saving the Family"

The state appears as a mediator or instrument of a plurality of interests on a problem such as wife battering, which emerges out of conflicts in the society at large. However, as I have suggested, policies are not formulated neutrally or arbitrarily, but come out of a framework in which certain options are considered and others discouraged or never even recognized. Egalitarian and political models of intervention with beaten wives, for example, or educational campaigns directed at battering husbands that seek to break down patriarchy, are outside the realm of state possibilities.

The state's overriding concern is to encourage the furthering of private accumulation of capital and the stabilizing of social relations, including necessary management of dissenting or troublesome groups. This requires that the state occasionally respond to demands for justice and welfare; for example, it may pass laws against battering, concede social services to victims, and eliminate legal protection of gender or marital status. But these concessions are implemented on the state's terms. In the context of the crisis of the family and women's place, this means the attempted smooth transition to new forms of gender domination, the reordering and relegitimizing of male authority and female acquiescence. "Saving the family" under various guises has again become a visible government priority.

The enormous changes in family life and consciousness threaten many people's beliefs in patriarchy; the world they grew up in seems to be in jeopardy. The turmoil also reveals most men's and some women's stakes in the old order, especially in the traditional family. The women's movement, particularly upon official ratification of a few of its milder demands, is becoming a primary target for fear and hostility toward all aspects of change. It is blamed as *causing* many of the historic developments (for example, the entry of many women into the labor market, the rising divorce rate) to which it has actually *responded*.

The redefinition of battering as a crime, which is accurately viewed as a fundamental and perhaps inevitable step toward the delegitimization of a husband's personal authority, has been opposed by many political right-wingers, neoconservative intellectuals, and religious fundamentalists (groups that also often oppose women's equal job opportunity, sexual and reproductive freedom, and equal political rights). One religious group in a northwestern city, for example, has distributed cartoons depicting the city's battered women's shelter as a vacuum cleaner sucking women out of the home, destroying the family.

Shelter support has briefly flourished as part of a liberal state strategy to respond to feminist demands and modernize family relations in order to integrate more people into the work force. However, that period may be at an end. Like abortion clinics and sexual counseling services, shelters may increasingly feel the effects of physical and fiscal attacks. Inflation and recession give rise to tax rebellion; social service budget cuts; and class, racial, and interest-

Dorie Klein

group polarization. Bowing to new alignments of power and interest, the state — and even some female activists and professionals — may bargain away tenuous feminist gains in a faltering economy and foundering national unity of purpose. The state may choose, under the cloak of nonintervention or laissez-faire, to move back toward direct reinforcement of traditional male authority and patriarchal relations. Women may be asked once more to sacrifice: for the good of their children, their husbands, their country.

Women may be chosen to be scapegoats, but this does not mean that women consent to act as such. They have always individually and collectively fought against their victimization, whether in private at the hands of abusive men or in the public arena of indifference. They have successfully raised the issue of wife battering against difficult odds. Efforts that arise in a patriarchal social order to ignore or neutralize the political issue of wife battering do not diminish — and indeed underscore — the significance of the public redefinition of the phenomenon of battering and the discovery of the domination behind it.

In sum, we have focused on the problem of battering as an aspect of an overall structure of patriarchy, which is shaped by capitalist modes of production and reproduction. We have seen how law, culture, and economics create both patterns of violence and societal responses. We have explored the emergence of battering as a social problem, as an aspect of feminist demands, and as a response to contemporary structural upheavals in family life. Finally, we have analyzed the nature and direction of state intervention and have suggested arenas of conflict at the present time. The issues raised in the course of this discussion are of sufficient importance to indicate that battering affects not just its immediate victims, but all women and men.

NOTES

1. The term *wife battering* will be used, rather than *spouse abuse* to emphasize that women, rather than men, are the primary victims of intimate violence. ''Husband abuse'' happens, but it is often relatively trivial in the eyes of both parties, and even more often it is done in self-defense. Child abuse and abuse of the elderly, while each a serious problem in its own right, are analytically quite separate and should not be lumped with wife abuse in a catch-all of domestic or family violence. Finally, the word *wife* is preferred to *woman* to describe the victim, whether legally married or

not, in order to focus not on the biological fact of gender but rather on the social relations of marriage or pseudomarriage.

2. The concept of patriarchy, which has had a number of interpretations, is used here to refer to any society in which male domination is a central institutional and cultural organizing principle, explicit or implicit. On this issue *see* Zillah Eisenstein, "Developing a Theory of Capitalist Patriarchy," and "Some Notes on the Relations of Capitalist Patriarchy," in *Capitalist Patriarchy and the Case for Socialist Feminism* (New York: Monthly Review Press, 1979), pp. 5–55.

3. C. Wright Mills, *The Sociological Imagination* (New York: Oxford University Press, 1959).

4. Lenore Walker, Address to the Conference on Violence Against Women and Children, University of Washington, Seattle, 4 October 1979.

5. U.S. Department of Justice, *Criminal Victimization in the United States 1977*, A National Crime Survey Report, Law Enforcement Assistance Administration (Washington, DC: U.S. Government Printing Office, 1979).

6. *See* James Bannon, "Presentation on Police Difficulties with Female Battering Cases" (Paper presented to the U.S. Civil Rights Commission, Hartford, Connecticut, September 1977). *See also* Police Foundation, *Domestic Violence and the Police* (Kansas City: Police Department, 1973); and James Bourdouris, "Homicide and the Family," *Journal of Marriage and the Family* 33, 4 (1971):667–76.

7. Marvin Wolfgang, *Patterns in Criminal Homicide* (New York: Wiley & Sons, 1958). *See also* Claudia McCormick, "Battered Women—The Last Resort," mimeographed (Chicago: Women's Correctional Center, 1977).

8. Murray Straus, Richard Gelles, and Suzanne Steinmetz, *Behind Closed Doors: Violence in the American Family* (Garden City, NY: Anchor, 1980), chapter 2. *See also* U.S. Department of Justice, *Intimate Victims: A Study of Violence Among Friends and Relatives*, A National Crime Survey Report, Law Enforcement Assistance Administration (Washington, DC: U.S. Government Printing Office, 1980).

9. On pornography's effects, *see* Diana Russell, "Pornography and Violence: What Does the New Research Say?" in *Take Back the Night: Women on Pornography*, ed. Laura Lederer (New York: William Morrow, 1980), pp. 218–38.

10. This is not generally understood by many researchers in the field. Straus, Gelles, and Steinmetz, for example, concentrate almost exclusively on interpersonal interaction. Therefore, it is not surprising that they come up with misleading interpretations of wife battering as just one instance of generalized family violence. *See* Dorie Klein, "Can This Marriage Be Saved? Battery and Sheltering," *Crime and Social Justice* 12 (1979):19–33; and R. Emerson Dobash and Russell Dobash, *Violence against Wives: A Case against the Patriarchy* (New York: Free Press, 1979), chapter 2, for critiques of the interactional and gender-neutral approaches.

11. Sophinisba Breckinridge, ed., *The Family and the State: Select Documents* (Chicago: University of Chicago Press, 1934), p. 109.

12. William Blackstone, *Commentaries on the Laws of England* (London: Houghton Mifflin, 1968), book 1, chapter 15.

13. Jacques Donzelot, *The Policing of Families* (New York: Pantheon, 1979). On the development of individual contractual legal rights, *see* Evgeny Pashukanis, *Law and Marxism: A General Theory* (London: Ink Links, 1978; orig. pub. 1929).

14. *See* Barbara Ehrenreich and Deirdre English, *For Her Own Good: 150 Years of the Experts' Advice to Women* (New York: Anchor, 1978).

15. James Bannon, "Law Enforcement Problems with Intra-Family Violence"

Dorie Klein

(Paper presented to the American Bar Association, Montreal, August 1975). *See also* Del Martin, *Battered Wives* (New York: Pocket Books, 1977); and Marjory Fields, "Wife Beating: Government Intervention, Policies and Practices" (Paper presented to the U.S. Commission on Civil Rights, Washington, DC, 30–31 January 1978) in *Battered Women: Issues of Public Policy* (Washington, DC: U.S. Commission on Civil Rights, 1978), p. 250.

16. I am grateful to Margrit Brückner, particularly for her talks to the Institute for the Study of Social Change, University of California, Berkeley, 1980–81, which helped me develop some of the thoughts expressed in this section.

17. *See*, for example, Dobash and Dobash, *Violence Against Wives*; Lenore Walker, *The Battered Woman* (New York: Harper & Row, 1979); and Mildred Daley Pagelow, "Battered Women: A New Perspective" (Paper presented to the International Sociological Association, Dublin, August 1977).

18. *See*, for example, Richard Gelles, *The Violent Home* (Beverly Hills: Sage Publications, 1972); Straus, Gelles, and Steinmetz, *Behind Closed Doors*; and Lee Bowker and Kristine MacCallum, "Women Who Have Beaten Wife-Beating: A New Perspective on Victims as Victors" (Paper presented to the American Society of Criminology, San Francisco, November 1980).

19. *See* Gresham Sykes and David Matza, "Techniques of Neutralization: A Theory of Delinquency," *American Sociological Review* 22 (December 1957): 664–70.

20. William Ryan, *Blaming the Victim* (New York: Random House, 1971). For examples, *see* Sue Eisenberg and Patricia Micklow, "The Assaulted Wife: 'Catch 22' Revisited," *Women's Rights Law Reporter* 3 (March 1977):138–61.

21. *See*, for example, Natalie Shainess, "Psychological Aspects of Wife-battering," in *Battered Women: A Psychological Study of Domestic Violence*, ed. Maria Roy (New York: Van Nostrand Reinhold, 1977), pp. 111–19; and John Gayford, "Battered Wives," *Medicine, Science and the Law* 15 (1975):4.

22. R. Emerson Dobash, "The Negotiation of Daily Life and the 'Provocation' of Violence: A Patriarchial Concept in Support of the Wife Beater" (Paper presented to the Ninth World Congress of Sociology, Uppsala, Sweden, August 1978).

23. *See*, for example, Straus, Gelles, and Steinmetz, *Behind Closed Doors*.

24. *See* Lillian Breslow Rubin, *Worlds of Pain: Life in the Working-Class Family* (New York: Basic Books, 1976); and Jessie Bernard, *The Future of Marriage* (New York: Bantam Books, 1972).

25. Cf. Talcott Parsons and Robert Bales, *Family, Socialization and Interaction Process* (New York: Free Press, 1955).

26. *See*, for example, Lucy Komisar, "Violence and the Masculine Mystique," in *The Forty Nine Percent Majority*, ed. Deborah David and Robert Brannon (Menlo Park: Addison-Wesley, 1976).

27. For sharing their insights with me, I wish to thank Dr. Anne Ganley, American Lake Veterans Administration Hospital, Tacoma; Dr. Vicki Boyd, Group Health Center, Seattle; Dr. Karil Klingbeil, Harborview Medical Center, Seattle; and Francis Purdy, Women's Support Shelter, Tacoma. The research findings of these clinicians are an excellent source of data on men who batter women.

28. Pagelow, "Battered Women."

29. Walker, *The Battered Woman*, pp. 92–93.

30. *See*, for example, Dobash and Dobash, *Violence Against Wives*.

31. Klein, "Can This Marriage Be Saved?" p. 28.

The Dark Side of Marriage

32. Dorie Klein, "Violence Against Women: Some Considerations on its Causes and on its Elimination," *Crime and Delinquency* 27, 1 (January 1981):65.

33. *See* Margaret May, "Violence in the Family: An Historical Perspective," in *Violence and the Family*, ed. J. P. Martin (Chichester: Wiley & Sons, 1978), pp. 135–67; and Erin Pizzey, *Scream Quietly or the Neighbors Will Hear* (Harmondsworth: Penguin, 1974).

34. *See* Susan Griffin, "Rape: The All-American Crime," *Ramparts* 10, 3 (1971):26–35; and publications of the Women's History Research Center, Berkeley, California.

35. *See* Martin, *Battered Wives*; and Betsy Warrior, *Working on Wife Abuse* (Cambridge, MA: Transition House [46 Pleasant St.], 1976).

36. I would like to express my appreciation to Dr. Patricia Morgan, Social Research Group, University of California, Berkeley, for sharing her knowledge in this area with me. Readers interested in state response to battering with special reference to the alcohol paradigm are referred to her work.

37. Morton Bard, *Training Police as Specialists in Family Crisis Intervention*, U.S. Department of Justice (Washington, DC: U.S. Government Printing Office, 1970). For a critique, *see* Fields, "Wife Beating."

38. On New York, *see* Fields, "Wife Beating." For California, *see The Legal Rights of Battered Women in California* (San Francisco: Voluntary Legal Services, State Bar Association, 1980).

39. Dobash and Dobash, *Violence Against Wives*.

40. Patricia Morgan, "From Battered Wife to Program Client: The Impact of the State in the Shaping of a Social Problem," *Kapitalistate* 9 (1981):17–40.

41. The work of Straus and his colleagues is the foremost example.

PART II

Women as Offenders

5

Exploring Female Crime Patterns

Problems and Prospects

NICOLETTE PARISI

Already it is an old refrain. Article after article begins with the trite comment that traditional research in criminology and criminal justice has ignored the female offender.[1] In the last decade, however, researchers have begun to compensate for this deficiency. The recent proliferation of books, articles, newsletters, courses, grants, commissions, and panels at conferences on women indicates the efforts being made to overcome the large gap in the literature. When we, predominantly female, researchers devote considerable attention to the female offender, we suggest that she is an "important criminal," and, at the same time, an "important person."[2] Regardless of the postulated impact of the women's movement on female crime,[3] it is clear that the interest in women's rights has influenced researchers in criminology and criminal justice to pay closer attention to the female offender.

A large part of this recent interest in the female offender has focused on female crime. A number of issues have surfaced along the following dimensions: the level of female crime; types of such crimes; changes in female crime patterns; characteristics of female criminal behavior (for example, weapon use, number and sex of partners in crime, sex of victim); victim and criminal justice personnel reactions to female crime; and interpretations of the figures on the relationship(s) between sex and crime. This chapter will examine these aspects of female crime[4] through a variety of data sources, with particular attention directed toward gaps in our knowledge of female crime and themes across the diverse research studies.

In order to investigate these questions concerning female crime (and, of course, crime in general), two types of data are used: official and unofficial statistics. A general critique of official and unofficial data bases is beyond the scope of this chapter. However, a brief review of these sources of data is necessary to highlight special problems posed in regard to using them to study *female* crime.

Official statistics are compiled by law enforcement and/or other criminal justice agencies. Official figures are based on the incident and/or the offender coming to the attention of the system. Data bases may be either *local* (for example, police department files, the Prosecutor Information System) or *national* (for example, *Uniform Crime Reports*, National Prisoner Statistics). Official data bases are assumed to reflect to some degree the amount and type of crimes committed. The filtering process has been traditionally seen as a serious problem for the study of female crime. Pollak's statements in 1950 regarding the "chivalry" of the system and similar comments over the last thirty years have caused researchers' concern that official statistics underestimate female crime to a larger extent than male crime.[5] Another serious deficiency is that the national official data systems lack specificity in their crime categories. Although this hampers any study of crime, it is particularly problematic for the study of female crime because assumptions about the character of female crime cannot be examined, but only surmised. For example, does an increase in female arrests for larceny indicate that females are being arrested for more cargo heists or more shoplifting?[6] Despite the obvious problems, official data have been until recently almost the sole source of information on female crime.

Unofficial statistics, the second type of data source, present information that is not hampered by bias in the screening decisions of law enforcement personnel. Such statistics include self-report stud-ies,[7] victimization surveys, attitudinal studies, and case histories/anecdotal accounts of offenders. These sources of data may be either national or specific to a particular group. The victimization surveys are national data bases using broad categories of criminal behavior. This deficiency is partially offset by detailed information on such specific incident characteristics as weapon use. However, another, more serious limitation exists: the definition of larceny excludes shoplifting, thus precluding comparative analysis of major official data (*Uniform Crime Reports*) and unofficial data (victimization surveys) in this crime category. Given the diverse speculation about female property crime in the last decade, this is a major difficulty. However, the victimization surveys are indeed useful in that they provide baseline information on the involvement of females in other categories of face-to-face crime across the United States. The other unofficial sources cannot provide estimates of the level of female crime, but can be used to supplement information on the nature of female participation and to explore explanations for female criminal behavior.

Two additional problems must be noted. First, both official and unofficial data sources are limited in terms of analyzing trends. This is particularly true of victimization surveys, which have a shorter history[8] than the *Uniform Crime Reports*.[9] The second basic problem involves the low base (the small number of crimes) for the incidence of female criminal behavior and calculation of rates of change.[10] Figures that appear to demonstrate large changes in the number and/or proportion of female arrests should be cautiously ex-amined. Often these "increases" in female crime are artifacts of low bases. Popular reports alleging great increases in the amount of female crime often make this mistake.[11]

THIS CHAPTER WILL review the patterns of adult female crime. The discussion begins with an investigation of data on the level of female crime, including type, range, seriousness of crime, and changes in female crime over time. Next, the discussion proceeds to the nature of female crime. In that section, female crime incident characteristics (such as role in the offense, weapon use, and sex of victim) are explored. Third, the reactions to female offenders by vic-tims and law enforcement personnel are briefly examined. Fourth, explanations of the relationship between female sex roles and

Nicolette Parisi

criminal behavior are reviewed and the evidence regarding these theories is highlighted. The chapter concludes with a discussion of the prospects for future research on female crime.

THE LEVEL OF FEMALE CRIME

It is possible to conceptualize and examine the volume of female crime in a number of ways. For example, the focus can be on the *amount* of female crime relative to that of males and/or to that of females in an earlier period. Second, the level of female crime can be examined in terms of the *versatility* (range) of female crime in comparison with that of males or that of females of an earlier period. Third, the *frequency* of commission can be explored through calculating and comparing ranks, intra- and inter-sex, between male and female crime rates. Analysis of the *seriousness* or *types* of crimes committed by males versus females or by females today versus females of an earlier period can also address the level of crime. Because accurate measurement of the level of female crime is very complex, the following analysis makes use of a number of these approaches.

To estimate the volume of female crime, it is appropriate to use both figures on arrests from the *Uniform Crime Reports* (UCR) and data on victimizations from the National Crime Surveys (NCS). It has been often observed that females commit fewer crimes than males. Despite Pollak's contention that females only *appear* to commit less crime than males because of the "masked" nature of the offenses,[12] the consensus is that males commit much more crime than females, excluding (of course) prostitution. The arrest data from the UCR[13] consistently support this view and, more recently, NCS data have as well. Hindelang's analysis of NCS data for 1976 confirmed that crime is essentially a male phenomenon across those categories of crime included in the NCS.[14] Comparing UCR and NCS figures, Hindelang found little support for Pollak's view that female criminality, if unmasked, would be comparable to that of males. In fact, the few differences that Hindelang observed in UCR and NCS data refuted Pollak's opinion that police hesitate to arrest females.[15] Thus, the volume of female crime is smaller than that of male crime regardless of whether we use official or unofficial statistics.

In terms of frequency of commission, males and females have

Exploring Female Crime Patterns

similar patterns across various crimes. In general, both males and females tend to commit property crimes more often than personal crimes. Moreover, despite some shifts in the rates of commission of various public order crimes (such as drunkenness, gambling, and narcotics), over time these crimes still compose a substantial portion of arrests of both males and females. Finally, both intra-sex and inter-sex rankings show marked consistency over time. Steffensmeier, for example, reports a rank order correlation between male and female arrests of .82 in 1965 and .84 in 1977.[16]

A ranking of offenses by sex provides an overview of the seriousness of male versus female criminal behavior. Calculating various measures of change[17] can also reveal whether the level of seriousness of female crime (in general or crime-specific) is high, low, or stable. In her classic work, *Sisters in Crime*, Adler postulated that violent personal crimes were increasing among females and the gap between male and female arrests for major crimes was decreasing.[18] On the other hand, Simon argued that female violent crime may be decreasing.[19] Neither view is confirmed by UCR and NCS data, which show only slight changes in the levels of violent or serious female crime.[20]

However, UCR data clearly point to increases in such female *property* crimes as larceny, fraud, forgery, and embezzlement. And according to Simon, these gains also indicate an increase in seriousness of female property crime because, increasingly, they are white-collar crimes.[21] Steffensmeier, however, challenged this supposition and defined them as "petty property offenses,"[22] although nothing in the arrest statistics *per se* provided evidence to support his position.[23]

Although the proportion of female arrests for larceny is greater today than in the past, and although the percent change is higher for females than males, females may not catch up with males in this crime category. In fact, Steffensmeier demonstrated that the large increases in female property arrests may have peaked.[24] Since 1975, the gains appear to have stabilized. Steffensmeier has posited that the increases in arrests of females for property crime may partly be a consequence of better methods of detection and changes in criminal justice policies.

Giordano, Kerbel, and Dudley reported increases in female larceny arrests in Toledo between 1970 and 1976 for both shoplifting and other types of larceny. Additionally, their data indicate that increases in female arrests for such other property offenses as forgery/counterfeiting and embezzlement/fraud should not be considered as support for Simon's view because such acts when committed by females are not occupation-related.

Public order crimes include gambling, prostitution, drug offenses, vagrancy, and drunkenness. Both male and female rates of arrest for drunkenness have declined, but not necessarily because the incidence has decreased; instead, decriminalization and shifting law enforcement priorities may be responsible.[25] Prostitution appears to be declining in relation to all female arrests.[26] Further, arrests of males for prostitution appear to be increasing.[27] Dramatic increases of drug arrests are evident for both males and females, both in frequency and in relationship to all other arrests.

The versatility or range of crimes committed by females is broad. In fact, the official and unofficial sources clearly demonstrate that females are involved in all crimes that males are (although, of course, not to the same extent). However, criminal versatility may also be defined as the range of crimes of an *individual subject*.[28] Does the career female criminal exhibit as much versatility as her male counterpart? And further, has the female criminal become more versatile over time? Although evidence on multiple crimes and career patterns of females is generally unavailable,[29] there is one study that indicates trends. Giordano, Kerbel, and Dudley studied arrest blotters in Toledo from 1890 to 1976. Among the data they collected was information on multiple charges. The rate of multiple charges for females per 100,000 population was 3.2 in 1890 and 422.1 in 1976. The comparable figures for males were 559.0 and 1855.4.[30] Additionally, the types of multiple charges varied over time. In recent years, females were combining a number of serious charges, not always including prostitution. Exploring these patterns systematically over time would provide a more accurate picture of many aspects of female crime levels.

INCIDENT CHARACTERISTICS

Beyond the overall and crime-specific quantitative differences between male and female criminal behavior, there is also assumed to be a qualitative difference in each sex's pattern of criminal behavior. It is often claimed that criminal behavior of females is distinguishable from that of males even within the same category (for example, larceny or murder).[31] The characteristics of female criminality have often been presumed to reflect the nature and role of females in

Exploring Female Crime Patterns

society. In this section, three issues will be explored: role in the offense; weapon use; and sex of victim. These issues were selected because: (1) theories of female crime frequently hinge on them; and (2) evidence on these factors is available from a number of sources.[32] Therefore, inspecting the findings from several data sources may allow us to discern if there is any consistency in the information on these aspects of female crime.

Role in the Offense

Opinions on the role of the female in crime are sometimes contradictory. One perspective is that a female offender does not act alone in crime, but needs a male partner to carry out *her scheme*.[33] Another view is that the female does not act alone or as a leader, but generally serves as an *assistant* to a more proficient male.[34] A number of studies have collected information on the number and sex of partners in crime.

Ward, Jackson, and Ward found that female inmates in California institutions in 1963 and 1968 tended to commit robbery and burglary with a partner, usually a friend or acquaintance. In contrast, inmates convicted of homicide and assault typically acted alone; if they had partners, they were slightly more likely to accompany a husband or lover than a friend or acquaintance.[35] Victimization data from NCS showed that female offenders tended to act alone or with other females, contrary to the popular accomplice theory.[36] Similarly, victimization data from twenty-six large cities indicated that both white and black female offenders tended to commit their offenses alone (79 percent and 61 percent, respectively), rather than with either male or female partners. Also noteworthy, female offenders were substantially more likely to be alone than male offenders.[37] Prosecutor Information System (PROMIS) data from Washington, DC, for 1974 and 1975 also repudiated the accomplice myth. Overall, females acted alone in over 70 percent of the arrests, a figure nearly identical to that for males. Moreover, except when committing robberies with others, females tended to have female accomplices as frequently as male. In contrast, across all crime categories, males working with partners overwhelmingly chose males.[38]

From these studies it is impossible to discern the particular relationship of the female criminal with her partner. Whether females were subservient when acting in concert with males cannot be determined. However, recent evidence (excluding the Ward,

Nicolette Parisi

Jackson, and Ward study) consistently demonstrates that the traditional image of females as accomplices of males is erroneous. It is also clear that if a group is involved, females tend to work with other females.[39]

Weapon Use

A female's choice of weapon (if any) is also supposed to reflect something about the nature and role of females in society. Both the location of the crime and strength of her victim are said to be important factors in the decision to use a weapon, and the type used. It is often claimed that females choose victims who are not prepared to respond (for example, drunk or asleep).[40] Additionally, the female criminal often selects a weapon related to her sex role (for example, a kitchen knife, ice pick, or other household implement).

The Ward, Jackson, and Ward California prison data separately examined the female's use of physical strength and choice of weapon (if any). Their 1963 and 1968 data showed that *one-fourth* of the female robbery inmates had used physical force and about *one-third* had used a gun. Interestingly, over half did not have any weapon at all during the robbery. They found that physical force was much more common in assaults and homicides (compared with robberies), and females convicted of these crimes generally used a weapon, especially a knife or household implement. This finding appears to confirm the prevalent notion that females use weapons related to their roles.[41] It should be noted, however, that this study did not contrast the findings with a similar group of male inmates.

The PROMIS data set for 1974 and 1975 included information on weapon use by males and females. About four-fifths of the males and females arrested for violent crimes used weapons. In robberies, females were less likely than males to use a weapon, but in simple assaults the reverse was true. Females tended to select weapons other than firearms (such as knives and ice picks) in violent crimes.[42] The large city victimization surveys from 1972 to 1975 also showed that females were less likely than males to use a weapon. These data indicated that guns were the least likely weapons of female offenders.[43] The classic impression regarding the use of weapons by female criminals appears to be substantiated in both data sets.

Wolfgang's study of homicide in Philadelphia between 1948 and 1952 (research based on police records) revealed that females

Exploring Female Crime Patterns

were twice as likely as males to stab their victims. Furthermore, males were substantially more likely than females to shoot or beat their victims.[44] These findings also support the traditional view of weapon use by females.

The actual level of weapon use cannot be estimated and these data should not be compared because of the many differences in the research. In the PROMIS and NCS data bases, the differences between males and females were not large (although the latter data set found a greater degree of weapon use than the former). Additionally the data do not reveal whether females use weapons to compensate for lack of equality in physical strength. However, the studies repeatedly confirm that females do choose less lethal weapons than males, and that location, among other factors, is related to the choice of the female's weapon.

Sex of Victim and Offender

The race component of the victim–offender relationship has been the subject of much research. In contrast, relatively little research has been directed toward the sex pairings of the victim and offender. Information about the sex of the victim can provide further evidence on the nature of female crime. For example, a common impression is that a female offender commits a violent crime usually against a male victim very familiar to her. Further, in order to be successful against a victim stronger than herself, the female may have to use a weapon or select a location and/or circumstances in which the victim is at a disadvantage. Unfortunately, there is not enough firm data to respond well to such theories. However, a number of studies and data bases include information on sex of victim–offender, which can provide the groundwork for further research in this area.[45]

To obtain data from the 1973–1976 NCS victimization surveys on victim–offender sex pairings, I recalculated Hindelang's table on reporting practices.[46] Male offenders typically had male victims, and females similarly chose members of their own sex. Intra-sex victimizations were 72 percent and 85 percent for males and females respectively, for the crimes of rape, robbery, aggravated assault, simple assault, and personal larceny. Table 5-1 shows that the proportion of males victimized by females increased from 9 to 29 percent as the seriousness of offense increased. The data do not support the stereotypical view that violent female offenders attack male in-

TABLE 5-1
Estimated Percentages of Crime Incidents,
by Sex of Offender and Victim,
United States, 1973–1976

	Offense Seriousness				Total
	1 (low)	2	3	4 (high)	
Male Offender:					
Male victim	70	68	78	75	72
Female victim	30	32	22	25	28
Female Offender:					
Female victim	91	84	78	71	85
Male victim	9	16	22	29	15

This source includes the following personal crime incidents: rape, robbery, aggravated assault, simple assault, and personal larceny.
Source: Table constructed from Michael J. Hindelang, "Sex Differences in Criminal Activity," *Social Problems* 27 (1979):151.

timates. In fact, in offenses of the highest level of seriousness, seven out of ten females had female victims. Explanations or assumptions about the character of female crime need to incorporate this finding and investigate further. However, the finding that females primarily victimize other females is consistent with the supposition that females choose victims who are not physically stronger than themselves.

To examine the inter-sex assumptions attached to violent female crime, UCR figures on arrests for murder and nonnegligent manslaughter were analyzed (Table 5-2). The UCR data for 1979 showed that 85 percent of the single (sole perpetrator) females murdered males, while only 26 percent of the single males had female victims.[47] In his 1948–1952 study of homicide in Philadelphia, Wolfgang similarly found that approximately 84 percent of the female offenders had male victims, while only about 25 percent of the male offenders had female victims.[48] Thus, homicide evidence establishes that females do tend to choose male victims, as purported by the theories.

Incident Characteristics Summary

Many other incident characteristics should be examined to obtain a

TABLE 5-2
Sex of Victim/Offender in
Murders and Nonnegligent Manslaughters,
United States, 1979

Sex of Victim	Single Offender		Multiple Offender	
	Male	Female	Male	Female
Male	74%	85%	88%	80%
Female	26%	15%	12%	20%
Total	100%	100%	100%	100%
	(10,387)	(2,021)	(3,537)	(371)

Source: U.S. Department of Justice, *Uniform Crime Reports 1979* (Washington, DC: U.S. Government Printing Office, 1980), pp. 8, 9.

more complete picture of the nature of female crime. These three were chosen because a number of data sources have addressed them and because they are critical to further, more detailed research work in this area of female criminality. None of the sources truly provides trend data (except, perhaps, the UCR homicide data) or any real measure of absolute levels. They do, however, provide information on relative levels, indicating that: (1) the accomplice theory is dubious; (2) sex roles (that is, the likelihood of a female being in a kitchen, and the like) affect the selection of a weapon; and (3) except for homicide, females do not choose male victims (which may imply that females tend to victimize subjects who are physically weaker than they).

REACTIONS TO FEMALE OFFENDERS

The victim's decision to report an incident to the police and the law enforcement officer's decision to take official action are often purported to be affected by the sex of the offender, in addition to other factors.[49] If all other factors are equal, official reactions are presumed to be less likely in cases involving female offenders. This, the so-called chivalry theory, however, has not been the subject of much research at the victim or police level, and existing evidence indicates that responses to female crime are more complex than the theory suggests.[50] This section reviews a number of studies that focus on the responses to female offenders by victims and police officers.

Nicolette Parisi

Hindelang analyzed the 1973 to 1976 NCS victimization data regarding variations based on sex of victim and offender in the decision to report an incident to the police.[51] Unexpectedly, Hindelang found that male victims were *more* likely to report personal crimes involving female offenders than male offenders. This pattern held across the four levels of seriousness of offense. On the contrary, female victims were *less* likely to report crimes involving female offenders than those involving male offenders. Furthermore, male victims were *more* likely than female victims to report female offenders. As Hindelang noted, if anyone is "chivalrous," it is the female victim.

A simulated study of shoplifting investigated reporting practices by varying the sex of the offender and other factors.[52] Sex of the shoplifter appeared to be a less important factor than physical appearance of the shoplifter in the decision to report the incident.

In terms of drug offenses, two studies provide information on police response to female offenders. Johnson, Petersen, and Wells combined self-report data and police files in their study of marijuana arrests.[53] Information on the circumstances of detection and arrest was analyzed to assess the probability of arrest by sex. Males were found to have a generally higher probability of arrest than females. However, the authors interpreted this finding not as evidence of "chivalry," but as a result of the "differential visibility" of females versus males. The males seemed more vulnerable to arrest because they had used marijuana in public places and had been more visible than females. Another study of police reactions to drug offenders found demeanor to be a determinant in the decision to arrest a female. DeFleur found that Chicago narcotics officers tended not to arrest females "if they behaved in expected stereotypic ways."[54]

In summary, the NCS victimization data and other evidence generally indicate that more serious crimes are likely to be reported to the police. Because female offenders tend to cluster in petty offenses, it may have initially appeared that females are less likely to be reported to the police. However, the chivalry theory was not confirmed at the victim's decision point when seriousness of crime was controlled. Police reactions to female offenders appear to be dependent on the place of occurrence and the offender's demeanor, especially in drug offenses. It should be obvious that more research must be done to investigate the dynamics of victim and police officer responses to female offenders.

Exploring Female Crime Patterns

EXPLANATIONS OF FEMALE CRIME

Over the years, a number of theories have been advanced to explain the extent and type of female participation in crime. According to Klein, the most influential theories up to early 1970s viewed

> . . . *criminality as the result of* individual *characteristics that are only peripherally affected by economic, social, and political forces. These characteristics are of a* physiological *or* psychological *nature and are uniformly based on implicit and explicit assumptions about the inherent nature of women.*[55]

Then in the mid-1970s the women's movement emerged as a favorite explanation for female crime. (Weis and others have observed, however, that the women's movement theory advanced by Adler is merely an update of earlier theories.)[56] At the same time, Simon proposed the *opportunity theory*, arguing that as more females enter the work force, their opportunity to commit crime expands. Furthermore, Simon postulated that these increased opportunities will result in females committing more serious property crimes (such as white-collar offenses) and less violent crimes.[57] The relationships of the women's movement and increased female participation in the labor force to female crime have been investigated by several authors.[58] This section reviews several studies that test and/or evaluate these recent explanations of the extent and scope of female crime.

Steffensmeier examined UCR arrest rates from 1965 to 1977 to assess the impact of the women's movement. He observed little difference between the pre-1970 and post-1970 rates and thus concluded that "the movement appears to have had a greater impact on changing the image of the female offender than the level or types of criminal activities that she is likely to commit."[59]

An attitude and self-report instrument administered to juvenile females by Giordano and Cernkovich attempted to investigate the possible link between delinquency and the women's movement. They concluded that liberated views were not related to crime.[60] Leventhal inquired about the impact of the women's movement at the adult level, using twenty-five incarcerated females in two New Jersey jails and twenty-five female students from a New

Nicolette Parisi

Jersey state college. An attempt was made to match the students with the confined population on personal and demographic characteristics. The female criminals had traditional perspectives on the role of females in society, while the female noncriminals were very "liberated."[61]

The opportunity theory is difficult to test directly. On the basis of crime-specific studies, Steffensmeier and Weis separately hypothesized that increases in female property crime result from traditional female sex roles and increased victim and law enforcement attention in such areas as shoplifting. They both concluded that these increases "reflect traditional sex-determined roles in legal and illegal marketplaces, from shopper to shoplifter, from passing good checks to passing bad ones, from being a welfare mother to being accused of welfare fraud, and so on."[62] However, there is little evidence directly supporting this perspective.

The study of Toledo arrest blotters over the last eighty years or so sheds some light on the opportunity theory. Giordano, Kerbel, and Dudley found that women's increased entry into the labor force is indeed related to female crime. In their view entry of older, married females into the work force put pressure on certain categories of females (young, single, minority), who then slid to an "even more unfavorable position in the labor market," and perhaps turned to property crime.[63] As described earlier in this chapter, their data on the content of female property crime appeared to support Weis and Steffensmeier, rather than Simon, by demonstrating that female property crime is generally an extension of the traditional female sex role.

To examine relationships between employment opportunities and female crime, Bartel analyzed data on arrests, commitments to state prisons, and time served, as well as census figures on labor participation, marital status, children, and so on.[64] For the thirty-three states in her data set, both percent of females in the labor force and percent married were positively related to property crime. Although this finding appears to support the opportunity theory, Bartel's regression analysis showed that labor force participation of only *single* females had a positive correlation with property crime; labor force participation of *married* females had no effect. Furthermore, an increasingly negative relationship between the proportion of married females in the labor force and property crime was observed as several variables on the number and age of children were entered into the equation. Therefore Bartel rejected the opportunity theory as an explanation for the increases in female arrests for property crime:

> *[W]hat the female criminal participation rate and the female labor force participation rate have in common is that they are negatively and significantly related to the women's . . . time at home, as measured by the average number of preschool children per family.*[65]

Thus, Bartel concluded that the increases in female crime were not directly related to female participation in the labor force, but rather to the decrease in the amount of time spent at home because of a decline in the average number of preschool children per family.

In summary, the explanations of female crime are only beginning to be tested. Those who have tried to examine the link between the women's movement and female crime have found little or no evidence of a relationship. Some studies also cast doubt on the opportunity theory. Before firmer interpretations of the data on female crime can be formed, more studies need to be conducted. Nevertheless, the direction of the studies discussed here demonstrates that we are turning away from psychological to socio-structural explanations. The study of sex roles will continue to play a key role in understanding female crime.

PROSPECTS FOR FUTURE RESEARCH

This review of the current research on female crime was not exhaustive. However, the findings from the *major* sources of data were examined to discover themes. In the process, gaps in our knowledge and deficiencies in the data were noted. This conclusion addresses avenues for further research, routes that must be explored in order to expand our knowledge of female crime.

It is noteworthy that in the last decade we have been able to use other sources in addition to the UCR arrest data to explore female crime. Both the UCR data and NCS victimization surveys can be used to establish *national baseline* data on the level of female crime. Once a baseline has been determined, *trend analysis* can be initiated, leading to *prediction* of future female criminal behavior. We are still at the elementary stage of developing these baselines. Fortunately, the NCS victimization data and UCR arrest data reveal

Nicolette Parisi

similar patterns of crime. Thus, depending on our needs, trend data may develop from either source (at least for incidents of face-to-face crime).

The earlier discussion of characteristics of female crime was tentative due to the lack of existing baseline data. This lack prevents both trend analysis and statistical comparison of the nature of female crime versus male crime or female crime in an earlier period. Assumptions are widespread concerning partners (number, sex, and relationship), weapons, sex of victims, provocation, and relationship and interaction between offender and victim; however, the sparse existing data allowed me to present only limited and isolated themes on three of these areas from a range of sources. More information on incident characteristics might come from extensive analysis of police files and interviews (case histories). Eventually, baseline information should be developed from more comparable data bases. Today, generalizations on the character of female crime are dubious and will remain so until trends can be investigated. However, such research will be impossible until a large amount of foundation work is accomplished.

Finally, theories explaining female criminal behavior have not been adequately explored. Although factors associated with female crime are tied to phenomena that are hard to isolate and measure, more effort should be directed to testing existing theories and developing new ones. The critiques of Adler and Simon are the beginning. Through surveys of females—of their attitudes and their patterns of criminality—we may discover the relationships (if any) that "liberated" ideas, economic pressures, and occupational opportunities have with female crime. Efforts for both prevention and treatment could be enhanced by this information. Special research attention should also be given to criminal justice agencies, to measure any changes in subtle or overt policies concerning female offenders.

NOTES

1. *See*, for example, Freda Adler and Rita J. Simon, *The Criminology of Deviant Women* (Boston: Houghton Mifflin, 1979), p. 2.

2. Freda Adler, *Sisters in Crime* (New York: McGraw-Hill, 1975), p. 162.

3. *See*, for example, Rita J. Simon, *Women and Crime* (Lexington, MA: D. C. Heath, 1975).

4. The focus of this essay is *adult* female crime.

5. Otto Pollak, *The Criminality of Women* (Philadelphia: University of Pennsylvania Press, 1950).

Exploring Female Crime Patterns

6. *See* Darrell J. Steffensmeier, "Sex Differences in Patterns of Adult Crime, 1965-77," *Social Forces* 58 (1980):344-357; and Darrell J. Steffensmeier, "Crime and the Contemporary Woman: An Analysis of Changing Levels of Property Crime, 1960-75," *Social Forces* 57 (1978):566-584.

7. Self-report studies are generally unavailable for adults and are usually limited to "a single time period, to less serious offenses and typically have no official data against which to compare the results." Michael J. Hindelang, "Sex Differences in Criminal Activity," *Social Problems* 27 (1979):144, n. 4.

8. Data from the national victimization surveys are available from only 1972 on. *See* Hindelang, "Sex Differences," pp. 147-150.

9. The FBI has been collecting information on arrests for decades. However, the earlier the time period, the more questionable the reporting practices and the less representative the data. Furthermore, most of the studies of female crime based on UCR data do not cover large periods of time. *See* comment by Peggy C. Giordano, Sandra Kerbel, and Sandra Dudley, "The Economics of Female Criminality: An Analysis of Police Blotters, 1890-1975," in *Women and Crime in America*, ed. Lee H. Bowker (New York: Macmillan, 1981), p. 66.

10. Darrell J. Steffensmeier, "Patterns of Female Property Crime, 1960-1978: A Postscript," in *Women and Crime in America*, p. 64.

11. *See*, for example, "Now the Violent Women," *Newsweek* 866 (6 October 1975):29; and "Crimes by Women Are on the Rise All Over the World," *U.S. News and World Report* 79 (22 December 1975):51.

12. Pollak, *The Criminality of Women. See* Dorie Klein, "The Etiology of Female Crime: A Review of the Literature," *Issues in Criminology* 8 (1973):21-23.

13. Most reports on the level of female crime rely on arrest data from the UCR.

14. Hindelang, "Sex Differences."

15. The differences were small, however.

16. Steffensmeier, "Sex Differences." *See also* Simon, *Women and Crime;* Dorie Klein and June Kress, "Any Woman's Blues: A Critical Overview of Women, Crime, and the Criminal Justice System," *Crime and Social Justice* 5 (1976):39; and Giordano, Kerbel, and Dudley, "Female Criminality," pp. 76-78.

17. Percent change may be calculated on the (1) base of the earlier year; (2) base of the total number of arrests; (3) base of the total number of arrests for each sex; (4) base of rates for the respective population groups; or (5) total percent change for both males and females. Caution should be used when interpreting changes, because a low base will affect the percent change dramatically if only a few more incidents are recorded.

18. Adler, *Sisters in Crime*, pp. 2, 3, 14.

19. Simon, *Women and Crime*, pp. 4, 14.

20. Steffensmeier, "Sex Differences"; Hindelang, "Sex Differences."

21. Simon, *Women and Crime*, p. 19.

22. Steffensmeier, "Sex Differences."

23. *See* Giordano, Kerbel, and Dudley, "Female Criminality," p. 67.

24. Steffensmeier, "A Postscript," p. 64.

25. Steffensmeier, "Sex Differences."

26. Steffensmeier, "Sex Differences," Table 1; Giordano, Kerbel, and Dudley, "Female Criminality," p. 77.

27. U.S. Department of Justice, Federal Bureau of Investigation, *Uniform Crime Reports 1979* (Washington, DC: U.S. Government Printing Office, 1980), p. 191 shows large increases (from a small base) in male prostitution arrests. Perhaps males are closing the gap in this category.

Nicolette Parisi

28. For a discussion of versatility in regard to juveniles, *see* Michael Hindelang, "Age, Sex, and the Versatility of Delinquent Involvements," *Social Problems* 18 (1971):527–528; and Joseph G. Weis, "Liberation and Crime: The Invention of the New-Female Criminal," *Crime and Social Justice* 6 (1976):17–27.

29. The larger the scope of any information system, the more likely it is for only the most serious charge to be recorded. Anecdotal and case histories have provided some information on career patterns of female criminals. However, whether the subject is typical or not cannot always be evaluated.

30. Giordano, Kerbel, and Dudley, "Female Criminality," pp. 76–79.

31. For a summary of a number of these classic perspectives of female crime, *see* Vernetta Young, "The Female Offender: Myth vs. Reality" (Unpublished paper, Criminal Justice Research Center, Albany, NY). *See also* Walter Reckless, *The Crime Problem* (New York: Appleton-Century-Crofts, 1950), p. 61.

32. Generalizations from the studies are not always appropriate. Data bases are often widely different (in terms of population, definitions, procedures, time periods, and so on), and extracting themes from their findings must be carefully done.

33. Pollak, *The Criminality of Women*, referred sometimes to the female as an "instigator." Simon makes a similar point in Adler and Simon, *The Criminology of Deviant Women*, p. 6.

34. Rita J. Simon and Navin Sharma, *The Female Defendant in Washington, D.C.: 1974 and 1975* (Washington, DC: INSLAW, 1979), p. 11.

35. David Ward, Maurice Jackson, and Renee Ward, "Crimes of Violence by Women," in *Crimes of Violence*, ed. Donald Mulvihill and Melvin Tuman (Washington, DC: U.S. Government Printing Office, 1969).

36. *See* Young, "The Female Offender."

37. Vernetta Young, "Women, Race and Crime" (Paper presented at the Academy of Criminal Justice Sciences, New Orleans, Louisiana, 1978). The proportion of white male offenders who acted alone was 65 percent, while the proportion of black male offenders in the same category was 49 percent (p. 16).

38. Simon and Sharma, *The Female Defendant*.

39. Several reasons might be used to explain the solitary female perpetrator. In "Sex Differences," Steffensmeier suggested that males are sometimes reluctant to work with females.

40. *See*, for example, Pollak, *The Criminality of Women*; and Ward, Jackson, and Ward, "Crimes of Violence by Women," pp. 871, 906.

41. Ward, Jackson, and Ward, "Crimes of Violence by Women," pp. 870–871.

42. Simon and Sharma, *The Female Defendant*, pp. 11–12, 40.

43. Young, "Women, Race and Crime."

44. Marvin Wolfgang, *Patterns of Criminal Homicide* (Philadelphia: University of Pennsylvania Press, 1958), p. 85.

45. The PROMIS data (Washington, DC) have incomplete information regarding sex of victim and cannot be included in this analysis. Simon and Sharma, *The Female Defendant*, p. 11.

46. Hindelang, "Sex Differences," p. 151.

47. U.S. Department of Justice, *Uniform Crime Reports 1979*, pp. 8, 9.

48. Wolfgang, *Patterns of Criminal Homicide*, p. 223.

49. Pollak, *The Criminality of Women*; Reckless, *The Crime Problem*, p. 61.

50. Meda Chesney-Lind, "Chivalry Reexamined: Women and the Criminal Justice System," in *Women, Crime and the Criminal Justice System*, ed. Lee H. Bowker (Lexington, MA: Lexington Books, 1978), pp. 197–219.

51. Hindelang, "Sex Differences," pp. 151–152.

52. Darrell Steffensmeier and Robert M. Terry, "Deviance and Respectability: An Observational Study of Reactions to Shoplifting," *Social Forces* 51 (1973):417–426.

53. Weldon Johnson, Robert Petersen, and L. Edward Wells, "Arrest Probabilities for Marijuana Users as Indicators of Selective Enforcement," *American Journal of Sociology* 83 (1977):681–699.

54. Lois B. DeFleur, "Biasing Influences on Drug Arrest Records: Implications for Deviance Research," *American Sociological Review* 40 (1975):101.

55. Klein, "The Etiology of Female Crime," p. 4.

56. Weis, "Liberation and Crime."

57. Simon, *Women and Crime*, p. 19.

58. For a general review of the purported link, *see* Susan Datesman and Frank Scarpitti, eds., *Women, Crime, and Justice* (New York: Oxford University Press, 1980), pp. 355–376.

59. Steffensmeier, "Sex Differences."

60. Peggy Giordano and Stephen Cernkovich, "On Complicating the Relationship between Liberation and Delinquency," *Social Problems* 26 (1979):467–481. The questionnaire was administered at three urban high schools and two state institutions for girls.

61. Gloria Leventhal, "Female Criminality: Is 'Women's Lib' to Blame?" *Psychological Reports* 41 (1977):1179–1182.

62. Steffensmeier, "Crime and Contemporary Woman," p. 580; Weis, "Liberation and Crime," p. 19.

63. Giordano, Kerbel, and Dudley, "Female Criminality," pp. 79–82.

64. Ann Bartel, "Women and Crime: An Economic Analysis," *Economic Inquiry* 17 (1979):29–51.

65. Bartel, "Women and Crime," p. 43.

6

Work and the Addicted Prostitute

MARSHA ROSENBAUM

Work is an integral part of an individual's life. Whether the work is highly paid or not paid at all, prestigious or demoralizing, the kind of work we do affects our lives, our survival, and our sense of ourselves. We generally think of work in occupational terms, but it far transcends the barriers of the traditional workplace. Work can include the unpaid artist's labor, the housewife's routine, the student's toil, and even the criminal's "hustle."[1]

This chapter is devoted to a discussion of prostitution among women heroin addicts. Prostitution, as has been noted by many researchers, is a common form of work for the woman addict.[2] In this analysis we first look at the initiation to prostitution and the woman's motivation for entering the occupation. Next, we discuss the work patterns of the heroin-addicted prostitute: the routines, job hazards, and ways in which the woman deals with the risks and dangers inherent in prostitution. We also discuss the handicaps that impair the work patterns of the addicted prostitute. We then look at the world of prostitution itself, which is at times part of and at times separate from the addict world. We examine the status of the woman addict in the prostitute stratification system and the

Marsha Rosenbaum

addict's own perception of her work and her place in the world of prostitution. Finally, we examine the way in which the woman comes to grips with her place in the prostitution world in an attempt to maintain her own sense of integrity and positive identity.

METHODOLOGY

This project was conducted in San Francisco between 1977 and 1980.[3] The total population interviewed consisted of one hundred women addicts. Ninety-five resided in the San Francisco Bay Area and five lived in New York City. Sixty-two were prostitutes. This project could be considered a "street study" because the women were primarily active, uninstitutionalized heroin users. The sample was procured through the posting of notices in areas of high drug use, a city prison, and a variety of drug treatment facilities. We also used the snowball method to locate members of neighborhoods and friendship groups. The sample population of women was split nearly equally between white (43 percent) and black (38 percent). There were also fourteen Latinas, one Asian, one Native American, and three Filipinos. The ages of the women ranged from twenty to fifty-three, with a median of twenty-eight.

All interviews were given completely voluntarily. They were conducted in our own interviewing office and the women's homes, with the exception of seventeen that were done in the city prison. A $20 remuneration was awarded the respondents. The in-depth life history method was used as the primary data collection tool.[4] Demographic statistics were collected in addition to the qualitative data.

The project personnel also spent time talking with addicts in "the field." We visited some of the women in their homes and accompanied our addicted associates on their daily rounds in their communities, including treatment facilities, "scoring" places, and "shooting galleries."[5]

GETTING IN

Financial gain, rather than social, sexual, or other motivations, is the overriding rationale for getting into prostitution. The financial necessity is usually (but not always) brought about by addiction to heroin.[6] We have found that there are three basic avenues through which addicted women get into prostitution: (1) *the independent mode* is taken by those who enter prostitution without reference to the wishes of husband or lover, either through conscious decision or by drift; (2) *the male-induced entree* occurs through encouragement by a boyfriend or spouse who sees the woman's prostitution as an activity through which they can both gain monetarily; and (3) *the covert entree* is taken against the husband or boyfriend's wishes, generally to assert financial independence.

The Independent Mode

Prostitution is often a faster way of making money than many legitimate options open to women addicts, such as domestic, clerical, custodial, and restaurant work.[7] As one women told us:

> *The first time I turned a trick, I wasn't using at the time. The guy I was with knew some girls—some working girls that had books—$100 tricks. That sounded a lot better to me than making $20 a day working in a restaurant. That's how I got into it. I needed the money.*

Most women begin to prostitute because both the financial need and the social opportunity are present. Often a woman's prostitution begins in her own neighborhood with boys who are personally known to her.[8] As another woman said:

> *The first time I got paid for it, I was about thirteen. This guy thought he was going to take me up into the hills and do it in the backseat . . . so we get up there and he's trying his little things and everything and I say, "Gee, I really need some money." So he gave me $20.*

For the addict who got into the heroin world via the hippie trip, prostitution was the natural progression from "free love" to paid sex.[9] As a woman who claimed that she hated prostitution, but needed the money for college, said: "I nearly got sick to my stomach, but I used to do it because I had a goal in mind. I figured, 'Why not? Instead of free fucking, why not get paid for it?' " As a runaway, this woman had lived in a crash pad in Haight Ashbury in

Marsha Rosenbaum

the late 1960s and had subscribed to the hippie ethic of casual sex. She had become involved with heroin after the use of such "counterculture" drugs as marijuana, LSD, amphetamines, and barbiturates. When she became addicted to heroin and was in greater need of money to support her habit, she found that she could use her sexuality for financial gain and turned to prostitution.

Numerous researchers have noted that individuals become involved with crime when they find themselves in close association with other criminals. Such was the case with most prostitutes in the study population. Women who live where many prostitutes work may begin to consider experimenting with it themselves. Often their friends and neighbors are prostitutes. According to one of our informants: "When I was in Boston and I was young, I fell in with a lot of hookers. They were using, but I wasn't yet. They wanted to turn me out . . . and take me around with them. Finally one day I needed $20 or $30, so I did it." Another woman added:

> I was separated from my husband and living in Hunter's Point [a high crime area] on welfare. I had my children with me—my two children. I used to go down the street, down the hill to the store, and a lot of sailors would come out from the Naval Shipyard and they would be whistling and all that bit, and one thing led to another. I took them up on it, accepted their money. That's how it turned out, gradually—not realizing that I [was] putting a label on me. . . .

For the woman addict, the independent entree into prostitution occurs without reference to the wishes of a male intimate, but merely because there is financial need, social opportunity, and close proximity to such activity. This avenue best characterized the women in the population of addicts studied.

The Male-induced Mode

Some women are encouraged to go into prostitution by male acquaintances who stand to gain financially from their earnings. As one woman noted:

> When we were real young and hanging out with these black dudes, we wouldn't do nothing for them. We were

Work and the Addicted Prostitute

virgins. They was already preparing us, getting us to learn how to make money. They'd be telling us for hours, "If you love your old man, you'd be out there making him some money."

Very few women in this study, however, described encounters with pimps who were successful hustlers making good, consistent money. Instead, most of the coaxing was done by small-time "would-be" pimps. There is good reason for this, as will be described in detail later. Many of the addicted women interviewed in this sample were too young and inexperienced to be of interest to a businessman (which is, ultimately, what the successful pimp actually is) or too addicted to be able to put together the dress and demeanor of a career prostitute who might qualify for work in the stable of a successful pimp. Therefore, once addicted, women are of little interest in the larger prostitution scene and instead are occasionally enticed by would-be pimps. One woman told of being coaxed into prostitution by a dishwasher at a restaurant in which she was a short-order cook:

He took me out and we smoked a couple of joints of weed, drinking Hawaiian Punch 'til the late half of the night. He's showing me all the advantages of being a prostitute —nice clothes and nice jewelry. All I have to do is go out and sell a little ass. Well, I said, "Okay." I finally gave in. But I already had my mind made up about that. So, that's the way I started in.

Thus, although occasionally an addict is induced by a man to prostitute, the man is usually a friend, sometimes a lover, but very rarely the kind of pimp who can put her in a situation in which she (and he) can make good money. For the addict/prostitute, male-induced entree is, then, uncommon.

The Covert Entree

While some of the women in the study population had been coaxed into prostitution by male acquaintances and friends who hoped to gain by their work, the women who were seriously involved with men—either husbands or boyfriends—claimed that they had to prostitute secretly because their men did not approve and had vetoed the idea. For these women, prostitution was used to gain money and in-dependence *in spite of* a male intimate's wishes. Typically:

> *I just needed money. When we were dealing, I was turn-ing tricks and my husband didn't know it. I just wanted money—my own pocket money. He wouldn't give me any.*

Another woman described a relationship that, like others in which the man opposed the woman's prostitution, seemed strikingly tradi-tional: the man appeared to have the bulk of the power and sought to control and dominate the woman by limiting her finances.

> *I was turning tricks and he couldn't handle it. He was just like my husband now. We were fighting all the time. He didn't want me turning tricks. But I didn't want to live off him forever. I wanted to be able to try making some of my own money.*

Another woman told us:

> *I still feel guilty about that [prostitution] because it broke him [her old man] up. But, hey, I had no other choice but to do it. I did it when I had my kids. No one turned me out. I needed the money. In fact, I've always hooked alone. In fact, the men that I have had in my life always were dead set against it.*

In general, relationships between addicted men and women fall into two major categories: in some a rather traditional relationship is maintained in spheres of both work and home; in others, a tradi-tional relationship is maintained at home, but not in the world of work.[10] A woman whose relationship to a male addict falls in the second category is given license, often encouraged, to prostitute. Covert prostitution is a result of the more traditional relationship between the woman addict and her male partner (lover or spouse). Men in a totally traditional relationship (at home and at work) try to prevent their women from going into prostitution because they feel that it lessens their own control over the women's sexual favors. Moreover, they do not want to share the societal stigma of prostitution by having a sexual partner who is a prostitute. Women with such spouses try to keep their prostitution a secret in order to preserve their partner's sense of sexual exclusivity in the relationship.

It also often happens that a man who was initially opposed to his woman's prostitution becomes financially needy and begins to condone the activity when he realizes that it might bring money to both of them. However, some women keep their prostitution a secret from their man not because they fear his disapproval, but because they fear he will get too used to the idea, attempt to exploit their hustle more fully, and take their only source of pocket money.

THE THREE MODES of entree into prostitution among women addicts —independent, male-induced, and covert—indicate that above all, this line of work is embarked upon by women who are in need of quick money. Two of the three modes, independent and covert, show us that these women are themselves resourceful, and not the passive, male-dominated creatures too often pictured in the literature. That only a small number of women in the study population had been induced into prostitution by men also indicates that passivity is not characteristic of most addict/prostitutes.

Having described how women addicts get into prostitution, we turn next to a discussion of the nature of their work: routines, hazards on the job, and coping mechanisms.

WORK PATTERNS

In the world of prostitution, the ideal work routine is consistent and patterned. The few women in the study population who considered themselves successful prostitutes talked about their routines, one relating that:

> *I usually go downtown from 4 to 8 P.M. I go down to make my quota—about $150. If I make $100, I'm happy. I won't leave until I make at least $100 and then I'll leave. That's every day. I also have regulars. I just go down and call them. I have somebody coming over tonight.*

The routines considered best are those in which the woman is not working on the street. She either has exclusive, regular customers or works out of a massage parlor. If a woman has regular customers, it is possible for her to earn $100 a day. In these instances the woman and her trick use the telephone to arrange meetings, and the encounter is less threatening for both parties. Many women begin relationships with regulars through work in massage parlors. One woman, who prides herself on having regulars, offered a "recipe" for successful hooking:

> *A hooker has got to be able to talk to people. She's got to be able to make a guy feel comfortable. Comfortable more than anything else. She's got to make him feel relaxed and appreciated. She's got to take him through a fantasy that he's very good sexually, try to build up his ego and things like that. As for looking beautiful or pretty or anything like that, just build up what you do look like. If your thing is hippie, make yourself an interesting looking hippie. Make yourself an interesting looking whatever-it-is-you-are.*

As we can see from this recipe, the successful prostitute is ambitious and professional. She has her wits about her and "keeps her act together." In this way she succeeds at her occupation from her own perspective and from that of her clients. As another woman noted:

> *I've got tricks that give me money and I haven't seen them in six months. Like Christmas, I got $500 just from my tricks, and some of them I haven't seen in six or seven months because I don't turn tricks now. Very, very seldom. I might turn two tricks every six months, but I was good to them when I was working. I didn't let myself go like a lot of girls do. I never stole a nickel from them ever. I was always there when I said I was going to be there, so I can go to them anytime and get $20 or $30 if they have it. It's good to do that.*

This kind of organized and routinized prostitution is difficult for a heroin addict. Her habit creates numerous problems, primarily ongoing chaos in her life. She rarely knows whether she will have enough money to buy drugs, where she will find them, or what the quality will be. If she does succeed in scoring drugs, successful ad-

ministration becomes problematic. Furthermore, the activities connected with heroin use tend to take up a great deal of time. The
woman therefore cannot devote much attention to her occupation—other than just being "out there" sporadically.[11] All the work
that the woman addict does, including prostitution, takes the form
of "odd jobs" rather than occupation or profession.[12] The woman
may burgle today, forge tomorrow, and prostitute next week; the
variables are the availability of the jobs and her skills. If a friend is
planning a burglary and the woman happens to be around, she might
go along and take a cut of the "score." If it is possible to pick up
some checks, the woman might use them temporarily as a forger. In
addition to the opportunity to hustle, the woman needs a few outside skills. She has to be agile and alert, for most hustles entail fast
movement. The possession of more refined skills such as safe-
cracking is truly an asset that enables the addict to select more profitable odd jobs.

Prostitution is readily available to the woman heroin addict,
for the neighborhoods in which she generally locates for their low
rent and easy access to drugs are usually also areas of high prostitution. However, for prostitution, she must maintain at least a
moderately attractive appearance and certainly a keen eye for risk
and danger. Unfortunately, the addicted prostitute is often "sick"—
withdrawing from heroin because she is unable to buy it—and hence
becomes slovenly in her appearance and/or unguarded in her approach to both tricks and police. Therefore, heroin-addicted street-
walkers tend to be unable to succeed as prostitutes. On the subject
of unsuccessful prostitutes, Goode point out:

> They don't have the ambition or the motivation—or the
> stomach—to work day in and day out, full-time, full-tilt,
> at a job that is unappealing to them. When an opportunity
> comes along, they quit. Instead of turning five or ten
> tricks a day, they might turn two or three. Instead of
> walking the streets five, six, or seven days a week, they
> will walk two or three. They use prostitution just to get
> by, to tide them over until something better comes along,
> until they meet a man they like, until they earn a little
> money to coast for a while.[13]

Such women, and most of those in our sample, are unsuccessful
because they fail to retain customers and often spend time in jail or

prison. Yet many women addicts continue as prostitutes because it is one of the few financial options (albeit a meager one) open to them.

A key aspect of the prostitute's work routines (whether she is addicted or not) is *safety*. The prostitute knows the hazards of non-directed streetwalking and therefore values a regular routine, regular customers, and a protected turf. The danger and risks work in two ways—for the prostitute *and* her trick. Since part of the addict's chaotic life is withdrawal, she often goes out on the street in desperation. There is always the temptation, when a woman is withdrawing and generally living with a heroin habit, to steal from a trick. One woman talked about the hazards of such behavior and the overriding importance of abstaining from stealing in order to establish regular clientele:

> *Like in the Tenderloin, it got very hot for awhile 'cause all the girls were ripping tricks off, and when the girls start ripping tricks off, that's when the cops start coming around. I don't rip tricks off because I want them to be regular customers.*

Yet it sometimes happens that a woman gets too desperate and cannot resist the temptation to take a little more money from a john:

> *Business wasn't that good. I didn't like it. I was used to places where men come to you. Business was so bad that occasionally I'd rip somebody off. One time, the john was in the shower. He had given me $50 and I took the other $50 in his pants.*

When individual prostitutes get a reputation for ripping off tricks or even when a neighborhood gets such a "name," women tend to be unable to establish ongoing relationships with johns. They fail to have regulars and to build up the clientele that would help to ensure safety in the dangerous world of street prostitution. This lack of regulars and the dependence on strangers as tricks contribute to the disruption of the woman's work routine, and her life is made even more chaotic and dangerous. Each encounter has the potential for disaster. Many women told us "war stories" about their encounters with violent tricks or police. As an example of the dangers of prostitution, one woman reported the following incident:

> One time, my last date, I already had $150, and I was get-
> ting ready to go home. Then up comes this car and chesty
> me, stupid me, I just get in the car. The guy says, "How
> much?" and I says, "$30." Okay, car date. I just jump in
> the backseat, took the money. He got in the backseat,
> pulls out an ice pick and puts it up against my neck and
> he ripped me off completely. Took my money, the money
> he gave me, plus me, you know? See, so you do take
> chances every time you do that. That's why I like my
> regulars. I know them.

For the woman addict, prostitution is an "odd job" fraught with
dangers and risk. To reduce the dangers of prostitution, some
women feel that working with and for men is beneficial. However,
when a woman relinquishes her status as a "free agent," she tends
to have to work much harder than her man—whether he is formally
her pimp, or more informally, her lover. In these situations, prostitution may become safer, but the addict/prostitute works longer
hours and makes less money. As one woman described this situation:

> When we got so hot in Oakland, when he and I got so hot,
> I was coming out and hustling on the street to make
> money. I had to make $250 for him and $250 for me. I had
> to make $500 a day on the street every day of the week.

Another woman described a situation in which her man forced her
to shoot ritalin (a psychoactive drug that produces a mood-elevating
effect):

> I didn't like ritalins, but he wanted me on them so I
> would go out and work the streets. I had him with me for
> protection—I don't like being alone. I was giving him my
> money and he'd get me high when I wanted. It didn't last.
> It was nice at first and then he started pulling shit. He'd
> say, "If you don't bring in $200–$300, I'm going to beat
> the shit out of you and you won't get fixed."

It is ironic that although most women get into prostitution independently or in spite of the wishes of a man, the actual work patterns of the addict and the risk in the world of heroin/prostitution

force her to accept the protection and domination of men. Whereas she may *enter* prostitution because she has the opportunity to do so and needs the money, once she has been in "the life" for a time, she finds that tricks are to be feared and that other men are often the only means of protection. The price of this protection (in whatever form it takes) is her independence.

Several researchers have argued that the woman addict has an advantage over men addicts because she has prostitution as an easy fallback.[14] Yet when one examines the work patterns of the addicted prostitute, it seems clear that the ongoing threats of being arrested by an undercover policeman posing as a john, ripped off by a trick, or exploited by a pimp all prevent the job of prostitution from being "easy." Instead it is risky, dangerous, demoralizing, and not particularly lucrative. Yet for the *addicted* prostitute there is no way out. She must utilize this kind of work because of the desperation of her heroin habit. And to make matters worse, she must cope with life in a world in which she ranks lowest in the stratification system, as discussed in the following section.

STRATIFICATION

In the world of prostitution, individual status is determined by physical appearance, location of solicitation, and status of clientele. Since prostitution is a fee-for-service arrangement, the "higher-quality" prostitute can charge more than the lower-quality prostitute. Financial success is the reward for quality. The prostitute who works strictly out of a book (a call girl) is regarded as more prestigious than the prostitute who works in expensive hotels. The streetwalker is the lowest rank, with the downtown hotel streetwalker ranking above those who solicit in ghetto neighborhoods. This geographic and stylistic stratification has racial overtones. Because there are a disproportionate number of blacks in poorer neighborhoods and because they are unable to pay as much as johns in richer parts of town, prostitutes see them as less desirable clientele. Similarly, black women who solicit in such neighborhoods are expected to accept less money than other prostitutes, particularly if they are suspected to be addicts. One black woman explained:

> I must be prejudiced or something, but I always would rather do something with a Caucasian. They don't talk

Work and the Addicted Prostitute

that $10–$15 stuff. I did one and I'd get $25–$30 for just one. When I was dealing with blacks, my own race, it was $15 or $20, which wasn't that far off from $25, but if I just needed it, I would take it. I have taken it, but $10 is no good . . . no good.

On the other hand, the clientele of call girls are often high-status men. The "date" is arranged through the john's business associates or colleagues. One woman told us that:

I've got regulars now. They just call me up and I go down or they come over and I've got a couple. One's a senator who I won't mention, and another guy is a big time dude. I know what he is. He's Japanese. Three hundred dollars a trick for fifteen minutes.

The prostitute who works the downtown hotel might be dated by conventioneers or other out-of-town middle-class men. However, the *addict's* work space, often the neighborhood in which she lives, attracts other drug users and lower-class ghetto dwellers. Her customers, then, are not as affluent as those of other prostitutes. Accordingly, this kind of john is less preferred:

The streets is a whole different trip in San Francisco— different than working a book. A book means phone numbers. The clientele is different with books—you know them. They don't want anybody to know. They're nicer. You don't have to worry about getting your ass kicked or getting the money from them. You don't have to ask for the money first like you do on the street here.

The woman's physical appearance is one indicator of the occupational stratification of prostitution. The less she looks like the stereotypical prostitute—tight clothes, heavy makeup, flamboyant appearance—the more she will be paid. The call girl, as exemplified by Jane Fonda in *Klute*, would rarely be mistaken for a prostitute. The streetwalker, at the lowest end of the stratification system, is easily identified because she so readily fits the stereotype. One woman described the different modes of appearance in this way:

Some of those girls in Oakland are righteous thugs . . . standin' on the street corner leanin' up against a post in

Marsha Rosenbaum

*body suits and jackets and boots and black stockings.
That's it. They don't play that in Chicago, where I
worked. I was wearin' evening gowns and shit. You don't
walk around there with no body suits, standin' on no
street corners.*

The addict often begins her activities in prostitution as a higher-
ranking prostitute. This is especially true for white women. She
may get customers from her work in massage parlors or contacts
with other prostitutes with "books." All goes relatively well for the
addict/prostitute as long as she can "keep it together": keep up her
appearance and work "respectable" areas. However, usually her addiction ultimately prevents her from keeping it together. As noted
earlier in the section on work patterns, her appearance may become
slovenly or she may begin to work in an indiscreet manner, attracting police. As one woman observed:

*I wanted to keep it as discreet as possible. I wasn't stand-
ing out there talking to other girls when I would go out.
And I wouldn't go out in jeans. I seen all kinds of whores
comin' through that jailhouse tank, and you should see
them. . . . If I knew I was goin' out, I would try to make
myself appealing, even if I had to do that and come back
and take what I got on off and put on some dirty clothes.*

Our data indicate that in addition to neglecting her appearance, the
addict/prostitute eventually begins to work neighborhoods in
which her drug connections reside. In this way she is never too
geographically far from a fix. In these neighborhoods, however, only
the low-paying johns will solicit her. Possibly most important in the
"slippage" of the addict/prostitute is the reality of her habit and the
frequency of her experience with withdrawal symptoms. When she
is sick, the addict will take less money for a date. As one woman
said:

*After I had been recognized as using drugs, guys wouldn't
offer me $25 or $50 or $35. They broke it all the way
down to $15 or $10. After things had gotten so hard, well,
I'd just have to take it and drop the old pride. I knew
something wasn't right. That was just about it. After feel-*

*ing like that, when you get to the point where you start
feeling like you are about to lose your womanhood, it's
time to slow down or quit or do something.*

Another woman said:

> *It's a big difference. Like if somebody came up and offered
> me $20 when I wasn't hooked, I'd say, "Get lost." But
> when I was hooked, $20 would get me a fix. That's the
> difference. That's why in the Tenderloin, people come up
> and say, "$10," and they can get away with it. And some
> bitches, they get so hooked, they'll take $5 or $10.*

Women who realize that obvious addiction makes them less
desirable and more vulnerable to price negotiation often try to con-
ceal their stigma. They try to strike a delicate balance. They are
more desperately in need of money than nonaddicted prostitutes;
therefore, they don't want to scare off potential tricks by looking
too high-priced. Yet they also don't want to appear too strung out
and available or they will not be able to make enough money to get
by. Restraint becomes the key:

> *If you are hooking and if you've got a habit . . . you don't
> make it any secret that you are a prostitute. You dress up
> nice, but not too nice, because if you dress up too nice,
> you'll scare them away because they'll think you want
> too much money. They always try to hustle you down to
> $15 or $10 because they figure you are strung out and you
> need the money quick, and they try to take advantage of
> that. You have to give them the idea that you're not
> strung out, that you don't use at all and that you're just
> out there hustling because you need rent money or some-
> thing. That you need the money, but you're not desperate
> at the moment . . . and usually you'll get the money you
> need.*

Another indication of the low status of addict/prostitutes is their rejection by high-status pimps. As noted earlier, a boyfriend or other
male associate sometimes may try to get a cut of the woman's "action"; however, such pimps are small-time. They have little to offer

Marsha Rosenbaum

the addict/prostitute and more to gain from the liaison than she does. High-status, successful pimps, on the other hand, can offer the addict/prostitute protection and material goods. But high-status pimps do not like to have addicts in their stables, because addiction often causes such women to get sloppy, earn less money, bring more risk, and become more expensive to maintain.

Addict/prostitutes' work patterns, which are very different from those of nonaddicted prostitutes, provide another indicator of their low rank in the stratification system. Their work patterns resemble those of other addicts, consisting of "odd jobs" and lacking an occupational orientation. Jennifer James, whose work on prostitution has opened up some new avenues of thought, underscores this difference in the following passage:

> *The styles of the addict/prostitute and nonaddicted prostitute are very different. The addict cares little about her clothing, her man is often on the street with her, she rarely works with another woman, she is careless about whom she chooses as customers and from whom she tries to steal, and frequently gets arrested as a result. She usually works the same area regardless of the threat of arrest once she has become known by the police. This style of work clearly differentiates her from professional prostitutes who are careful about clothes, who consider having their man anywhere in the working vicinity as being low-class, who usually work with another woman, and are careful with customer choice, stealing, and the police. These women are much less likely to be arrested than the addicts and always move to another town or area of the city if they feel they are known by the police. The addict/ prostitute is afraid to move because of the importance of her drug connection.*[15]

Thus, the sporadic and often sloppy work patterns of the addicted prostitute—and the attitudes of key figures in the world of prostitution—force her to occupy a low position. She is demeaned by pimps, johns, and other prostitutes; yet, she must continually walk the streets in order to survive and, most important to her, support her heroin habit. In the following section we look at the ways in which addict/prostitutes deal with their social ranking at the bottom of the world of prostitution—how they manage to maintain integrity despite their low status.

Work and the Addicted Prostitute

WORK AND IDENTITY

It would seem logical that the addict/prostitute's low status in the worlds of both prostitution and addiction would diminish her sense of self-esteem. We found, surprisingly, that this was not the case, due to the nature and importance of work in shaping identity.

The fact that addicts do not see themselves as "career" prostitutes is apparently what saves them from having to face their degraded status in the world of prostitution. For the woman addict, prostitution is not a career, not even an occupation. It is just one of many "odd jobs" that she does in order to survive; hence, she does not identify with any one job or hustle. All of them, yet none of them, reflect her "real self." The addicted prostitute turns tricks now and then simply because she needs the money. Despite her increasing inability to "keep it together," her low pay, and her position at the bottom of the prostitution hierarchy, the addict/prostitute maintains a positive sense of self by turning the system on its head and redefining her work. She merely needs money for drugs; from that perspective of necessity comes her scorn of the *nonaddicted* woman (prostituting *voluntarily*), whose motives seem more suspect than her own.

Another irony lies in the addict/prostitute's attitude toward pimps. As noted earlier, the addict/prostitute is unwelcome in most stables, a factor that keeps her status low. Many women addicts, however, value independence and regard the traditional prostitute's domination by a pimp as undesirable. Again the system is turned on its head. Rather than seeing the pimp as protection, a sexual attraction, and a source of prestige, the addict/prostitute who works on her own denigrates such relationships, characterizing them as basically exploitative. She refuses, in essence, to accept the traditional definitions of herself as *deviant* because she turns tricks, and as *undesirable* because she does not have a pimp. In fact, she may look down on prostitutes who have pimps. As one woman reported:

> I tell all those whores I met in jail that you people are sick. You think I'm going to go out there and whore all day long, go home and give my nigger all this money? And then you people say, "Look what my daddy bought me." Daddy didn't buy it. You bought it. You went out there and worked all day long. I whore for myself. I'd rather go in and pick up a gun and rob somebody rather than be a whore and give my money to a man.

Marsha Rosenbaum

Women addicts see themselves primarily as ''junkies,'' controlled by heroin, often against their own will. They define their prostitution, in whatever form it takes, as strictly business—a way to make the very necessary money to buy drugs. They see themselves as involuntarily involved in prostitution. The following statement represents the way many addict/prostitutes we studied feel about their work: ''Yeah, I've turned tricks, but I don't consider myself a prostitute. I always got pretty embarrassed about it. I'd tell the guy, 'Hey man, I'm not really into this, but I do really need the money.' '' Another woman put it more succinctly: ''I don't like it. I'm not very proud of it. Let's put it that way. But the money I've made in one day is more than a person makes in a week.''

CONCLUSION

Most women addicts (62 percent of the study population) prostitute at some time during their heroin careers. Their entree is usually the independent mode, although occasionally a mate will instigate it. We have also observed that women sometimes prostitute covertly, in spite of a mate's dislike of this kind of work. Whatever the mode of entree, however, addicted women enter prostitution because they need money quickly, often desperately.

Although prostitutes see the occupational or career form of prostitution as ideal in terms of safety and monetary gain, the addict is unable to attain such career status because of her habit. Her world is too chaotic: she needs to work in the neighborhood of her drug connection, where dangerous and low-paying johns solicit her; the pace of her lifestyle causes her appearance to deteriorate; and her desperation causes her to steal from tricks, thereby preventing the establishment of regular clientele. Hence, she is degraded in the world of prostitution and addiction—the ''junkie/whore''—and generally disparaged by the larger society.

Yet the woman maintains a positive self-concept, despite great odds, because she does not regard prostitution as her career. It is merely an ''odd job,'' like many others she has—a job that enables her to survive and, above all, to buy drugs. The addict/prostitute is primarily an addict. This emphasis enables the woman to retain some semblance of self-respect in a world in which she is so thoroughly degraded.

Thus, although the label ''prostitute'' carries with it a host of negative connotations, society's label is not the only factor that

Work and the Addicted Prostitute

determines the identity of the addict/prostitute. In a phenome-
nological sense, the *meaning* of one's activities—especially those
activities centering around one's work—plays a central role in shaping self-concept. One is not just a carpenter, a physician, a judge, or
a prostitute; occupational labels only partially determine what individuals feel about themselves. It is necessary to learn the *meaning*
of the individual's participation in the occupation, profession, or
odd job. Is there total identification with the role, or is the work just
a way to get by financially? Is it consonant with the individual's
values and goals, or just a way to survive? If it merely ensures survival, we should expect the individual to attach little significance to
her work and to be at least somewhat immune to outsiders' attitudes toward it. Thus the addict/prostitute can maintain self-
respect despite mearger positive reinforcement.

NOTES

1. *See* Studs Terkel, *Working* (New York: Avon Books, 1974); Peter Letke-
mann, *Crime as Work* (Englewood Cliffs, NJ: Prentice-Hall, 1973); Gene Miller, *Odd
Jobs: The World of Deviant Work* (Englewood Cliffs, NJ: Prentice-Hall, 1978); Edwin
Sutherland, *The Professional Thief* (Chicago: University of Chicago Press, 1937); Ed
Preble and J. J. Casey, "Taking Care of Business: The Heroin User's Life on the
Street," *International Journal of the Addictions* 4 (1969): 1–24; and Bert Sackman et
al., "Heroin Addiction as an Occupation: Traditional Addicts and Heroin-Addicted
Polydrug Users," *International Journal of the Addictions* 2 (1978):1–3.

2. *See*, for example, R. Ball and J. R. Lilly, "Female Delinquency in an Urban
County," *Criminology* 14 (1976):279–281; C. Chambers et al., "Narcotic Addiction
in Females: A Race Comparison," *International Journal of the Addictions* 5
(1970):257; W. Cuskey et al., "Survey of Opiate Addiction Among Females in the
United States Between 1850 and 1970," *Public Health Review* 1 (1972):8–39; J.
Densen-Gerber et al., "Sexual Behavior, Abortion and Birth Control in Heroin Ad-
dicts," *Contemporary Drug Problems* 1 (1972):783; C. A. Eldred and M. M.
Washington, "Female Heroin Addicts in a City Treatment Program: The Forgotten
Minority," *Psychiatry* 38 (1975):75; E. Ellinwood et al., "Narcotic Addiction in
Males and Females: A Comparison," *International Journal of the Addictions*
1(1966):33; S. Fiddle, "Sequences in Addiction," *Addictive Diseases*
2(1976):553–557; Paul Goldstein, *Prostitution and Drugs* (Lexington, MA: Lexington
Books, 1979); James Inciardi and C. Chambers, "Some Aspects of the Criminal
Careers of Female Narcotics Addicts" (Paper presented to the Southern Sociological
Society, Miami Beach, FL, 1971); Jennifer James, "Prostitution and Addiction: An In-
terdisciplinary Approach," *Addictive Diseases*, 2 (1976):611; Marsha Rosenbaum,
"Sex Roles Among Deviants: The Woman Addict," *International Journal of the Ad-
dictions* 16 (1981):3; Alan Sutter, "The World of Righteous Dope Fiends," *Issues in
Criminology* 2 (1966):177–182; J. Weissman and K. File, "Criminal Behavior Pat-

Marsha Rosenbaum

terns of Female Addicts," *International Journal of the Addictions* 11 (1976):6; Lewis Yablonsky, *Synanon: The Tunnel Back* (New York: Macmillan, 1965); and Margaret Zahn and John Ball, "Patterns and Caues of Drug Addiction Among Puerto Rican Females," *Addictive Diseases* 1 (1974):203–214.

3. Funded by the National Institute on Drug Abuse, Grant No. 1 R01 DA 703-0. "The Career of the Woman Addict," Marsha Rosenbaum and John Irwin, Co-Principal Investigators; Sheigla Murphy, Research Assistant.

4. The interviews were lengthy (two to three hours in duration) and semistructured. They followed the woman's life from childhood to the present. Subject areas pertinent to drugs were explored in complete detail. The interview guide was continually expanded as the data suggested new areas of exploration. For a full discussion of the data-gathering and analysis techniques, *see* Leonard Schatzman and Anselm Strauss, *Field Research: Strategies for a Natural Sociology* (Englewood Cliffs, NJ: Prentice-Hall, 1973); Barney Glaser and Anselm Strauss, *The Discovery of Grounded Theory* (Chicago: Aldine, 1970); and Barney Glaser, *Theoretical Sensitivity* (Mill Valley: The Sociology Press, 1978).

5. "Scoring places" are locations where drugs are purchased; a "shooting gallery" is a place where drugs are administered.

6. Jennifer James, who has explored entree into prostitution, notes that although the argument continues over whether prostitution causes addiction or vice versa, the issue remains unresolved. Ultimately, money is the key factor. *See* "Female Addiction and Criminal Involvement (Paper presented to the Pacific Sociological Association, Victoria, British Columbia, 1975).

7. *See* Marsha Rosenbaum, *Women on Heroin* (New Brunswick, NJ: Rutgers University Press, 1981), pp. 62–85.

8. For an interesting discussion of entree into prostitution via the neighborhood, *see* Nanette Davis, "The Prostitute: Developing a Deviant Identity," in *Studies in the Sociology of Sex*, ed. James M. Henslin (New York: Appleton-Century-Crofts, 1971).

9. *See* Marsha Rosenbaum, "Becoming Addicted: The Woman Addict," *Contemporary Drug Problems* (Summer 1979):141–167.

10. *See* Marsha Rosenbaum, "When Drugs Come in the Picture, Love Flies Out the Window: Love Relationships Among Women Addicts," *International Journal of the Addictions* 16, 7 (1981):1197–1206.

11. *See* Marsha Rosenbaum, "Women Addicts' Experience of the Heroin World: Risk, Chaos, and Inundation," *Urban Life: A Journal of Ethnographic Research* 10 (April 1981):65–91.

12. For an excellent discussion of "odd jobs," *see* Miller, *Odd Jobs*.

13. Erich Goode, *Deviant Behavior: An Interactionist Approach* (Englewood Cliffs, NJ: Prentice-Hall, 1978), p. 334.

14. *See* Dan Waldorf, *Careers in Dope* (Englewood Cliffs, NJ: Prentice-Hall, 1973).

15. James, "Prostitution and Addiction," p. 611.

7

Murdered Women and Women Who Murder

A Critique of the Literature

WILLIAM WILBANKS

The academic literature on women and murder is surprisingly sparse, given the seriousness of the crime and the mushrooming literature on women and crime in general. The major treatises on women and crime devote little attention to homicide, and nowhere in that literature will one find a systematic description of the patterns and trends of homicides by or against women. This chapter attempts to fill this gap by reviewing the data and critiquing the existing literature. It concludes with a series of recommendations as to the direction future research should take if our knowledge of female involvement in homicide is to be expanded.

Dominated by mythology and sex stereotypes on the one hand and by a virtual lack of scholarly attention on the other, the existing literature often focuses on the psychology of women involved in homicide, either as victims or offenders. It pays particular attention to their alleged sickness, weakness, fragility, and vulnerability. The etiological literature is dominated by psychiatrists and psychologists; little attention is given to explaining the sociological data on female involvement in homicide. This disregard for apparent patterns and trends in the data has led to theories that emanate from bias and stereotype.

Despite the lack of attention to patterns and trends, some facts about homicides involving females are beginning to come into focus. Whether women are the victims or offenders, homicides in which they are involved are mainly "family affairs." Strangers are usually not involved in such cases; those who kill or are killed by women are frequently male relatives. The chapter explores some factors that may explain the domestic nature of homicides involving females.

Females are much more frequently homicide victims than offenders—twice as often, in fact. Both homicide victimization and arrest rates for women are increasing, but not as fast as comparable rates for men. If we focus on victimization alone and look at rates for different categories of females, it becomes clear that nonwhite women have the highest homicide victimization rates. (Race is, in fact, the best predictor of homicide victimization, outstripping even the factor of sex.) Murders involving women of all races, whether the women are victims or offenders, are very likely to be intraracial events. Finally, women are unlikely to kill other women. They are killed by men in the overwhelming majority of cases, just as they tend to kill men rather than members of their own sex.

THE CHAPTER BEGINS with a discussion of the extent to which the inconsistent definitions of *homicide* and *murder* determine the data upon which explanations of female homicide are based. From there it proceeds to a description of the various types of data bases that serve as the foundation for descriptive and theoretical treatises on female involvement in homicide. A section on patterns and trends reviews current information on homicides committed by and against women (both at one point in time and over time), followed by an historical overview and critique of attempts to explain why women kill and are killed. In conclusion, I recommend priorities for future research into female involvement in homicide.

DEFINITIONAL PROBLEMS IN HOMICIDE STUDIES

Three definitional issues emerge from a review of the literature on women and homicide. First, many discussions do not utilize the same terminology or equivalent samples of cases. For example, some writers speak of "murder" while others speak of "homicide." Second, some writers speak of the "murder rate for females" without indicating whether the arrest rate of female offenders or the victimization rate of females is being discussed. Third, the labeling of a death involving a female as a "killing," "accident," "homicide," or "murder" is part of a political process. Obviously, the nature of the data collected on homicide by or against females largely depends on how deaths are labeled. The following sections address each of these issues in turn.

Inconsistent Definitions

Any discussion of homicides should be preceded by a definition of terms. As Wolfgang has pointed out,[1] some writers use the terms *homicide* and *murder* interchangeably, as if the definitions were the same. *Homicide*, the more inclusive term, refers to the killing of one human being by another.[2] This term covers both criminal and noncriminal (justifiable and excusable) homicides. *Murder* is a criminal homicide that involves both intent and premeditation. Some states distinguish between *first-degree* murder (generally requiring both intent and premeditation) and *second-degree* murder (requiring intent but not premeditation). *Manslaughter* is a type of criminal homicide, but is not considered murder. Other types of criminal homicide that are not considered murder are vehicular homicide and negligent homicide.[3]

An example of confusion of terms appears in an article by Rasko, who claims to report on a study of *homicides* although her sample is limited to criminal homicides (or perhaps even to murders; the article is not sufficiently clear on the composition of the sample).[4] On the other hand, some writers speak of female "murderers" when some of the cases they discuss appear to involve manslaughter rather than murder.

The distinction among terms and the proper labeling of samples of women who kill are not simply a matter of semantics.

William Wilbanks

The characteristics, motives, and so on of women who commit justifiable homicides are likely to be quite different from those of women who commit murder (or for that matter, manslaughter). Writers should be clear as to whether they are attempting to explain why women kill (homicide) or why women kill with premeditation and intent (murder).

Unclear Statistics Regarding Victims versus Offenders

Some writers who discuss female homicide are not clear as to whether they are speaking of female victims or female offenders.[5] It is not uncommon to read of the rising "murder rate" for females without having any indication as to whether this means the female arrest rate or the female victimization rate. Since the overall rate of women who *are killed* is twice the arrest rate of women who *kill*, this distinction is quite important. For example, in examining the now-common argument that the women's movement has caused the female "murder rate" to increase, it is crucial to specify whether the argument involves the female arrest rate or the female victimization rate.

Political Aspects of Labeling Deaths

Perhaps the most important definitional problem involves determining whether deaths will be designated as "homicides" or "murders." The labeling of a death as "killing," "accident," "homicide," or "natural death" is a political decision. Thus, "homicide" and "murder" rates are a result of political decisions that determine which deaths are to be considered homicides, and which murders.[6] The literature consistently reports that males are more frequently homicide (or murder) offenders than females; yet if abortions were considered murder (as many people today advocate), female offenders might far outnumber males. Similarly, if all the deaths of children due to neglect or abuse were considered to be "murder," the numbers of female offenders might be greatly increased. Furthermore, Godwin suggests that the female murder rate would double or triple if women who *instigate* such acts were considered murderers. He asserts that many women "use men as their murder weapon" and thus commit murder by "remote control."[7]

In like manner, the female victimization rate is partly a function of whether deaths are labeled as homicide or murder. If deaths resulting from traffic accidents involving defective automobiles were labeled as criminal homicide (as advocated by some writers),[8] the number of females "murdered" would be greatly increased. And, if all of the deaths of females that occur as the result of unnecessary surgery were considered murder, the number of female victims would increase dramatically.[9]

IN CONCLUSION, I am not recommending that those who write of women and homicide use the term *homicide* rather than *murder* (or vice versa); the female offender rate rather than the victimization rate; or any particular definition of *murder*. I do suggest, however, that authors be sensitive to these definitional issues and avoid misuse of terms. Those who compare female to male homicide rates and patterns should also be sensitive to the third point raised above, for the ratio of male to female "murder" is partly a function of the type of deaths considered to be murder.

DATA BASES FOR HOMICIDE STUDIES

Authors who discuss women and homicide utilize case examples and rates drawn from one or more of several data bases. Five data bases commonly serve as the foundation for descriptive and theoretical studies of female involvement in homicide. These data bases are: (1) the *Uniform Crime Reports* (UCR); (2) the National Center for Health Statistics (NCHS); (3) city studies; (4) prison studies; and (5) "anecdotal" studies. Each has its own advantages and disadvantages.

The Uniform Crime Reports (UCR)

Figures on female involvement in murder and nonnegligent manslaughter are reported by local police jurisdictions to the FBI and published in the annual *Uniform Crime Reports* (UCR). Murder and nonnegligent manslaughter include all murders, but exclude involuntary manslaughter, justifiable homicide, and excusable homicide. The UCR reports both victimization and offender statistics. What is generally termed the "FBI murder rate" is a victimization rate; although it is not broken down by sex, a table is presented each year on the number of victims by age, sex, and race. The UCR also reports on the number (but not the rate) of arrests each year for murder and nonnegligent manslaughter by sex and age.

The primary strength of this data set is that it provides national data on female murder and nonnegligent manslaughter offenders and victims. Furthermore, FBI data tapes (available to researchers) enable those interested in more information on female involvement to compute rates for female victims and offenders by jurisdiction at one point in time and over time. Finally, because the FBI collects additional data on each event of murder and nonnegligent manslaughter (reporting on age, sex, and race of offender and victim; type of weapon; circumstance; and victim–offender relationship), it is possible to obtain descriptive data on all murder and nonnegligent manslaughter involving females. Thus, one could look at the pattern of murder and nonnegligent manslaughter for all females of a particular age, race, and jurisdiction.

The major disadvantage of the murder and nonnegligent manslaughter figures reported by the FBI is that the UCR does not routinely report its figures by sex. Moreover, the arrest data in the supplementary data tapes are of questionable validity; often such reports are not updated with each new arrest.

Although a number of published studies refer to UCR figures, none to date has utilized the vast amount of information on the FBI data tapes. Analysis of the tapes would overcome two major disadvantages of the figures that are currently reported—that rates are not broken down by sex in victim data and that rates are not even reported in the arrest data.

The National Center for Health Statistics (NCHS)

The second source of national data on female involvement in homicide is published by the National Center for Health Statistics (NCHS), which collects information from death certificates. Each death certificate includes a cause of death coded according to a classification scheme developed under the auspices of the United Nations.[10] The NCHS publishes national homicide victimization rates by sex and age. Rates for the United States can be compared to rates for other nations provided in United Nations publications.[11]

The strength of this data base lies in its national scope and in the potential (as yet untapped) for separate analysis of homicides involving females. Use of data tapes on death certificates available from NCHS would make possible specification of homicide events by weapon choice (poison, firearm, knife, and so on); age, sex, and race of victim; jurisdiction; and time of incident (day, month, and year). The major weakness of this data base is that it (unlike the FBI data base) provides no information on offenders. Published studies to date have not utilized the data available on the NCHS data tapes to describe female victimization in the United States. However, a number of authors do report the victimization rates by sex and age that are published by NCHS.

City Studies

The third type of data base utilized by those who have studied female offenders and victims involves information on individual jurisdictions. Jurisdictional studies generally draw on death certificate data from local medical examiners (thus all homicides) or reports from local police (thus murder and nonnegligent manslaughter). Since far more data is available at the local level than is reported to the FBI and NCHS, these studies of reported cases are much richer in detail.

The prototype for this type of study is the 1958 study by Marvin Wolfgang, *Patterns of Criminal Homicide*. Wolfgang examined all criminal homicides occurring in Philadelphia in 1948–1952 and presented victimization and offender rates by sex, age, and race. He also presented data on the patterns of homicides involving females (type of weapon, alcohol use, location, and so on). A number of other "city studies" have followed this format, reporting data on female involvement in homicides for a single jurisdiction.[12]

The strength of jurisdictional studies is that they enable the researcher to gather more detailed information on each case. Knowledge of the identity of the offender in each case allows for the collection of data on disposition. For example, one study was able to discover that husbands who killed their wives were given much more severe sentences than wives who killed their husbands.[13] Researchers who are primarily interested in the circumstances of the case, the motive of the offender, and the disposition have tended to utilize city studies.

The major weakness of this type of data base is the lack of comparative data from other jurisdictions. For example, the Wolfgang study is difficult to interpret: the situation may be unique to that jurisdiction or common to all jurisdictions. Thus the "depth" of data available via city studies must be balanced against the lack of "breadth"—the absence of comparative data.

Prison Studies

The fourth type of data base involves murderers in prison. Three of the most prominent studies of female offenders involve samples of women who were convicted of murder and incarcerated in a particular prison. Two of these (Ward et al. and Suval and Brisson) relied solely upon case files, while the third (Totman) also utilized interviews.[14] The major advantage of this data source is that it provides considerable detail on the nature of the event and the characteristics of victim and offender with relatively little effort. (It is much more time-consuming to follow all cases in a jurisdiction through to disposition to determine the number and nature of cases involving female offenders.)

However, this type of sample is subject to some serious biases. Obviously it is not representative of all offenders in a particular jurisdiction; those not caught, charged, convicted, or sentenced to prison are not included. Furthermore, a sample of offenders present at a particular time is likely to overrepresent serious (long-term) offenders, since those with shorter sentences are less likely to be "caught" at the time the sample is drawn. Thus the three studies cited above do not necessarily provide an accurate sample of women who commit murder (or homicide). For example, one cannot assume that because 90 percent of the offenders studied by Suval and Brisson had IQs under ninety that this characteristic can be generalized to any population of offenders.

"Anecdotal" Studies

The fifth and final type of data base involves a collection of cases from various sources (such as newspapers or history books), with no attempt to secure a representative sample for a particular jurisdiction. Such studies rely upon the "anecdotal" method of proof, reporting examples to prove a particular point. A number of popular works (including Ann Jones's *Women Who Kill*, a major new treatise on female offenders)[15] rely upon anecdotes. The obvious criticism of this data source is that the cases reported are not representative of any group of offenders and may merely reflect the bias of the author.

Murdered Women and Women Who Murder

TABLE 7-1
Murder and Nonnegligent Manslaughter
Victimization Rates by Age, Sex, and Race
for the United States, 1979
(rates are per 100,000 population)

	Male	Female	White	Black[a]	Both Sexes Both Races
0–1	5.75	4.42	3.29	12.73	5.09
1–4	2.75	2.78	1.94	5.94	2.76
5–9	1.20	0.91	0.78	2.08	1.05
10–14	1.28	0.90	0.80	2.48	1.09
15–19	12.97	4.62	6.19	22.01	8.86
20–24	25.90	7.88	10.57	51.35	16.95
25–29	29.44	7.64	10.56	65.56	18.50
30–34	26.18	5.76	9.03	60.07	15.86
35–39	22.74	5.56	8.10	52.16	13.96
40–44	20.20	4.98	7.49	43.79	12.40
45–49	17.26	4.74	7.01	36.23	10.85
50–54	14.81	3.26	5.49	33.95	8.83
55–59	12.19	2.57	4.49	29.18	7.16
60–64	10.25	2.99	4.26	25.79	6.39
65–69	8.70	2.91	4.02	16.63	5.48
70–74	7.23	3.32	3.80	15.57	4.97
75–up	6.84	3.74	3.86	15.22	4.86
All ages	14.81	4.30[b]	5.90	30.13	9.42

Male/Female rate ratio = 3.4:1
Black/White rate ratio = 5.3:1

Source: The number of victims in each category upon which the rates are based are taken from *Uniform Crime Reports* (1979), p. 10. The population figures (for the denominator of the rate) are taken from *Current Population Reports*, series P-25, no. 800 (April 1979).

[a]"Black" is equivalent to Negro and does *not* include other nonwhites.

[b]The rate of 4.30 for females is equivalent to a ratio of 1:23,256 (meaning that in 1979 one female in 23,256 was the victim of murder or nonnegligent manslaughter). The ratio is obtained by dividing 100,000 by the appropriate rate.

IN SUMMARY, these five types of data bases have various strengths and weaknesses. Depth of information is best provided by the use of city studies and prison studies. Breadth of data and cross-jurisdictional information can best be obtained through the use of NCHS or UCR data. The weaknesses of the anecdotal method are so great that primary reliance upon this type of data base should be avoided. Selected cases, however, can be used to illustrate facts established through more representative samples.

PATTERNS AND TRENDS IN HOMICIDES AGAINST AND BY FEMALES

The literature on women and homicide concentrates on female offenders and the homicide events in which they are involved, paying less attention to female victimization. This emphasis cannot be explained by the relative amounts of data available on offenders versus victims; contrary to the impression one might gain from the literature, more data are available on victims than offenders. In most cities, researchers have access to information on female victims from medical examiners and the police; although data on offenders are also available, collection requires much more work. For example, to gather information on a cohort of female homicide offenders, a researcher can usually collect data on all homicide events for a given period of time from police files. Furthermore, the quality of data on offenders that is available from the police is inferior to that available on victims from death certificates.

Apparently, female murderers are much more interesting to researchers than female murder victims. The female killer seems to be an anomaly: men are expected to be aggressive and violent, but women are not. On the other hand, the female victim is *not* an anomaly; because women are viewed as vulnerable and passive, we are not surprised when females are victimized. Gender stereotypes about women, then, appear to have affected researchers' approach to the subject of women and homicide. Susan Brownmiller, in her important work on rape, suggests that women are trained to be victims by the socialization imposed by a male-dominated society.[16] Interestingly enough, although many of the authors of books and articles on female offenders are women, few women have focused on female homicide victims. Female researchers, too, have been affected by gender stereotyping.

Murdered Women and Women Who Murder

This next section briefly reviews the data on homicide cases involving either a female offender or a female victim.

Overall Homicide Victimization and Offender Rates

The two sources of data on national homicide victimization rates, NCHS and UCR, report similar figures. According to NCHS, the national homicide victimization rate for 1975 was 10.0 per 100,000. This is equivalent to a ratio of 1:10,000; that is, according to NCHS, one resident in every 10,000 was the victim of homicide in 1975.[17] According to the second source, the UCR, the national murder and nonnegligent manslaughter victimization rate for 1979 was 9.42 per 100,000 (see Table 7-1). This second rate is lower because it excludes justifiable homicides. As Hindelang has suggested, the closeness of fit across states of the FBI murder and nonnegligent manslaughter rate and the NCHS homicide rate gives us more confidence in the validity of both sets of figures.[18]

The NCHS rates for the nation as a whole, available from the year 1900, indicate that the victimization rate has risen from approximately one (per one hundred thousand) in 1900 to ten in 1979.[19] The UCR murder and nonnegligent manslaughter rates, published since 1935, began at approximately seven (per one hundred thousand) in 1935; declined to approximately five in 1963; and then began a consistent, sharp rise to approximately nine in 1979.[20] Both national sources, then, indicate that the homicide victimization rate has risen in recent years.

Offender rates are found less often in the literature because it is far easier to count victims than offenders (many cases are not cleared). Furthermore, whereas a single county medical examiner or coroner maintains records of all homicide deaths in a county, there may be several police departments in the same county, each maintaining its own records on offenders. Although the FBI does collect data on arrests for murder and nonnegligent manslaughter, this is not an "offender" rate because no arrest is made in approximately one-fourth of all homicide cases. Table 7-2 indicates that the murder and nonnegligent manslaughter arrest rate for 1979 was 8.93 per 100,000. Because this figure represents only about 75 percent of the offenders, we may assume that the offender rate for 1979 was actually around 12.0. Note that the arrest rate has actually declined from 10.31 in 1974 to 8.93 in 1979. Thus, homicide victimization rates appear to be increasing while arrest rates are decreasing.

William Wilbanks

TABLE 7-2
Arrest Rates for Murder and Nonnegligent
Manslaughter and Negligent Manslaughter by Sex
for the United States, 1963–1979
(rates are per 100,000 population)

	Murder and Nonnegligent Manslaughter			Negligent Manslaughter	
	Males	Females	Both Sexes	Males	Females
1979	15.82ᵃ	2.38	8.93	_____	_____
1978	15.97	2.50	9.06	_____	_____
1977	15.18	2.45	8.65	2.70	0.32
1976	14.05	2.33	8.04	2.80	0.29
1975	15.94	2.80	9.20	3.09	0.37
1974	18.07	2.93	10.31	2.99	0.40
1973	16.19	2.74	9.21	3.52	0.43
1972	16.29	2.82	9.38	3.37	0.43
1971	16.09	2.97	9.36	3.20	0.44
1970	14.71	2.54	8.47	3.65	0.42
1969	13.94	2.37	8.00	4.10	0.44
1968	12.33	2.24	7.15	3.99	0.43
1967	10.76	2.00	6.27	3.83	0.40
1966	9.72	1.83	5.67	3.81	0.49
1965	9.27	1.88	5.48	3.90	0.39
1964	8.16	1.68	4.84	3.75	0.39
1963	8.13	1.70	4.83	4.01	0.42

1979 Male/Female rate ratio = 6.6:1
1963 Male/Female rate ratio = 4.8:1

Source: The number of arrests for each year are taken from tables in the annual *Uniform Crime Reports* entitled "Total Arrests by Sex, 19——." For each of these annual tables there is a notation as to the population serviced by the agencies reporting the data in the table. Since an examination of population figures by sex for the U.S. from 1960 to 1978 indicated that the percentage of males was fairly constant at 48.7 percent, the population for males in each year was estimated by multiplying the estimated population for the table by .487. A similar procedure was utilized to obtain a population figure for females in each year (multiplied by .513). Though there are some problems with this method of calculation, the figures given above are probably more accurate in indicating a trend than the trend data found in the tables of the *UCR*, as the latter do not account for increases in population.

ᵃThe rate of 15.82 for males in 1979 is equivalent to a ratio of 1:6,321 (meaning that in 1979 1 male in 6,321 was the victim of murder or nonnegligent manslaughter). The ratio is obtained by dividing 100,000 by the appropriate rate.

Murdered Women and Women Who Murder

Homicide Victimization and Arrest Rates for Women

Because the focus of this chapter is on homicides by and against women, it is important to compare victimization and arrest rates for women with those for men and the population as a whole. The national victimization rate for women in 1975 (as reported by NCHS) was 4.0 per 100,000, which contrasts with a figure of 10.0 for all persons and 16.0 for men. Thus, 1 woman in 22,727 was the victim of a homicide in 1975.[21] The national murder and nonnegligent manslaughter victimization rate for women in 1979 was 4.30 (see Table 7-1).

Klebba has presented NCHS female victimization rates from 1950 (2.5) to 1973 (4.5) and has indicated that while the female victimization rate increased by 80 percent, the male rate increased by almost 100 percent—from 8.4 to 16.7.[22] Here, Klebba found no evidence to indicate that violent crime *against* women is increasing faster than that against men. (The UCR does not consistently report the number of murder and nonnegligent manslaughter victims by sex; therefore, no annual murder and nonnegligent manslaughter victimization rate can be computed.)

The female arrest rate for murder and nonnegligent manslaughter for 1963 to 1979 is presented in Table 7-2. Note that the female rate has increased from 1.70 to 2.38 per 100,000 (an increase of 40 percent), while the male rate has increased from 8.13 to 15.82 (an increase of 95 percent). Adler's contention that female violence is increasing as a result of the women's liberation movement is thus confirmed only in the sense that the female arrest rate for murder and nonnegligent manslaughter is increasing.[23] However, the fact that the male arrest rate is increasing at a faster pace poses a problem for her popular theory.

In a 1951 study published in Copenhagen, Veli Verkko formulates and tests static and dynamic "laws" of sex and homicide.[24] The static law asserts that the female homicide rate (with respect to both female victims and female offenders) remains constant *across countries*, the variation in overall rates across countries being a function of differing male rates. Similarly, the dynamic law states that *over time* in the same country the female rate of crimes against persons remains stable, with the variation in the overall rates being a function of the changing male rate. Verkko suggests that the stability of female rates cross-sectionally and longitudinally is due to the fact that the woman lives "in a somewhat different and more peaceful atmosphere than the man, and that the factors influencing her, also, are not nearly so subject to changes as those affecting a man." Further, he views the regularity of rates as being a function of the "different qualities of men and women."[25]

There appears to be little evidence to support either of these two "laws." For example, Curtis found no support for the static law in his examination of homicide rates in several countries and across cities in the United States.[26] Moreover, a recent review of this literature and analysis of new data have failed to confirm either law.[27]

Female Homicide Rates by Age

As stated earlier, the female homicide victimization rate for 1975 was 4.4 per 100,000 population. However, this figure varied sharply by age. Females aged 20 to 24 had the highest rate (7.6), those aged 5 to 9 the lowest (0.9). However, females under 1 year of age had a relatively high rate (5.1). The rate declined across age groups from 25 to 74, but then increased slightly in the three oldest groups.[28] The male pattern across the ages was similar to that for females, with the highest risk group aged 25 to 29 (a rate of 31.5). Females aged 20 to 24 are at a higher risk than other females, due to their association with males of the same approximate age. The relatively high female risk rate for children under 1 apparently reflects the battered child syndrome. Thus, the structural position of females of various ages appears to affect their rates of homicide victimization.

One should not assume from these figures that a particular individual who is under 30 today will have a reduced risk of victimization as he or she grows older. Klebba has demonstrated through an analysis of male birth cohorts that the peak age of homicide victimization for birth cohorts from 1888–1892 to 1938–1942 was not 20 to 24 or 25 to 29 but whatever age the cohort happened to be in 1972.[29] Thus it does not follow that the peak age of risk for a particular individual over a lifetime is 20 to 24. Although no comparable research has been conducted with females, it is likely that the belief that 20 to 29 is the peak age of risk is the result of cross-sectional data being used to the exclusion of longitudinal data (cohort studies).

Murder and nonnegligent manslaughter victimization rates by sex and age are reported in Table 7-1. The pattern of rates across age groups for males and females is similar to that found in NCHS rates.

Murdered Women and Women Who Murder

Note that the male/female rate ratio is 3.4:1 (3.4 males are the victims of murder and nonnegligent manslaughter for every female victim).

Although figures on the sex and age of victims of murder and nonnegligent manslaughter are not consistently reported in the annual volumes of the UCR, homicide rates by sex and age have been reported by NCHS since 1968. The pattern of variation across age groups for females (and males) in NCHS figures has always been fairly consistent. However, in earlier years the peak age for female victimization appears to have been older; the peak age in 1968 and 1969 was 30 to 34, while the peak age in 1970 and 1971 was 25 to 29. Moreover, the distribution of rates across age groups is much "flatter" for females than for males. (The peak rate for young males may be several times the rate for younger and older age groups, while the peak rate for females aged 20 to 29 may be only marginally larger than that for other age groups.) That male victimization rates are less flat may be due to the impact of the so-called subculture of violence on young males, many of whom constantly try to prove their manhood. (Many die making this point.)[30]

The UCR reports arrest figures for murder and nonnegligent homicide by sex and age in separate tables; therefore, no rates can be computed from those tables by sex *and* age. However, other studies indicate that offender rates across age groups follow a pattern somewhat similar to that of victimization rates.[31] It does appear that women become murderers at a somewhat older age than men. Blum and Fisher maintain that there is a pronounced delay in the rise and peak of the female offender age distribution and that there is also a slower decline beyond the peak age.[32]

Although there is currently little data on the topic, it would be interesting to learn what female age groups are experiencing the greatest increase in arrest rates. If the increases in female arrest rates are largely a function of increasing arrests for young people of both sexes (with the rates for older women remaining stable), one might argue that the women's liberation movement has had more of an impact than current data indicate.

Female Homicide Rates by Race and Race/Age

Female victimization and arrest rates also vary markedly by race. The NCHS figures for 1975 indicate that the white female victimization rate was only 3.7 per 100,000, while the nonwhite rate was 13.8, greater than the 9.1 for white males; the nonwhite male rate was 62.6. Therefore, the rank ordering of the four sex/race groups is as follows: nonwhite males, nonwhite females, white males, white females. Race, then, is a better predictor of victimization rates than sex.[33]

Shin et al. report NCHS victimization rates by sex/race from 1940 to 1974. Over this twenty-five-year period, the four sex/race categories showed the following increases: white males, 86 percent (5.0 to 9.3); white females, 123 percent (1.3 to 2.9); nonwhite males, 36 percent (57.1 to 77.9); and nonwhite females, 23 percent (12.6 to 15.5).[34] Therefore, the percentage increases in female victimization rates appear to have been largely due to the large increase experienced by white females.[35]

Even greater variation is found in female victimization rates when one examines race/age subgroups. The NCHS figures for 1975 indicate that the rate for white females ranges from 0.8 for those aged 5 to 9 to 4.8 for those aged 20 to 24, while rates for nonwhite females range from 1.5 for those aged 5 to 9 to 26.3 for those aged 25 to 29. However, the variation across race/age subgroups is even greater for males (1.0 to 150.4 for nonwhite males and 1.0 to 15.7 for white males).

As these data make clear, it is extremely important, when we study victimization patterns of offenders, to probe differences between age and race categories. These differences reveal that young adult women and nonwhite women have much higher rates of victimization than other females. Yet if we go further and compare female with male rates, we find that even young, nonwhite adult females are victimized far less than young, nonwhite adult males.

Victim–Offender Homicide Relationships

One of the most striking features of homicides against and by females is their intrafamily setting. However, it is likely that this characteristic is more typical of female offenders than female victims: females may often be the victim of a felony-related murder (such as robbery or rape), but are rarely involved as the perpetrator in a felony-related murder. Blum and Fisher suggest:

> *While murder in general is a very personalized crime, in the vast majority of cases taking place between people who know each other, female murder appears to be an*

Murdered Women and Women Who Murder

especially intimate act. That is, women are more likely than men to murder another family member—particularly a husband or child; outside of husbands and children, the only significant choice for women appears to be a lover.[36]

The UCR publishes data on both "circumstance" (felony type; romantic triangle; argument over money, property, and so on) and "relationship" (husband, wife, acquaintance, neighbor, stranger) but does not break down this data by sex. Thus one cannot learn from the UCR the extent to which circumstance and relationship vary by sex of the victim or offender. However, the UCR does present figures that allow computation of percentages for victim–offender relationships by sex and sex/race. Table 7-3, which was derived from 1979 UCR figures, suggests that when the offender is female, the victim is male in 80.3 percent of the cases. Similarly, when the victim is a female, the offender is a male in 90.0 percent of the cases. The table also indicates that males are more likely to kill males (79.6 percent of cases) and to be killed by males (72.0 percent of cases). On the other hand, females are also more likely to kill males and to be killed by males.

When subgroups by race and sex are considered, it appears that white females usually kill white males (82.4 percent of cases) and black females usually kill black males (81.0 percent of cases). In like manner, white females are usually victimized by white males (82.3 percent) and black females are usually victimized by black males (82.0 percent). It should also be noted that Table 7-3 indicates that it is more likely that a female will kill another females (19.7 percent) than it is for a female to be killed by another female (10.0 percent). Finally, the rarest victim-offender relationships found in Table 7-3 involve female offenders who kill female victims of another race: only 0.8 percent of the victims of black female offenders were white females and only 0.6 percent of the victims of white female offenders were black females.

Table 7-3 also presents data on the extent to which murder and nonnegligent manslaughter is interracial. Note that white offenders kill white victims in 93.7 percent of single victim-single offender cases, but that black offenders kill black victims in 89.1 percent of the cases. In cases in which the victim is white, 10.7 percent of the offenders are black. (The corresponding interracial figure in cases having a black victim is only 5.0 percent.) White citizens may

William Wilbanks

TABLE 7-3
Victim–Offender Relationship by Sex and Race and Sex/Race (by Percentage) of All Murder and Nonnegligent Manslaughter Cases Involving a Single Victim and Single Offender for the United States, 1979

	Offender is White Male	Offender is White Female	Offender is Black Male	Offender is Black Female
Victim is White Male	74.4%	13.6%	10.0%	0.7%
Victim is White Female	82.3%	5.1%	10.2%	0.6%
Victim is Black Male	4.7%	0.9%	73.0%	21.1%
Victim is Black Female	2.3%	0.5%	82.0%	15.2%

	Victim is White Male	Victim is White Female	Victim is Black Male	Victim is Black Female
Offender is White Male	67.6%	26.2%	4.5%	0.6%
Offender is White Female	82.4%	10.7%	5.4%	0.8%
Offender is Black Male	8.9%	3.2%	67.2%	20.1%
Offender is Black Female	2.4%	0.8%	81.0%	15.5%

Murdered Women and Women Who Murder

	Offender is Male	Offender is Female
Victim is Male	72.0%	28.0%
Victim is Female	90.0%	10.0%

	Victim is Female	Victim is Male
Offender is Male	79.6%	21.4%
Offender is Female	80.3%	19.7%

	Offender is White	Offender is Black
Victim is White	87.9%	10.7%
Victim is Black	5.0%	94.7%

	Victim is Black	Victim is White
Offender is White	93.7%	5.2%
Offender is Black	10.3%	89.1%

Source: The figures upon which these percentages are based are taken from *Uniform Crime Reports*, 1979, p. 8. Percentages should be read across rows (rather than down columns). The total of percentage figures across rows will approach but not reach 100 percent, because some victims and offenders were Native Americans, Chinese, Japanese, or "other" and some involved persons of unknown sex.

perceive that they are more likely to be killed by a black offender because they are aware that blacks have a much higher homicide offender rate than whites. However, due to the intraracial nature of murder and nonnegligent manslaughter, whites are in fact more likely to be killed by whites and blacks more likely to be killed by blacks.

No data are currently published that would indicate trends in victim–offender relationship in homicides involving females as offenders. However, it would be interesting to determine the extent to which the increase in homicides by females in recent years involves strangers. It could be that because females are less confined to their homes today, they release their aggression increasingly upon non–family members. In other words, it may be that the absolute rate of murders by females will remain the same, but that the pattern (target) of victimization may change.

In a similar vein, it would be interesting to determine the extent to which the victim–offender relationship has changed over the past few years in cases involving female victims. It is likely that many (most?) females fear strangers more than family members, and yet statistics indicate that the female is more likely to be killed by a family member. However, it may be that victimization of females by strangers is increasing at a much greater pace in recent years than victimization by family members. If this is the case, females today are correctly perceiving a marked increase in the chance of being killed by a stranger.

Weapon Use

Both NCHS and the FBI collect and store data on the type of weapon used, but neither reports a breakdown of this variable by sex. The 1979 UCR, for example, reports that 63 percent of all cases of murder and nonnegligent manslaughter were committed with firearms, but we do not know what percentage of female offenders use guns. However, it is likely that the figure is less than 63 percent because women less frequently own or have experience with guns. Like the UCR, most city studies do not break down crime method by sex; thus, data are sparse on this point. Although there is a common stereotype of a woman wielding a kitchen knife, the extent of this stereotype's accuracy is unknown. One study of incarcerated female murderers found that women were as likely to use a knife as a gun, but this finding is difficult to interpret given the biased nature of the sample.[37]

Murdered Women and Women Who Murder

There are also no published data on the percentage of female homicide victims who are killed by various types of weapons. However, it is quite possible that much of the increase in female homicide victimization in recent years is due to a disproportionate increase in homicides involving guns. That is, some data indicate that most of the increase in homicides in recent years (male and female victims combined) is due to more killings involving guns; the rate of homicides involving other weapons has remained relatively stable.[38]

Published data on female offenders' choice of weapon over time are also lacking. This type of information (which is available in NCHS and FBI tapes) could shed light on the importance of guns (their availability or women's willingness to use them) in the increasing homicide rate for female offenders. It probably takes more strength (and courage?) for a woman to attack a man with a knife than a gun. Therefore, an increase in male homicides by women might indicate that women are killing at a higher rate because guns, easier weapons to use, are becoming more available to them.

Location

Neither NCHS nor the FBI collects data on location of the homicide event. Data on incident characteristics are therefore limited to what can be found in city studies. (Data from incarcerated samples are too biased.) In his Philadelphia study, Wolfgang presents data on location by sex and finds that female offenders and victims are likely to kill or be killed at home. (The reverse is true for males.)[39] This finding is what one would expect; most homicides involving females as victims or offenders involve family members, and thus are likely to occur in the home.

Simon has suggested that because the women's movement leads women out of the home, there will probably be a decrease in female-perpetrator homicides involving family members (and, thus, the home).[40] It may be, as Simon suggests, that the level of frustration diminishes for women who are able to get away from the confinement of home and children. Of course, this decrease may be offset by more homicides committed by females outside the home—a possibility not recognized by Simon. And for women who move about the community, the risk of victimization by strangers in settings other than the home may increase.

The currently available data on the location of homicides involving women are extremely limited. Had we more detailed information, we would be better able to determine whether the women's movement has affected the number of female homicide victims and offenders.

Alcohol Involvement

The only study that reports on alcohol use by the homicide offender and victim by sex is that by Wolfgang.[41] He found that alcohol was present in 56 percent of the male victims but in only 42 percent of the female victims. More significantly, he found that alcohol was present only in the *victim* in less than 3 percent of the 139 criminal homicides involving female victims. In other words, if the victim was female and had been drinking, the offender was almost certain to have also been drinking. In addition, Wolfgang found that 49 percent of the female offenders had been drinking, while 57 percent of the male offenders had been drinking. Thus, both female offenders and victims were less likely to have been drinking than their male counterparts.

Two studies of incarcerated female murderers found that female offenders were less likely to have been drinking than male offenders.[42] Ward et al. found that 61 percent of the victims of female offenders were helpless, ill, drunk, off-guard, asleep, or infirm.[43] However, it may be that this condition of the victim was a primary factor in the woman being sent to prison. There are no published data on trends over time in the presence of alcohol in victims and/or offenders by sex.

Prior Record of Offender

Only the Wolfgang study presents data on prior record of homicide offenders by sex. He found that 52 percent of female offenders had no previous arrest record, in comparison to 46 percent of the male offenders.[44] Furthermore, those females who had been previously arrested had fewer arrests than their males counterparts, and they were less likely to have been arrested for a prior offense against person. Wolfgang suggests that these data indicate that females are less a part of the subculture of violence than are males. Supporting Wolfgang, one prison sample found that 75 percent of female offenders had no prior record.[45] Thus it appears from the few available data that female homicide offenders are more likely than males to be first offenders.

Murdered Women and Women Who Murder

Mental Condition of Offender

Perhaps the most interesting and controversial "fact" about female murderers is that they tend to be (or are perceived to be) more disturbed than their male counterparts. Blum and Fisher cite several studies that tested male and female murderers and found females to be more psychotic or "psychiatrically ill."[46] In addition Blum and Fisher review the literature on infanticide (usually written by psychiatrists); it generally views mothers who kill their children as schizophrenic, but fathers who kill their children as nonpsychotic.

Blum and Fisher question the validity of this "scientific evidence," pointing to a study that found that college students saw female killers as more deranged than equivalent males (even though the event and background information were the same for both sexes). Gender stereotypes create the belief that violence is incompatible with traditional female roles. Therefore, observers may attribute mental illness to the female murderer because they think that a "rational" woman would not behave in such a masculine way; the attribution of mental illness to female offenders often involves a tautology.

If it is indeed true (as some suppose) that female killers are sometimes penalized more leniently than male killers, this phenomenon could be a product of the belief that the former are more mentally disturbed. That is, their behavior is so out-of-role that they may be considered "crazy" and hence treated more sympathetically by the courts.[47] Moreover, when wives kill husbands, prosecutors may seek lesser charges on the belief that the husband somehow deserved his fate. That is, if the victim appears to have been partly to blame, the prosecutor may attribute less blame to the female offender.[48] In either case, the mental condition attributed to the female offender may serve to reduce her punishment.

Summary of Patterns and Trends

A number of themes about women as murderers and as murder victims emerge from the preceding review of the literature. Each must be taken into account by anyone who proposes to explain why women kill or are killed. It seems appropriate to summarize what we know about women and homicide before we review etiological theories in the following section. We know that:

1. There are over three times as many male victims of murder and nonnegligent manslaughter as female victims.

2. Over six times as many males as females are arrested for murder and nonnegligent manslaughter.
3. The victimization and arrest rates for males are increasing faster than those for females.
4. The distribution of victimization and arrest rates across age groups is much "flatter" for females than for males.
5. Race is a better predictor of victimization and arrest rates than sex. (That is, nonwhite females have higher rates than white males.)
6. Homicides by and against females are primarily intersexual. (Females are more likely to kill and be killed by males.) However, such homicides are also predominately intraracial.
7. Female offenders are perceived as being more disturbed than male offenders.

It is obvious that there are a number of areas in which so little information is currently available that no conclusions can be drawn. For example, we know little about differences between the sexes in terms of weapon use, prior record, alcohol use, and location of the assault.

A NOTE ON ETIOLOGICAL VIEWS

As stated earlier, little attempt is made in the literature to explain why women are killed. Even the literature that attempts to explain why women kill is not as massive as one might expect, given the seriousness of the crime and the degree of attention paid to the male killer. Historically, both popular and academic treatises on female murderers have reflected the sexist view that female killers are motivated by different forces than male killers. Whereas males have been seen as turning to crime for economic reasons or through poor socialization, the motivations of females have been attributed to physiological and psychological factors peculiar to their sex.[49]

Works by popular writers contain "grimly amusing homicidal anecdotes" portraying female murderers as evil and stealthy, driven by an "hysterical sexually-inspired madness."[50] However, this stereotype of the female killer is not limited to popular works; such authors as Lombroso, Thomas, and Pollak present a somewhat similar view, thus providing "scientific" credibility for the stereotype.[51] Although some writers have recently challenged the sexist stereotype of the female offender, it is probably still strong in the mind of the layperson.[52]

In the past few years, more attention has been paid to the female homicide offender by psychiatrists than by members of any other discipline. For example, psychiatrists have authored numerous journal articles on infanticide, a crime that appears to be dominated by women.[53] The psychiatric view of the female killer as mentally disturbed seems to be accepted by most laypersons, who reason that a woman would have to be crazy to kill her own child. However, the fact that laypersons accept tautological reasoning is not proof of its validity.

Biological explanations continue to appear in the literature on women and homicide. Daniel Glaser, for example, has suggested that half of the assaultive acts committed by women occur during menstruation and the four days preceding it; he claims that this is "perhaps the highest correlation of crime with a physiological condition that has been established."[54] Similarly, Lieber suggests that there is a correlation between the phases of the moon and homicide and that this "lunar effect" is more pronounced for women during menstruation.[55] There is, however, little persuasive evidence for these biological theories.[56]

Although sociologists are noticeably absent from the list of academics who have attempted to explain why women kill, one recent work, *Women Who Kill* by Ann Jones, does claim to be a sociological analysis of female homicide offenders.[57] This work provides a strong critique of the sexist etiological views set forth by other writers; however, it fails to provide the promised sociological analysis. Jones never gives the reader a systematic theory of why women kill, but focuses instead on the reaction of a male-dominated society to the women who do kill.

The only book devoted to a sociological explanation of why women kill is Jane Totman's *The Murderess: A Psychosocial Study of Criminal Homicide*. Totman presents a sociological analysis of murder based on interviews with several incarcerated women. Although her sample is quite biased, her methodology deserves attention. Totman argues (correctly, I believe) that because most current theories of crime are created via the deductive method, they do not fit the facts to be explained. Totman suggests that a more valid approach would be to utilize an inductive method, beginning with a tentative hypothesis and then examining a number of cases to see if

William Wilbanks

they can be explained by the hypothesis. The hypothesis should be reformulated until all cases are explained. This approach has been used by academics in other fields,[58] but only Totman has used it in the study of why women kill. It seems particularly necessary in this field of inquiry, which has suffered from sparse data and deductive theories.

However, the data to be explained inductively should be expanded beyond information pertinent to individual cases (Totman's approach) to include sociological findings set forth at the conclusion of the preceding section of this chapter. A theory developed in this manner would be "grounded" in the sense that it would emanate from the facts to be explained. In summary, the facts to be explained must be set forth and then an effort made to develop an explanatory theory. To date, there has been little effort to set forth both individual and sociological data and almost no attempt to devise theory to explain those data. This critique of current methodology has some obvious implications for future research.

ISSUES FOR FUTURE RESEARCH

It should be clear from the preceding sections that there is a sizable gap between what is known about women and homicide and what could and should be known before adequate theories can be proposed for why women kill and are killed. Although a number of facts *are* known, much remains unknown. Moreover, those who wish to devise explanations for female involvement in homicide (as either victims or offenders) should proceed inductively so that theory will fit facts. To close the gap and work toward sounder theory, researchers should follow these recommendations:

1. Future research should attempt to discern the patterns of homicide events involving female victims or offenders. Patterns involve characteristics of the offender (prior record, attitudes toward violent resolution of conflict, use of alcohol, psychological profile, attitude toward victim prior to assault, and so on); characteristics of the victim (prior record, prior relationship to offender, use of alcohol, and so on); and characteristics of the event (availability of weapon, presence of audience, nature of interaction between victim and offender

Murdered Women and Women Who Murder

before the assault, and so on). The description of patterns should include consideration of changes over time. Such changes in homicide patterns could be used, for example, to determine the extent to which increased victimization may be a function of more homicides involving guns.

2. The attempt to gain greater "depth" of information (as suggested above) should be matched by efforts to obtain "breadth"—that is, data obtained in one jurisdiction should be compared with those found in other jurisdictions, both in this country and abroad. One way of achieving breadth would be coordination of research in various cities so that a uniform format could be utilized to gather data. Currently it is almost impossible to compare results from city studies due to the different data collection formats. Second, data from the NCHS and FBI national data tapes (which do use a uniform format) could be utilized to calculate arrest and victimization rates by sex and jurisdiction. Such analysis would allow us to determine a number of sociological facts about female involvement in homicide. For example, it may be that female offender rates are quite stable across jurisdictions, with the variance in overall rates being a function of varying male arrest rates. On the other hand, the patterns of female involvement may vary sharply from jurisdiction to jurisdiction. We might discover that higher rates for female offenders in some cities are due to a large number of killings outside the family context (that is, that only "domestic" killings are stable across jurisdictions). Similarly, female victimization and arrest rates might be found to be correlated with such factors as inflation or male unemployment. This examination of the sociological facts of homicide should be longitudinal as well as cross-sectional; in other words, research should attempt to determine the changes over time in the relationship of sociological variables.

3. Theory development and testing should be grounded in both individual case data and sociological data obtained through the research recommended above. Theories of female assaultive behavior that have already been formulated should be tested, especially the highly suspect one that proposes relationship with the menstrual cycle.

178

William Wilbanks

NOTES

1. Marvin E. Wolfgang, *Patterns in Criminal Homicide* (Philadelphia: University of Pennsylvania Press, 1958), p. 26.

2. On the legal definition of various types of homicide, *see* R. M. Perkins, "The Law of Homicide," *The Journal of Criminal Law, Criminology and Police Science* 36 (1946):391–454.

3. On vehicular homicide, *see* Jack Barker, "The Fallacy and Fortuity of Motor Vehicle Homicide," *Nebraska Law Review* 41 (1962):793–815.

4. Gabriella Rasko, "The Victim of the Female Killer," *Victimology* 1 (1976):396–402.

5. This type of error by writers is discussed and illustrated in Wolfgang, *Patterns.*

6. Philip E. Devine, *The Ethics of Homicide* (Ithaca, NY: Cornell University Press, 1978), p. 203. *See also* Joel Swartz, "Silent Killers at Work," *Crime and Social Justice* (1975):15–20; and Jeffrey H. Reiman, *The Rich Get Richer and the Poor Get Prison* (New York: John Wiley & Sons, 1979).

7. John Godwin, *Murder U.S.A.: The Ways We Kill Each Other* (New York: Ballantine Books, 1978), pp. 118–124.

8. G. Clark, "Corporate Homicide—New Assault on Corporate Decision-Making," *Notre Dame Lawyer* 54 (1979):911–924.

9. Reiman, *The Rich Get Richer,* pp. 73–75.

10. *International Classification of Diseases,* 8th rev. ed. (Washington, DC: HEW, NCHS, 1965). Mortality data can be found in annual volumes of *Vital Statistics of the United States.*

11. Figures on homicide for nations in the U.N. can be found in annual editions of *The Demographic Yearbook* and *World Health Statistics Annual.*

12. For a listing of such city studies, *see* William Wilbanks, "Homicide and the Criminal Justice System in Dade County," *Journal of Crime and Justice* (Summer 1979):58–72.

13. Ibid.

14. David A. Ward, Maurice Jackson, and Renee Ward, "Crimes of Violence by Women," in *The Criminology of Deviant Women,* ed. F. Adler and R. Simon (Boston: Houghton Mifflin, 1979), pp. 114–138; Elizabeth M. Suval and Robert C. Brisson, "Neither Beauty nor Beast: Female Criminal Homicide Offenders," *International Journal of Criminology and Penology* 2 (1974):23–34; Jane Totman, *The Murderess: A Psychosocial Study of Criminal Homicide* (San Francisco: R and E Research Associates, 1978).

15. Ann Jones, *Women Who Kill* (New York: Holt, Rinehart & Winston, 1980).

16. Susan Brownmiller, *Against Our Will: Men, Women and Rape* (New York: Simon and Schuster, 1975), p. 309ff.

17. *Vital Statistics of the United States, 1975,* vol. II: Mortality, part A (Hyattsville, MD: 1979), pp. 1–24, 1–42.

18. Michael J. Hindelang, "The Uniform Crime Reports Revisited," *Journal of Criminal Justice* 2 (1974):1–17.

19. A. Joan Klebba, "Homicide Trends in the United States, 1900–74," *Public Health Reports* 90 (1975):195–204.

20. Hindelang, "The Uniform Crime Reports Revisited."

21. *Vital Statistics of the United States, 1975.*

22. Klebba, "Homicide Trends."

23. Freda Adler, *Sisters in Crime: The Rise of the New Female Criminal* (New York: McGraw-Hill, 1975), pp. 2, 3, 24.

24. Veli Verkko, "Static and Dynamic 'Laws' of Sex and Homicide," in *Studies in Homicide,* ed. Marvin Wolfgang (New York: Harper & Row, 1967), pp. 36–44.

25. Verkko, "Static and Dynamic," pp. 41, 44.

26. Lynn A. Curtis, *Criminal Violence: National Patterns and Behavior* (Lexington, MA: D. C. Heath, 1974), p. 34.

27. William Wilbanks, "A Test of Verkko's Static and Dynamic 'Laws' of Sex and Homicide," *International Journal of Women's Studies* 4 (1981):173–180.

28. William Wilbanks, "Trends in Violent Death Among the Elderly," *International Journal of Aging and Human Development* 14, 3 (1981):167–175.

29. Klebba, "Homicide Trends."

30. M. E. Wolfgang and F. Ferracuti, *The Subculture of Violence: Towards an Integrated Theory in Criminology* (London: Tavistock, 1967).

31. *See,* for example, Wolfgang, *Patterns,* pp. 65–78; and Wilbanks, "Homicide and the Criminal Justice System," p. 70.

32. Alan Blum and Gary Fisher, "Women Who Kill," in *Violence: Perspectives on Murder and Aggression,* ed. I. Kutash et al. (San Francisco: Jossey-Bass, 1978), pp. 187–197.

33. *Vital Statistics of the United States, 1975,* pp. 1–42.

34. Yongsock Shin, Davor Jedlicka, and Everett S. Lee, "Homicide Among Blacks," *Phylon* 38 (1977):398–407.

35. No data on arrest rates for murder and nonnegligent manslaughter by sex/race subgroups can be obtained from the annual volumes of the UCR. Thus, there are no data currently published that indicate the trend in arrest rates across various sex and race groups.

36. Blum and Fisher, "Women Who Kill," p. 192.

37. Ward et al., "Crimes of Violence."

38. Blum and Fisher, "Women Who Kill," p. 192. *See also* William Wilbanks, "Trends in Violent Death in a Southern Metropolitan County: A Study of Dade County (Miami) Florida, 1956–1978" (Unpublished, 1979; available from the author, Dept. of Criminal Justice, Florida International University, AC-I-284, N. Miami, FL 33181.)

39. Wolfgang, *Patterns,* pp. 364–367, 99ff., 106–109, 368. *See also* Ward et al., "Crimes of Violence," p. 117.

40. Rita James Simon, *The Contemporary Woman and Crime* (Rockville, MD: National Institute of Mental Health, 1975), p. 4.

41. Wolfgang, *Patterns,* pp. 136–141, 369–371.

42. Suval and Brisson, "Neither Beauty," pp. 30ff.; Ward et al., "Crimes of Violence," p. 120.

43. Ward et al., "Crimes of Violence," p. 120.

44. Wolfgang, *Patterns,* pp. 175–184.

William Wilbanks

45. Ward et al., "Crimes of Violence," p. 129.

46. Blum and Fisher, "Women Who Kill," p. 193. *See also* Carol Smart, *Women, Crime and Criminology: A Feminist Critique* (Boston: Routledge & Kegan Paul, 1977), p. 145.

47. Ronald A. Farrell and Victoria Lynn Swigert, "Legal Disposition of Inter-Group and Intra-Group Homicides," *The Sociological Quarterly* 19 (1978):565–576.

48. Franklin Zimring and S. O'Malley, "Punishing Homicide in Philadelphia—Perspective on the Death Penalty," *University of Chicago Law Review* 43 (1976):227–252.

49. Smart, *Women, Crime and Criminology*, p. 18.

50. Jones, *Women Who Kill*, p. xv; Gerald Sparrow, *Women Who Murder* (New York: Abelard-Schuman, 1970), pp. 43, 47.

51. For a description and critique of the views of Lombroso, Thomas, and Pollak, *see* Dorie Klein, "The Etiology of Female Crime: A Review of the Literature," *Issues in Criminology* 8 (1973):3–30.

52. Smart, *Women, Crime and Criminology*; Klein, "The Etiology"; Totman, *The Murderess*; Jones, *Women Who Kill*.

53. For a review of this literature, *see* Marie W. Piers, *Infanticide* (New York: W. W. Norton, 1978).

54. Daniel Glaser, *Crime in Our Changing Society* (New York: Holt, Rinehart & Winston, 1978), p. 150.

55. Arnold L. Lieber, *The Lunar Effect: Biological Tides and Human Emotions* (Garden City, NY: Anchor Press, 1978), pp. 27, 54.

56. It is quite possible that such a relationship does exist, but only because females who endorse such an idea exercise less self-control (that is, it may be a self-fulfilling prophecy).

57. Jones, *Women Who Kill*, p. xvi.

58. Barney G. Glaser and Anselm L. Strauss, *The Discovery of Grounded Theory: Strategies for Qualitative Research* (Chicago: Aldine, 1967). *See also* Donald R. Cressey, *Other People's Money* (Belmont, CA: Wadsworth, 1953).

8

Delinquency Causation in Female Offenders

MARGUERITE Q. WARREN

The intent of this chapter is to consider in a preliminary way several crime-causal theories in terms of their adequacy in explaining female crime. In the research to be reported, the assumptions of four crime-causal theories—social control, cultural deviance, psycho-dynamic, and strain—were assessed for appropriateness against the case record material of a small sample of adolescent females committed to a state correctional agency. In addition, to assess the differential appropriateness of the theoretical perspectives for subgroups of the sample, five categories of female delinquents were distinguished with respect to meeting the theoretical assumptions.

In conducting the study, two specific questions were asked: (1) do the assumptions regarding crime causation and characteristics of delinquents hold better for some causal theories than others when applied to a female delinquent sample, and (2) do the assumptions for a particular theory hold better for some subtypes of female delinquents than for others?

The four crime-causal theories were chosen because they con-

Marguerite Q. Warren

tinue to be frequently used and cited as explanatory of delinquency. Social learning theory has been one of the most utilized explanations for delinquency in recent years,[1] but it is not assessed in this study because the case files from which the study data were obtained do not include information necessary to identify individual learning sequences. Although such other perspectives as mixed strain/subcultural theories could also have been used,[2] the analysis was restricted to "purer" theories to keep the number of perspectives as small as possible.

Some might argue that the sociological theories do not apply at the individual level of analysis. However, Monahan and Splane have recently pointed out that many of the sociological theories, including strain, cultural deviance, and social control, invoke such psychological constructs as motives, aspirations, internal definitions, beliefs, attachments, self-concepts, and so on. The theories assume that system-level determinants lead to internal states and processes that then explain crime.[3] This assumption of relevant internal states and processes appears to support a study conducted at the individual level of analysis.

Little crime-causal theoretical work has been done on female offenders. Two studies have considered the usefulness of opportunity (or strain) theory in explaining delinquency of females. Datesman, Scarpitti, and Stephenson compared nondelinquent high school students and delinquent youths appearing in juvenile court, and found that perceptions of limited opportunity were more strongly related to female involvement in delinquency than to male involvement. Cernkovich and Giordano found that general blocked opportunity (based on education/occupation) was more strongly associated with the delinquency of females than was gender-based blocked opportunity (restrictions based on female gender).[4]

In a study more related to social control and psychodynamic theories, Datesman and Scarpitti also used their data to assess the etiological relevance of broken homes. A number of previous studies have reported evidence that deficient family relations are more relevant for female delinquency than male delinquency.[5] However, Datesman and Scarpitti showed this model to hold for status offenses only and for whites (but not blacks), for person and property offenses. In other words, they found the broken home hypothesis to be based primarily on the normative model of white family structure.[6]

STUDY PROCEDURES

Theoretical Perspectives

To determine whether any of the commonly used explanations for male delinquency may be used to explain female delinquency, we begin by examining each of the four theoretical perspectives for causal assumptions and the assumed characteristics of the offender population. Table 8-1 presents these assumptions.

Intake Material

The data for the study consisted of the intake material from case folders of 25 adolescent females, compiled during each youth's stay in the Reception Center of the correctional agency. Although the case files contained information collected during the two- to five-year commitments of the youths to the state agency, only the intake data were used in this study because a major intent of the intake process was to determine the causal factors in each youth's delinquent behavior. The intake data were collected during the 1960s, and the sample of 25 cases is part of a larger sample of more than 250 female delinquents participating in an experimental program in California, the Community Treatment Project (CTP).[7] Although the study population took part in the experimental program, the data used for the study reported here were based primarily on information collected routinely for all youths committed to the California Youth Authority.

Two documents provided most of the data used for this study: the parole agent's Initial Home Visit (IHV) report and the report of the Reception Center staff for consideration by the Youth Authority Board. The IHV report recorded information obtained directly from the youth's family. Data were obtained concerning the youth's behavior in the home; attitudes toward the family, school, and peers; developmental problems; school problems; employment; and social history of each parent and sibling, including criminality and mental illness. The Reception Center report is a ten- to twenty-page report summarizing all of the information collected on each youth during a four- to six-week assessment. This report included a review of the probation report, a listing of the prior record, and a social history developed by a social worker. Demographic data were

Marguerite Q. Warren

TABLE 8-1
Theoretical Perspectives Concerning Female Delinquency: Assumptions Regarding Delinquency Causation and Characteristics of Offender Population

Perspective	Assumptions	
	Regarding Delinquency Causation	Regarding Characteristics of Offenders
Social control theory[a]	1. Absence of internalized norms and rules governing behavior (inadequate socialization) 2. Absence of effective external controls in social groups or institutions 3. Belief that society's laws are irrelevant or unimportant 4. Weak or missing attachment to family 5. Weak or missing attachment to friends 6. Lack of commitment to school 7. Lack of commitment to career 8. Lack of involvement in conventional activities	1. Low aspirations 2. Membership in weakened family 3. Inadequate socialization 4. Few (if any) close, meaningful relationships 5. Lack of success in school or other such endeavors 6. Parental rejection 7. Acceptance of conventional values

Cultural deviance theory[b]	1. Delinquency is enactment of permitted or required roles and rules
	 2. Values at odds with the dominant culture (if evidence of no values, rate "no")
	 3. No evidence of remorse
	 4. Apparent comfort with delinquent behavior/values
	 5. Overriding need for group approval
		1. Conformity to a deviant subculture
		 2. Self-concept other than that of a norm violator
		 3. Lower-class status (if "yes":
		   a. No evidence of psychological problems
		   b. No evidence of defective socialization)
		 4. Middle-class status (if "yes":

Delinquency Causation in Female Offenders

Perspective	Assumptions	
	Regarding Delinquency Causation	Regarding Characteristics of Offenders
	6. Attachment to friends 7. Deviance learned through interaction with other deviants 8. Delinquency result of expression of focal concerns (trouble, toughness, smartness, excitement, fate, and autonomy) 9. Delinquency occurs with others (if only evidence is sexual activity, rate "no data")	Evidence of psychological instability) 5. Strong ties with the subculture and its values 6. Acceptance by peers 7. Reliance on peers as primary group, rather than family 8. Peers as major path to learning techniques and values of crime

Psychodynamic theory[c]	1. Breakthrough of impulses (i.e., weak ego/ superego controls)
	2. Adaptation to stress (symptoms of coping problems)
	3. Delinquency as neurotic behavior
	4. Compulsive need for punishment
	5. Substitute gratification
	6. Repressed traumatic event(s)
	7. Displaced hostility
	8. Private meaning for crime
	  a. Little interest in material gain
	  b. Motivation beyond peer approval
	9. Crime as a violation of own standards/ values
	10. Bonds pervaded with ambivalence
		1. Anxiety, guilt, inner conflict
		2. Negative life script; self-defeating goals
		3. At least partially prosocial goals *and* means
		4. Nondelinquent self-concept

Strain theory[d]	1. Middle-class values 2. Only socially induced pressures toward	1. Definition of delinquency same as societal definition

Perspective	Assumptions	
	Regarding Delinquency Causation	Regarding Characteristics of Offenders
	delinquency (no individual pathology) 3. Self-perception as having limited access to the means of obtaining conventional goals (leads to an individual feeling of strain) 4. Blocked opportunities due to a cultural imbalance (leads to state of alienation, anomie, and frustration) 5. Delinquency releases tensions generated by discrepancy between aspirations (high) and expectations (low) 6. Criminal actions motivated by the frustrated economic or status wants they gratify 7. Criminal behavior usually economic and rational	2. No evidence of individual pathology 3. Lower-class status 4. High aspirations 5. Crimes usually economic and rational 6. Concept of the source of failure as external; resultant sense of injustice

[a]Travis Hirschi, *Causes of Delinquency* (Berkeley: University of California Press, 1969).
[b]Edwin Sutherland, *Principles of Criminology* (Philadelphia: J. B. Lippincott, 1947); Walter Miller, "Lower-Class Culture as a Generating Milieu of Gang Delinquency," *Journal of Social Issues* 14 (1958):5–19.
[c]Gisela Konopka, *The Adolescent Girl in Conflict* (Englewood Cliffs, NJ: Prentice-Hall, 1966).
[d]Strain theory is sometimes referred to as *limited opportunity theory* and also as *anomie theory. See* Robert Merton, "Social Structure and Anomie," *American Sociological Review* 3 (1938):672–682.

presented and medical, educational, and employment histories were reviewed. Tested academic achievement, IQ, and educational problems were noted. Behavior during the Reception Center stay was described by the living-unit counselors, and a chaplain's report was included. If psychological and/or psychiatric evaluations were requested, reports of these assessments were available.

These two documents were used for testing the theoretical assumptions in all cases. In a few of the cases, treatment plans developed by a parole agent were also consulted in order to fill out the picture on a particular youth. The procedure involved the reading of the case materials by the author and a graduate student. After reading the intake material on a case, the two raters independently searched for evidence for each assumption of each theoretical perspective. Five ratings were possible for each assumption:

Yes–evidence for the assumption was present and clear.

No–evidence for the assumption was not present.

Somewhat—evidence was mixed. For example:

> Item: Person has faced parental rejection.
>
> Evidence: the youth has been openly rejected by the father, but not by the mother. (A "somewhat" rating could also mean some evidence for the assumption seemed present, but that the evidence was not strong or clear.)

Nonapplicable–for cultural deviance theory, different assumptions were made for lower-class and middle-class youth regarding individual pathology. If the youth being rated was from the lower class, the middle-class items were considered "nonapplicable."

No data—absence of relevant information in the case file.

During a preliminary period, the two raters discussed the meaning of each of the assumptions as well as the kinds of evidence that might be used appropriately in rating the assumptions. For the rating of the sample cases, high interrater agreement was obtained.[8] If the raters disagreed on a rating, the material was reviewed and a final rating was determined jointly.

In terms of demographic factors and offense characteristics, the study sample was fairly similar to the population from which it was drawn, the total CTP population. At the time of intake into the California Youth Authority, the youths resided in San Francisco, Sacramento, or Stockton and ranged in age from 13.0 to 18.1, with a mean of 15.6. The racial composition of the study sample was 48 percent white, 20 percent black, 16 percent Hispanic, and 16 percent other. The commitment offenses included drug and alcohol violations, burglary and petty theft, vehicle theft, prostitution, vagrancy, battery, assault with deadly weapon, and status offenses. Ten of the young women were committed for status offenses only. As is usual when commitment to a state agency occurs as a result of status offenses only, the records included large numbers of such behaviors as running away, being beyond control, and failing in several foster homes.

I-Level Subtypes

Because the study focused not only on the relevance of the causal theories for an overall female sample, but also on their relevance for subgroups of the sample, the twenty-five cases were selected to represent five types of female delinquents as classified according to a theory of ego development. This theory, the development of interpersonal maturity (I-level), has been used to describe numerous correctional populations.[9] It focuses on understanding the growth and development of human personality and has been used as a frame of reference for understanding delinquents.[10] The theory proposes that individuals develop through a series of stages (a milestone sequence) that can be defined. As individuals proceed along this growth continuum, their view of themselves and others, and of the interactions among individuals, increases in complexity. Few, if any, individuals (in either delinquent or nondelinquent populations) reach the theoretically defined last stage. Rather, they stop somewhere along the way.

The stage of an individual's growth can be identified and used to categorize each individual. Further, subdivisions can be made within each maturity level category according to the person's ways of dealing with his or her view of the world. In such a manner, nine categories of delinquent youths have been identified. These categories have been shown over the past two decades to be useful in understanding delinquency and in conducting research on offender populations.[11]

All youths (both male and female) in the CTP were classified during the intake process. As a result, the cases for this study could be chosen to represent the five most frequently occurring I-level subtypes. Descriptions of the five subgroups of young women are presented below in order of their frequency of occurrence in the total CTP population.[12]

1. Conflicted/Anxious. This subgroup of female delinquents is also called "neurotic." Along the ego developmental continuum, these young women have reached a stage of social maturity in which they

Delinquency Causation in Female Offenders

operate from an internalized value system that they use to judge themselves and others, to model themselves after persons they respect, to understand cause and effect relationships, to perceive needs and motives in others, to accept the concept of accountability for their own behaviors, and so on. But in addition, as the label *conflicted* suggests, individuals so classified have a good deal of internal wear-and-tear involving anxiety, guilt, a "bad me" self-image, "negative life script," distorted perceptions, and dysfunctional behavior. Delinquency has some private meaning; it does not represent simply a material gain or a response to cultural pressure. It may involve the acting out of a family problem, an identity crisis, or a long-standing internal conflict.

Within the *conflicted* category, one of two subtypes is identified as "anxious." Individuals in this group show a number of symptoms of emotional disturbance, such as chronic or intense depression or anxiety, or psychosomatic complaints. The tensions and fears of these girls usually result from conflicts produced by feelings of failure, inadequacy, or underlying guilt.

2. Conflicted/Acting-out. Individuals in this subgroup are similar to the group described above with respect to social maturity and other personality dynamics. However, rather than openly expressing the symptoms of anxiety, the "acting-out" subtype shows primarily the defense against anxiety. This subtype has little tolerance for conscious anxiety and often attempts to deny (to herself and others) feelings of inadequacy, rejection, or self-condemnation. Individuals so classified may do this by verbally attacking others, by using boisterous distractions, by playing a variety of "games," and so on. During the individual's initial period of incarceration, such defenses (i.e., the acting-out to prevent the feelings of anxiety) do not work very well; therefore, the person appears more agitated than is usually the case.

Both types of *conflicted* youths are typically from neurotic families in which at least one of the parents also carries a great deal of guilt and a "bad me" self-image. Family life is characterized by poor communication, "skeletons in the closets," and a feeling on everyone's part that other family members are not meeting (unspoken) expectations. Often, the delinquent youth seems to bearing the family burden or making a rescue attempt. The primary feeling that permeates the family is one of ambivalence: members

Marguerite Q. Warren

care about each other, but they also feel that they are not cherished and have somehow been hurt.

3. Power-oriented. These youths, also called "counteractive," have reached a stage of social maturity in which they underestimate the complexity of others; do not operate from an internalized value system, but instead seek external structure in terms of rules and formulas; and perceive the world and their role in it along a power dimension. In addition, as the terms *power-oriented* and *counteractive* suggest, they are often aggressively counteractive to power, attempting to undermine or circumvent the intent of authority figures. Typically, such persons do not wish to conform to standards set by anyone else and often attempt to take on a power role for themselves.

Persons in this subtype do not have close or trusting relationships with others. They usually try to create an image of emotional indifference, imperturbability, and invulnerability. Sometimes, especially under stress, they appear openly angry and threatening. They are often described by correctional staff who try to control them as resentful, persistently annoying due to crude efforts at being the center of attention, verbally and/or physically explosive, suspicious, and/or grandiose in their thinking.

Young women in this group seem to pride themselves on their ability to manipulate or outsmart others. Many of them come from homes with a cold, brutal, and rejecting father and a weak, helpless, and superficial mother. The common front of invincibility and toughness frequently turns out to be a cover-up (of which the young woman is rarely conscious) for long-standing and extremely intense fears of (and primitive dependence on) the abusive parent. The girl's protective attachments to her family are missing; she is contemptuous of her mother and hates and fears the father.

The extent of her distrust of others means that peer attachments are also not available. Additionally, her manipulativeness and unwillingness to conform lead authority figures at school and in youth agencies to reject her. And she has no belief system that disallows delinquency. The *power-oriented* girl defines herself as cynical, "cool," smooth, delinquent, powerful, invulnerable—a definition that is not inconsistent with offense behavior.

4. Passive Conformist. Individuals classified in this category have reached the same stage of social maturity as that described for the *power-oriented* group. However, they differ in their orientation toward the power dimension. The *passive conformist* youth views others as powerful and herself as weak. As the label suggests, individuals so classified are dominated by the need for social approval, responding with almost automatic compliance to whoever they think has the power at the moment; they overestimate the power and adequacy of others, seeing themselves as helpless and childlike. They consider themselves to be lacking in social know-how and usually expect to be rejected by others, no matter how hard they try to please. Although such persons long to be accepted by their peer group, they usually rate no more than fringe membership.

The family situation for *passive conformist* girls seems to present a picture of instability and inconsistency. There appears to be some concern for the youth by a parent; however, the parent is unable to provide a stable structure for growth. In many cases, there is also a rejecting parent, whose approval the youth cannot win. Throughout childhood, the youth has not seen love and strength combined in either parent.

Although a girl of this type presents herself as sincere, cooperative, and well intentioned, she also admits that she has no capacity to control herself or her environment. She feels that she is dependent on the rules of others for keeping out of trouble. She wants to be a "good person" and hopes that others will be helpful and understanding. With this self-definition, it is clearly a matter of chance whether the "helpful" others will encourage delinquency or law-abiding behavior.

5. Cultural Conformist. The young woman classified in this category has reached a stage of social maturity similar to that of the *power-oriented* and *passive conformist* youths. However, her reaction style differs in some important ways. Although she deals with her perception of the external power structure in a conforming way, she is more selective in her choice of a reference group than is the *passive conformist*. As a *cultural conformist*, she does not conform indiscriminately to whoever appears to have the power at the moment; instead, she conforms only to those individuals and groups that look, sound, and behave in familiar ways—usually the delinquent peer group. They appear to perceive adults as irrelevant to their lives, although they may align themselves with other siblings as well as delinquent peers. They appear tough rather than weak and seem comfortable with a delinquent label.

The family structure for this type of youth is often unstable, the mother having her hands full coping with her own emotional needs as well as trying to provide financially for her children. The children may have had different fathers; at any rate, typically a series of father-figures have come through the home. Often, one or both of the parents, as well as the siblings, have criminal records.

THESE FIVE SUBTYPES do not make up equal proportions of female delinquent populations. However, for purposes of this study, five of each group were chosen at random from the pool of cases in each subtype. This procedure provided an opportunity to determine whether any of the causal theories appeared to hold for subgroups of the offender population, even though they might not hold well for the total sample. To prevent any bias due to preconceived ideas about the relationship between the theories and the classification categories, the graduate student chosen to make the second ratings was not familiarized with the maturity level theory and subtype categories.

FINDINGS

As mentioned earlier, two main questions were asked of the data: (1) do the assumptions regarding crime causation and characteristics of delinquents hold better for some causal theories than others; and (2) do the assumptions for a particular theory hold better for some subtypes of youths than for others. The findings, presented below, follow this separation.

Do Assumptions Regarding Crime Causation and Offender Characteristics Hold Better for Some Causal Theories Than Others?

Using all 25 sample cases in the analysis, the assumptions of *social control theory* held up best. In the individual case with the poorest fit between case material and assumptions of social control theory, 30 percent of the assumptions were supported. In the best fit case, 97 percent of the assumptions held. The mean assumption-support rating for the 25 cases was 67.2 percent for social control theory.

Across all 25 cases, the specific social control assumptions holding for the largest proportion were: (1) there is an absence of ef-

Delinquency Causation in Female Offenders

fective external controls in social groups or institutions (23 cases); (2) the individual has not met with success in school or other such endeavors (21 cases); (3) the individual comes from a weakened family (19 cases); and (4) involvement in conventional activities is missing (18 cases).

In rating the total cases on applicability of *cultural deviance theory*, a mean of 42.7 percent of the assumptions held, with a range of 6 percent to 94 percent on individual cases. The assumptions holding for the largest proportion of the 25 cases were: (1) the individual is from the lower class (18 cases); (2) the individual learned deviance through interaction with other deviants (13 cases); (3) delinquency always occurs with others (13 cases); and (4) the individual's self-perception is not that of a norm violator (13 cases).

Using the total cases for rating the assumptions of *psychodynamic theory*, a mean of 37.7 percent of the assumptions held, with a range of 6 percent to 94 percent on individual cases. The assumptions holding for the largest proportion of the 25 cases were: (1) the individual shows little interest in material gain from delinquency (18 cases); (2) cause of delinquency is beyond just peer approval (14 cases); (3) crime is caused by breakthrough of impulses (i.e., weak ego or superego controls) (12 cases); and (4) the individual sees herself as basically nondelinquent (11 cases).

For total cases, *strain theory* assumptions held up most poorly of the four perspectives. A mean of only 20 percent of the assumptions held, with a range of 0 percent to 38 percent for individual cases. Those assumptions holding for the largest proportion of the 25 cases were: (1) the individual is from the lower class (18 cases); (2) definition of delinquency is the same as societal definition (10 cases); (3) the individual exhibits no individual pathology (8 cases); and (4) only socially induced pressures toward delinquency exist (8 cases).

Therefore, the assumptions regarding crime causation and characteristics of delinquents *do* hold better for some causal theories than others for female delinquents generally. The assumptions of social control theory appear to be more generally applicable across cases; two-thirds of the assumptions hold for the average case, and the top four hold for 18 or more of the 25 cases. Strain theory shows the poorest fit of its assumptions to the case material, with only one-fifth of its assumptions holding for the avarage case. Only the assumption that the individual is from the lower class held up for more than 10 of the 25 cases. Cultural deviance and psychodynamic theories showed somewhat similar patterns, with about 40 percent of their assumptions holding for the average case.

Do Assumptions for a Particular Theory Hold Better for Some Types of Female Delinquents Than for Others?

Two procedures were used to answer this question. The first involved simply identifying the causal theory receiving the highest rating (i.e., the theory for which the highest proportion of assumptions held) for each of the five subjects in each of the five subtypes. For three of the subtypes, *conflicted/anxious*, *power-oriented*, and *passive conformist*, the pattern was completely clear. All five individuals classified as *conflicted/anxious* showed their highest ratings in psychodynamic theory. All five classified as *power-oriented* showed their highest ratings on social control theory. Similarly, those classified as *passive conformist* had their highest ratings on social control theory. The rankings of the theories for proportions of assumptions met for each subject in each subtype are shown in Table 8-2.

For the other two subtypes, *cultural conformist* and *conflicted/acting-out*, the patterns were somewhat less clear. four of the five youths classified as *cultural conformist* showed their highest ratings on cultural deviance theory, with one individual showing a slightly higher rating on social control theory than on cultural deviance theory. The patterns for those individuals classified as *conflicted/acting-out* were mixed, with two cases showing highest ratings on psychodynamic theory. The other three cases in this category again showed highest ratings for social control theory. For one of the latter three cases, the psychodynamic theory received the second highest rating, but the cultural deviance theory received the second highest rating in the other two cases.

Strain theory assumptions did not receive highest ratings for any subtype nor for any individual delinquent; for only one individual did the theory receive the second highest rating.

The second procedure used to assess the appropriateness of the various theoretical assumptions involved developing for each of the subtypes of youths a numerical indicator of the extent to which the assumptions of each theory held. The numerical indicator was a ratio of the total "fit" score to the total possible score. For the com-

Delinquency Causation in Female Offenders

TABLE 8-2
Rankings of Theories According to Proportion of Assumptions-met for Each Individual within Five Subtypes

Delinquents in Each Subtype	Ranking of Theories			
	Social Control	Cultural Deviance	Psychodynamic	Strain
Conflicted/anxious				
Case A	3.0	2.0	1.0(78%)[a]	4.0
B	2.0	4.0	1.0(72%)	3.0
C	2.0	3.0	1.0(66%)	4.0
D	2.0	4.0	1.0(66%)	3.0
E	3.0	2.0	1.0(62%)	4.0
Conflicted/acting-out				
Case F	2.0	4.0	1.0(94%)	3.0
G	2.0	4.0	1.0(81%)	3.0
H	1.0(77%)	4.0	2.0	3.0
I	1.0(77%)	2.0	3.5	3.5
J	1.0(63%)	2.0	3.0	4.0
Power-oriented				
Case K	1.0(97%)	3.0	2.0	4.0
L	1.0(93%)	3.0	2.0	4.0
M	1.0(93%)	2.0	3.0	4.0
N	1.0(83%)	2.0	4.0	3.0
O	1.0(60%)	2.0	4.0	3.0
Passive conformist				
Case P	1.0(86%)	4.0	2.0	3.0
Q	1.0(80%)	2.0	4.0	3.0
R	1.0(73%)	2.0	4.0	3.0
S	1.0(73%)	3.5	2.0	3.5
T	1.0(70%)	2.0	4.0	3.0
Cultural conformist				
Case U	2.0	1.0(94%)	4.0	3.0
V	3.0	1.0(89%)	4.0	2.0
W	2.0	1.0(89%)	3.0	3.0
X	2.0	1.0(75%)	3.0	4.0
Y	1.0(77%)	2.0	4.0	3.0

[a]Proportion of assumptions-met indicated for each first-rank theory.

bined five members of each subtype, the "fit" score allowed one point for each assumption met and a half point for each assumption partially met. For example, for a perfect "fit" score to occur for social control theory, all fifteen assumptions of the theory (see Table 8-1) would have to be met by all five members of the subtype. The ratios of "fit" scores to possible scores are shown in Table 8-3.

Marguerite Q. Warren

TABLE 8-3
Differential Applicability of Four Causal Theories
to Five Subtypes of Female Delinquents
Ratio of Theoretical Assumptions-met to
Total Assumptions Tested

Offender Subtypes	Theories			
	Social Control	Cultural Deviance	Psychodynamic	Strain
Conflicted/anxious	.55	.27	.78	.22
Conflicted/acting-out	.69	.33	.59	.16
Power-oriented	.91	.38	.25	.13
Passive conformist	.89	.45	.26	.26
Cultural conformist	.73	.93	.14	.30

As suggested in the analysis of the first question, social control theory showed a generally high level of assumptions-met scores across the five subtypes and the highest scores for three subtypes: *conflicted/acting-out*, *power-oriented*, and *passive conformist*. Assumptions-met scores were generally low for cultural deviance theory except for the *cultural conformist* subtype, for which the score was very high. For psychodynamic theory, only the score for the *conflicted/anxious* subtype was high, with that of the *conflicted/acting-out* group moderate, and other scores low. As expected from previous analyses, assumptions-met for strain theory were low for all subtypes.

Therefore, there is considerable evidence that the causal assumptions of particular theories hold better for some types of female delinquents than for other types. For both cultural deviance and psychodynamic theories, a subtype of female delinquents can be identified for which a large proportion of assumptions hold. For social control theory, two subtypes fit especially well. For strain theory alone, no matching subtype of female delinquents is identified.

DISCUSSION

This study is best seen as pilot work because of the small number of subjects involved. Its results can be thought of as hypothesis-developing rather than hypothesis-testing. In this context, a number

Delinquency Causation in Female Offenders

of questions can be raised about the assumptions of the theoretical perspectives and about delinquent females.

Social Control Theory

Beginning with the theories of crime causation, we can ask why social control theory appears to be so generally applicable across subtypes of youths. One possibility is that the theory is social-psychological in nature; that is, it combines environmental and personal dimensions in either one area or the other. According to social control theory, an individual may become delinquent because the social environment does not provide effective external controls and/or because the individual has been inadequately socialized. These alternatives permit the theory to account for a larger range of patterns of juvenile behavior.

Social control theory assumptions best fit the case material for the subtypes *power-oriented* (12 percent of the total CTP female population) and *passive conformist* (7 percent). While this finding makes complete sense in terms of the characteristics of the *passive conformist* subtype, it seems—in at least one respect—at odds with the description of the *power-oriented* subtype. Because this type of individual does not have a belief system that disallows delinquency (*see* pages 188–192), the social control assumption that the person accepts conventional values appears a contradiction. In fact, it is this assumption, rated as not-met in four of the five young women classified as *power-oriented*, that keeps the relationship between theory and subtype from being even closer to unity.

Aside from this one assumption, however, there is indeed an excellent fit between social control theory assumptions and the characteristics of the *passive conformist* and *power-oriented* subtypes. An interesting aspect of this finding is that these two categories are found at the lower of the two social maturity levels represented by the five subtypes. At this lower maturity level, individuals have not yet internalized a set of behavioral standards; instead, they make decisions as to how to behave through immediate interactions with the world around them. This means, of course, that they are much more vulnerable to either peer pressures toward delinquency or an absence of external controls than those who have developed internal standards.

When we ask where social control theory works least well, the answer seems to be found in the *conflicted/anxious* category. This subtype of youths is the only one to have a greater number of assumptions-not-met than assumptions-met by social control theory. These individuals are well socialized, using internalized standards to evaluate their own behavior and that of others. Because these internalized standards tend to be prosocial, the individual is typically loaded with guilt and anxiety, judges herself harshly, and sometimes seems to seek punishment as a relief for these feelings. This pattern does not fit the assumptions of social control theory as well as those of the less complex subtypes. Because the *conflicted/anxious* category includes the largest proportion of any of the categories in the total CTP study population (45 percent), we would not predict that, based on this small sample, social control theory will not offer the best explanation of delinquency in a large number of female cases.

Cultural Deviance Theory

Cultural deviance theory often does not fit well with the subtype characteristics; however, when it does fit, it works very well indeed. The assumptions of the theory seem to characterize only the *cultural conformist* subtype. The assumptions that fit particularly well are lower-class patterns, with a focus on the peer group as both the primary source of gratification and status and the path to learning techniques of delinquency. The expression of focal concerns of the lower class as a path into delinquency and the absence of individual pathology also characterize the *cultural conformist* subtype.

Cultural deviance assumptions fit least well with the *conflicted* subtypes. However, all of the subtypes except *cultural conformist* have a far greater number of assumptions-not-met than assumptions-met. The selection of equal numbers of each subtype for study tends to give a distorted picture of the number of female delinquents classified as *cultural conformist*. Of the five subtypes included in the study, this subtype represents the smallest proportion of the CTP female population, only 3 percent. Thus, while the hypothesis concerning the appropriateness of cultural deviance theory for the *cultural conformist* category seems a powerful one, we will not expect to find our theoretical explanation applying to very many cases.

One can speculate as to why so few females enter into delinquent activities through the *cultural conformist* path. This subtype represents a larger portion of the male delinquent population. Cultural deviance theory places great emphasis on peers as the reference group for youths. Morris found that delinquent behavior is relatively more accepted by peers for males than for females, and that female delinquency is generally regarded more critically than male delinquency by delinquents and nondelinquents of both sexes.[13] Thus, disapproval of their reference figures may reduce the delinquency of *conformist* girls.

Psychodynamic Theory

It is not surprising to find that psychodynamic theory fits best with *conflicted/anxious* youths. After all, the type of psychodynamic theory called "psychoanalysis" has been used to explain "neurotics" at least since Freud. What is perhaps more surprising is that the psychodynamic assumptions do not hold as well for the *conflicted/acting-out* subtype. Three of the individuals in this subgroup had higher assumptions-met scores for social control theory than for psychodynamic theory. However, the lack of fit with psychodynamic theory should not be exaggerated; in fact, the five cases in this category produce together more assumptions-met than not-met, in contrast to the two *conformist* subtypes and the *power-oriented* group. For individuals in these last three subtypes, very few assumptions of the psychodynamic perspective were met.

As described earlier, although anxiety, guilt, and inner conflict are present in individuals of the *conflicted/acting-out* subtype, these feelings are not as visible as they are in persons classified as *conflicted/anxious*. An individual of the *acting-out* subtype suppresses these symptoms as much as possible, and exhibits them only in the form of defenses against anxiety. When the defensive structure is working relatively well, the person may be saying, "Nervous? Who, me?" or "Guilt? Never heard of it." Many clinical papers have been written on the "neurotic acting-out" individual. There are suggestions that such individuals may be frequently mislabeled as "psychopathic."[14]

In our study, suppression of the neurotic symptoms by those categorized in the *conflicted/acting-out* subtype meant that fewer of the psychodynamic items appeared to hold than in the case of the *conflicted/anxious* subtype. To the extent that our hypothesis holds concerning the appropriateness of psychodynamic theory for both the *conflicted* subtypes, we will expect to find a large number of

Marguerite Q. Warren

female delinquents for whom this theory will hold. The *conflicted/ anxious* subtype includes a large proportion of the population, as indicated above, and the proportion of the female delinquent population falling into the *conflicted/acting-out* subtype is also relatively large (29 percent).

Strain Theory

Why does strain or opportunity theory appear to fit the case material so poorly? The primary reason seems to be that the youths in this sample (and in the larger population from which it comes) did not commit economic and rational crimes. Perceptions of blocked opportunities and subsequent frustration were not found in the cases. Only one of the twenty-five cases was rated as having high aspirations, an important assumption of strain theory. It is conceivable that a larger sample of the female delinquent population would produce some cases for which the strain assumptions would hold. Very few prostitution activities were found in this sample, and prostitution represents the kind of activity in which we might expect to find strain assumptions operating. It is also possible that strain assumptions might be met more often in a population of adult female offenders.

IN INTERPRETING THE FINDINGS of the study, it is important to remember that the sample included only young women who were sent to a state correctional agency, rather than a broader population of all young women who commit delinquent acts. It is interesting to speculate on whether the same patterns would occur in the broader group. It is possible, for example, that weak parental bonds, an important assumption of social control theory, are more characteristic of youths committed by the courts than they are of delinquents generally. The "neurotic" patterns of the *conflicted/anxious* subtype might characterize fewer individuals in the broader group; therefore, the psychodynamic theory might apply less often. Patterns of minor shoplifting that rarely lead to a state correctional system might characterize a large number of the broader delinquent group, possibly making strain theory more applicable. Should these findings occur, however, they would not alter the major theme of this chapter: that theories may be differentially applicable to subgroups of the delinquent population. However, the proportions of the various subtypes in the broader population might vary considerably from those of the court-committed population, thus

Delinquency Causation in Female Offenders

changing the proportions to which the theories most appropriately apply.

In summary, when we assess the utility of the various crime causal theories for understanding female delinquency, it seems clear that—of the four perspectives studied—social control theory receives most support for the total sample of female delinquents. However, the delinquent behavior of two of five subtypes of the sample seems better interpreted by two other theoretical perspectives. In the case of young women classified as *cultural conformist*, cultural deviance theory appears more satisfactory than social control theory. This is of considerable importance theoretically. However, because this subtype includes such a low proportion of the CTP female delinquent population and because the proportion of social control assumptions met by the individuals classified as *cultural conformist* is still high, the implications of including this subgroup in an overall control theory explanation of female delinquency are not seriously negative.

A serious distortion is introduced for only the subtype *conflicted/anxious*, by utilizing social control theory to explain female delinquency in an across-the-board fashion. Not only does psychodynamic theory fit this subtype much better than social control theory, but also the distortion is compounded by the fact that this subtype is the most frequently occurring of the five subgroups, representing almost half of the CTP female population. Thus, while a large portion of female offenders meet the assumptions of social control theory well or very well, almost half of the population is better explained by the psychodynamic theory.

The study thus offers sufficient support for the idea of differential applicability of crime causal theories so that future research along these lines is encouraged. Rather than attempting to identify the one "correct" theory to explain female crime while falsifying the others, future research might better aim to ascertain which theoretical perspective is best suited to explain which patterns of female crime.

NOTES

1. *See*, for example, Albert Bandura, *Social Learning Theory* (Englewood Cliffs, NJ: Prentice-Hall, 1977).

2. Albert Cohen, *Delinquent Boys* (Glencoe, IL: Free Press, 1955); Richard Cloward and Lloyd Ohlin, *Delinquency and Opportunity: A Theory to Delinquent Gangs* (Glencoe, IL: Free Press, 1960).

Marguerite Q. Warren

3. John Monahan and S. Splane, "Psychological Approaches to Criminal Behavior," in *Criminology Review Yearbook*, ed. E. Bittner and S. L. Messinger, vol. 2 (Beverly Hills: Sage Publications, 1980).

4. Susan Datesman, F. R. Scarpitti, and R. M. Stephenson, "Female Delinquency: An Application of Self and Opportunity Theory," *Journal of Research in Crime and Delinquency* (July 1975):107–123; S. A. Cernkovich and Peggy Giordano, "Delinquency, Opportunity, and Gender," *Criminology* 70(1979):145–151.

5. For example, California Youth Authority, *A Comparison of Admission Characteristics of Youth Authority Wards, 1970–1976* (Sacramento, CA, 1977).

6. Susan Datesman and F. R. Scarpitti, "Female Delinquency and Broken Homes: A Reassessment," *Criminology* 13 (1975):33–55.

7. For a description of the Community Treatment Project, *see* Ted Palmer, "California's Community Treatment Program for Delinquent Adolescents," *Journal of Research in Crime and Delinquency* 8 (1971):74–92. The project involved a random assignment of youths to community based and institutional treatment. The young women in the study sample include individuals from both assignments.

8. Reliability figures were in the eighties and nineties for the various assumptions.

9. M. Q. Warren, "The Impossible Child, the Difficult Child, and Other Assorted Delinquents: Etiology, Characteristics and Incidence," *Canadian Psychiatric Association Journal* 23 (1978):41–61.

10. I-level theory is not a crime causal theory except to the extent that the theory proposes that the meaning of delinquent behavior varies according to developmental state (I-level) and preferred ways of interacting with the world (subtype). For descriptions of the theory, *see* Clyde Sullivan, M. Q. Grant, and J. D. Grant, "The Development of Interpersonal Maturity: Applications to Delinquency," *Psychiatry* 20 (1957):373–395; and M. Q. Warren, "Intervention with Juvenile Delinquents," in *Pursuing Justice for the Child*, ed. M. Rosenheim (Chicago: University of Chicago Press, 1976).

11. *See*, for example, M. Q. Warren, "Correctional Treatment and Coercion: The Differential Effectiveness Perspective," *Criminal Justice and Behavior* 4 (1978):355–376; M. Q. Warren and M. J. Hindelang, "Differential Explanations of Offender Behavior," in *Psychology of Crime and Criminal Justice*, ed. H. Toch (New York: Holt, Rinehart and Winston, 1978); T. N. Ferdinand, "Female Delinquency and Warren's Typology of Personality Patterns: An Evaluation," *social Work Research and Abstracts* (1978):32–41; Phillip Harris, "The Interpersonal Maturity of Delinquents and Nondelinquents" (Ph.D. diss., State University of New York, Albany, 1979); and Kathleen Heide, "Classification of Offenders Ordered to Make Restitution by Interpersonal Maturity Level and by Specific Personality Characteristics" (Ph.D. diss., State University of New York, Albany, 1981).

12. M. Q. Warren, "The Female Offender," in *Psychology of Crime and Criminal Justice*.

13. Ruth Morris, "Attitudes Toward Delinquency by Delinquents, Nondelinquents, and Their Friends," *British Journal of Criminology* 5 (1965):249–265.

14. M. Hammer and M. B. Ross, "Psychological Needs of Imprisoned Adult Females with High and Low Conscience Development," *Corrective and Social Psychiatry* 23 (1977):73–78.

PART III

Women
as
Defendants and Prisoners

9

Are Females Treated Differently?

A Review of the Theories and Evidence on Sentencing and Parole Decisions

NICOLETTE PARISI

The importance of "being female" in the postadjudication phase of the criminal justice system is the subject of some debate.[1] The controversy centers around what role sex plays in sentencing and parole decisions. Following a brief discussion of discrimination and disparity, the chapter proceeds to outline the major perspectives on, and explanations for, the presumed differences (or lack of differences) in dispositions of males versus females. Key studies are then reviewed to explore the existence and direction of disparity by sex. The chapter concludes by arguing that sex *should* be considered in sentencing decisions.

DISCRIMINATION AND DISPARITY

One of the major controversies in sentencing concerns differential treatment of offenders. Although the term *discrimination* has developed negative connotations, it merely means, "differentiation." If justifiable on legally relevant criteria, differentiation is permissible in sentencing and parole decisions. However, *disparity* refers to unwarranted differences in dispositions among groups with similar characteristics. If the differences are linked to such factors as race, religion, or class, then *disparity* is the appropriate term to describe the unjustifiable variation. Of course, the differences could be either advantageous or disadvantageous for those being sentenced.

Prior to analysis of sentencing and parole decisions in terms of disparity based on the sex of the offender, two caveats should be noted. First, decisions made at prior points in the criminal justice system will determine the character of the sentenced population. Penalties that are disparate (based on unjustifiable factors) may stem from bias in the screening process by victims, police, and prosecutors. Judges may be only partly responsible. Second, unjustifiable differences often disappear when legally relevant factors are considered. In general, females may be charged with, and convicted of, less serious offenses than males and may be less likely to have prior criminal records. Even in the same category of offense, females may be less likely thn males to commit serious types of crimes. For example, within the larceny category, shoplifting and cargo heists are primarily female and male behaviors, repsectively. These two considerations—bias in screening and the level of seriousness of female crime—should be kept in mind throughout the chapter.

MAJOR PERSPECTIVES ON THE IMPACT OF SEX

There are three perspectives or models that purport to reflect the impact of sex on sentencing and parole decisions. According to the "preferential" perspective, females receive more advantageous treatment than males. The second perspective, the "punitive" model, refers to disadvantageous dispositions for females at sentencing and parole. The third, or "equal" treatment, perspective claims that males and females receive similar treatment in similar cases. The explanations behind these three perspectives are described in more detail in the following section.

Are Females Treated Differently?

Preferential Treatment

The preferential[2] (or paternalistic[3]) perspective postulates that female offenders are treated more leniently than males. According to this view, females are more likely than males to receive probation, to receive shorter sentences, to serve shorter terms, and to complete probation or parole without revocation. Simon, Steffensmeier, and Crites have explained this leniency in terms of several theories about the nature of female crime, attitudes of the judiciary, and attitudes of parole officials.

The most popular interpretation of preferential treatment attributes it to "chivalry." Male judges and prosecutors treat females more leniently, it is argued, because our society has taught them to approach females in a fatherly, protective manner and to assume that females have an inherently submissive, domestic nature.

A second explanation for preferential treatment, not necessarily independent from that of chivalry, is labeled "naiveté." Simon, for example, has pointed out that judges are thought to compare "women defendants with other women they know well—namely their mothers and wives, whom they could not imagine behaving in the manner attributed to the defendant."[4] As a result, judges sentence females leniently. A variation of the naiveté theme has been noted by Steffensmeier, who argues that naiveté comes into play when females are perceived to be "less capable than men of committing criminal acts."[5] This view may be expanded to the perception that *female* offenders are generally not *dangerous* offenders.[6] Naiveté is a particularly interesting explanation of preferential treatment because it appears to contradict another assumption about the sentencing of females: some argue that by the sentencing stage, minor female offenders have been "chivalrously" filtered out to a greater degree than minor male offenders, so that only the most serious female offenders remain.[7] Suppositions about judicial naiveté appear to be inconsistent with the implications of the chivalry argument.

"Practicality" has also been identified as a rationale behind preferential treatment. This explanation focuses on the fact that females are typically responsible for their children.[8] If the mother is incarcerated, care of the children becomes a major issue; this consideration, it is claimed, results in more lenient dispositions of females with children.

Another assumption that may lead to the preferential perspective is the belief that females are more "susceptible to rehabilitation."[9] Steffensmeier found this view to be a major explanation for sex-based "differential sentencing" and ironically instrumental in affirming different legislative sentencing structures for males and females. Sentencing schemes that provide special "rehabilitative" terms for females are cited in support of the *punitive* perspective as well (as we shall see in the next section). But it has also been argued that a consequence of the theory that females are more likely to be rehabilitated than males may be more lenient sentences for females.

Although not distinct from the naiveté position, another theory associated with the preferential perspective on the treatment of females focuses on the character of female crime.[10] Female crime is often purported to differ in kind as well as quantity from male crime (see *Chapter 5*). The number and sex of accomplices, type of weapons used, relationship between offender and victim, role in the offense, degree of provocation, and other incident characteristics are theoretically consistent with the preferential model of sentencing females. However, to the extent that these traditional assumptions about female crime are accurate, females are not receiving preferential (disparate) treatment, but justifiably differential (equal) treatment.

Finally, an argument can be made that judges treat females more leniently because they assume that opportunities for rehabilitative programs are limited in female institutions.[11] The small numbers of female prisoners in each state apparently prevent a wide range of rehabilitative programs from seeming cost-effective or necessary. To the degree that this reason lies behind the preferential perspective, it is a self-fulfilling prophecy: there are not enough females for diversified programs because judges do not send females to correctional facilities in great numbers.[12]

A number of explanations, then, have been proposed to support the view that females are treated preferentially by the courts. These include chivalry, judicial naiveté, practical considerations relating to child care, females' supposedly greater potential for rehabilitation, the nature of female crime, and the rehabilitative potential of female prisons. The empirical evidence for the preferential perspective is evaluated later in this chapter.

Punitive Treatment

Differences in dispositional decisions can also be in a negative direc-

Are Females Treated Differently?

tion. The punitive (disadvantaged or prejudicial)[13] perspective holds that females are treated more severely than males in like cases. That is, female offenders are more likely than males to be incarcerated, to receive and serve longer sentences, and to have their probation or parole revoked.

This negative response to female offenders can be attributed to two main explanations. Some argue that females are treated punitively because the female criminal is perceived to be "unladylike"; she does not, in other words, conform to sex-role expectations.[14] Judges are presumably more likely to "throw the book" at such women, treating them more harshly because they have not conformed to male expectations of what females should be.[15] Chesney-Lind has observed that when "a woman commits 'male' crimes . . . the advantage of being female deteriorates rapidly, and, in some cases, the courts are responding more harshly to female than male behaviors."[16] This attitude implies that females who commit such violent offenses as aggravated assault receive either more severe sentences than males in like cases or less preferential treatment than that accorded females convicted of other types of crimes.

It can also be argued that punitiveness is a consequence of "misguided attempts to 'protect' females."[17] Protection is considered necessary because females are not as strong as males. Does protection lead to more severe dispositions for females than males? Benevolent attitudes did form the rationales for sentencing structures providing separate (and generally, more severe) sentencing formulas for females. Ironically, then, at times benevolent objectives have been pursued by punitive means.[18]

In sum, several explanations have been offered in support of the punitive perspective. Female offenders may elicit punitive responses because they fail to conform to sex-role expectations. Or, perhaps, female criminals are treated more punitively than males out of misguided benevolence.

Equal Treatment

Unlike the previous two perspectives, the equality model holds that there are no sex-related differences between males and females at sentencing.[19] Data that appear initially to support either of the differential (and disparate) positions may actually reflect problems in measurement. Moreover, rather than sex of the offender affecting the disposition, other (often legitimate) factors may explain the dif-

Nicolette Parisi

ferential sentencing patterns. *Justifiable* differential decisions are neither preferential nor punitive.

The equal treatment perspective in a sense has been institutionalized by recent sentencing reforms—presumptive sentences, sentencing and parole guidelines, and mandatory sentences. Because these reforms aim at reducing or eliminating discretion, they eradicate whatever impact (positive or negative) sex of the offender may have had on sentencing.[20] However, as we argue more fully in the conclusion, these reforms that are intended to reduce disparity may not have the desired effect (or *should* not have the desired effect) in regard to the male/female issue. Reduction or elimination of discretion may sometimes restrict or prevent the decision maker from considering relevant factors (such as role in the offense or amount of property taken) as well as legally irrelevant factors (such as dependent children). Efforts to enhance equality, them, may actually formalize or compound disparity to the detriment of female offenders.

EVIDENCE ON THE EFFECT OF SEX IN SENTENCING

Data on the impact of sex in sentencing decisions can be presented through analysis of three types of data: sentencing, prison, and parole data sets. Comparisons of findings from studies based on these types of data should be made cautiously, due to differences in research designs, definitions of terms, agency policies and practices, and so on. Most important, certain populations of offenders have inherent biases; incarceration and parole populations typically contain more offenders with convictions for very serious offenses and/or prior criminal records than do sentencing populations. Nevertheless, we will try to extract certain themes from the data: Are females treated differently than males? If so, what is the direction of that differential treatment, and is the differentiation justifiable or unjustifiable?

Data on Differential Dispositions

With one exception,[21] general sentencing studies and studies focusing on female offenders have found that females are more likely than males to receive probation or suspended sentences. Using different jurisdictions and time periods, Green, Nagel and Weitzman, Sutton, Pope, and Simon and Sharma all found that female offenders were more likely to receive probation than males.[22] But, as mentioned above, the conclusion that females receive preferential (disparate) treatment needs to be carefully investigated in terms of offense, prior record, and other relevant criteria.

Green's study of sentencing practices in Philadelphia in the mid-1950s collected information on offense, prior record, and sex. However, Green presented data on prior record only in terms of "no prior felony conviction" and on type of offense only in terms of felony/misdemeanor. For both broad categories of offenses, Green reported no differences in type or length of sentence for males or females who had *no prior convictions for a felony.*[23] Green's Philadelphia data seem to support the equality model. It should be recognized, however, that Green did not examine many other categories of offenders: those with prior records or those with different types of criminal behavior (for example, property versus personal offenses).[24] Thus, generalizations based on this study supporting the equality model are dubious.

Another classic study analyzing the impact of sex on sentencing is the Nagel and Weitzman research. Their data were based on a nationwide 1962 survey of indigent defendants. Nagel and Weitzman used the data to assess the direction of differential treatment of females in felonious assault and grand larceny cases. However, neither prior record of the offender nor characteristics of the offense (other than the two broad categories) were controlled. On both type of sentence (probation) and length of sentence (less than one year), females, when compared with males, seemed to have received preferential treatment.[25] Nagel and Weitzman, comparing the proportion of females receiving probation for assault and for grand larceny (44 and 64 percent, respectively) with that of males (36 and 43 percent, respectively), concluded that more lenient treatment was awarded to females in grand larceny cases. They also concluded that females convicted of "more manly" crimes (that is, assaults) were more likely to receive sentences equal to those of males in similar cases. However, it should be noted that *both* males and females were less likely to be confined for grand larceny. The kinds of behaviors subsumed under grand larceny are varied, and the significant difference in dispositions for males and females may be due to differences in the type of crime. This widely published and reviewed study is problematic in many ways,[26] and yet it is often used to support the overall conclusion that judges are paternalistic.[27] In reality, as Hagen noted, the Nagel and Weitzman data seem to justify the conclusion that sex "plays a negligible role in the sentencing decision."[28]

In 1966, Baab and Furgeson collected information on felony sentencing practices from a sample of Texas counties.[29] Despite opinion to the contrary,[30] their study investigated the impact of sex (as well as other variables) on disposition *after all other variables had been taken into account.* This study of felony sentencing included thirteen categories of offenses and a number of measures of prior record. Disposition was measured along an interval "scale of increasingly severe dispositions, ranging from pecuniary fine to death." The data showed that "being female" resulted in "chivalrous" treatment—less severe sentences in like cases. It should be noted that this study was conducted in felony courts; thus, its findings should not be generalized to less serious offenses.

Chiricos, Waldo, and Jackson conducted a study of the Florida sentencing procedure that permitted judges to place felong offenders on probation while withholding adjudication.[31] Withholding adjudication is advantageous to the defendant because the person who completes probation satisfactorily will have no criminal conviction. The researchers found no relationship between sex of the offender and the withholding of adjudication. They had expected to find that females received preferential treatment (were more likely to have adjudication withheld) in comparison to males. To explain the apparent lack of differential treatment of the sexes, Chiricos, Waldo, and Jackson surmised that preferential treatment probably still occurred because the females who reached the disposition stage were likely to be higher risks than males. Less serious female offenders, they assumed, had been screened out at a greater rate than males. Thus, preferential handling apparently still existed, and unmeasured factors probably made the females " 'greater risk' cases than the males" at the sentencing stage.[32]

Pope's study of felony sentencing in twelve California counties between 1969 and 1971 is often cited as one of the strongest studies of the impact of sex on sentencing.[33] Controlling for prior record (none, minor, or major), type of offense (violent, property, drug, or other), criminal status at arrest, level of court, and urban/rural area, Pope was able to overcome some of the deficiencies of previous studies. In terms of type of sentence, after standardization,[34] Pope found no differences in the disposition of males and females sentenced in superior courts. However, differences in sentencing were still observed for males and females in urban lower courts. Analysis of length of sentence uncovered no differences by sex in lower courts; however, in urban and rural superior courts, males were more likely than females to be sentenced to terms of over six months. It should be noted, however, that offense was not controlled in the analysis of length of sentence.

It is clear from this review that previous research has generally failed to control adequately for the type of offense and specific behavior of the offender.[35] Two sentencing studies have tried to compensate for the disadvantages of using the criminal offense label by measuring offenses along the Sellin-Wolfgang scale of offense seriousness. Simon and Sharma, using 1974 PROMIS data for Washington, DC, controlled a variety of offense and offender characteristics through multiple regression analysis. These factors accounted for about 20 percent of the variation in disposition; sex "was of practically no predictive power."[36] Thus, in like cases, females received sentences similar to those of males. In contrast, Curran found that females in her Dade County (Miami) Florida study received less severe sentences than males in 1971 and 1975–76, "even with the effect for differences in offense seriousness, total counts, and criminal history controlled."[37]

A sentencing study conducted by Engle included information on each offender convicted in Philadelphia in 1964. Offenses were grouped into twenty-seven crime categories, and sentences were coded along an interval scale according to severity of sentence. Engle reported that overall, females sentenced in Philadelphia received less severe dispositions than males.[38] Investigating the effect of sex after controlling crime group, Engle found that females received significantly less severe dispositions for burglary, firearms violations, aggravated assault, possession of drugs, and sale of drugs. Even in the crime group that included mainly female offenders (that is, prostitution), females tended to receive less severe dispositions than males. There were only two crime categories in which females tended to get more severe sentences—offenses against police and public order, and miscellaneous offenses. The absence of lenient treatment for some of these offenders may have been due to the perception that resisting arrest is not appropriate for females (it is, perhaps, unladylike). If so, the finding supports the sex-role explanation of the prejudicial perspective.[39] It should be pointed out that prior record and other important variables were not controlled.

Nicolette Parisi

Therefore, although there was evidence of differential treatment, we cannot conclude that this treatment was necessarily disparate.

Data on Differential Periods of Incarceration

Earlier in this section, it was noted that a sample of incarcerated persons provides a narrow perspective on sentencing practices because this type of data includes only the most serious offenses and high-risk offenders. Further, an incarceration data set can be used to investigate sentencing patterns in terms of length of sentence and time served. Whether there is disparate treatment of male and female offenders along these two dimensions can be assessed only by controlling legally relevant factors.

The preferential perspective, to review, predicts that females receive shorter sentences and serve less time than males. An Alabama prison study of 149 females and 217 males who had parole hearings between June 1973 and May 1975 found that the average sentence for females was indeed shorter than that for males.[40] After offense was controlled, females still tended to have been sentenced to shorter terms than males, although females received longer sentences than males in drug violations. When the study examined time served, females again fared better than males: they were more likely to be granted parole and to have served less time than males.[41] When prior record was controlled, however, the preferential pattern held only for those with no, or one, prior felony conviction.

The Uniform Parole Reports collects information on persons paroled from state correctional institutions throughout the United States. Like the Alabama Law Project, the Uniform Parole Reports indicated that females released to parole in 1976 had served less time than males.[42] However, as a group, female parolees were substantially more likely than males to have been originally convicted of willful homicide and involuntary manslaughter, theft/larceny, and a miscellaneous category of offenses (forgery, fraud, sex offenses, drug violations). The shorter period of incarceration may reflect the fact that almost half of the females had been convicted of the miscellaneous offenses, which tend to be ranked low in seriousness. Without controlling for offense, prior record, and other relevant factors, no conclusions should be drawn as to whether the differential periods of incarceration truly indicate disparate treatment.

Are Females Treated Differently?

Data on Differential Revocation

The Uniform Parole Reports can be used to determine the success or failure of males and females on parole. These data consistently show that female parolees have similar or slightly higher success rates compared with males during one-, two-, or three-year follow-up periods.[43] This pattern holds across offense and prior record.[44] In terms of types of failures, for 1974–76 one-year follow-up periods, the largest differences were observed in the category, "return to prison with a new major conviction." Females were somewhat less likely than males to be returned for this reason. There were no significant differences between male and female parolees in the technical violation category. Although differences were not large, females tended to abscond at a greater rate than males.[45]

Summary

Despite problems with research designs, limitations due to broad offense categories, and failures to consider prior record and other relevant factors, the data consistently show some degree of differential treatment of females at aggregate levels. However, when controls are introduced, contradictory results appear. Although it is fair to conclude that the direction of differential dispositions is most often advantageous, it occasionally appears that negative (punitive) treatment is accorded females for "manly" crimes. Improved research designs and collection of data assumed to be particularly relevant to sentencing females will improve our ability to address the issue of differential treatment. More definitive conclusions about the existence and direction of disparity may then follow.

AN ARGUMENT IN FAVOR OF DISPARITY

Sentencing studies have generally not empirically explored the possible sources of disparate dispositions; they merely conclude that such disparity appears to exist based on their data. In the earlier sections of this chapter, a number of alternative explanations were posed for preferential or punitive models of disparity. One of these explanations, "practicality," focused on the female offender's responsibility for dependent children. We have little evidence establishing the effect (if any) of the existence of dependent children on

Nicolette Parisi

the sentencing of males versus females. Some scholars would probably argue that it is a factor that should be ignored in the sentencing decision. In this section, however, I argue that the presence of dependent children is a factor that *should* be considered at sentencing. Women with dependent children should receive more lenient sentences than men who have committed similar offenses, if such a decision benefits society as a whole.

Assume, for the purpose of argument, that (1) disparity on the basis of sex exists in some crime categories; (2) that disparity is preferential treatment resulting in leniency for females in certain crime categories; and (3) that evidence exists to support that children (especially young children) affect the decision to be more lenient with females than males. Can a case be made that this disparate sentencing practice should continue?

In today's society, males do not typically have major responsibility for their children. From a child's infancy, the child-raising duties are primarily allocated to the mother. Although both mother and father are equally capable, society is not yet prepared to recognize or accommodate this. Why should the judiciary blindly impose equal treatment on parents, when the rest of society does not? If the judiciary treats both parents alike, then it may be the children (innocent third parties) who suffer; furthermore, society may pay the eventual price. The liabilities (in terms of the impact on the children, who may have less supervision, less care, and so on) may be costly. If protection of society is weighed by the judge, consideration should be given to the consequences of incarcerating a mother. If, or when, both parents are expected to be equally responsible for children, the existence of children can be abandoned as a factor to weigh in the sentencing decision.

CONCLUSION: RESEARCH AND REFORMS

In addition to generally improving research designs, researchers studying the role of sex in sentencing must pay particular attention to certain issues. Prospects for determining the impact of sex will continue to be limited if certain deficiencies in prior research are not specifically addressed. First, offense behavior must be more carefully defined. Broad categories of offenses impede efforts to determine whether differential dispositions are disparate. Second, data must be collected on certain factors that assumedly describe the differing nature of female crime (see *Chapter 5*). Third, more investigation should focus on less serious offenses, which have been overlooked in most studies. This is an important aspect of research because the existence and direction of differential treatment may not be uniform across all categories of crime.

Finally, research on this topic may be affected by sentencing reforms. The purpose of presumptive sentences, mandatory terms, and sentencing and parole guidelines is, in part, to decrease disparity. However, in the case of females, these reforms hinder consideration of factors relevant to the seriousness of the crime (for example, role in the offense), females may be disadvantaged. Furthermore, as we have suggested, failure to consider the needs of dependent children may ultimately harm society. Until males take (and are treated as having) equal responsibility for child-raising, the welfare of dependents should be a factor in sentencing decisions involving female offenders.

NOTES

1. Rita J. Simon, *Women and Crime* (Lexington, MA: D.C. Heath, 1975); Darrell J. Steffensmeier, "Assessing the Impact of the Women's Movement on Sex-Based Differences in the Handling of Adult Criminal Defendants," *Crime and Delinquency* 26 (1980):344–357; Meda Chesney-Lind, "Chivalry Reexamined: Women and the Criminal Justice System," in *Women, Crime and the Criminal Justice System*, ed. Lee H. Bowker (Lexington, MA: Lexington Books, 1978); Laura Crites, "Women in the Criminal Court," in *Women in the Courts*, ed. W. Hepperle and L. Crites (Williamsburg, VA: National Center for State Courts, 1978); Laurie E. Ekstrand and William A. Eckert, "Defendant's Sex as a Factor in Sentencing," *Experimental Study of Politics* 6 (1978):90–112; Mark C. Clements, "Sex and Sentencing," *Southwestern Law Journal* 26 (1972):890–904; Freda Adler, *Sisters in Crime* (New York: McGraw-Hill, 1975).

2. Simon, *Women and Crime*; David B. Rottman and Rita J. Simon, "Women in the Courts: Present Trends and Future Prospect," *Chitty's Law Journal* 23 (1975):24–32.

3. Stuart S. Nagel and Lenora J. Weitzman, "Woman as Litigants," *Hastings Law Journal* 23 (1971):171–198; Debra A. Curran, "Judicial Discretion and the Sex of the Defendant" (Paper presented at the Southern Political Sciencek Association November 1979).

4. Simon, *Women and Crime*, p. 49.

5. Steffensmeier, "Sex-Based Differences," p. 350.

6. Steffensmeier, "Sex-Based Differences"; Nagel and Weitzman, "Women as Litigants," p. 180; Helen Gibson, "Women's Prisons: Laboratories for Penal Reform," *Wisconsin Law Review* (1973):212.

7. Marilyn Haft, "Women in Prison: Discriminatory Practices and Some Legal Solutions," *Clearinghouse Review* (May 1974):3; Adler, *Sisters in Crime*, p. 240; Katharine Krause, "Denial of Work Release Programs to Women: A Violation of Equal Protection," *South Carolina Law Review* 47 (1973-1974):1459; Linda R. Singer, "Women and the Correctional Process," *American Criminal Law Review* 11 (1973):302; "Brief on the Woman Offender," *Canadian Journal of Corrections* 11 (1969):39.

8. Simon, *Women and Crime*, p. 49; Steffensmeier, "Sex-Based Differences," p. 349; Crites, "Women in the Criminal Court," p. 71.

9. Steffensmeier, "Sex-Based Differences," p. 352; Nagel and Weitzman, "Women as Litigants," p. 180.

10. Crites, "Women in the Criminal Court," p. 171; Steffensmeier, "Sex-Based Differences," p. 351.

11. Steffensmeier, "Sex-Based Differences," p. 353.

12. Crites, "Women in the Criminal Court," p. 171.

13. Simon, *Women and Crime*; Rottman and Simon, "Women in the Courts"; Nagel and Weitzman, "Women as Litigants"; Ekstrand and Eckert, "Defendant's Sex."

14. Vernetta D. Young, "The Female Offender: Myth vs. Reality," mimeographed, p. 14; Clarice Feinman, "Sex Role Stereotypes and Justice for Women," *Crime and Delinquency* 24 (1979):88.

15. Simon, *Women and Crime*, p. 52.

16. Chesney-Lind, "Chivalry Reexamined," p. 217.

17. Ekstrand and Eckert, "Defendant's Sex," p. 25.

18. Chesney-Lind, "Chivalry Reexamined," p. 212; Clements, "Sex and Sentencing," pp. 895-900; Eta Anderson, "the 'Chivalrous' Treatment of the Female Offender in the Arms of the Criminal Justice System: A Review of the Literature," *Social Problems* 23 (1976):353-355.

19. Ekstrand and Eckert ("Defendant's Sex," pp. 98, 106) point out that the equality model has been overlooked. They state that "some verification of unequal treatment due to sex is necessary prior to considering models that specify its direction." Hagan's review of the data on sentencing indicated that the equality model was most strongly supported. *See* John Hagan, "Extra-Legal Attributes and Criminal Sentencing: An Assessment of a Sociological Viewpoint," *Law and Society Review* 8 (1974):357-384.

20. For comments on the impact of sentencing reforms on females, *see* Joan Potter, "In Prison, Women Are Different," *Corrections Magazine* 4 (December 1978):15, 17, 18; Stephen Gettinger, "Fixed Sentencing Becomes Law in Three States: Other States Wary," *Corrections Magazine* 3 (September 1977):23; and Simon, *Women and Crime*, p. 70.

21. "Alabama Law Review Summer Project 1975: A Study of Differential Treatment Accorded Female Defendants in Alabama Criminal Courts," *Alabama Law Review* 27 (1975):709. This study found no difference in type of sentence, but preferential treatment in length of incarceration.

22. Edward Green, *Judicial Attitudes in Sentencing* (London: Macmillan, 1961); Nagel and Weitzman, "Women as Litigants"; L. Paul Sutton, *Variations in Federal Criminal Sentences: A Statistical Assessment at the National Level* (Washington, DC: U.S. Government Printing Office, 1978); Rita J. Simon and Navin Shar-

Are Females Treated Differently?

ma, *The Female Defendant in Washington, DC: 1974 and 1975* (Washington, DC: INSLAW, 1979); Carl E. Pope, *Sentencing California Felony Offenders* (Washington, DC: U.S. Government Printing Office, 1975).

23. Green, *Judicial Attitudes*, pp. 53, 122.

24. Furthermore, the male and female populations may have had different characteristics. The data showed that substantially more males than females had been convicted of burglary, while substantially more females than males had been convicted of drug violations. Another factor to consider before reaching any conclusions is that the sample was drawn in 1956–1957, when the Muncy Act provisions may have strongly affected the sentencing selection of judges.

25. Nagel and Weitzman, "Women as Litigants," p. 173.

26. *See* Chesney-Lind, "Chivalry Reexamined"; and Steffensmeier, "Sex-Based Differences."

27. Simon, *Women and Crime*; Steffensmeier, "Sex-Based Differences"; Crites, "Women in the Criminal Court."

28. Hagan, "Extra-Legal Attributes," p. 375.

29. George W. Baab and William Furgeson, "Texas Sentencing Practices: A Statistical Study," *Texas Law Review* 45 (1967):471–503.

30. Curran, "Judicial Discretion"; Chesney-Lind, "Chivalry Reexamined."

31. Theodore Chiricos, Phillip Jackson, and Gordon Waldo, "Inequality in the Imposition of a Criminal Label," *Social Problems* 19 &1972):553–572.

32. Chiricos, Jackson, and Waldo, "Inequality," p. 557, n. 4.

33. Pope, *California Felony Offenders*.

34. "Test factor standardization" can be used to control several independent variables in order to assess whether they have an effect on the relationship between a focal independent variable and the dependent variable. *See* Pope, *California Felony Offenders*, p. 15.

35. I am using "type of offense" here to refer to the usual crime categories—robbery, larceny, and so on. "Specific behavior" refers to the offender's particular actions under the legal label of the offense—whether the robbery was *armed* robbery, the larceny *shoplifting*, and so on.

36. Simon and Sharma, *The Female Defendant*, p. 34.

37. Curran, "Judicial Discretion," pp. 14, 20. Curran analyzed the data by time period (1965–66, 1971, and 1975–76). Sex was *not* a factor in the 1965–66 period; however, "chivalry" was evident in the other two periods.

38. Charles Donald Engle, "Criminal Justice in the City: A Study of Sentence Severity and Variation in the Philadelphia Criminal Court System" (Ph.D. diss., Temple University, 1971), p. 260.

39. *See*, for comparison, Nagel and Weitzman, "Women as Litigants."

40. Alabama Law Project, p. 717.

41. Alabama Law Project, p. 723.

42. National Council on Crime and Delinquency, *Characteristics of the Parole Population 1977* (San Francisco, NCCD, 1979), p. 6, Appendix B. Moseley and Gerould report that females paroled in 1970 served less time than males even when offense was controlled. *See* William H. Moseley and Margaret H. Gerould, "Sex and Parole: A Comparison of Male and Female Parolees," *Journal of Criminal Justice* 3 (1975):52–54.

43. Michael Gottfredson, Michael Hindelang, and Nicolette Parisi, eds.,

Nicolette Parisi

Sourcebook of Criminal Justice Statistics 1977 (Washington, DC: U.S. Government Printing office, 1979), pp. 664, 668; National Council on Crime and Delinquency, *Parole Population*, pp. 10–12, Appendix B.

    44. Gottfredson, Hindelang, and Parisi, *Sourcebook 1977.*

    45. National Council on Crime and Delinquency, *Parole Population*, pp. 10-12.

10

Female Delinquents in a Suburban Court

ANNE RANKIN MAHONEY
CAROL FENSTER

In general, across jurisdictions and over time, girls have been less likely than boys to come into juvenile courts, just as women have been less likely than men to appear in criminal courts. Now, as the women's liberation movement focuses attention upon the equality of men and women, some researchers who study female criminality report an increase in the frequency and seriousness of female crime. They argue that changes accompanying the women's movement have altered the patterns of female criminality—that as women become more aggressive and competitive, this new assertiveness is reflected in a rise in official rates of female delinquency and crime and in a wider range of offenses, particularly those formerly dominated by males. They note also that the response of crime control officials is changing, these officials being less likely to treat males and females differently. In other words, as males and females approach equality in other dimensions of activity, they also become more similar in their patterns of criminality and the ways in which they are treated by the justice system. As a result, contend some researchers, more girls are coming to court on more serious charges, and the court's treatment of them is becoming increasingly harsh.

Some writers argue, however, that it is too early to observe changes in patterns of criminality because the women involved in crime were socialized into traditional sex-role values as children; furthermore, they are predominantly from lower socio-economic groups, which have been less influenced by the women's movement than middle- and upper-class groups.

The purpose of this chapter is to explore the patterns of male and female delinquency over a ten-year period in a juvenile court of an affluent suburb. If the women's movement has changed the pattern of female crime, it may be more noticeable in an adolescent population from an Anglo middle-class community where boys and girls are more likely to grow up in an environment that stresses equal opportunities.

Three propositions will be tested for this population: (1) that official rates of female delinquency are rising more rapidly than the rates for males; (2) that girls' offenses are becoming more serious; and (3) that the dispositions for females are becoming more severe. In order to test these propositions, three data-collection procedures were used. One involved a tabulation of the number of petitions for status offenses and delinquency for boys and girls from monthly court logs for each year from 1969 through 1978 and for the first seven months of 1980. The second involved the coding of court records for all girls and a random sample of boys in 1969, 1972, 1975, and 1978. Third, observational data from 1980 hearings in the same court are used to provide descriptive material on female delinquents now coming before the court.

The chapter includes a discussion of the relevant literature on female delinquents, presentation of the research findings from the study of youths in a suburban court, and a discussion of the meaning of the research for our understanding of female delinquency.

REVIEW OF THE LITERATURE

On Increasing Frequency and Seriousness of Female Crime

Studies of crime and delinquency have consistently shown that males are more numerous in criminal populations than women. In the past, delinquent acts of males have been greater in number and in level of seriousness than those of females. Cernkovich and Giordano[1] reviewed several studies and found that while official male delinquency has traditionally included a variety of offenses, official female delinquency has been limited to a much narrower range of activities.[2] Males have been primarily responsible for the more violent delinquent acts and property crimes, while females' misconduct has largely been limited to incorrigibility, various sex offenses, running away from home, and shoplifting.[3]

Although more males are arrested than females, some research shows that the gap between arrest rates is narrowing. Adler reports that in the early 1960s the annual ratios of male to female delinquents was over fifty to one; by the mid-1970s, it has shrunk to about five to one.[4] Some studies[5] show that females are more likely than males to be taken into custody for status offenses, but Giordano's analysis of *Uniform Crime Reports* (UCR) shows that there is a substantial increase in arrest rates for girls under eighteen years of age for more serious delinquency charges. During 1960 to 1973, the arrest rate increased 265 percent for all offenses, 393 percent for violent crimes, and 334 percent for property crimes. This contrasts with increases of 124, 236, and 82 percent respectively for males in the same age group.[6] Giordano acknowledges the limitations of using UCR data, buttressing her argument with the results of a recent comparison at a state institution of self-reported delinquency for 1960 and 1975. The comparison shows a significantly greater involvement of the 1975 females in almost every offense category.[7] Noblit and Burcart also use UCR data to show that the rates of arrest and the seriousness of offenses for female juveniles have increased faster than those of males. Using a shorter time period than the Giordano study, 1960–1970, they illustrate that the arrest rates for both juvenile and adult females increased significantly more than they did for males. The rate for females almost tripled, while the rate for males did not quite double.[8]

Other writers disagree that there has been a sharp increase in female crime. Steffensmeier and his associates,[9] in their reports of a reanalysis of UCR data, suggest not only that the purported increase in female crime may be exaggerated, but that the trend toward increase was in motion long before 1968–1969, the date generally accepted as the start of the women's liberation movement.[10] In three separate articles on adult property crimes, adult violent crimes, and juvenile crimes, Steffensmeier contends that previous analyses of

Anne Rankin Mahoney & Carol Fenster

UCR data (for example, those by Adler and Simon)[11] have overlooked two issues: whether the rate of increase in female arrests is greater than increases in the U.S. female population during the same period, and whether the rate of increase in female arrests is greater than the increase for males.

Using the adjusted UCR data for 1960–1975, Steffensmeier et al. show that for violent crimes, the gap between adult males and females has remained about the same.[12] Using the same adjusted UCR data for property crimes, Steffensmeier concludes that although there has been an increase in adult female property crime, this increase lags behind that of adult males except for larceny/theft and fraud/embezzlement. And for juveniles during 1965–1977, Steffensmeier and Steffensmeier use UCR data to show that although females made arrest gains in larceny, running away, and liquor violations, gains in other offense categories leveled off. Their review of juvenile court statistics and self-report studies shows a similar pattern of female delinquency, but includes increases for marijuana use and drinking as well. On the basis of these findings, Steffensmeier concludes that the "new female criminal" is more of a social invention than an empirical reality.[13]

Even if it is possible to show clear increases in the frequency and seriousness of female delinquency, it is unclear whether the increases can be attributed to changing behaviors by the females themselves or to changing attitudes of legal officials. Several self-report studies show that although girls do report less delinquent activity than boys, the difference between self-reported rates for boys and girls is considerably less than the difference between official delinquency rates for boys and girls.[14] Given this differential, changes in arrest or reporting practices could in themselves account for substantial "increases" the delinquency rates of girls.

On Increasing Severity of Dispositions for Female Delinquents

There is very little literature on differential changes in dispositions for girls and boys over time, although there is a considerable literature on the differential treatment of males and females by the juvenile justice system at each stage of processing. Chesney-Lind has recently provided an excellent summary of research on differential treatment of girls at each stage of the process and throughout the history of the juvenile court.[15]

Female Delinquents in a Suburban Court

Several studies suggest that juvenile judges mete out more severe dispositions to females than to males. Gibbons and Griswold found that males and females in the state of Washington were dismissed from juvenile court jurisdiction in about the same proportions, but that females were more likely than males to be institutionalized.[16] In Wisconsin, Terry also found that girls brought before the juvenile court were more often institutionalized than boys, even though they were also more likely than males to be placed under informal supervision by the probation department.[17] Neither of these studies was able to control adequately for type of offense or prior record. Datesman and Scarpitti found in their analysis of 1,103 juveniles appearing before a juvenile court over a seven-month period that males receive more severe dispositions than females on criminal offenses, but that females receive more severe dispositions than males on noncriminal status offenses, especially if they have a prior record.[18]

Some studies show that adult females receive more lenient treatment in the courts than males who commit the same type of offense,[19] while others show that males and females are treated similarly in certain types of courts when offenses and prior record are controlled.[20]

OVERALL THE RESEARCH on criminality of girls suggests that the official crime rate for girls is rising and that girls are now coming into court on a wider range of charges than they did ten or twenty years ago. It is not clear from the literature, however, how much of an increase there is or whether it comes from changed behavior of the girls or a greater willingness of law enforcement officials to take girls into custody and charge them with delinquent acts. The research on dispositions for girls gives some evidence that girls have in the past been treated more harshly than boys by the courts. The more severe treatment has occurred primarily through the sexualization of girls' offenses and the use of charges for status offenses which, although technically less serious than delinquency charges, in the past have led more often to institutionalization and longer periods of out-of-home placement. Very little research has been reported regarding the changes in dispositions for girls over time. This chapter examines whether changes similar to those described in the literature in regard to arrest rate, offense type, and disposition can be detected for girls in a suburban juvenile court over a ten-year period.

Anne Rankin Mahoney & Carol Fenster

METHODOLOGY AND SAMPLE

The data for this study are drawn from the records of male and female delinquents whose petitions were filed in a suburban juvenile court during the years of 1969 (the first year for which complete data on juveniles are available) through 1978. These records provide total numbers of juveniles processed by the court over this ten-year period. From these data it is possible to determine whether the frequency of female delinquency has increased more rapidly, remained the same, or decreased relative to that of male delinquency. For 1969, 1972, 1975, and 1978, records were examined for all girls and an equal-sized sample of randomly selected boys. In all, the records of 655 cases were included in the study: 60 females and 59 males from 1969; 66 females and 67 males from 1972; 69 females and 68 males from 1975; and 133 females and 133 males from 1978. The records for the four years were examined to determine: (1) whether the incidence of serious offenses committed by females is rising faster than that of males; and (2) whether the court's processing of delinquents varies by sex and type of offense.

Informal interviews with probation counselors in this court and several hundred hours of juvenile courtroom observations provided a context that helped to explain the trends or variations in the data. The observations took place during the first part of 1980. At least one hearing was observed for 40 of the 103 girls who came through the court on delinquency petitions during the first seven months of 1980.

The characteristics of the youths in the sample drawn from the court records over the ten-year period are similar to the characteristics of the youths observed in the courtroom. The average age for the boys and girls in the sample drawn from the court records was fifteen years. It was the same for the 1980 observation sample. For both the record sample and the 1980 observation sample, the percentages of youths who were not represented by attorneys ranged from 50 to 75 percent, with girls less likely to have legal counsel than boys. Youths represented by legal counsel were much more likely to retain a private attorney than a public defender, possibly because of the relatively high incomes of these youths' families.

The data were drawn from a juvenile court within a suburban county that is generally regarded as relatively affluent. In 1977, the median household income was $24,943.[21] However, there are several sections within the county that have fairly high concentrations of poverty, family disruption, and delinquency. As a result, children who come before the court may represent a wide variety of social and economic backgrounds, but most children come from middle-income families. The population of the county is predominantly Anglo and this is reflected in a juvenile court populalation that is typically 90 percent Anglo, 1 percent black, and 8 percent Chicano.[22]

Census data show that the ratio of boys to girls in this county is roughly one to one, with no indications that this ratio had varied during the last ten years.[23] Thus, we are relatively sure that any changes in the proportions of boys and girls brought into court during the past ten years are due to factors other than changes in their proportions in the county population.

FINDINGS

Data from the suburban juvenile court under study were used to test three propositions: (1) the proportion of delinquents who are girls will increase over the ten-year period of 1969–1978; (2) there will be an increase over the ten-year period in the proportion of females who are charged with more serious rather than less serious offenses; (3) the dispositions of female delinquents and status offenders will move from being less severe than boys' dispositions to being more similar to boys' dispositions.

1. Is Female Delinquency Increasing?

In order to test the first proposition, the percentage of delinquency petitions filed on girls was compared for each year of the ten-year period. Table 10-1 utilizes data from monthly logs that record names and offenses of youths upon whom petitions are filed. The table shows that during 1969–1978, the proportion of delinquent females more than doubled, rising from 7 percent in 1969 to 16 percent in 1978. Data from the first seven months of 1980 show a rise to 18 percent. On first appearance, these findings provide some support for the first proposition, although the increase is not large. However, the increase may be due primarily to a general decrease in the use of status offense petitions by the court over the ten-year

Anne Rankin Mahoney & Carol Fenster

TABLE 10-1
Percentage of Delinquency Petitions, Status Offense Petitions, and Total Petitions Filed on Girls
from 1969 through 1978 and for the First Seven Months of 1980

	Delinquency		Status Offense		Total Petitions	
	% Girls	Total	% Girls	Total	% Girls	Total
1969	7	204	45	89	19	293
1970	10	153	60	76	27	229
1971	7	194	63	81	24	275
1972	9	325	46	87	17	412
1973	12	276	60	94	24	370
1974	8	378	57	91	18	469
1975	13	363	64	39	18	402
1976	9	523	60	62	14	585
1977	18	430	48	65	22	495
1978	16	506	50	105	22	611
1980[a]	18	565	0	0	18	565

[a]First seven months.

period. In 1969, they made up nearly 33 percent of all petitions. By 1978, they accounted for only 17 percent of all petitions. Petitions for status offenses in this jurisdiction are fairly equally divided between boys and girls. (This is in sharp contrast to other studies that report that most status offenders are girls.) By 1980 there were no petitions filed on status offenders, as a result of state legislation in 1979 that decriminalized them.

A substantial number of youths in this court and elsewhere are involved in both delinquency and status offenses. When both status offenses and delinquency are present, Chesney-Lind and others suggest that girls in particular may be more likely to be charged with status offenses than delinquency.[24] But since Chesney-Lind's investigation, federal and state legislation has limited detention and disposition alternatives for status offenders; therefore, police officers may elect to bring a child in on a delinquency charge because if entails less hassle. These changes in charging practices, if they occur, confound efforts to determine whether girls are committing more delinquent offenses than in the past, because there is no way to sort out whether girls are committing more delinquent acts or are simly being more frequently charged with them.

Courtroom observations in 1980 suggest that many females

coming into court are taken into custody for delinquent acts, but have exhibited types of behavior that could have been filed as status offenses prior to 1979. For example, many of the girls are runaways and commit offenses to maintain their runaway status. Two of the three burglary cases observed, for instance, involved girls burglarizing their own parents' homes and taking food and clothing to prolong their runaway status. If such cases had been filed prior to the 1979 legislation that eliminated status offenses, the child could have been brought into court either as a status offender for running away *or* as a delinquent for committing burglary.

Table 10-1 gives some indication in the last column that the increase in the percentage of delinquency petitions filed on girls over the last ten-year period may indeed be the result of a greater tendency to charge for delinquency rather than status offenses. It shows that the percentage of total petitions filed on girls remains remarkably stable over the ten-year period, moving from 19 percent in 1969 to 27 percent in 1970 and 22 percent in 1978.

2. Is Female Delinquency Becoming More Serious?

The second proposition, that girls' offenses are becoming more serious, can be tested by examination of Table 10-2, which separates misdemeanors and felonies. It shows that delinquent girls are far more likely than boys to come into court on misdemeanor charges, and much less likely than boys to come in on felony charges. The difference between boys and girls does not change substantially from 1969 to 1978. In 1969, 32 percent more boys than girls were charged with felonies; in 1978, 29 percent more boys than girls were charged with felonies. During 1969–1978, there is a 20 percent increase in girls' felony charges and a 17 percent increase in boys' felony charges. This increase, essentially the same for both sexes, probably can be partially attributed to inflation: both boys and girls engaged primarily in property offenses, which are classified as misdemeanor or felony on the basis of the property damaged or stolen. As the value of items increases through inflation, offenses are also inflated from misdemeanors to felonies. Table 10-2 does not provide support for the second proposition. There is no indication in the table that girls' offenses compared with boys' offenses are becoming more serious.

Observations of 1980 court cases also do not support the proposition that girls' offenses are becoming more serious. Like those of

Anne Rankin Mahoney & Carol Fenster

TABLE 10-2
Percentage of Charges by Sex and Year
for Juvenile Males and Females

	1969		1972		1975		1978	
Charges	Male	Female	Male	Female	Male	Female	Male	Female
Misdemeanor	60%	92%	60%	83%	55%	74%	43%	72%
Felony	40%	8%	40%	17%	45%	26%	57%	28%
	100%	100%	100%	100%	100%	100%	100%	100%
Total Number	43	12	47	18	60	38	109	72

This table does not include drug charges, most of which were misdemeanor charges. Our sample included the following drug cases: in 1969, 4 boys and 0 girls; in 1972, 2 boys and 3 girls; in 1975, 3 boys and 1 girl; and in 1978, 3 boys and 5 girls.

the 1969–1978 group, the delinquency allegations for the 1980 group are concentrated in the less serious offense categories, primarily minor forms of theft. Of the 103 petitions filed against females between January and July 1980, 55 percent were theft allegations. During courtroom observations, we were able to observe at least one hearing for 40 of these 103 cases; of these 40 cases, 53 percent were theft related. Since the kinds of thefts engaged in by both groups are very similar, a description of the 1980 cases should serve to illustrate the relatively benign nature of female theft compared to male theft.

The 1980 theft-related cases fall into two categories: (1) theft by means of shoplifting items from department or discount stores; and (2) theft by means of stealing money, usually from an employer. The first type, shoplifting, was more common. The items most often stolen by girls were clothing, particularly sweaters, skirts, pants, shoes, purses, and jewelry. Boys also stole clothing, but they were much more likely to take such items as radios, tape decks, or stereo equipment. The girls tended to steal items worth less than $50, although two cases involved the theft of clothing valued at over $500.

The second kind of theft, stealing money from one's employer, occurred much less often. In one such case, the girl (with a female accomplice) used her employee position to write fraudulent receipts, refunds, and so on, and managed to take nearly $100 over several months. Her accomplice took a smaller amount of money. Boys also use their employee positions to steal from their employers, but the boys we observed more often took merchandise (record albums, tapes) rather than money.

For personal crimes, the courtroom observations provide further evidence that girls' offenses are not becoming more serious. Of the 103 delinquency petitions filed on girls during the first seven months of 1980, only 9 percent were personal crimes. Furthermore, two-thirds of these were third-degree assaults, a relatively minor form of personal crime classified as a misdemeanor in this court. Actions typically classified in this manner include hitting, biting, shoving, kicking, and so on. Observations show that victims of these assaults are frequently acquaintances of the delinquent and that confrontations usually arise from arguments occurring on school grounds or nearby parks and recreation areas. Neither the frequency of occurrence nor the nature of these personal crimes varied significantly between the 1969–1978 and 1980 groups, providing little reason to believe that girls' personal crimes have become more serious since 1969.

Overall, courtroom observations confirm the conclusion that girls' offenses are not becoming more serious. Over the years, females have been most likely to engage in minor forms of theft and the very small proportion of personal crimes they do commit are not serious.

3. Are Dispositions of Female Juveniles Becoming Harsher?

There are several dispositional options available in the court under study. One is a dismissal. However, because the court operates on a District Attorney Intake Model and the district attorney makes the initial decision about which cases to file in juvenile court and which cases to refer to the juvenile diversion program (a program of counseling/supervision for firt-time and/or nonviolent offenders), dismissal rarely occurs because the district attorney feels the case is weak. It is used more often to clear the docket of a case of a youth who has other, more serious cases pending in other counties, or of a case involving a youth who has moved away or cannot be located.

A second possible disposition is acquittal in either a bench or jury trial. Only one youth whose case was included in this study

Anne Rankin Mahoney & Carol Fenster

was acquitted. A third and frequently used disposition is the reserved adjudication, in which a youth is assigned to a probation counselor for a six-month period of supervision. If the youth behaves satisfactorily during this period (that is, does not have any more petitions filed against him/her and complies with the terms and conditions of the supervision order), the judge may then terminate the supervision period without finding that the youth is a delinquent. This enables the youth to avoid a delinquency record.

Finally, the judge may find that the youth is a delinquent and adjudicate him/her as such. Any number of options are open to the judge at this point; the youth might be fined, be required to spend a specific period of time in the juvenile detention center, be placed on probation for a period of time not to exceed two years, or receive any combination of these dispositions. The most severe disposition is commitment to the State Department of Institutions, where a child is evaluated and may ultimately be placed in a juvenile correctional institution. Throughout the ten-year data-collection period, the most frequent dispositions were dismissals of the entire petition, reserved adjudication, adjudication with a two-year probation term (with no accompanying fines or confinement in detention centers), and commitment to the Department of Institutions. Only four youths whose cases were included in this study were fined or sentenced to the detention center for punishment.

Table 10-3 shows dispositions for delinquent boys and girls by year. Only those with no prior record are considered in order to control for the effect of record upon disposition. The analysis is also limited to youths who live within the court's jurisdiction because nonresident youths who are taken into custody in the county usually are returned to their county of residence for disposition. A total of 62 percent of the delinquent boys and 57 percent of the delinquent girls in the study were in-county youths.

The table shows no clear pattern of change over time. It does not support the proposition that girls are treated more severely than boys, nor does it support the proposition that they were treated more severely in 1978 than they were in 1972, the earliest year in which there were enough resident girls to show dispositions.

A large proportion of both boys and girls were charged with theft, and we thought that perhaps some differences in dispositions between boys and girls could be seen if only one category of delinquency were considered. However, the pattern of dispositions for theft for in-county boys and girls was similar to that for delinquency offenses in general and showed no pattern of either discrimination between boys or girls or change over time.

TABLE 10-3

Percentage of Dispositions by Year for Delinquency Petitions Filed on Males and Females Residing in the Court's Jurisdiction and Having No Previous Record

Disposition	1969		1972		1975		1978	
	Male	Female	Male	Female	Male	Female	Male	Female
Dismissal	30%	100%	29%	13%	13%	8%	28%	43%
Reserved Adjudication	39%	0%	43%	56%	63%	67%	38%	42%
Adjudication: Probation	26%	0%	28%	31%	12%	25%	31%	15%
Adjudication: Department of Institutions	5%	0%	0%	0%	12%	0%	3%	0%
	100%	100%	100%	100%	100%	100%	100%	100%
Total Number	24	1	21	16	24	12	39	33

DISCUSSION AND CONCLUSION

Efforts to study changes in official rates of girls' delinquency over time are hampered by many problems. One problem is that the number of girls in the court system continues to be small and the quantitative research methods most usually relied upon by social scientists for analysis of data from records have serious limitations when used with small populations. The study of female delinquents, like that of such other small segments of the population as ethnic minorities, gifted children, or never-married women, necessitates the development of a wider range of methodologies and the use of nonstatistical techniques that do not limit studies of women to large populations.

An additional problem is that it is difficult to study a specific change in a juvenile court because the court itself, particularly in certain states, has undergone many changes during the last ten years. The *Gault* decision in 1967, which granted substantial legal rights to juveniles, set in motion a whole range of changes in juvenile codes and court practices throughout the country. Federal legislation in 1974 in regard to the deinstitutionalization of status offenders sent yet another wave of legislative change through state juvenile justice systems. In addition, many jurisdictions have modified record-keeping and staffing procedures; such changes may in-

Anne Rankin Mahoney & Carol Fenster

fluence dispositions during a particular time period in ways a researcher would never suspect.

It is important to keep these research difficulties in mind as we consider the findings set forth here. Even so, it is hard to make a case based on these data to support either the proposition that female delinquency is rising much more rapidly than male delinquency, or the proposition that females are now being treated more severely by the juvenile court. The small increase in female delinquency found in the study over the ten-year period appears to reflect, in part, a movement away from the use of status offenses. The percentage of total petitions filed on girls over the period studied did not increase. Furthermore, there is nothing in these data to suggest that the seriousness of the girls' crimes has increased. Court observation confirms that most girls coming into court have engaged in relatively minor property offenses. This study found that no girls, in comparison with five boys, were committed to the Department of Institutions. A study of dispositions over time gives no indication that dispositions for girls have increased in severity. There is, therefore, little indication in this suburban court that the women's liberation movement has triggered a crime wave among juvenile women.

NOTES

THIS CHAPTER WAS PREPARED under Grant Number 79-JN-AX-0034 from the National Institute for Juvenile Justice and Delinquency Prevention, Law Enforcement Assistance Administration, U.S. Department of Justice. Points of view or opinions stated herein do not necessarily represent the official position or policy of the U.S. Department of Justice. Special thanks are extended to Susanna Bozinovski and Susan Stuber for their help in collecting these data.

1. Stephen A. Cernkovich and Peggy C. Giordano, "A Comparative Analysis of Male and Female Delinquency," *The Sociological Quarterly* 20 (1979):131–145.
2. C. B. Vedder, *The Juvenile Offender* (New York: Doubleday, 1954); W. Wattenberg and F. Saunders, "Sex Differences Among Juvenile Offenders," *Sociology and Social Research* 39 (1954):24–31; C. E. Shaclay, "Sex Differentials in Juvenile Delinquency," *British Journal of Criminology* 5 (1965):289–308; E. Doleschal, "Review: Hidden Crime," *Crime and Delinquency Literature* 2 (1970):546–572; M. Gold, *Delinquent Behavior in an American City* (Belmont, CA: Brooks/Cole, 1970); R. W. Jongman and G. J. A. Smale, "Unrecorded Delinquency Among Female Students," *Tijdschrift Voor Criminologie* 14 (1975):1–11; J. R. Haggart, "Women and Crime," *Humboldt Journal of Social Relations* 1 (1973):42–47.

3. Freda Adler, *Sisters in Crime: The Rise of the New Female Criminal* (New York: McGraw-Hill, 1975); G. H. Barker and W. T. Adams, "Comparison of the Delinquencies of Boys and Girls," *Journal of Criminal Law, Criminology and Police Science* 53 (1962):470-475; Meda Chesney-Lind, "Judicial Enforcement of the Female Sex Role: The Family Court and the Female Delinquent," *Issues in Criminology* 8 (1973):51-59; Susan K. Datesman and Frank R. Scarpitti, "Unequal Protection for Males and Females in the Juvenile Court," in *Women, Crime and Justice* (New York: Oxford University Press, 1980), pp. 300–319; Lois G. Forer, *No One Will Listen: How Our Legal System Brutalizes the Poor* (New York: John Day, 1970); W. B. Miller, "The Molls," *Society* 11(1973):32–35; C. O'Reilly, F. Cizon, J. Flanagan, and S. Pflanczer, "Sentenced Women in a County Jail," *American Journal of Corrections* 30 (1968):23–25; C. B. Vedder, *The Juvenile Offender*; C. B. Vedder and D. B. Somerville, *The Delinquent Girl* (Springfield, IL: Charles C. Thomas, 1970).

4. Adler, *Sisters in Crime*, pp. 87–88.

5. Chesney-Lind, "Judicial Enforcement of the Female Sex Role"; P. C. Kratcoski, "Differential Treatment of Delinquent Boys and Girls in Juvenile Court," *Child Welfare* 53 (1974):16–22; W. Reckless and B. Kay, *The Female Offender; Report to the U.S. President's Commission on Law Enforcement and the Administration of Justice* (Washington, DC: U. S. Government Printing Office, 1967).

6. Peggy C. Giordano, "Research Note: Girls, Guys, and Gangs: The Changing Social Context of Female Delinquency," *Journal of Criminal Law and Criminology* 69 (1978):126–132.

7. Peggy C. Giordano and Stephen A. Cernkovich, "Changing Patterns of Female Delinquency" (Paper presented at the Annual Meeting of the Society for the Study of Social Problems, New York City, August 1976).

8. George W. Noblit and Jane M. Burcart, "Women and Crime: 1960-70," *Social Science Quarterly* (1976):651–657.

9. Darrell Steffensmeier, Renee Hoffman Steffensmeier, and Alvin Rosenthal, "Violence and the Contemporary Woman: An Analysis of Changing Levels of Female Violence, 1960–1974" (Paper presented at the Annual Meeting of the American Sociological Association, Chicago, August 1977); Darrell Steffensmeier, "Crime and the Contemporary Woman: An Analysis of Changing Levels of Female Property Crime, 1960–1975," *Social Forces* 57 (1978):566–584; Darrell J. Steffensmeier and Renee Hoffman Steffensmeier, "Trends in Female Delinquency," *Criminology* 18 (1980):62–85.

10. K. Oppenheim Mason and J. Czajka, "Change in U.S. Women's Sex-Role Attitudes, 1964–1974," *American Sociological Review* 41 (1976):576–596; Rita J. Simon, *The Contemporary Woman and Crime* (National Institute of Mental Health, Center for Studies of Crime and Delinquency, Rockville, MD: U.S. Government Printing Office, 1975).

11. Adler, *Sisters in Crime*; Simon, *The Contemporary Woman*.

12. Steffensmeier et al., "Violence."

13. Steffensmeier, "Crime," pp. 566–584.

14. Gold, *Delinquent Behavior*; Joseph Weis, "Liberation and Crime: The Invention of the New Female Criminal," *Crime and Social Justice* 6 (1976):23.

15. Meda Chesney-Lind, "Guilty by Reason of Sex: Young Women and the

236

Anne Rankin Mahoney & Carol Fenster

Criminal Justice System," in *Women and the Law: The Social-Historical Perspective*, ed. D. Kelly Weisberg (Cambridge, MA: Schenkman, 1982).

16. D. C. Gibbons and M. J. Griswold, "Sex Differences Among Juvenile Court Referrals," *Sociology and Social Research* 42 (1957):106–110.

17. R. M. Terry, "Discrimination in the Handling of Juvenile Offenders by Social Control Agencies," *Journal of Research in Crime and Delinquency* 4 (1967):218–230.

18. Datesman and Scarpitti, "Unequal Protection."

19. Linda Singer, "Women and the Correctional Process," *American Criminal Law Review* 11 (1973):295–305; H. Kritzer and T. M. Uhlman, "Sisterhood in the Courtroom: Sex of Judge and Defendant in Criminal Case Dispositions," *Social Science Journal* 4 (1977):77–78.

20. E. Pope, "Sentence Dispositions Accorded Assault and Burglary Offenders: An Exploratory Study in Twelve California Counties," *Journal of Criminal Justice* 6 (1978):151–165; J. Hagan, "Extra-Legal Attributes and Criminal Sentencing: An Assessment of a Sociological Viewpoint," *Law and Society Review* 8 (1974):357–383; C. Fenster and A. Mahoney, "The Effect of Prior Record Upon the Sentencing of Male–Female Co-Defendants" (Paper presented at the Annual Meeting of the American Sociological Association, New York City, September 1980).

21. National Planning Data Corporation, "Home Estimates by Census Tract" (Ithaca, NY, 1978).

22. Colorado Judicial Department, "Survey Report of Colorado Probation" (1976), Office of the State Court Administrator, 323 State Capitol, Denver 80203.

23. Denver Regional Council of Governments, "Population by Age Group Developed," A Report on Program Activities (1977), 2480 W. 26th Ave., Denver 80204.

24. Chesney-Lind, "Guilty."

11

Hard Times

*Custodial Prisons for Women and the Example
of the New York State Prison for Women
at Auburn, 1893-1933*

NICOLE HAHN RAFTER

The incarceration of women has received little attention from historians, penologists, or sociologists. What little research has been done on state-run female penal institutions has focused almost exclusively on one type, the reformatory. In their physical plants, women's reformatories fit a campus image (usually lacking walls and consisting of "cottages" grouped around central quadrangles); in their programs and rhetoric, women's reformatories generally stressed training and rehabilitation. The women's prison literature, in other words, insofar as it exists at all, has dealt primarily with "womanly" institutions that reflected a stereotype of the female criminal as relatively harmless, docile, and malleable.[1]

Although reformatories for women, established in many states between 1870 and 1930, did play a crucial role in the development of the women's prison system, they represented only part of the picture. Other penal institutions for females conformed to a very different style, one that might be called a ''custodial'' model. In striking contrast to the reformatory, the custodial model stressed security and demonstrated little interest in rehabilitation. Custodial institutions for female prisoners were more ''masculine,'' closely resembling maximum security prisons for men.[2] Furthermore, they usually incarcerated a type of female criminal (the felon) who was portrayed as ''masculine'' in the criminological literature, whereas women's reformatories tended to exclude all but the less threatening misdemeanants.

Although the custodial type of female prison has attracted little attention, it was in fact the first of the two styles of women's prisons to develop. In the nineteenth century, and perhaps the twentieth as well, the custodial model was more widely adopted across the United States than the reformatory. From the very start of our prison system, there were custodial units for female state prisoners either in wings of men's prisons or in separate buildings close by.[3] It was not until the last quarter of the nineteenth century that the custodial model began to be supplemented by that of the reformatory, which thereafter received the bulk of attention. The reformatory style, however, appears to have had little impact in the South, where few institutions for female prisoners deviated from custodialism, or in the West, which developed much of its women's prison system after the reformatory movement had passed. Moreover, many states that did establish a reformatory also ran a custodial prison for those women who, because of their age, offense, prior record, or history of disciplinary infractions in a reformatory, seemed beyond reform.

The almost exclusive focus on reformatories in the scholarly literature has produced a distorted picture of the history and nature of the women's prison system as a whole. It has obscured understanding of the origins of some of the problems faced by women's prisons today. And it has encouraged the view that the crimes and punishment of all women are relatively ladylike phenomena, quite different from the crimes and punishment of men.

To help correct such misconceptions, this study focuses on a particular custodial institution, the New York State Prison for Women at Auburn. This prison, operated from 1893 until 1933, coexisted with three state reformatories for women at Albion, Bedford, and Hudson, New York. Insofar as some states that operated custodial women's prisons did not also run reformatories, the New York example does not entirely fit with all cases. However, the

Auburn institution itself appears to have been typical of custodial women's prisons elsewhere, even those of states that held all their female prisoners under one roof.[4]

NEW YORK HAD NO FEMALE state prison of either the custodial or reformatory type between 1877 (when an older prison for women at Sing Sing was closed) and the late 1880s. After 1877, women who previously would have been sent to Sing Sing were assigned to county penitentiaries. In time, this sentencing practice became burdensome to the penitentiaries of the New York City area to which such women were most often sent, for although the prisoner's keep was paid by the state, their numbers became relatively large. The build-up in the number of female felons in the penitentiaries was one reason why, in the early 1890s, New York decided to establish a separate prison at Auburn to incarcerate this population.[5] At about the same time, it also established the three reformatories, but these were designed primarily for the reform of young misdemeanants. The new State Prison for Women, in contrast, was designated to hold older and second-term felons—women considered too far sunk in criminality to respond to reformative influences.

PHYSICAL PLANT

Like custodial prisons for women in many other states, the State Prison for Women at Auburn was established with a minimum of expenditure. Whereas the three New York reformatories were entirely new institutions, built specifically for women, the State Prison was located in an abandoned institution, the former Asylum for Insane (male) Criminals. The asylum had been part of the Auburn prison for men, the oldest maximum security prison in the country and an institution with a reputation for harshness.[6] However, the asylum stood on several acres of land separated from the regular men's section "by a high, thick wall, with only a wicket for passage between the two." The asylum inmates had recently been moved to a new asylum at Matteawan, New York; its main building was in good repair and "should be used by the State for some purpose," the State Superintendent of Prisons urged in 1892, "before damage and deterioration shall result from . . . non-occupancy."[7]

These quarters were typical of custodial women's prisons else-

Nicole Hahn Rafter

where in the United States not only in their low cost to the state, but also in their proximity to a men's prison. Unlike reformatories for women, which were totally independent institutions located on tracts of their own, women's prisons of the custodial type were often associated with men's prisons either through being physically attached (as at Auburn) or, if a separate unit, within the same walls. With the transfer of nearly one hundred women to Auburn from the county penitentiaries in May 1893, New York once again had a state prison for women.

In its physical plant, the State Prison for Women at Auburn was typical of other custodial women's prisons in that it was more closed than reformatories: instead of cottages and open spaces, it had rows of cells and almost no additional space for work, education, or recreation. And yet its quarters were not quite as secure or physically oppressive as those of the adjacent men's prison. The women's cells opened off corridors rather than being stacked in tiers; they had windows (albeit windows with bars); and there was generally less in the way of locks, concrete, and guards than would ordinarily have been found in prisons for men.

It would be a mistake, however, to conceive of custodial women's prisons as physically more pleasant than the men's prisons with which they were associated. Women's units of this type, because they were considered less important than either women's reformatories or men's prisons, were not as well maintained. The conditions at Auburn demonstrate that women's facilities were generally the last to be funded, and that female inmates often did without physical advantages (adequate utilities, consistent maintenance and repairs, modern workrooms, and so forth) enjoyed by male counterparts on the same site.

Within the State Prison for Women at Auburn were six "wards," each consisting of inmate rooms joined by a central corridor. In official prison reports, these rooms were described as "light, airy and comfortable"—and indeed they were roomier than the cramped and unventilated cells of the men's prison. But other than spaciousness, the plant of the women's prison had few virtues. Inspectors through the years called for overhaul of the heating system, which ceased to function in the further reaches of the building and in some winters stopped working entirely; the water and lighting systems also were targets of criticism. Madeline Doty, a prison commissioner who in 1916 posed as an inmate and spent several days incarcerated at Auburn, described air befouled by slop jars, scant supplies of washing water, and even scanter provision of drinking water.[8] Doty's description provides a glimpse of the prison's interior:

> *I was quickly transferred to a ward in another part of the building. This ward, like the first, had a very broad corridor resembling a large assembly-hall, off which on each hand opened the cells. At each end and in the middle of this big thoroughfare were great windows which, though painted, let in through the upper half a flood of light. In the middle of the hallway, in the recess made by a big baywindow, were two long, wooden tables. This space served as a dining-room for the twenty-seven women in the ward. Down past the rows of cells I was led. At the extreme end of the ward, leading off on the right and left, were two blind alleys. Down the one to the left we turned. Five cells opened on this narrow hallway, and into one of them I was thrust.[9]*

Although the Auburn Prison for Women used these quarters for forty years, the plant described by Doty remained much as it had been in the days it held the insane—a sign, perhaps, that authorities regarded its "hardened" female prisoners as closer to the demented than to normal male prisoners in their need for discipline, work, and recreation.

In the late 1920s a new structure was erected on the grounds of the women's prison. It was a shop building designated for men and built in anticipation of the day when the women's prison would be moved to another location.[10] (No such educational or vocational building was constructed for women at Auburn.) Meanwhile, the structure in which the female inmates resided was allowed to deteriorate, for state authorities planned to replace it before male prisoners inhabited that spot. Thus, while the women's area was less cramped and slightly more relaxed in terms of security, it was certainly not more comfortable physically, and it offered fewer advantages to the women than were available to men on the other side of the dividing wall.

ADMINISTRATION

Just as custodial women's prisons tended to be physically dependent on nearby prisons for men, they tended to be administratively dependent as well. The chief administrator was frequently the male warden of the nearby men's institution. Female officers were subordinate to him, and often they were older women, impoverished and poorly educated—women who would work for the low wages offered by women's prisons of the custodial type. In contrast, the typical reformatory was run entirely by women (many states required that the chief administrator of a women's reformatory be female);[11] and, because their aim was improvement, reformatories tried to hire young and relatively well-educated staff members who might serve as role models for inmates.

The legislation that established the New York State Prison for Women at Auburn provided for a matron and female assistants, but it fixed them in subordinate positions, specifying that "For the purposes of the government and management..., such State Prison for Women shall be deemed a department of the Auburn prison."[12] Assisting the male warden in the task of operating the women's institution were other males in prominent positions: the physician, clerk, and chaplain of the men's prison. The warden even had the power to appoint the assistant matrons. Thus, authority was firmly in the hands of men, with women officers being assigned to routine tasks.

Working conditions for these female officers were not calculated to attract well-educated women who might be interested in careers in prison administration. Salaries, for instance, were very low, the matron's being fixed at $1,200 yearly, those of her assistants at $300 or less. (In contrast, guards at the adjacent men's prison—male counterparts of the assistant matrons—received $600 annually.) The female officers were also provided with living quarters near the prison, but their overall recompense was, as the State Commission of Prisons complained in 1902, "entirely inadequate." Women who ran the early reformatories were also often poorly paid, but they had far more administrative authority and the creative challenge of attempting to put rehabilitation theory into practice.[13] Female officers at Auburn, on the other hand, had neither opportunity nor incentive to assume more than a caretaker role.

For the first twenty years of its operation, the Auburn women's prison was run by Mrs. Annie M. Welshe ("a dignified woman, mature in years," as described by the *New York Times* in 1895).[14] Welshe kept the prison scrupulously clean and maintained strict discipline, but did little else. She was succeeded by two other matrons, but in 1923 the matron's position was allowed to go unfilled, the physician of the men's prison thenceforth acting as "Superintendent in Charge" of the prison for women. By 1927 the State Prison for Women had only one reporting official—its teacher—who was female and not primarily an employee of the men's prison. These indications that female personnel were considered expendable were also signs that the Auburn Women's Prison aimed no higher than to fulfill custodial obligations. It would feed and clothe its inmates, and insure that they did not escape, but there its aspirations ended.

COMMITMENT LAWS AND PRACTICES

Criminological commentary of the late nineteenth and early twentieth centuries was dominated by two images. One showed the female offender to be a fundamentally "good" woman led astray by her own baser instincts or by a male consort. According to this kind of analysis, women committed crimes almost thoughtlessly, with little advance planning; they did not really "mean" to break the law and their offenses were relatively "soft" (sexual or petty property crimes). "Training" such women to be more "womanly"—more domestic, less sexual—would build up their defenses against future temptations. The second image that dominated the criminology of women, in contrast, portrayed the female offender as a basically "bad" woman: dark, large, hairy, aggressive—in a word, *masculine*. According to this second type of analysis, the female criminal was a serious social threat and beyond rehabilitation.[15]

These different understandings of the nature of the female criminal seem to have been shaped by, and in turn to have affected the development of, the bifurcated women's prison system, with its reformatory institutions for misdemeanants and its custodial institutions for felons. The laws that governed commitment to the State Prison for Women at Auburn made it clear that this prison was intended to isolate women who were beyond reform themselves and who might impede efforts to reform others. In contrast to most reformatory inmates, few Auburn women would have fit the stereotype of the female criminal as an impulsive, minor offender.

To insure that the reformatory populations would be likely to respond to rehabilitative programs, New York law generally excluded from such institutions women with felony records. Further, it specified that reformatory commitments might include women convicted of such "soft" (and hence, it was assumed, easily correctable) offenses as petit larceny, vagrancy, prostitution, and intoxication. Yet another hedge against unreformable commitments was provided by a stipulation excluding from the reformatories women over the age of thirty at the time of commitment.[16]

Women sent to the reformatories received indeterminate sentences of up to five years (later reduced to a maximum of three). The indeterminate sentence was part and parcel of the rehabilitative approach to criminals; it provided that release could be determined (within limits) by the prisoner's response to treatment. In theory at least, the amount of time to be served depended not on the offense, but on the rapidity of the prisoner's progress toward the state of being "cured" of criminal tendencies. The type of offender for whom the reformatories were intended, then, was conceived as errant, nonviolent, relatively new to crime, and curable.

In contrast to the laws governing commitment to the reformatories, New York's Penal Code provided that "Any woman over the age of sixteen who shall be convicted of felony in any court shall, when sentence imposed is one year or more, be sentenced to imprisonment in the State Prison for Women at Auburn."[17] This clause, in combination with the reformatory commitment laws, insured that Auburn inmates would be felons and either over thirty years in age or, if under thirty, likely to have a previous felony conviction. (They would, in other words, be women most likely to fit the image of criminal women as hardened and unreformable.) During the first years of the prison's existence, Auburn inmates received the determinate sentences associated with state prisons for men—sentences that were designed to punish, not rehabilitate. Later, as indeterminate sentences became nearly universal, women at Auburn also received such sentences. However, the minimum and maximum were determined by offense and not, as at reformatories, by the condition of needing a cure for criminality. Auburn sentences, in short, were more frankly punitive.

The reformatory movement developed a rhetoric of benevolence and, in its first flush of enthusiasm for itself, issued many promises of cure. These encouraged judges and social agencies to funnel commitments into the reformatories, many of which began to suffer from overcrowding not long after they were opened. The populations of custodial prisons for women, on the other hand, tended to remain small.[18] Their low numbers were no doubt partly a function of generally low rates of serious crimes by women. But as

Hard Times

shown in more detail below, the small populations of custodial women's prisons were probably also an effect of judicial reluctance to
commit to such "masculine" institutions women who appeared to
warrant gentler treatment.

Records pertaining to the Auburn women's prison indicate that
judicial reluctance to commit was one factor that kept that prison's population low. In the early years of the State Prison for Women, judges took advantage of a law giving them discretion to send
felons with terms of under five years to local penitentiaries instead
of to the prison. Some exercised this discretion when they
sentenced women, thus causing a good deal of bitterness among the
State Commissioners of Prisons, who worried about underutiliza-
tion of the women's prison with its capacity for 250 inmates. In
1901 the commission had the Penal Code amended to force judges to
send *all* female felons with sentences of a year or more to Auburn,
even though this might mean separating them by long distances
from families and friends. "If their friends were acquainted with the
prison for women at Auburn," the commissioners opined, "they
would ask as a favor that the unfortunates be sent there."[19]

Thus there was from the start a struggle between state prison
authorities, who wanted their prison full, and judges who felt
Auburn was an unsuitable place of commitment for all but the most
hardened women. This struggle continued, but after the opening in
1901 of the reformatory at Bedford (which could receive some young
first felons as well as misdemeanants), judges began committing
women to Bedford in preference to either the penitentiaries or
Auburn. Now state authorities blamed *Bedford* rather than the
penitentiaries for siphoning off women who might have been sent to
the prison. As the Superintendent of State Prisons ovserved with
irritation in 1903,

> For some reason, many women convicted in this State
> who might be sent to the State Prison for Women, at
> Auburn, are sent to other institutions. This is very greatly
> to be regretted. In its equipment and its resources for
> dealing with women under sentence it is not equalled by
> any other institution in the State.[20]

And, he tellingly added, the Auburn prison "can comfortably accommodate three times as many as are now confined there."[21] Despite its capacity of 250, the State Prison for Women seldom held

more than 120 inmates; frequently the population fell below 100. Prison officials had good reason to suspect that judges committed women to Auburn with less enthusiasm than to reformatories. We cannot identify, from this point in time, the criteria (other than offense seriousness, age, and prior record) that judges used when they decided to send women to Auburn or other institutions. Yet we can be fairly sure that they sometimes did use other criteria, and it seems quite possible that these included preconceptions about the characteristics of reformable and unreformable female offenders.

THE PRISONERS

The majority of the Auburn women were committed for property crimes, the modal offense within this category being grand larceny. However, crimes against persons usually ran a close second to property offenses, and if one looked a the institution's population as a whole (as opposed to those committed in the course of a particular year), one might have found a preponderance of offenders against persons. (For example, for ninety-nine inmates incarcerated at the State Prison for Women in 1927, forty-eight had been convicted of offenses against persons, thirty-eight of offenses against property.) Within the category of crimes against persons, the offense for which Auburn women were most frequently convicted was homicide.[22]

As noted earlier, one common stereotype of the female offender pictured her as a sex offender or minor property offender who strayed into criminal activity (or was led into it by a male companion) rather than seeking it deliberately. This stereotype of the ''womanly'' female offender had little in common with the image of Auburn offenders that emerges from that prison's records. In range and variety, their offenses were decidely unladylike; examples include arson for profit, assault with acid, bigamy, blackhand extortion, check forgery, pickpocketing and other types of professional theft, robbery in the first degree (sometimes committed with female accomplices), accessory to rape, and torture. Examination of cases *within* specific offense categories also indicates that the Auburn women did not fit with traditional concepts of the female offender as passive and impulsive. For example, the stereotype of the female-who-kills as someone who strikes back at her lover in self-defense is contradicted by some of the data on Auburn homicide offenders, whose victims included not only husbands and lovers, but also

children, parents, and other women. The means by which these women killed, moreover, included not only stabbing with the kitchen
knife with which the female homicide offender is often associated,
but also strangulation (in one case, of two men), bludgeoning, burn-
ing alive in an oven, and presenting a husband poisoned candy. If
any female prisoners conformed to the image of the gentle offender
it was those held at the reformatories; the Albion reformatory's prisoner registries, for instance, show that its inmates were convicted of
a narrow range of such mild offenses as drunkenness and fornication, offenses that seem pale in comparison to those of the women
at Auburn.[23]

In view of the greater seriousness of their crimes, we would expect women in a custodial prison like Auburn to serve longer terms
than those sent to reformatories, and this does indeed seem to have
been the case in New York State. Average time-served for Auburn
prisoners, of course, was increased by the high proportion of women
serving life sentences, and in some cases "life" meant many years
indeed. Case No. 60, for instance, one of the women transferred in
1893 to Auburn from a county penitentiary, had originally been
sentenced to the old prison for women at Sing Sing in 1865, at the
age of sixteen; when she arrived at Auburn, she had already served
twenty-eight years. Similarly, Case No. 65 had served seventeen
years, beginning at the old Sing Sing women's prison, before she was
transferred in 1893 to Auburn.

A second factor suggesting that women in the custodial institutions served longer sentences is the fact that their discharge dates
were keyed to their offenses. During its first years, the State Prison
for Women released inmates principally through "commutation"—
expiration of sentence with some time off for good behavior. Later,
parole became the primary means of release; however, the principle
that the punishment should be proportional to the severity of the offense still operated, working to hold serious offenders for long
periods.

Thus at least in the New York case, the custodial institution
seems to have held inmates longer than reformatories. However, we
should note that in one sense, reformatory inmates were sentenced
more harshly, for many of them were committed for relatively in-
nocuous offenses. For minor "crimes" like fornication and drunkenness—offenses for which men were punished but lightly, if at
all—reformatories throughout the country could hold women for
several years. Reformatory sentences ignored the principle that pun-

ishment should be proportional to the crime, and reformatory programs were designed to induce conformity to middle-class standards of female propriety.[24] In both respects, sentence to a reformatory was more repressive and inequitable than sentence to a custodial institution, where little effort was made to "improve" prisoners and the principle of proportionality still prevailed.

From data in the annual reports of the State Prison for Women, we can piece together a composite portrait of the Auburn inmates. In age, they averaged in their early or mid-twenties at the time of commitment, although the range was great, stretching from sixteen to over sixty. (Reformatory records indicate that during their early years of operation, the majority of their inmates were twenty-one years or younger.) A high proportion of the Auburn population was black—from one-quarter of the total population in the early years up to one-half in 1913. (New York reformatories for women, in contrast, received few women of color during their early years of operation.) Also well represented in the Auburn population were the foreign-born (primarily German and Irish), who usually constituted from one-third to one-half of the total population. In religion, the majority identified themselves as Protestants, but Catholics were not far behind numerically, and usually there were also several Jews. In view of their relatively advanced age at commitment, it is not surprising that the majority of Auburn women were married or widowed. (In this respect, too, they differed from reformatory inmates, who tended to be unmarried.)[25]

In sum, the Auburn prisoners bore little resemblance to the "soft" female offender who dominated the literature on reformatories. Judges avoided sending women to this institution. When they did sentence prisoners to Auburn, they apparently made their decision partly on the basis of characteristics associated with the stereotype of the female offender as hard and masculine. This was a stereotype that Auburn women might well have seemed to fit: serious offenders with long sentences, they were relatively mature and often either foreign-born or nonwhite. They were, in short, women who probably seemed incapable of resocialization to meet middle-class standards of womanliness.

PROGRAM

One of the strongest contrasts between the custodial women's prison and the reformatory lay in the former's relative indifference to those training and treatment programs that provided the reformatory's raison de'être. This is not to say that the custodial prisons offered no programs at all; like most men's prisons, they usually attempted to provide instruction to illiterates and work that (in theory at least) might prepare inmates to hold jobs after release. Nor, on the other hand, was the ambitious rhetoric of the reformatory always matched in practice when it came to educational programs. But while the differences in program between the two types of women's prisons were not entirely clear-cut, they were nonetheless *key*: the goal of providing rehabilitative programs—a goal that affected reformatories in their architecture, routine, allocation of resources, and hiring practices—had very low priority in custodial institutions. The latter took an interest in programs only to maintain discipline, and they valued smoothness of operation above the expanded opportunities of inmates. Custodial institutions allocated few funds for educational or vocational programs, and their administrators did not conceive that such programs, even if well funded, would produce much in the way of results.

Vocational

The programs of the two types of female penal institutions *did* resemble one another in the area of vocational training. Reformatory and custodial practices approximated each other in this area because they were based on similar assumptions about the types of work appropriate to women—needlework, cleaning, food preparation, and personal care.

At the State Prison for Women, the main industry for the forty years of the institution's existence was the sewing of bedding. Mattresses, pillows, and hemmed blankets were the chief products, the manufacture of which occupied roughly half the population at any one time. The other half of the population was kept busy with institutional maintenance: cooking, cleaning, domestic service for the matron, laundry (for not only the women's prison, but the warden and hospital of the men's prison as well), mending, nursing, and gardening. To work in the gardens surrounding the main building of the women's prison was probably the inmates' most prized activity, as it gave them a chance to be active and outdoors. Large quantities of vegetables, particularly cabbages and turnips, were harvested each year, Probably the least popular assignment was to work at the handlooms, obsolete machines noted for "their racket and discomfort to the inmates working along side of them.'' On these looms inmates produced immense lengths of toweling— 6,000 yards in 1900, for example.[26]

While work programs that featured sewing, cleaning, and food preparation were also common in reformatories, institutions of this type were less concerned about the costs of vocational programs. Indeed, reformatories often insisted that moral profit to inmates, not financial benefit to the institution, should be the first consideration in planning work programs for prisoners. Auburn and other custodial prisons for women, in contrast, usually looked for a way to keep inmates busy at the least possible expense. Some also maintained the ancient tradition of men's prisons of expecting inmate industries to produce a profit.[27] The State Prison for Women at Auburn, for example, usually turned a small profit (up to $1,500 in 1900). For a while, this prison adhered to yet another men's prison tradition by paying its industrial workers, albeit poorly at one-and-a-half cents a day.[28] This tradition was also ignored by most women's reformatories, which trained inmates to be domestics rather than factory workers.

Educational

There was greater discrepancy between the two types of female penal institutions in their educational programs. When funding permitted, reformatories hired several teachers, and they usually gave class attendance a prominent place in the day's schedule. But custodial prisons like Auburn spent little on teaching staffs, and in scheduling they gave industrial work precedence over classroom activities. For its first fifteen years, the school at Auburn operated only in the evenings, and it was taught not by a hired teacher, but by educated inmates supervised by the head teacher of the men's prison. A paid female teacher joined the staff early in the twentieth century. She instituted a typing program (although there was only one typewriter), and from then on the school played an increasingly important role in the life of inmates. But it never assumed the dominant place in institutional life taken by education in reformatories.

DISCIPLINE

In terms of discipline there were also great differences between the two types of women's prisons (though less in practice, no doubt, than in theory). Custodial prisons for women dealt with discipline in the relatively straightforward, rule-dominated manner of large men's prisons. Little interest was shown in the reformatory ideal of giving inmates opportunities to develop a sense of responsibility; rather, the emphasis fell on obedience and conformity.

This emphasis was congruent with the traditions of the Auburn prison as a whole, which had a long and at times infamous history of harsh discipline. Soon after the women's section was established in 1893, a *New York Times* feature story described it and the adjacent men's prison as "old school" in their regulation of prisoners, with "iron-clad rules of discipline." Warden James C. Stout, who supervised both the men's and women's prisons, was characterized as a no-frills, no-nonsense keeper. Furthermore, the *Times* went on, the "silent" system that forbade prisoner communication was, in 1895, still enforced in the shops and mess hall of the men's prison. It seems also to have been enforced in the women's prison and to have endured there even longer, for nearly twenty years after the *New York Times* report we learn from Madeline Doty, the prison commissioner who posed as an inmate, that silence was enforced at all times except during a daily ten-minute walking period. According to Doty, the penalty for whispering was three days in solitary confinement, loss of good time (the time off they had earned for good behavior), and a fine of fifty cents daily; silence was enforced even in the industrial areas. Doty described the harsh enforcement:

> There were fifty of us in the workroom, with three matrons keeping guard. They sat at high desks, glaring. . . .[29]

Discipline at the Auburn prison for women, as at penal institutions the world over, was achieved through both positive and negative rewards. Positive rewards consisted of promotion to better "grades" in which one might wear solid-colored rather than striped dresses and enjoy such privileges as decorating one's room with a rug and white bedspread. From time to time at Auburn, systems of badges were instituted; for example, in 1903 the matron founded a Society of the Red Badge of Courage, awarded red badges in return for strict obedience, and convened a meeting of the Society once a month. Negative consequences at Auburn included being assigned to "cold, damp cells in the basement," solitary confinement in the institution's jail, loss of good time, and fines. Doty pointed out that although inmates were paid a pittance for their labor, "as a fine of fifty cents a day for each day of punishment is imposed, it is seldom a prisoner has any funds on release, even after a long term." Such punishments were the consequences of insolence, rule-breaking, and emotional outbursts. That the authorities at the State Prison for Women also worried about homosexuality is indicated by Doty's observation that "one of the many unwritten prison rules...is that any form of greeting between inmates is considered immoral, evidence of what is termed 'lady love,' and promptly punished."[30]

ROUTINE

Routines of custodial women's prisons were more monotonous than those of reformatories, their monotony flowing from a number of sources. One was architectural: such institutions tended to have less space for programs and recreation. Another was the custodial approach itself, which discouraged those visits and gifts from benevolent outsiders that sometimes enlivened routines in reformatories.[31] Third, as noted earlier, the absentee-warden system of the custodial women's prison meant that the female subordinates who were in charge of daily routine had little authority or incentive for innovation.

Even the few events that did interrupt the monotony of cell time at Auburn had a cheerless aspect. Normally inmates were allowed half an hour of daily exercise in the yard. Doty describes them as wearing overshoes, capes, and knitted hats called "fascinators." "We resembled a group of dejected little orphans suddenly grown old as round and round the yard we marched." Another break was provided by chapel services featuring organ music by the reverend's daughter and hymns sung by the inmates. Members of the local Women's Christian Temperance Union would visit occasionally, distributing religious tracts and flowers. In 1912 a series of "entertainments" was organized, but these probably were more edifying than entertaining: they included celebration of Columbus Day with readings; a music program featuring "vocal solos, pianologues and violin solos"; a Christmas presentation by the East Auburn WCTU; and a play performed by the inmates of Ward V called "The Colored Suffragettes." There were also un- planned interruptions of routine, as when an inmate gave birth, became deranged and was transferred to Matteawan, or committed suicide. Such events, no doubt, were central topics in the inmates' whispered conversations.[32]

Hard Times

Given the bleakness of life at Auburn, it is little wonder that a Prison Survey Committee of 1920 described this prison as lacking in "vitality." To this committee, the State Prison for Women was like "an old ladies' home, or . . . a well-conducted county almshouse. The atmosphere was one of quiet routine. . . ."[33]

There were, however, three events that interrupted the usual calm of the State Prison for Women. One was the reappearance in 1913 of Madeline Doty, returning after her few days in the guise of an inmate to exhort prisoners and staff to institute major changes. In the tradition of Progressive reformers (and in frank emulation of Thomas Mott Osborne, who had similarly approached the reform of men's prisons), Doty urged more intercourse with the outside world and a system of inmate self-government. Prisoners, she instructed, should take an active role in all aspects of institutional life, from improving the food to discipline. But despite Doty's enthusiasm, several mass meetings of inmates, and a few innovations in routine, Auburn soon slipped back into its old ways. Doty blamed the backsliding on the older matrons who, she claimed, were fearful that they would lose their jobs if inmates assumed too much responsibility. However, it is unlikely that the reforms recommended by Doty would have succeeded even if the matrons had all been as youthful and independent as she. Doty herself soon tired of the effort to enliven a routine whose monotony was inherent in the concept of the prison.[34]

The second and third events to disrupt the usual monotony of life at the State Prison for Women were two related riots in the adjacent men's prison—the most serious prison riots in New York state history before Attica. In the first, which began on 28 July 1929, male inmates armed themselves from the prison's arsenal, set large areas of the men's prison on fire, and attempted a mass escape. A contemporary report states:

> *For five hours the battle raged, but in the end the guards, reenforced by State troopers and militiamen, drove the prisoners to cover with machine-guns, rifles and tear gas bombs. A check-up then showed that four convicts had escaped, two prisoners had been killed, and three guards, a fireman, and twelve convicts wounded.*[35]

During the second riot in the men's prison, which began the following December, the principal keeper and eight inmates were killed;

control was restored by state police armed with gas and guns. Neither riot spilled over the dividing wall into the women's prison, but the effects there of nearby fires, teargassing, and gun battles were probably dramatic.[36]

REMOVAL TO BEDFORD

In 1933, the New York State Prison for Women was relocated to the grounds of the Bedford reformatory, where it remains today. Among pressures contributing to this change, most important seems to have been the severe overcrowding in the men's section of Auburn. This overcrowding, a prime precipitator of the riots of 1929, drew the attention of prison authorities to the adjacent women's prison, which had never reached capacity and was growing in population more slowly than any other prison in the state.[37]

But there were also positive reasons for wanting to shift the females to Bedford. First, the change would locate the women's prison closer to New York City, from which most of its inmates were committed. Second, the population of the Bedford reformatory was at a low point, and its superintendent was interested in finding new sources of commitments. A third factor influencing the choice of Bedford was the state's recent purchase of property directly across the road from the reformatory. This land had been used for female prisoners back in the days when it was owned by John D. Rockefeller, Jr., who had bought it with the idea that the state should hold female prisoners there and study them to learn the causes of crime. Several dilapidated buildings remained, and prison authorities planned to renovate them to hold female prisoners once again.[38]

Transfer of the Auburn felons to Bedford probably would not have taken place had the women's reformatory movement not been on the wane. After sixty years of enthusiasm for creation of a separate system of female reformatories, the movement had finally lost its momentum. As the optimism of the Progressive period subsided, the reformatory movement—like many other Progressive causes—was virtually abandoned. No longer did it seem a matter of urgency to keep reformatory women totally isolated from older, more serious offenders like those held at the State Prison for Women. The stereotypes of the female offender as either feminine and curable or masculine and unreformable now carried less force.

Removal of the female inmates from Auburn to Bedford had been discussed since 1913, the year in which the Superintendent of State Prisons first suggested that the women's prison be appropriated for use by men. The plan for removal was developed fully in 1920 when the influential Prison Survey Committee urged the state to buy the Rockefeller property for relocation of the Women's Prison.[39] (The head of the Prison Survey Committee, Adolph Lewisohn, was a business associate of William Rockefeller, brother of John. Purchase of this land for $175,000 from John D. Rockefeller, Jr., was completed in 1923.)[40] To overcome potential resistance to the plan, the Prison Survey Committee argued that the differences between inmates held at the Auburn women's prison and the Bedford reformatory were actually small. According to the committee:

> *The difference lies rather in the names of the institutions than in the character of the inmates. One is supposedly a state's prison for women, the other presumably a reformatory. [But] each has its mental defectives, its border-line cases, its easily-managed types and its hardened or difficult types. . . .*
>
> *It makes little difference whether one is at Albion, Bedford, or Auburn. . . .*[41]

Such statements minimized real differences and also signified the weakening of the distinction between two types of female criminals. The most significant point, however, is that the members of the committee, leaders in prison reform, were now abandoning the reform ideology. Their interest had shifted from rehabilitation to system management.

In 1931 the legislature finally authorized relocation of the State Prison for Women to Bedford. The new institution was to receive the same types of offenders as Auburn had, and to hold them apart from reformatory inmates; however, the new prison would be managed by the superintendent of the reformatory. In the same year the legislature stopped postponing the expense of remodeling of the "Rockefeller Group" of buildings and appropriated $225,000 for this purpose.[42] With transfer of women to Bedford in 1933, the State Prison for Women at Auburn was closed.

LINKAGE OF THE TWO varieties of female penal institutions on one site and under one management in 1933 provides us with a date for

Nicole Hahn Rafter

what was, in effect, the end of the two types of women's prisons in their pure form. (Similar amalgamations of female felon and misdemeanant populations occurred in a number of other states in the early 1930s.) Thereafter, the two models merged and their confluence eventually produced the women's prison system as we know it today, with its mixed mode of custodialism and nurturance.

The traditions that had evolved with the custodial model, however, lived on. Their strength and persistence is indicated by the fact that even in the new quarters at Bedford, inmates of the state prison for women (renamed Westfield State Farm) continued to receive care more similar to that which they had known at Auburn than that typical of the reformatory: almost no provision was made for their education, job training, or recreation.[43] Despite changes, the custodial style persists today; we see signs of it in the fact that women's prisons are often the last to be funded, in the fact that their plants are often more poorly equipped that those of men's prisons, in the relative weakness of their programs, and in the system's failure to produce more top female administrators. It is particularly in the customary neglect of women's prisons that the custodial tradition continues.[44]

Although the custodial and reformatory models have today merged, it is also possible to distinguish, for analytical purposes, inheritances from the old reformatory style. We see this legacy in such contemporary aspects of female incarceration as its characteristically low security; its tendency to provide living quarters that (to the outsider, at least) resemble college dormitory rooms rather than cells; and in its paternalistic aspects, such as its tendency to treat female inmates as errant children. Particularly in the ways in which the current prison system treats female offenders as "softer" than men does the reformatory tradition persist.

The women's prison system is not, then a monolith. The merger of its two quite different traditions or styles created its present ambiguous character of being *both* harsher and milder than the prison system for men. The scholarly tradition that has ignored women and women's institutions if they did not conform to stereotypes associated with the "good" woman blinds us to historical realities about the development of the women's prison system—and of the prison system as a whole. It obscures sources of problems that plague the women's prison system today. And it contributes to a process by which criminology and penology perpetuate sex stereotypes and thus actually distort their own subject matter.

Hard Times

NOTES

THE RESEARCH REPORTED here is part of a larger investigation of the origins of the women's prison system funded by the National Institute of Justice. This chapter on the State Prison for Women at Auburn, New York, is primarily based on such official records as the annual reports of the institution. However, data on the State Prison for Women were also collected from prisoner registries held by the New York State Archives, and some use is made of that data here. A number of people made helpful comments on earlier versions of this chapter, among them Eleanor Little, Lou Lombardo, Gary Marx, Elena Natalizia, Stephen Pfohl, and Claudine SchWeber.

1. Until recently, the most comprehensive study of state prisons for women was one that dealt exclusively with reformatories, published in Holland in 1931: Eugenia Cornelia Lekkerkerker, *Reformatories for Women in the United States* (Batavia, Holland: Bij J. B. Wolters' Uitgevers-Maatschappij, 1931). During the last fifteen years scholars in various social sciences have begun to pay slightly more attention to the incarceration of women, but their focus has generally remained fixed on the reformatory-type of prison. *See*, for example, Rose Giallombardo, *Society of Women: A Study of a Women's Prison* (New York: John Wiley & Sons, 1966); and Estelle B. Freedman, *Their Sisters' Keepers: Women's Prison Reform in America, 1830–1930* (Ann Arbor: University of Michigan Press, 1981).

2. The men's prison system, too, had a subsystem of reformatories, and these were inspired by the same ideology of rehabilitation that gave birth to the reformatory prison for women. However, reformatories for men bore little resemblance to those holding women: they were closer to the maximum security type of prison for older men (indeed, reformatories for males were sometimes themselves maximum security institutions), while women's reformatories more closely resembled reformatories for juveniles. That women were conceived as more childlike is, I think, significant; it underscores my basic point that criminal justice is shaped by sex stereotypes and, in turn, reinforces them.

3. For descriptions, *see* Dorothea Lynde Dix, *Remarks on Prisons and Prison Discipline in the United States*, 2d ed. (1845; repr. Montclair, NJ: Patterson Smith, 1967); E. C. Wines and Theodore W. Dwight, *Report on the Prisons and Reformatories of the United States and Canada* (Albany: Van Benthuysen & Sons, 1867); and W. David Lewis, "The Ordeal of the Unredeemables," in *From Newgate to Dannemora: The Rise of the Penitentiary in New York, 1797–1848* (Ithaca, NY: Cornell University press, 1965), ch. 7. My discussion has dealt with only state-supported prisons for women; some of the remarks about custodial prisons, however, also apply to locally run jail units for women.

4. The first of the four state female prisons established by New York in the late nineteenth century was the House of Refuge for Women at Hudson, which received its first inmates in 1887; however, in 1904 this institution became a training school for girls. The Western House of Refuge at Albion opened in 1893. The New York State Reformatory for Women at Bedford was established in 1892, but was not ready to receive prisoners until 1901. In contrast to the other two reformatories, Bedford admitted some felons as well as misdemeanants. For a study of a custodial

women's prison in a state that had only one institution for female state prisoners, *see* Nicolas Fischer Hahn, "Female State Prisoners in Tennessee: 1831-1979," *Tennessee Historical Quarterly* 39, 4 (Winter 1980):485-97.

5. In 1893, just before the State Prison for Women was established at Auburn, New York's penitentiaries held a total of 155 females (New York State Governor, *Annual Message, 3 January 1893:181#82); see also* "To Help Fallen Women," *New York Times,* 2 January 1892:8. That the Women's Prison Association of New York also brought pressure to bear on the legislature to establish the reformatories and the institution at Auburn is indicated by "Care of Women Prisoners," *New York Times,* 25 January 1891:3.

6. The harsh character of the Auburn men's prison is indicated by the fact that the first electric chair was installed and used there in 1890, not long before the women's prison was established.

7. New York State Commission of Prisons, *Annual Report 1896*:42 ("only a wicket"); New York Superintendent of State Prisons, *Annual Report 1892*:23.

8. New York State Commission of Prisons, *Annual Report 1898*:68 ("airy and comfortable"); ibid., *Annual Report 1908*:92 (heat, light, water); Madeline Z. Doty, *Society's Misfits* (New York: Century, 1916), esp. pp. 25-26, 46.

9. Doty, *Society's Misfits,* p. 39.

10. New York State Commission of Correction, *Annual Report 1928*:15.

11. This was true, for example, at the New York Reformatory for Women at Bedford until, in 1921, as a result of a series of disastrous female superintendents, the law was changed to permit appointment of a male; see New York *Laws of 1921,* Ch. 485.

12. New York *Laws of 1893,* Ch. 306, sec. 12.

13. New York State Commission of Prisons, Annual Report 1902:14-15. That the women who ran reformatories were not necessarily better paid was pointed out to me by Miss Eleanor Little of Guilford, Connecticut. Miss Little began her long career at Pennsylvania's Sleighton Farms, an institution for girls. In the second decade of the twentieth century she became psychologist at the recently opened New Jersey reformatory for women, Clinton Farms, an institution superintended by May Caughey. Miss Little writers, "May Caughey's salary when she began at Clinton was $1,200 per year. Mine as I remember was $600 maximum. My beginning salary at Sleighton Farms was $300." (Personal communication of 11 October 1980.)

14. "An Old School Prison—The Institution at Auburn the First This State Built," *New York Times,* 8 December 1895:25.

15. The image of the typical female criminal as "soft" dominated the literature on female criminality in the Progressive period; *see,* for example, Jean Weidensall, *The Mentality of the Criminal Woman* (Baltimore: Warwick & York, 1916). An early and typically condemnatory discussion of the female offender as "hard" and "masculine" appeared in Francis Lieber's "Translator's Preface" to Gustave de Beaumont and Alexis de Tocqueville, *On the Penitentiary System in the United States* (1833; repr. Carbondale, IL: Southern Illinois University Press, 1964), pp. 8-13; *see also* Caesar Lombroso and William Ferrero, *The Female Offender* (1895; repr. New York: Philosophical Library, 1958). Madeline Doty's treatment of Auburn women in *Society's Misfits* is curious in that it presents these "hard" prisoners as "soft" and reformable; here we see the power of the Progressive ideology of reform. For recent analyses of the influence of sex stereotypes on the criminology of women, *see* Dorie Klein, "The Etiology of Female Crime: A Review of the Literature," in *The Female Offender,* ed. Laura Crites (Lexington, MA: Lexington Books, 1976), ch. 1;

and Nicolas F. Hahn, "Too Dumb to Know Better: Cacogenic Family Studies and the Criminology of Women," *Criminology* 18, 1 (May 1980):3–25.

Although these stereotypes of "the" female offender have less power today than they did at the turn of the century, they continue to appear in the criminological literature and to affect theories of female crime and punishment. Indeed, the fact that when women's prisons are studied at all, attention is given almost exclusively to institutions that began as reformatories, indicates the continuing investment in the notion that female offenders are "feminine."

16. New York *Laws of 1881*, Ch. 187, secs. 7-8.

17. New York *Laws of 1893*, Ch. 306, sec. 9.

18. This generalization must be qualified, however, because the size of the population in custodial institutions differed markedly among the states at any one time and because these populations tended to expand over time. Furthermore, few custodial units for women were as spacious as Auburn. Hence, even those with relatively small populations could be horribly overcrowded.

19. New York State Commission of Prisons, *Annual Report 1896*:5–7; ibid., *Annual Report 1898*:68–69; ibid., *Annual Report 1899*:17; ibid., *Annual Report 1902*:82 (1901 change in law); ibid., *Annual Report 1896*:43 ("If their friends…").

20. New York Superintendent of State Prisons, *Annual Report 1903*:19–20.

21. Ibid.

22. This paragraph is based on information in the prison's annual reports. At a later time these data will be tested against those collected directly from the prisoner registries.

23. This paragraph is based on as yet untabulated data collected directly from the prisoner registries of the Auburn prison and Albion reformatory (New York State Archives). The Bedford reformatory, because it could receive both felons and misdemeanants, probably had a more mixed population; however, because the original prisoner records from Bedford have been lost, that institution is not included in the comparison here. A classic description of the woman who commits homicide appears in Marven E. Wolfgang, *Patterns in Criminal Homicide* (Philadelphia: University of Pennsylvania Press, 1958).

24. *See* Freedman, *Their Sisters' Keepers.*

25. Information on Auburn in this paragraph is based on the official data published in the prison's annual reports; at a later time it will be tested against data collected from the prisoner registries. Information on the reformatories is based on unpublished data collected from the Albion reformatory records and on official records covering the first ten years of operation of all women's reformatories in the northeastern and midwestern United States.

26. New York State Commission of Prisons, *Annual Report 1918*:93 ("racket and discomfort"); ibid., *Annual Report 1900*:28.

27. This tradition also influenced reformatory industries, but was less important to reformatories than to custodial institutions.

28. Ibid., *Annual Report 1900*:28; Doty, *Society's Misfits*, p. 53. That women were not paid at all for their work in later years is indicated by New York State Commission of Correction, *Annual Report 1928*:58, which argued that "as the men in the industries in the men's prison receive compensation, these [female] inmates should also receive it."

29. "An Old School Prison," *New York Times*, 8 December 1895:25; Doty, *Society's Misfits*, pp. 17-18, 24-25, 51.

30. Doty, *Society's Misfits*, pp. 90-90 ("damp cells"), 53 (fines), 47-48

(homosexuality); New York Superintendent of State Prisons, *Annual Report 1903:166* (Society of the Red Badge of Courage); New York State Commission of Prisons, *Annual Report 1918:93* (harshness of punishments at the State Prison for Women).

31. *See*, for example, New York State Reformatory for Women at Bedford, *Annual Report 1910:29*, noting that one women from as far away as Chicago had donated $50 to help the reformatory produce a play and that the play's author had donated another $25.

32. Doty, *Society's Misfits*, p. 49; New York Superintendent of State Prisons, *Annual Report 1913:199-200* (list of "entertainments" for 1912).

33. New York State Prison Survey Committee, *Report* (Albany: J. B. Lyon, 1920), pp. 366-67 (hereafter cited as Lewisohn Committee, *Report*).

34. Doty describes her futile efforts to reform the routine in the chapter of *Society's Misfits* benefits on p. 66. For the famous model she was following, *see* Thomas Mott Osborne, *Within Prison Walls* (New York: D. Appleton, 1916).

35. "New York State's Prison Revolts," *Literary Digest* 10 (August 1929):8.

36. For more on the riots, *see* Winthrop D. Lane, "Prisons at the Breaking Point," *Survey 62*, 11 (1 September 1929):557-58, 584-89; and Elizabeth B. Croft, "New York State Prisons and Prison Riots from Auburn and Clinton: 1929 to Attica: 1971" (Master's thesis, School of Criminal Justice, State University of New York at Albany, 1972). That the riots did not spill over into the women's prison is indicated by Shelia Tucker, "Cat Eye Annie," *Citizen Advocate* (Auburn, NY), 2 November 1974.

37. New York State Department of Correction, *Annual Report 1932:7*.

38. Lewisohn Committee, *Report*, p. 374 (closer to New York City, and thus transportation costs would be lowered); New York State Commission of Correction, *Annual Report 1934:76* (underpopulation leads superintendent to advertise Westfield State Farm to committing magistrates in an illustrated brochure); ibid., *Annual Report 1928:24*; and New York State Commission on Prison Administration and Construction, *The Correctional Institutions for Women* (Albany: J. B. Lyon, 1932), p. 29 (Rockerfeller property). For background information on Rockerfeller's involvement with Bedford, *see* Katherine B. Davis's "Introduction" to Weidensall, *The Mentality of the Criminal Woman*.

39. New York Superintendent of State Prisons, *Annual Report 1913:22, 127-28*; Lewisohn Committee, *Report*, esp. p. 372.

40. *New York Times*, 15 February *1923:19*.

41. Lewisohn Committee, *Report*, pp. 365-66.

42. New York State Commission on Prison Administration and Construction, *The Correctional Institutions for Women*, p. 29.

43. New York State Commission of Correction, *Annual Report 1934:79* (only teacher at the prison is an inmate and the prison lacks library materials); ibid., p. 83 ("The women of the Prison group knit a great deal").

44. For ways in which the current women's prison system fails to measure up to that for males, *see* Ruth M. Glick and Virginia V. Neto, *National Study of Women's Correctional Programs* (Washington, DC: U.S. Government Printing Office, 1977).

12

Female Patients and the Medical Profession in Jails and Prisons

A Case of Quintuple Jeopardy

NANCY STOLLER SHAW

The terms *double* and *triple jeopardy* are often used to describe the condition of poor and minority women in a racist, sexist, and economically oppressive society. Women in prison who have health problems are jeopardized in their attempts to solve them by these and two additional factors: being prisoners and being patients. As prisoners they are in those institutions that accord the fewest rights to, and sanction the most oppressive treatment of, their inmates. And as patients they are expected to submit without objection or question to the authority of experts—health workers and physicians. Summing these factors up, we can say that the female prisoner is in *quintuple* jeopardy when she encounters the medical profession. To understand how this works and how it can be resolved to the patient's ultimate advantage, we must first know something about the women in American prisons.

261

Nancy Stoller Shaw

Female prisoners are young; most of them are under twenty-nine years of age. The 80 percent who are misdemeanants and unsentenced women have a median age of twenty-four. Similarly, the median age of felons is only twenty-seven.[1] Only 36 percent of incarcerated women are white (although whites constitute 82 percent of the U.S. population). Over 50 percent of the prisoners are black, 9 percent are Hispanic, 3 percent are Native American, and 2 percent are from other ethnic groups. All minority groups are over-represented.[2] Most women arrestees and prisoners come from poor families and are at a bare survival level at the time of incarceration.[3]

Their crimes are overwhelmingly economic in nature, with property and related offenses constituting over 75 percent of all female arrests.[4] Naturally, women confined for such misdemeanors as prostitution or small-scale shoplifting differ somewhat from those women convicted of computer fraud, major stock market machinations, and other serious crimes. Yet the majority of women are more similar than divergent in several salient ways: they share their gender; they are predominantly poor; most have children; most are from Third World and native backgrounds; and they are all incarcerated at the will of the state.

HEALTH NEEDS AND HEALTH CARE

Female inmates arrive at jail or prison with a normal variety of health needs, all of which must be met inside the correctional institution. It is the essence of incarceration that one cannot go out to the grocery store, the drug store, the clinic, the dentist, and certainly not to the health food store. If a prisoner's needs cannot be met in the *carcel* or at a designated health-care location (such as a hospital with guards or a locked ward for prisoners), those needs simply will not be met. This is true for such routine outpatient or clinic-type services as dental work; most gynecological services (including PAP smears), general checkups, and prenatal and postnatal care; and for such specialized services as drug and alcoholism treatment, psychiatric care, and dietary assistance. But, one might ask, do the women have serious or significant problems requiring much care? Are they not rather a healthy group of people? The answer is that they arrive with some health problems and develop others at the institution.

Because women in prison are predominantly poor and nonwhite, they suffer from the health ailments common to people from their economic and racial backgrounds; they are generally in worse health than citizens of higher economic status or those who are white.[5] Data collected by HEW in 1979 demonstrate that minorities and the economically disadvantaged have higher rates for four of the chronic diseases that are leading causes of mortality: heart disease, cancer, stroke, and diabetes.[6] They also have especially high mortality rates for diabetes and cirrhosis of the liver. Although they suffer injuries at the same rate as the advantaged population, the impact of the injuries is usually far greater. Recent surveys of dental needs support the generalization that 50 percent more nonwhites than whites are in need of dental care. In the area of gynecological and obstetrical health, minority women have higher rates of teenage pregnancy, maternal mortality, and untreated venereal disease. Most of this differential is a result of unequal access to such health-care services as birth control, legal abortion, and general medical care. Inferior nutrition further jeopardizes the pregnancies and infants of poor and nonwhite women.

General Medical Needs

In New York City, the women's jail population is 80 to 95 percent nonwhite. A study of this population in 1975 found that 72 percent of the women arriving at the jail had at least one current medical problem. The most frequently observed problems were drug addiction, psychiatric illness, hypertension, and respiratory ailments. Seventeen percent also had recent physical injuries.[7]

Incarceration exacerbates existing illnesses; leads to the development of new problems; and causes a general physical, mental, and emotional deterioration. Studies of sentenced women throughout the United States reveal that well over half also have abnormalities of the vulva, vagina, cervix, uterus, or ovaries,[8] although venereal disease rates on admission appear to be similar to those of the general population of single women.[9] Multiple pelvic exams, poor diet, and erratic medical follow-up on vaginal infections probably contribute to this high rate of gynecological disease. Another consequence of incarceration for women is abnormal weight gain. For example, the average woman of normal weight at the state prison in Connecticut gains fifteen pounds in her first three months of incarceration.[10] The same pattern is found at other institutions. It is caused by required meal attendance, poor diet, boredom, distress, and lack of exercise.

Emotional Problems Stemming from Loss of Children

Incarceration also results in multiple emotional shocks for the female prisoner. She is more often than not the sole support of her child or children, from whom she is now inevitably separated.[11] She is also more likely to have children and more of them, than is the average American female who is similarly a head of household.[12] Such a situation in which there is loss of job and household, sudden and perhaps permanent separation from children, and typically no outside "partner" to handle her free world needs, inevitably weakens the female prisoner and her dependents.

Female prisoners' separation from their children affects not only those with existing sons and daughters, but also those who are pregnant and may give birth in prison. Knowledge of the inevitable and lengthy separation from the child and the possible permanent loss influences abortion decisions, prenatal self-care and care by others, hospital plans, and decisions concerning breast feeding. Separation of newborns and mothers can have drastic emotional consequences for the child–mother relationship. It may also put the baby at an added health risk due to loss of breast feeding protections. Finally, it frequently raises the stress level of the woman. Modern obstetrical practice, including twentieth-century hospital birth arrangements with nurseries and bottle feeding technology, may have been a causal factor in the loss of the age-old right of mothers to keep their children with them in prison. Regardless of its historical origins, the current and widespread practice in the United States is to separate imprisoned mothers from their children completely except for limited visits.[13]

Overuse of Psychotropic Drugs

In most American correctional institutions, the use of psychotropic medication is common, with percentages of those under such medication on any given day averaging over 25 percent in many institutions and up to 100 percent in others.[14] Such prescribing patterns are indicative either of widespread mental and emotional problems among incarcerated women, or of the use of medication as a form of social control. The rate of psychiatric medication ranges from two to ten times higher for incarcerated women than for men, depending on the institution involved.[15] Studies of these prescribing patterns indicate sexist evaluation and prescription routines. For example, Shaw, Meyer, and Browne found that at Rikers' Island in a typical month in 1978, 15 percent of the female population was on psychotropics as compared to only 2 percent of the male population. Staff explanations of this difference focus on greater frequency of drug addiction and prison-induced emotional problems in women, and the assertion that overprescribing for women is a general social phenomenon that should draw no special attention.[16] The following statement was made in 1979 by the psychologist in charge of the mental health services for New York's female inmates:

> *All I can say is that the quantity of medication consumed by female offenders compared to the male offenders is really not significantly different than the amount of psychotropic medication consumed by females as compared to men in free society. Women for whatever reason, and I don't mean to be pointing fingers or saying anything disparagingly about them, use more medication. And that's an empirical fact.*[17]

Indignities of Custody and Punishment

Jails are punitive, not helping, institutions. The model of the 1950s and 1960s, with rehabilitation as the most important goal, has been officially discarded by many correctional systems. Thus, the traditional functions of retribution and containment are becoming the predominantly acknowledged purposes of prison. The impact of this custody and punishment orientation on the prisoner ranges from the acceptance of a low-quality health environment (seen as "all the prisoners deserve") and routine use of vaginal and rectal searches (daily for some court-goers) to physical and mental abuse, forced medication, denial of exercise, and intentional neglect. Female prisoners are sexually abused; demeaned; infantilized; and denied access to the vocational training, education, prison work, and work furlough opportunities afforded men.

Meanwhile, they are expected to behave in accord with traditional female sex-role patterns, which include pleasant submission to these inequalities and indignities. In contrast to this expectation is the fact that many jailed women are locked up precisely because they have refused to accept their designated lots. Most have been willing to break laws and take chances. As women and as mothers, they have fought against difficult odds and survived. Researchers report that most female prisoners have a positive self-concept and feel they have good survival skills.[18] This discrepancy between the prisoners' orientations and the realities of prison life produces a permanent struggle for self and social control. It is ironically tragic that prisons aim to crush the very characteristics that women need in the struggle for a dignified existence.

In this context, then, what hope does a woman have to receive adequate medical care from the prison doctor? The physicians and other health personnel in prisons vary widely in experience, competence, and attitude toward prisoners. As part of the general professionalization movement among service workers of all types, jail health workers, ranging from aides to internists, are upgrading their status. This process has included the recruitment of new workers fighting for more adequate health service funding, reorganization, and the hiring of more paraprofessionals.

QUINTUPLE JEOPARDY

When female prisoners seek medical care, five factors—gender, race, class background, legal status, and social role as patient—mitigate against equal and open communication between the patient and the health worker.

1. Gender

Sexism produces both a prejudiced view of female intelligence and stereotyped notions of appropriate behavior and public roles. Researchers have found that in physicians' offices female patients are treated differently than men. Basically, they are not taken seriously.[19] This practice also occurs in jails, even if the health services are fairly progressive.[20] Sexist notions affect both the prisoner and the health worker, regardless of the latter's sex. These stereotypes include notions about female criminality, sexuality, and sex-appropriate diseases, as well as behavior and role requirements. For example, at Rikers' Island in New York City, jail physicians object to women using obscene language; however, they tolerate such vocabulary from male prisoners, whose comments

Female Patients and the Medical Profession in Jails and Prisons

they view as an unpleasant but normal attribute of masculinity. In my own prison research I have found that when physicians are female, those who identify themselves as feminists are best able to critique their own diagnostic and planning behavior with female patients. Only those health workers who are comfortable with assertive, independent women are able to enjoy working with female prisoners.

2. Race

Racism causes the minority prisoner to hang back instead of speaking up, complaining, or discussing health matters with the medical worker or physician, especially when that person is white. The individual health worker may be a committed supporter of racial equality, but the overall structure of prison and jail existence is racially organized. Minority women are arrested, convicted, and incarcerated at higher rates than are whites. They are assigned to lower-status jobs and receive less pay. They have unequal access to educational and work furlough programs. They are sometimes denied the right to form organizations. And in some institutions, they are still segregated, although now by unofficial strategies. In prisons in which black women predominate as prisoners, white inmates are sometimes housed separately for "protective purposes." Such procedures foster racial conflict. Because prisoners *expect* racial stereotypes and prejudice (even if the health staff is not biased), communication is hindered and diagnoses may therefore be inaccurate.

3. Class Background

The prisoners' impoverished condition—their lack of social, financial, legal, and educational resources—prevents them from acting effectively in problematic situations. The impact of socioeconomic factors on health care in prison can be seen in several ways. The few prisoners who are wealthy or middle-class can arrange for better options: outside physicians for "second opinions" and lawyers to argue their health needs. They can afford health-oriented commissary items that not only help them physically, but also impress clinic health workers. The workers, for their part, are not usually trained to understand either the past or current impact of poverty on the prisoners' lives. Consequently, they may assume that ill health

Nancy Stoller Shaw

is a product of willful neglect, when the true explanation is poverty. The gap in education and personal values between most prisoners and their physicians may be so broad as to be uncrossable without special programs. For example, I was told by several health workers at a prison in New York City that women prisoners did not care about their health—otherwise, they would have taken care of their teeth and had better preventive care outside jail. Some staff maintained that the prisoners were "too lazy" to go to health clinics or private physicians outside and merely waited until incarcerated to attend the more convenient in-jail clinic. In other jails, I have met health workers who were offended by prisoners' language (including grammar), tattoos, style of dress, welfare status, and occupation.

4. Legal Status

Because the prisoner is legally detained, she is basically dependent on the state and its agents—the jail, the courts, the health department, the parole board—for survival and release. She is dependent and consequently powerless in her needs for food, clothing, heat, and shelter; communication with friends, family, and children; the satisfaction of health needs; and the provision of physical security. Additionally, she must rely on staff evaluations for release from the institution. In many cases *medical* personnel—particularly psychiatrists and other mental health staff members—have the added power of influencing the release process. Such power has a corrupting influence on the relationship between the prisoners and those providing the services.

5. Social Role as Patient

The doctor–patient relationship, often difficult to manage by *any* health-care consumer, is usually *more* difficult for incarcerated females. In the United States, in order to provide a guaranteed market, consumer desires for goods and services are constantly stimulated. A person who is sick is encouraged and even required to assume the role of health-care consumer. Ordinarily, a sick person's primary route to health is consumption of medical services provided by profit-producing bureaucracies. All patients suffer from powerlessness when confronting medicine, the wealthiest and most powerful of professions. This powerlessness has been well documented by the *American Health Empire, Health and Medical*

Care in the U.S., and the works of Eliot Friedson, among others.[21] The dependency and submission of any medical patient is intensified for the prisoner because she is incapable of going elsewhere to satisfy her medical needs and because physicians' decisions affect classification, in-prison movement, and release. It is difficult to overstate the impact of such medical decisions—one negative psychiatric report can be used to justify an extra year in prison. A doctor's refusal to authorize sick-time can result in either forced work or, if the prisoner refuses, punitive detention.

THESE FIVE FACTORS jeopardize the ability of the female prisoner/patient to get what she may need from the health-care system. It might be argued that many people (not only those who are prisoners) do not understand their medical needs—for example, what medication is necessary to cure a particular illness. This does not, however, contradict the fact that mutual negotiation and communication improve the chances for a successful diagnosis and plan. The best diagnoses are made following a free and extensive exchange of information between equals. To devise the best therapeutic plans, doctors must rely not only on their medicine, but on their ability (and their willingness) to communicate with patients. In correctional institutions, however, the physician has so much power and the prisoner so little that goodwill is not enough to overcome the power discrepancies. Successful resolutions of medical problems throughout the prison, as well as on an individual case basis, require institutional changes that guarantee the prisoner her right to speak freely and to protect and care for her own body. These are the same guarantees that the women's health and patients' rights movements seek for all people. In prisons, such guarantees can be initiated by staff, prisoners, or outside advocates.

ADDRESSING THE PROBLEMS

Montefiore Hospital's Rikers' Island Health Service in New York City provides an example of a prison medical service that attempts, through staff education and the hiring of young and ethnically diverse physicians and paraprofessionals, to develop a caring, informed staff that will be better able to listen to and work with male and female prisoners. By contracting with a private institution, the city hopes to encourage the predominance of medical (over *institu-*

Nancy Stoller Shaw

tional) values when prisoners have health problems. However, this program fails to address the nature of the jail experience itself and its consequences for physical and emotional health. The staff are encouraged to work on an individual basis with prisoners, but this approach is inadequate. Race, class, sex, incarceration, and professional dominance continue to operate against the patient/prisoner and her abilities to speak her mind and protect her interests.

Other local and national projects have also begun to address the question of inmate–staff power as it relates to health care. These include:

1. The Project on Legal and Ethical Issues in the Delivery of Health Care within Detention and Correctional Institutions. Run by the Department of Social Medicine, Montefiore Hospital and Medical Center (Bronx, NY), this project is staffed by a legal/medical/social science/activist mixture of persons. It has organized inmate health committees and workshops, and conflict resolution conferences for professionals. Currently, it is working with inmates and staff at Bedford Hills, New York State's main prison for women.[22]
2. The National Prison Project of the American Civil Liberties Union (Washington, DC). This project focuses on the federal courts, constitutional issues, and the development of case law. It has supported prisoners' health suits throughout the United States.[23]
3. Prisoner Health Advocates (San Francisco). This organization brings physicians and other health professionals to work in prisons and jails. In addition to public education work, they recruit experts for testimony in court cases and find persons who can give prisoners second opinions on specific health matters.[24]
4. Legal Services for Prisoners with Children. Also in San Francisco, this organization provides direct legal services primarily to female prisoners and organizes outside support and public education programs. It addresses custody, health, and "conditions" issues in courts, prisons, and other institutions (such as hospitals) that deal with prisoners.[25]
5. Prisoners' Rights Project, Legal Aid Society (New York City). This is an active, statewide project providing legal services to prisoners eligible for public defenders. It attempts to advance case law and fight for better prison conditions, and has brought a number of issues to the U.S. Supreme Court.[26]

Female Patients and the Medical Profession in Jails and Prisons

These projects are only a few of those currently focusing attention on conditions in women's jails. Other public education and action groups—such as the Southern Prison Ministry, American Friends Service Committee, Unitarian Universalist Service Committee, Women Free Women in Prison, and *Through the Looking Glass*[27]—rely more heavily on mass organizing, public education, and the electoral process to make changes. Although I cannot address their strategies in detail in this chapter, it is important to be aware of the similarities among these groups. The major commonality is a multifaceted approach to change. All pursue prisoner education in health and other areas, development of inmate health and grievance committees, organization of outside and inside support for prisoners, legal backup, provision of more alternatives to incarceration, and continuing critiques and exposes of the punitive and inhumane conditions in American prisons and jails.

These and other organizations have been most successful in protecting the health of the incarcerated female when they have focused on issues of power and powerlessness. Health care for women in prison cannot be divorced from the prison context. Nor can it be separated from the fact that the women are poor and nonwhite. Successful organizing addresses racism, sexism, class, and medical and legal oppression simultaneously. Changes in one area but not another can produce only a temporary appearance of improvement. A jail health service may be able to cure yeast infections, but what good is that if the institutional diet continues to produce the poor health that makes women susceptible to the infection? A health staff member may be considerate of a woman's story about her migraine headache, but if the jail has a rule against speaking in Spanish, the inmate may never be able to communicate the problem. Thus it is necessary to address all these issues when trying to improve, even in a limited way, the health conditions in women's prisons.

NOTES

1. Government Account Office (GAO), *Female Offenders: Who Are They and What Are the Problems Confronting Them?* (Washington, DC: U.S. Government Printing Office, 1979), GGD-79-73.

2. R. Glick and V. Neto, *National Study of Women's Correctional Programs* (Washington, DC: National Institute of Law Enforcement and Criminal Justice, 1977).

Nancy Stoller Shaw

3. U.S. Bureau of Prisons, *Female Offenders in the Federal Prison System* (Washington, DC: U.S. Government Printing Office, 1977); GAO, *Female Offenders*.

4. GAO, *Female Offenders*. *See also* Rita James Simon, *The Contemporary Woman and Crime* (Washington, DC: National Institute of Mental Health, 1975).

5. U.S. Department of Health, Education, and Welfare, Office of Health Resources Opportunity, *Health Status of Minorities and Low Income Groups* (Washington, DC: U.S. Government Printing Office, 1979), HRA-79-627. Additional statistics in this paragraph are drawn from this report.

6. "Disadvantaged," as defined in HEW's *Health Status of Minorities and Low Income Groups* (p. 19), refers to an aggregate based on income, education, sex, population density, age, and membership in a racial/ethnic minority group.

7. L. F. Novick, R. Della Penna, M. S. Schwartz, E. Remmlinger, and R. Lowenstein, "Health Status of the New York City Prison Population," *Medical Care* 15 (1977):205.

8. B. Anno, *Analysis of Inmate/Patient Profile Data* (American Medical Association Program to Improve Medical Care and Health Services in Jails, 1977).

9. H. Ris and R. W. Dodge, "Gonorrhea in Adolescent Girls in a Closed Population," *American Journal of Diseases of Children* 123 (1972):135.

10. Judith Resnik and Nancy Shaw, "Prisoners of Their Sex: Health Problems of Incarcerated Women," in *Prisoners' Rights Sourcebook: Theory, Litigation and Practice*, ed. Ira Robbins, vol. II (New York: Clark Boardman, 1980).

11. Glick and Neto, *Women's Correctional Programs*, p. xviii.

12. GAO, *Female Offenders*, pp. 10–15.

13. *See also* Ann Stanton, *When Mothers Go to Jail* (Lexington, MA: Lexington Books, 1980); and "On Prisoners and Parenting: Preserving the Tie That Binds," *Yale Law Journal* 87 (1978):1408, 1423 (n. 74), 1424 (n. 79).

14. Resnik and Shaw, "Prisoners of Their Sex," pp. 337–339. *See also* Glick and Neto, *Women's Correctional Programs*, pp. 67–68.

15. Resnik and Shaw, "Prisoners of Their Sex," pp. 337–338.

16. Nancy S. Shaw, Irene Browne, and Peter J. Meyer, "Sexism and Medical Care in a Jail Setting," *Women and Health* 6, 1/2 (Spring/Summer 1981).

17. Ibid.

18. On the subject of self-esteem, *see* Glick and Neto, *Women's Correctional Programs*, p. 18.

19. *See* K. Armitage, L. Schneiderman, and R. Bass, "Response of Physicians to Medical Complaints in Men and Women," *Journal of American Medical Association* 24 (1979):2186. *See also* K. J. Lennane and R. J. Lennane, "Alleged Psychogenic Disorders in Women as Possible Manifestation of Sexual Prejudice," *New England Journal of Medicine* 2881 (1970):288–293.

20. Shaw, Browne, and Meyer, "Sexism and Medical Care in a Jail Setting."

21. *See*, for example, Barbara Ehrenreich and John Ehrenreich, *American Health Empire* (New York: Random House, 1970); Vincent Navarro, *Health and Medical Care in the U.S.* (Farmingdale, NY: Baywood, 1973); and Eliot Friedson, *Professional Dominance: The Social Structure of Medical Care* (New York: Atherton, 1970).

22. Funded by National Science Foundation and Montefiore Hospital and Medical Center.

23. Funded by the ACLU.

24. Funded by members.

25. Funded by benefits and foundation grants.

26. Funded by New York Legal Aid Society.

27. Women's and Children's Prison Newsletter, P.O. Box 22061, Seattle, Washington.

PART IV

*Women
as
Practitioners
and Professionals*

13

"The Government's Unique Experiment in Salvaging Women Criminals"

Cooperation and Conflict in the Administration of a Women's Prison— The Case of the Federal Industrial Institution for Women at Alderson

CLAUDINE SCHWEBER

Women convicted of federal crimes were first housed together in 1927 at the newly constructed Federal Industrial Institution for Women in Alderson, West Virginia. Until that time, the Department of Justice had contracted to board federal women convicts at such state facilities as the House of Correction in Rutland, Vermont, or the Kentucky State Reformatory in Frankfort. When Alderson was completed at the cost of $2.5 million, it consisted of five hundred acres of land on which Georgian-style buildings were arranged in a horseshoe pattern on two tiered slopes called the upper and lower campus. The first superintendent, Mary Belle Harris, was appointed in 1925; the prison began operating two years later. By

Claudine SchWeber

the official opening day in November 1928, over two hundred inmates and staff lived on the grounds. Alderson remained the only
federal women's prison until 1955.[1]

The fight for a separate facility for federal women offenders had
been carried on since 1923 by a nationally based coalition of women
with power or influence in the federal government, and by women
outside government involved in penal reform and women's groups.
This women's network served two purposes: first, it rapidly moved
the federal prison project from the 1923 idea to legislation, site
selection, appropriations, design and construction, and staffing by
1927; second, it provided the institution's leadership, particularly
Superintendent Harris, with a power base that could be called upon
for assistance if problems developed. As Dr. Harris was later to remind her bosses during one particularly severe dispute, Alderson
"was a 'cause' before it was established."[2]

The work of the women's coalition was made easier by the
receptivity of Congress and federal officials to the idea of
establishing such a women's prison. This climate was due in part to
the successful model offered by state reformatories for women. Between 1870 and 1925, seventeen such facilities had been opened to
get women out of the jails, workhouses, and prisons that also
housed men. Females were always a small proportion of the inmate
population. They were neglected and abused; mixed with first offenders and repeaters, young and aged; and often placed in filthy and
disease-ridden facilities. Reports of physical and sexual abuse were
rampant. Penal reformers in the Progressive tradition argued that
male institutions ignored the special needs of women, that women
criminals had often been men's pawns, and that only a nonmale environment could provide the special attention necessary to women
who had been denied such consideration outside.[3] The government
was receptive to the idea of a federal women's prison because its arrangement for boarding federal prisoners in state facilities around
the country was becoming impractical by the 1920s due to rising
costs, abuses by state officials, and occasional riots by women inmates who claimed that as federal prisoners they were entitled to
better treatment.[4]

From the beginning, Alderson acquired a national reputation as
a "Ladies Seminary" that worked, a successful "society of women
working together under the guidance of other women."[5] Between
1925 and 1930, Alderson's administrators set about the creation and

operation of the model women's "re-educational institution."[6] In this mission, the administrators were given free rein and strongly supported by superiors in the Department of Justice, particularly the Assistant Attorney General for prisons, Mabel Walker Willebrandt.

This era of independence and cooperation ended in 1930 with the creation of the Bureau of Prisons as the agency directly responsible for federal prisoners. To the five federal wardens of the time this change meant not only a new set of (all male) bosses, but also superiors whose mission included the reining in of the autonomous prison operations—Alderson's included.[7] After 1930 Alderson's relation to its superiors was characterized by continual conflict from which few areas were immune. In part, the struggle flowed from the Bureau's push to consolidate its authority and to limit institutional autonomy. In part, it flowed from the fact that "in many instances, the only point in the whole [federal] system where [the Bureau] met any resistance was at [Alderson]."[8] Most important, the men at the Bureau disagreed with the women of Alderson's contention that as a women's institution it should be exempt from many policies and practices that had been devised for the largely male inmate population of the system.[9] Whereas Alderson's correctional superiors in the 1920s included a powerful woman, Willebrandt, who agreed with the women-oriented approach, leadership of the Bureau of Prisons during the 1930s was composed of men who did not. Conflict was inevitable.

The cooperation/conflict period offers an opportunity to examine how women administrators operated during times of protection and siege. It also represents a unique era in which the women's institution functioned as the last relatively independent operation in the federal correctional system. After Harris's departure, no federal prison would again enjoy the autonomy that the periods of cooperation and conflict represented.

PHASE I. COOPERATION: "THE GOVERNMENT'S UNIQUE EXPERIMENT IN SALVAGING WOMEN CRIMINALS"[10]

The Federal Industrial Institution for Women (FIIW) was authorized by Congress in the Act of 7 June 1924 "for the confinement of female persons above the age of eighteen years, convicted of an of-

fense against the United States . . . , [and] sentenced to imprisonment for more than one year." The institution's mission was
clearly stated:

> *To provide for the instruction of the inmates . . . in the*
> *common branches of an English education, and for their*
> *training in such trade, industry, or occupational pursuit*
> *as will best enable said inmates on release to obtain self-*
> *supporting employment.*[11]

In carrying out this mission, the institution was to be assisted by an
Advisory Board of four prominent citizens appointed by the president to "recommend ways and means for the discipline and training
of such inmates. . . ."[12] Alderson's Advisory Board, unique among
the federal prisons but modeled after those of state women's institutions, would later become an important source of support for Alderson's administrators in their power struggle with the Bureau of
Prisons.

The Act of 1924 assigned to the Attorney General very broad
responsibilities in the managerial and fiscal operation of the institution. However, the exact location of the facility was not as yet determined. It was to be decided by three parties: the Attorney General,
the Secretary of Labor, and the Secretary of the Interior. Moreover,
the remaining sections of the act, including budget, staffing, and
construction, were to go into effect only after the site selection was
accomplished.[13]

This seemingly unusual situation was not the result of
congressional displeasure with women or with the Attorney
General. Instead, the language was part of a strategy laid out several
months earlier to obtain passage of the federal women's prison
statute. The plan's architect and floor manager was Mabel Walker
Willebrandt. As Attorney General John Sargent told those assem-
bled at the opening ceremonies:

> *[Mabel Willebrandt] has watched over, cared for and*
> *fought for [Alderson] as a mother for her child. Like a true*
> *mother, she knows those who are sent here have done*
> *wrong . . . but [she] cannot believe that any of them is*
> *wholly bad or devoid of some instinct, which if . . . prop-*
> *erly cultivated, will . . . produce a useful life.*[14]

"The Government's Unique Experiment"

Willebrandt's position was critical to the enterprise. As Assistant Attorney General in the United States Department of Justice, she was responsible for three areas: tax litigation (other than customs), prohibition, and prisons. Willebrandt was considered very bright, hard-working, effective, and loyal, despite her relative youth and newness to the legal profession. She was only thirty-two and four years out of law school at the time of her appointment by President Harding in August 1921. She had come from Los Angeles, where she specialized in defending women and drafting such legislation as the California married women's property act, in addition to carrying on a private practice and actively participating at the highest levels of Republican party activities in the state. Willebrandt was particularly well known to many Americans in the 1920s because her defense and enforcement of prohibition laws during her eight-year tenure (August 1921–June 1929) was frequently front-page news.[15]

Although Inspector of Prisons Ellen Foster (1908–1911) was the first person to urge direct federal control of women prisoners, and the Justice Department even toyed with the idea of opening a women's wing at Leavenworth in 1912, the project lay dormant for a decade until Willebrandt's arrival. Within a year of her appointment, Willebrandt was actively pursuing the establishment of a federal prison for women. The first attempt was a January 1923 bill proposing that such an institution be established at Mount Weather, Virginia. Mount Weather had the advantage of already being government property; it was an abandoned United States weather installation that could be inexpensively converted to a prison facility. While there appears to have been no opposition to the idea of a federal women's prison, the bill was defeated in May 1923 due to intense pressure from congressional families who worried that the value of their summer homes in the Mount Weather area might decline.[16]

The second attempt was successful. In December 1923 another bill was introduced, which passed on 7 June 1924. It diffused the site issue by calling only for the "establishment of a federal women's industrial institution" to be located at a site chosen by the Attorney General and the Secretaries of Labor and Interior. Although acreage, construction, and staffing were left undefined, overall responsibility was assigned to the Attorney General's office, which thus obtained jurisdiction over virtually everything. In essence, this act gave

Willebrandt, as the Attorney General's assistant for prison matters, control of the project.[17]

To arrive at this successful end, Willebrandt had mobilized existing national support among communities interested in housing the prison, among Progressive penal reformers, and especially among middle- and upper-class women's organizations with their thousands of well-connected members.

Soon after the first bill was introduced in January 1923, people from all over the country had written Willebrandt and members of Congress offering to sell land for the prison. She used this mail as evidence that there was widespread support for the idea of a federal women's prison.[18]

At the same time, West Virginians had begun to lobby intensively to have the prison in their state. Representatives of the Alderson Chamber of Commerce, the C & O Railroad, the Prisoners' Relief Society, and local women's clubs commuted between West Virginia and Washington, DC, to lobby congressional representatives and ambitious West Virginians in the federal government. At the center of this activity was Lena Lowe Yost, president of the West Virginia chapter of the Women's Christian Temperance Union, and a woman well connected in both West Virginia and Washington, DC. In addition, the political leverage of the 1924 elections was not lost upon the supporters of the women's prison. That political event offered West Virginians a special opportunity: in 1924, the Republican Calvin Coolidge was opposed by Democrat John W. Davis of West Virginia.[19]

In September 1923, three months after the Mount Weather defeat, women's groups and penal reformers met in Washington, DC, at a conference sponsored by the General Federation of Women's Clubs (GFWC) at their national headquarters. The official purpose was to "consider ways and means of providing adequate care for women convicted of offenses by the Federal courts. . . ." However, since everyone present favored the women's prison, the real purpose was to affect the prison legislation that would be introduced in the next session of Congress beginning December 1923. Twenty-two organizations representing women's groups, political parties, unions, and penal reformers participated in this meeting. Also involved were state corrections officials working with women prisoners, including Jessie Hodder of Massachusetts and Florence Monahan of Minnesota; Katherine Bement Davis, formerly Corrections Commissioner in New York City; and such government of-

"The Government's Unique Experiment"

ficials as Mabel Willebrandt and Heber Votaw, Superintendent of
the Federal Prisons. A committee, chaired by Willebrandt, recommended that the federal women's prison be constructed on the cot-
tage plan, on a minimum of 500 acres, to house no more than 700
inmates; that the prison should be called the Federal Industrial Farm
for Women until a more precise name was selected; "that the head
of the institution be a woman"; and that the December bill
authorize the Justice Department to select a site, draft the legislation, and prepare the appropriations details. The recommendations
were unanimously approved.[20] In addition, the legislative representative of the GFWC agreed to convene other organizations' representatives as soon as the bill was ready in order to get endorsements.
The GFWC also agreed to send each of its 12,000 clubs a copy of the
bill and to ask each individual member to write her legislator twice
in support. The GFWC was already on record in favor of the
women's prison bill, having voted at their May 1923 Council
meeting to work actively for the legislation.[21]

The process by which Alderson was completed followed
precisely the plan set out in 1923. First, the Act of 1924 made few
changes from the 1923 recommendations, although one significant
point was omitted: that a woman must head the institution.[22] Second, legislators were bombarded with pressure to approve the
measure. Letters, visits, telegrams, memoirs, and speeches testify
to the intensity of the women's campaign. Alice Ames Winter,
president of the GFWC, contacted such important friends as Mrs.
Grace Coolidge on behalf of the bill. Julia K. Jaffray, the coordinator
of the September 1923 meeting, was not only an active GFWC
member but also executive secretary of the National Committee on
Prisons and Prison Labor, an organization of prominent New
Yorkers concerned with prison reform; she mobilized its forces in
support of the federal women's prison. Furthermore, many of the
organizations at the 1923 meeting, already joined together as
members of the Women's Joint Congressional Committee, continued to work through this coalition to promote legislation of interest to women.[23] Third, once the legislation passed in June 1924,
the follow-up details were controlled by the Justice Department,
and thus Willebrandt.

Site selection was the first task, since the act made funding
contingent upon it. At least twenty places were in varying degrees of
competition for the prison. When coordination problems among the
three men charged with site selection threatened to delay the pro-

cess until the next Congress convened and the results of the 1924 election would be reflected in committee changes, Willebrandt acted quickly. On 23 January 1925 she urged Attorney General Harlan Fiske Stone to take the initiative in choosing a location, assuring him that Secretaries Davis (Labor) and Work (Interior) would concur, since their connection with this project was temporary. One week later, 29 January 1925, the choice of Alderson was formally presented to Congress.[24] Willebrandt is reported to have been seen running into Union Station, Stone's site selection letter in hand, to obtain Davis's and Work's signatures because they were departing on a business trip that would not be completed until after Congress had adjourned.[25]

Two weeks after the site was chosen, Willebrandt and her staff were on to the next task, financing the prison. On 11 February 1925, they appeared before the House Appropriations Committee with the first request for $909,100, which was granted 4 March 1925. The first contract was let 31 December 1925. Road building began in the fall of 1925, using inmates from Atlanta and Leavenworth penitentiaries; this contingent of 200 men remained at Alderson for almost five years, camped on the lower perimeter. Additional funds of $1,509,300 were approved in July 1926, bringing the total allocation to $2,418,400. The first housing units were completed in April 1927, a year after construction had begun. The first fifteen inmates, "the early settlers," arrived 30 April 1927, although the official opening did not take place until 24 November 1928, when all the major construction was completed.[26]

Another task, the appointment of a superintendent for Alderson, was completed within two weeks of the first financial appropriation. Willebrandt recommended that Stone appoint Mary Belle Harris, an educated and experienced woman. Prison administration was Dr. Harris's second career. Until 1914, when she was forty, Harris had been a scholar and teacher of Latin and the Classics, having earned a Ph.D. in Sanskrit and Indo-European Philology from the University of Chicago in 1900. In 1914 she was appointed warden of the Women's Workhouse on Blackwell's Island in New York City by Corrections Commissioner Katherine Bement Davis, a University of Chicago classmate. Harris continued to work in the penal field. She was sworn in as Alderson's superintendent on 12 March 1925, remaining in the position for sixteen years, until her retirement from federal service in 1941.[27]

Like the work that had created a federal women's prison by

1925, Alderson's design, construction, and administration were largely controlled by women. Supported by Willebrandt and accompanied by Jaffray and others, Harris spent 1925 to 1927 supervising architects and engineers in the physical creation of "The Government's Unique Experiment in Salvaging Women Criminals."[28] A largely female staff supervised and ran the entire operation. Women were housed in cottages complete with private dining rooms with tablecloths, living rooms with curtains, and a scattering of vases with fresh flowers from the gardens. Inmate councils ran the cottages, prisoners operated the farm and dairy, and the better educated prisoners taught others—all with relatively little supervision, few escapes, or serious disciplinary problems. A half-day in class was encouraged and work assignments were plentiful. County fairs, nature hikes, and baseball games provided additional leisure and physical activities. Is it any wonder that Alderson was widely hailed as a ladies' seminary? Here was seeming proof that despite some setbacks at Elmira or Norfolk, the reformatory movement's principles were on target.[29]

Part of this applause reflected the admirers' surprise that this society of women could function so well. However, neither Harris, her staff, Willebrandt, nor the women's network had any doubt that only in a society of women could the inmate's reform take place. These reformers believed that men were part of the problem, that women's criminality was largely due to their economic and psychological dependence, usually upon men. The solution, they argued, was an institution run by and for women. Consequently, male staff were kept to a minimum and male supervisors at a distance. While Harris saw no problem with male subordinates, she had once urged female colleagues not to take a back seat to anyone, particularly male bosses who tried to tell women how to "manage their own sex." Such circumstances, Harris advised in 1921, might require women to quit their posts, thereby permitting the men to make the predictable mess alone.[30]

In the 1930s Harris had cause to remember this advice. The federal prison structure changed; instead of Willebrandt as a supervisor, Harris had several male bosses controlling policy and funding. Inasmuch as their mission included wresting control away from the many autonomous prison operations, conflict with autonomous Alderson was inevitable. But Harris did not quit. Instead, she turned to the women's network and to other allies for help in the struggles that followed.

Claudine SchWeber

TABLE 13-1
Chronology of Major Events Relating to the
Establishment of the Federal Women's Prison
at Alderson, West Virginia

Date	Event
1908	J. Ellen Foster, Inspector of Prisons, Department of Justice, first looked at conditions of federal women prisoners in state prisons.
1921 August	Mabel Walker Willebrandt appointed Assistant Attorney General in the Department of Justice by President Harding (1921–1929 tenure).
1923 January	First bill to establish a federal prison for women, at Mt. Weather, introduced in the House of Representatives (by W. Goodykoontz, R–WV) and in the Senate (by C. Curtis, R–KS).
May	Mt. Weather bill defeated in Congress.
September	Twenty-three penal organizations and women's groups met at General Federation of Women's Clubs headquarters in Washington, DC.
December	Second bill to establish a women's prison introduced in the Senate (by C. Curtis, R–KS) and later in the House (by T. Lilley, D–WV).
1924 January	Senate and House Judiciary Committees held hearings on the women's prison bill and recommended passage.
June	Enabling Act established the Federal Industrial Institution for Women.
1925 January	Alderson recommended as site for women's prison.
March	First appropriations approved ($909,100). Mary Belle Harris sworn in as superintendent.
August	First contingent of male prisoners arrived to build roads.
December	First meeting of Board of Advisors. First building contract let (completed April 1927).

PHASE II. CONFLICT:
". . . THE ONLY POINT IN THE WHOLE SYSTEM WHERE WE MET ANY RESISTANCE WAS AT [ALDERSON]"[31]

The years 1925–1930 were pioneering ones at Alderson. When Dr. Harris was appointed in 1925, there were no buildings, no staff, no inmates—just a congressional mandate, a location, and the first appropriation of nearly one million dollars. Harris and the staff controlled the planning, construction, development, and staffing of the institution. As Harris wrote in her autobiography:

> *It was rather a solemn responsibility to open a new institution and inaugurate new policies, especially at an institution which was so much in the public eye, as this promised to be.*[32]

This era of splendid isolation ended in 1930 as a result of two major changes in the federal bureaucracy. First was the resignation of Mabel Walker Willebrandt from the Justice Department, effective 30 June 1929. Without this powerful protector and patron, the financial and administrative independence that Alderson had enjoyed could not be sustained. Second was the creation of the Bureau of Prisons, effective 14 May 1930. Henceforth, the new agency, instead of a single Assistant Attorney General such as Willebrandt, would control the administration, operation, and funding of the institutions in the federal penal system. Sanford Bates, whom Willebrandt had lured from Massachusetts a year earlier to become the Superintendent of Prisons, was named Director of the Bureau, assisted by James V. Bennett, Austin McCormick, and W. T. Hammack.[33]

Alderson was most directly affected by the new agency's mandate to centralize control of prison operations. After more than a decade of severe problems and scandals in the men's facilities, Congress had recommended that the Bureau forcefully establish a cohesive and professional federal penal system. Although this solution was directed at problems in men's prisons, Alderson was not considered exempt from the policies and directives of Bates and company. Harris believed otherwise: that the point of the last fifty years of prison reform was that women offenders should be handled

Claudine SchWeber

differently than men.[34] So while Bates and his staff worked to create an integrated federal prison system, Harris and her staff fought to retain Alderson's individuality and autonomy.

The struggle began almost immediately upon Bates's accession and continued throughout the decade until Harris retired in 1941. The issues included such relatively minor disagreements as the one over titles: the Bureau decided to call all institutional chief executives "Warden," but Harris and her assistant, Helen Hironimous, preferred "Superintendent," the title used in state women's prisons.[35] Also included were questions concerning industrial output and wages for inmates. The industries battle, which was especially intense, acrimonious, and lengthy, shall be explored in detail later. Through all the disputes Harris always maintained that the appropriate standard for Alderson's operation was not consistency with other federal facilities; instead, she insisted that the correct model be "the progressive women's institutions throughout the country."[36]

A. Staff Issues

The hiring and firing of staff was one area of conflict. During the cooperative years, Harris and her assistants had chosen the entire staff, paying particular attention to "filling all the positions possible . . . by women" and hiring only those few men necessary to do heavy lifting and hauling, maintenance of the boiler plant, and road and building construction. Like her colleagues in the state women's reformatories, Harris felt strongly that "anyone who wished to work [at Alderson] would have to accept the fact that the order came from women."[37]

This power of staff selection was severely limited after 1930 by creation of the Bureau of Prisons and establishment of the Civil Service system in 1936. As a consequence, Harris's recommendations were scrutinized and finalized by the Bureau's Director. Bates complained that Harris was uncompromising, that while he had been willing to support her selections "in some instances against the recommendations of [his] staff," she had not been equally accommodating. Instead,

> *You and your institution . . . have continually taken the attitude that supervision from Washington was a thing to be tolerated and that you and your institution were fully*

"The Government's Unique Experiment"

capable of managing the institution without "inter-
ference" from Washington.[38]

Furthermore, Bates claimed that Harris did not "get along
with [some of the] personnel who were selected as competent people and sent to you," that she continued to retain a number of
employees "who do not overexert themselves," and that when the
Bureau sent a man to assist with operational problems, she "be-
littled" the offer of such assistance.[39]

Alderson and the Bureau also clashed over the hiring of
medical personnel. In 1932, for example, the Alderson Advisory
Board requested a replacement for the incumbent dentist, a woman
named Dr. Calder. Bates consulted with the Public Health Service
(PHS) over the matter, and responded that the PHS suggested that
"it might be wise" to send both a male dentist and a male doctor;
the Alderson Board reacted negatively. In October 1932,

> [The Board unanimously withdrew] its recommendation
> of February that the position of Dentist be open to both
> men and women . . . [and] suggested that in the mean-
> time an attempt be made to secure longer hours of service
> from the present incumbent. . . . [Furthermore] seeing
> strong objections to the appointment of a resident male
> physician . . . [the Board] recommends that the present
> policy of having a resident woman medical officer be con-
> tinued.[40]

Bates's angry reaction was immediate. A week later he wrote to
Harris:

> You put us in an extremely embarrassing position [with
> the Public Health Service] by entirely reversing your
> policy with reference to the incumbents in the position of
> medical officer and dentist. . . . Dr. Treadway has been
> unable to find a female dentist and we were of the belief
> that you would not oppose his plan to substitute a male
> dentist for Dr. Calder.
>   You now pass a vote not only opposing the appoint-
> ment . . . but you also go further and urge us not to
> disturb Dr. Calder in her position. I certainly should not
> blame the Public Health Service if they took the position
> that you did not know just what you did want. . . .[41]

Relations between Alderson and the Bureau were such that even Harris's periodic attempts at compromise went awry and further increased the strains, as in the case of obtaining replacements for the inmates from Atlanta and Leavenworth prisons. These men had been constructing roads, digging foundations, and doing other heavy labor at Alderson since 1925. They lived in camp tents on Alderson's lower perimeter, controlled by a male supervisor. The inmates were scheduled to leave in late 1930. Harris was concerned that the work continue, and thinking that Bates approved, she recommended to the Alderson Board that the camp be retained despite the many problems caused by the presence of men on the grounds of a women's prison—a suggestion that the Board approved in early 1930.

Bates, however, was opposed to the continued use of male inmates so close to females. Although he did not offer replacement workers, he wrote Harris to raise questions about the potential problems of this situation and to lament the Board's approval of this matter "without much debate or objection."[42] Harris immediately responded with a somewhat apologetic letter, telling Bates that she thought he had favored the camp. She defended her own support (which "might be interpreted as a backward step in view of the struggle women have had to get their institutions separated from men's") on the grounds that at Alderson "the situation is exactly reversed, inasmuch as the men would be kept here to do the work of the women's institution." In any case, she wrote Bates, she was "perfectly willing to do whatever you think is best for the institution," and urged him to make a quick decision on camp workers versus new employees.[43] The Alderson Board also reversed its original stand, supporting Harris as usual. More than a year later no additional assistance was forthcoming and the camps were disbanded. Instead, the Bureau began to send (male) federal inspectors to Alderson to determine whether it could be run more efficiently and at a lower cost.[44]

B. Inmate Issues

In addition to staffing decisions, those regarding inmates also needed Bureau approval after 1930. Four examples indicate the diverse and continuing nature of the disagreements and accommodations between Alderson and the Bureau in this area: inmate privileges, inmate transfers, disposition of escapees, and inmate readmissions.

In 1931 the Bureau disallowed the practice whereby inmates sold products to each other. Apparently a fairly extensive cigarette and liquor sale had been going on at the male prisons. At Alderson, however, the women sold items they made at the prison (scarves, handkerchiefs, candy).[45] Harris and the Alderson Board argued that the new rules "worked real hardships" on the women and, therefore, an exception should be made for Alderson, one that "would bring [it] in line with the progressive women's institutions throughout the country."[46] Bates agreed to consider such a plan if it was presented to him, but the evidence suggests that the 1931 policy did not change.[47]

As for inmate transfers, in early 1932 Harris wrote Bates asking that an inmate who was a continual disciplinary problem and a "malignant influence" on inmate morale be transferred. While Bates agreed to this request, he warned that it would not "establish a [precedent] for the transfer of other prisoners in the future . . . [because] Federal prisoners should be taken care of in our own institutions as far as possible."[48]

Alderson and the Bureau also clashed over the disposition of escapees. The issue of disciplinary transfers was far more difficult for Harris than other prison wardens because Alderson was the only federal women's facility. In 1934, the Alderson Board considered the case of a woman who had escaped, been captured, and returned. The Board recommended that instead of pressing charges in federal court (the usual procedure), institutional punishment and loss of time off for good behavior ("goodtime") were sufficient. Assistant Director James Bennett was furious at this usurpation of authority by Harris and the Alderson Board. In a strongly worded memo to Bates, Bennett warned that:

> [Y]ou have advised every institution and Dr. Harris specifically that the Superintendent . . . ought to present all such cases to the court for such action as it thought proper . . . this is a sound policy . . . [and you] should in this instance overrule the Advisory Board and inform Dr. Harris that the case should be presented to the court.

At the top of the memo was Bates's handwritten reply:

> *Ordinarily this would be so but Alderson is exception to all rules. I think the decision right in this instance.*[49]

Lastly, Alderson and the Bureau also fought over inmate admissions. In late December 1937, Harris received a pitiful letter from a former inmate who had been in an automobile accident that had left her severely crippled and, after months of hospitalization, addicted to drugs. The woman wanted to arrange to be convicted of possession under the Harrison Act (although her drugs were legally prescribed), on the condition that she be sent to Alderson to be cured of her addiction. A sympathetic note from Assistant Superintendent Helen Hironimous advised the woman of the procedure used in past cases of this kind, and indicated Harris's support in this instance. A brief letter to the Director of the Bureau (by then, James Bennett) requested approval for this action, while a copy of the correspondence was sent to the appropriate United States Attorney. Unfortunately, Bennett was neither sympathetic nor agreeable. A telegram was immediately sent to the U.S. Attorney stating that the Bureau "could not authorize [Miss X's] commitment to Alderson on account of overcrowded conditions. . . ." At the same time, Bennett wrote Harris that this woman could not be accepted at Alderson because:

> *I think it would be a very bad precedent. I don't think we ought to bargain with ex-inmates at the time they are placed in custody and I don't think we ought to accept a permanent custodial problem of this kind.*

As to the appropriateness of such negotiations with the U.S. Attorney by institutional heads, Bennett warned:

> *In the future I would appreciate it if you would, when such cases are brought to your attention, correspond with the U.S. Attorney through this office.*[50]

C. Institutional Management

Along with disagreements over staff and inmate issues, another dispute concerned the administration of the women's prison. The Bureau's goal was accountability, consistency, and efficiency among all federal facilities. Toward that end, several members of the Bureau of Efficiency (from whence had come Bennett) had been hired in the Washington office. These men were sent to inspect institutional operations and to assist in correcting the problems they uncovered. Among the complaints about Alderson was the "mess" in the physical plant; the "waste and inefficient management" of the farm; the high per capita cost of operating Alderson in comparison with the other (men's) prisons; and Harris's continual rebuttal of suggestions by the Washington men for improvement.

When Harris complained about the offensive manner and inaccuracies of the Bureau's farm supervisor, Mr. Forristal, Bates responded with a three-page litany of evidence and anger about the overall "lax and inefficient management" of Alderson, including "leaky steam pipes; inefficient boiler room operation; buildings heated way beyond necessity; retention of unnecessary staff on the payroll; and resistance to the full development of prison industries." The crux of Bates's complaint was that Alderson's (mis)management was also expensive. Forristal's farm recommendations were in the interest of the "lower cost administration and greater productivity" mandate of the Bureau, which was also indicated by the forced reduction of Alderson's per capita daily costs from $1.25 in 1930 to $0.78 in 1936.[51]

Thus, creation of the Bureau meant that Alderson, like other federal facilities, had lost control of staff, inmate, operational, and budgetary decisions. Harris's view of the Bureau's emphasis on cost-effectiveness is made clear in lectures she gave on "The Great Gawd Budjhut and his Consort Purrcapita," in which help was denied to the needy because it was not cost-effective.[52] After 1930 the bottom line was that the Bureau of Prisons in Washington was the boss and there was "no reason why Alderson should be exempt."[53]

D. Prison Industries

Of all the battles between Alderson and the Bureau, the one concerning prison industries was the most acrimonious. This war contained the themes, tactics, and philosophical differences articulated in the above disputes, as well as a personal conflict between two independent, strong personalities, each fiercely committed to the cause—James Bennett of the Bureau and Mary Harris of Alderson.

The Bureau's determination to develop productive and profitable industries in all of its institutions was guided by Assistant Director for the Industrial Department, James V. Bennett. Bennett had come to the prison system in 1928 from the Bureau of Efficiency, where his responsibilities had included advising the Justice Department on cost-cutting measures it could take in the federal prisons. The 1930 legislation that created the Bureau included authority for the central office to create new shops and to consolidate the moneys from prison industries throughout the system into one fund. In 1934 Federal Prison Industries was created as a wholly owned government corporation with authority to sell its products only to other federal agencies. Prison industries were to be self-supporting and profitable operations, run in a businesslike manner to provide inmates with job training and to inculcate those habits and values deemed necessary for successful employment outside. Industries were to use the profits for reinvestment, for new industries, and for subsidizing other prison programs. In order to accomplish these objectives, it was determined that, among other measures, at least 20 percent of the inmate population at each institution was to be assigned to industries work.[54]

The arguments over appropriate production levels in the garment factory were bitter. As with other disputes and developments, Harris reported the issues and her position to the Alderson Advisory Board, which sustained her recommendations, communicated its concern to the Bureau, and in at least one well-documented case sought the intervention of the Attorney General on Alderson's behalf. Assistant Bureau Director W. T. Hammack was very perceptive when he warned Bates in 1930 that the Alderson Board might embarrass the Bureau unless its scope of operations was checked.[55]

The Bureau's contention was that Alderson's garment factory, like the industries in men's facilities, should be profitable, productive, and self-supporting. By March 1931, several additional power sewing machines had been installed so that more women could be assigned to the work on a full-time basis.[56] In this connection, Bennett also wanted to halt Alderson's policy of allowing industry inmates to attend classes or to work part-time, arguing that "unless the same woman worked on the same machine the entire working day" the industry would be neither profitable nor productive "from the business point of view."[57] Harris and the Alderson Board strongly objected, arguing that the Bureau's plan: (1) disrupted prison operations by requiring a sizable proportion of the available inmate work force to be assigned to industry; (2) ignored the realities of such operational commitments as spring farming needs, since contracts for garments were due in the spring when farming demands were greatest; and (3) subverted the institution's mission as defined by Congress in 1924, to educate and train inmates and to fit the institution's various offerings to each inmate's needs. The Bureau's plans, argued Harris and her allies, would turn the institution into a factory where the inmate would be fitted to the industry's needs. Dr. Lewellys Barker, chairman of the Alderson Board, warned at one meeting that:

> [T]he minute you have something come which compels you to put women into certain activities and restrain them from others, you come into a clash with the prime purpose of the institution. If you have enough inmates who are well suited to that kind of work and who need a trade of that kind, it would be exceedingly good to have them in a factory there; but if you are doing it to make money and compel women to work there regardless of their needs, the question of the readjustment policy of the institution is at stake.[58]

Bennett was certainly not much impressed with the assumption that Alderson existed to provide women with a variety of opportunities. Nonetheless, Bates and Bennett attended an Alderson Board meeting in January 1931 to assure the members that the purpose of the industry was not merely to make money, but also to offer inmates skills and good work habits. The Board agreed to nothing, urging instead that the smaller scale industries of women's institutions be considered as the model for Alderson. Harris closed the meeting with a commitment to "keep a fixed number of women [working] the machines . . . ,"[59] a reminder that control of industries policy was inseparable from control of inmates and the institution.

Both sides returned to these battle themes for the duration of the industries war. The Bureau complimented, cajoled, criticized, and threatened in its attempt to get Alderson's full compliance. Harris compromised on some points, such as the right of an industry to

Claudine SchWeber

exist and the addition of new machines; gave in on some others, such as a wage incentive plan; and continued to resist most of the Bureau's plans on the grounds articulated in 1931.

When Bureau pressure became especially intense, as in the 1932 dispute over industries output, Harris turned to the Alderson Board members and to their contacts for additional help. In this instance, Bates had written to Harris that he was pleased with her acceptance of the value of the sewing industry. However, he and Bennett were "disappointed" in the shop's low production level and the consequent poor financial returns, despite substantial orders, because this meant that Alderson's factory could become a "burden upon the earning of our other shops." Furthermore, inasmuch as the main problem seemed to be "excessive overhead" caused by taking inmates out of industry work to attend classes—in laundry theory, reading, candy making, table service, and so on—Bates asked:

> [Isn't there] some way by which these girls who must necessarily go to school not be assigned to the shop at all, or that a schedule more conducive to the efficient operation of the shop be evolved[?][60]

Perhaps anticipating Harris's reply, Bates's last paragraph warned:

> I do not like to issue instructions to the effect that no one who is assigned to the [factory] should be removed except for sickness, appearance before the Parole Board, or disciplinary reasons, but I, nevertheless, am sympathetic with the feeling of our industrial department that these are the only causes which should be allowed to interfere with the operation of the industry.[61]

Harris took immediate steps to prevent such actions by Washington. First, in a reply letter, Harris spent one paragraph on the production levels issue and four pages lecturing Bates and company on the special status of Alderson and on the differences between men's and women's institutions. She concluded by warning Bates et al.:

> I do not see how the Institution can carry out its legal purposes and also turn itself into a power machine factory. . . . Any gain in profits for the power room would be more than offset by the deliberate abandonment of the Institution's principles. . . . We . . . hope that you will not

change the established policy of the Institution, which is to assign each woman to the work that will enable her to fit into the necessities of her home environment, keeping house for her family or earning a livelihood after leaving Alderson.[62]

Second, Harris sent the correspondence to the Advisory Board, whose members wrote to Bates to express concern that Alderson's founding principles not be subverted. Third, the Alderson Board contacted others who might help Alderson. Dr. Barker, for example, sent a "personal and confidential" note to Mabel Willebrandt, who still maintained an office in Washington, enclosing Harris's letters and expressing his fear that:

[U]nless the main principles upon which Alderson was founded are adhered to, we shall be taking a very serious step backward. Moreover . . . unless Dr. Mary Harris can be backed up by the department in her efforts to approach the ideals mentioned I . . . question . . . whether the present members of the advisory board would regard it as worthwhile to continue their services.[63]

Willebrandt passed this correspondence to the Attorney General, who queried Bates about the problems. In May 1932, Bates wrote his superior that:

I believe this situation is now pretty well ironed out. [At the last Board meeting no one] raised the question . . . as to any lack of support for the principles of the institution.[64]

It was thus a philosophic war, not merely a power struggle between Alderson and the Bureau. The situation was undoubtedly worsened by the fact that Alderson alone, of all the federal prisons, consistently and continually challenged Bureau policies.[65] Alderson stood out not only because Harris was a vigorous opponent, but also because by early 1930 the Bureau had replaced all the wardens with men of its own preference—except Harris. Indeed, Harris's tenacity and contacts enabled her to remain at Alderson a year beyond the mandatory retirement age,[66] assuring that the Alderson–Bureau conflict was in force until early 1941.

Claudine SchWeber

CONCLUSION

Alderson's record of cooperation and conflict mirrored the shifts in federal correctional power from women to men, from autonomous prisons to a centralized system, and from a penology of individual treatment to one based on system needs. It was a shift that Alderson persistently resisted. Resistance was accomplished by using contacts with such supporters as Willebrandt, the Alderson Board, and later Eleanor Roosevelt; by extensively publicizing Alderson's programs and successes;[67] by using the Alderson Board as a "board of trustees . . . [securing] the backing of an official body" for institutional positions;[68] by forcing some disputes to be viewed as attacks upon the institution's founding principles; and by periodically causing the Bureau to answer to outsiders, such as the Attorney General and Board members, for its actions.

Before 1930, Alderson was virtually unchecked in operating a women-run, women-centered environment that offered a variety of educational, social, and vocational opportunities considered crucial to the rehabilitation of women offenders. Afterwards, Alderson's leadership was confronted with a male-run, system-oriented supervising agency that did not view women inmates as a population distinct from other inmates; did not see state facilities, even the progressive ones for women, as the appropriate model for the federal system; and included in its penal philosophy, particularly that of Bennett, "the conviction that the retributory or punitive element is an important one."[69] In 1930, two years before Harris so widely attacked the Bureau for attempting to subvert the institution's principles, Bennett had written the following to Bates about Harris's philosophy:

> It is just pure *"bunk"* it seems to me for anyone to say that an inmate at Alderson believes that time spent there is an opportunity and not a penalty for some offense. The most silver tongued orator, or the greatest high pressure salesman never could convince an inmate in full command of their intellect that their incarceration was a reward laid in their laps by fortuitous circumstance . . . the very moment restraint enters the picture, then the idea of privilege leaves it.
>
> Moreover, I think it is perhaps dangerous philosophy for anyone to believe that he or she is

"The Government's Unique Experiment"

operating an institution for the purpose of providing opportunities for those who offend society. . . .[70]

Hearing such penal blasphemy from the young efficiency experts of the new Bureau probably irritated the older, more experienced Alderson women even further.[71]

The government's "experiment" at Alderson involved more than the rehabilitative program with women prisoners. It also involved the administration, by women, of a relatively autonomous institution focused on the specific needs of incarcerated women. Once the Bureau was created, the experimental conditions changed. The question became, could this women-operated, autonomous prison and its philosophy effectively function in an overwhelmingly male, integrated system? By the early 1940s, after a decade of conflict between the women in Alderson and the men in Washington, the answer was clear: no, the experiment was over.

NOTES

I WANT TO THANK the following persons and agencies for their support: Carolyn Wadsworth Harris, legal guardian of the Mary Belle Harris papers, for her hospitality and accessibility; the National Endowment for the Humanities, for the Summer 1979 and Spring 1981 Faculty Research Fellowships; and Howard Kitchener and the staff of the Research Office of the Federal Prison System, for their continual assistance with the Alderson project. Opinions and analyses are my own.

1. Mary Belle Harris, *I Knew Them in Prison* (New York: Viking, 1936), pp. 245–403; Claudine SchWeber, "Pioneers in Prison," *Federal Probation Quarterly* (September 1980):30–36. Women were also briefly housed at the Federal Reformatory in Seagoville, Texas, during World War II (28 August 1940 to 25 June 1942). Bureau of Prisons, *Statistical Report, Fiscal Year 1975* (Washington, DC: Department of Justice, Bureau of Prisons, 1977), pp. 115–119.
2. Mary Belle Harris to Sanford Bates, 11 March 1932, file 4-9-0, Box 658, Record Group 129, Department of Justice files, National Archives. (References to National Archives Correspondence hereafter cited as *A* to *B*, date, Box #, Archives.)
3. For an analysis of institutional philosophy and practices in the Progressive era, *see* David J. Rothman, *Conscience and Convenience* (New York: Little, Brown, 1980).
4. SchWeber, "Pioneers"; "Put Down Prisoners' Strike at Riverside" (Rutland, 1927), clipping from a 1927 inmate file, Alderson Inmate Records #1–#3010 (1927–1935), Record Group 129, Bureau of Prisons, Department of Justice, Washington National Records Center (Suitland, Maryland). (References to material from these inmate files hereafter cited as Alderson Inmate Records, *year.*)
5. Representative Kopp asked Captain O'Connor, Superintendent of Prisons,

Claudine SchWeber

"Alderson, that is a sort of Ladies' Seminary?" during the 1929 appropriation hearings. U.S. House of Representatives, "Hearings Before the Special Committee on Federal Penal and Reformatory Institutions (7 to 15 January 1929)," 70th Cong., 2nd sess., in "The Alderson Saga" (c. 1925–1935) (Unpublished scrapbook; Warden's office, Federal Correctional Institution, Alderson, WV; Ware Torrey, "Women at Alderson Institution Prepared for Useful Careers," *Washington Star* (16 September 1928), VII, p. 1.

6. Mary Belle Harris, "A Re-Educational Institution: The Federal Industrial for Women," in *University of Chicago Magazine* (April 1934?):207–210.

7. After 1930, the wardens reported to Bureau officials in Washington, who in turn reported to the Department of Justice, Attorney General's office. The existing federal prisons of 1930 were: the penitentiaries at Atlanta (GA), Leavenworth (KS), McNeil Island (WA); a young men's reformatory at Chillicothe (OH); and Alderson (WV); *see* Gregory Hershberger, *The Development of the Federal Prison System* (Washington, DC: Federal Prison System, U.S. Department of Justice, 1979), pp. 6–9.

8. Sanford Bates to Mary Harris, 10 January 1936, "personal and confidential," in Mary Belle Harris Personnel file, National Personnel Records Center (St. Louis). (References to these records hereafter cited as MBH/NPRC.)

9. Minutes of (Alderson) Advisory Board Meeting, 11 October 1931, Box 658, Record Group 129, Department of Justice files, National Archives. (References to Advisory Board minutes hereafter cited as Adv. Bd. Mtg., *date*.)

10. Raymond P. Brandt in *St. Louis Post-Dispatch* (18 August 1929), Sunday Magazine, p. 3.

11. Act of 7 June 1924, Public Law 68-209 (commonly called "The Enabling Act"), secs. 1, 5.

12. Ibid., sec. 7. The Alderson Advisory Board was discontinued 5 January 1975. "Alderson Advisory Board File," Director's Office, Federal Prison System, Washington, DC.

13. Public Law 68-209, secs. 1, 2.

14. "Alderson Institution Dedicated," *New York Times* (28 November 1928), II, p. 5.

15. Dorothy Brown, "Mabel Walker Willebrandt," in *Notable American Women*, ed. Barbara Sicherman and Carol Hurd Green (Cambridge: Harvard University Press, 1980), III, pp. 734–737; Mabel Walker Willebrandt Personnel file, National Personnel Records Center (St. Louis). (Reference to these records hereinafter cited as MWW/NPRC.) Governor Smith of New York called Willebrandt "Prohibition Portia."

16. Harris, *I Knew*, pp. 260–261; U.S. House of Representatives, "Hearings," (*supra* note 5), Appendix I, p. 204; Boxes 658 and 659, Record Group 129, Department of Justice files, National Archives. *See* Table 13-1, p. 286, for chronology of Alderson's establishment.

17. Public Law 68-209.

18. Box 658, Record Group 129, Department of Justice files, National Archives.

19. Some correspondence for the 1923–1925 period existed. It showed the work done by various segments of the West Virginia community to have the women's prison located in the state. Such people included C. R. Crawley, the C & O Railroad manager; E. Chase Bare, the Chamber of Commerce secretary; E. E. Dudding, president of the Prisoner's Relief Society; Lena Lowe Yost, president of the

"The Government's Unique Experiment"

Women's Christian Temperance Union chapter; and Judge Mary O'Toole, a former West Virginian in Washington, DC. The correspondence was contained in a box housed at the Warden's Office, FCI Alderson. Since 1976 when I saw the papers and made copies of several of them, the box has disappeared.

20. *Federal Prisoners, Report of a Conference on Federal Women Prisoners, held September 21, 1923, at the General Federation of Women's Clubs,* n.p., Archives of the General Federation of Women's Clubs, Washington, DC. (References to this report hereafter cited as GFWC 1923.) Some of the attending groups were: American Association of University Women, National Women's Trade Union League, Women's Christian Temperance Union, Democratic National Committee, Republican National Committee, American Federation of Teachers, and National Committee on Prisons and Prison Labor. Note that before 1930, the total federal oversight in corrections consisted of a Superintendent of Prisons and an Inspector of Prisons reporting to an Assistant Attorney General in the Department of Justice. Other committee members were: Mr. Heber Votaw, Superintendent of Federal Prisons; Dr. Katherine B. Davis, General Superintendent of the Bureau of Social Hygiene; Mrs. J. D. Hodder, Superintendent of the Massachusetts Reformatory for Women; Mrs. Fannie French Morse, Superintendent of the New York Training School for Girls; Dr. Valerie H. Parker, Director of the Department of Protective Measures, American Social Hygiene Association; Mrs. Mina Van Winkle, Director of the Women's Bureau of the Metropolitan Police Department; Dr. Mary Wolfe, Superintendent of the Pennsylvania Village for the Feebleminded; Dr. E. Stagg Whittin, Executive Director of the National Committee on Prisons and Prison Labor.

21. The GFWC had endorsed the principle of a federal prison for women at their May 1923 Council Meeting in Atlanta; *see* Mary White Wells, *Unity in Diversity: The History of the General Federation of Women's Clubs* (Washington, DC: General Federation of Women's Clubs, 1953), pp. 207–208; and GFWC *Federation News* (June/July 1923):13.

22. Public Law 68-209. Note that this omission made it possible to appoint a male warden at Alderson for the first time on 1 June 1976. Since then, all Alderson wardens have been men.

23. Boxes 658 and 659, Record Group 129, Department of Justice files, National Archives; MWW/NPRC (*supra* note 15); GFWC *Federation News* (October 1923):9; Obituary of Julia K. Jaffray, *New York Times* (23 May 1941), p. 21.

24. Heber Votaw to the Attorney General, 14 July 1924, file 4-9-01, Box 658, Record Group 129, Department of Justice files, National Archives; Mabel Walker Willebrandt to Harlan Fiske Stone, 29 January 1925, Papers of Harlan Fiske Stone, Manuscript Division, The Library of Congress. Alderson contributed 200 free acres, a serious consideration in its favor. Harris, *I Knew*, p. 251; James Bennett, *I Chose Prison* (New York: Viking, 1970), p. 129.

25. Harris, *I Knew*, p. 251.

26. Ibid., pp. 254–274; Sanford Bates to Mary Harris, 21 January 1930, Box 658, National Archives; Mary Harris to Sanford Bates, 3 May 1930, Box 658, National Archives; "Report of Superintendent to the (Alderson) Advisory Board," Adv. Bd. Mtg., 12 October 1930.

27. Claudine SchWeber, "Mary Belle Harris," in *Notable American Women,* vol. III, pp. 315–317.

28. Brandt, *St. Louis Post-Dispatch* (*supra* note 10).

29. SchWeber, "Pioneers"; Harris, *I Knew*, pp. 254–274, 334–371; Rothman,

Claudine SchWeber

Conscience, pp. 379–421; Eugenia Lekkerkerker, *Reformatories for Women in the United States* (The Hague: J. B. Wolters, 1931), pp. 131–186.

30. SchWeber, 'Pioneers''; Harris, *I Knew*, p. 281; "Women Will Drop Erring Girls If Men Interfere," in (Philadelphia) *Public Ledger* (21 May 1921), n.p., clipping in a scrapbook in the Mary Belle Harris papers currently held by niece Carolyn Wadsworth Harris of Pennsylvania. (References to materials from this collection hereafter cited as MBH/WWH.)

31. Sanford Bates to Mary Harris, 10 January 1936, MBH/NPRC and MBH/WWH.

32. Harris, *I Knew*, p. 259.

33. Boxes 658 and 659, Record Group 129, Department of Justice files, National Archives; MWW/NPRC.

34. Hershberger, *Developments*, pp. 6–7. The scandals included the discovery in 1928 that Warden John Wilson Snook of Atlanta was operating a thriving bootleg whiskey operation in the prison. In order to obtain evidence against the powerful Snook (appointed by the state's U.S. Senator as was the custom before 1930), Willebrandt sent undercover FBI agents to the prison. This was an effective, but very controversial, tactic. *See* MWW/NPRC; and H. Park Tucker, "A History of the Atlanta Federal Penitentiary 1901–1956" (Unpublished, 1956; available at the Bureau of Prisons Library), pp. 225–250, 280. On the authority of the new Bureau, Sanford Bates wrote, "The new organization was given carte blanche to work out a modern prison system for the Federal Government." *See* Sanford Bates, *Prisons and Beyond* (Freeport, NY: Books for Libraries Press, 1936), p. 133; and Adv. Bd. Mtg., 11 October 1931.

35. The outcome was a compromise: *Warden* was to be the official title, but *Superintendent* would be used in "routine and informal correspondence and reference." James Bennett to Mary Harris, 1 November 1937, and Mary Harris to James Bennett, 4 November 1937, MBH/NPRC.

36. Adv. Bd. Mtg., 11 October 1931.

37. Harris, *I Knew*, p. 281.

38. Sanford Bates to Mary Harris, 10 January 1936, MBH/NPRC and MBH/WWH.

39. Ibid.

40. Adv. Bd. Mtg., 16 October 1932.

41. Sanford Bates to Mary Harris, 24 October 1932, Box 658, National Archives.

42. Sanford Bates to Mary Harris, 21 January 1930, Box 658, National Archives.

43. Mary Harris to Sanford Bates, 27 January 1930, Box 658, National Archives.

44. Adv. Bd. Mtg., 12 October 1930; A. H. MacCormick to Sanford Bates, 17 March 1931, Box 658, National Archives.

45. Alderson Inmate Records, 1927–1930.

46. Adv. Bd. Mtg., 11 October 1931.

47. Alderson Inmate Records, 1930–1935.

48. Alderson Inmate Records, 1932.

49. James Bennett to Sanford Bates, 15 May 1934, Box 658, National Archives.

50. Alderson Inmate Records, 1938. Helen Hironimous became Alderson's

warden at Harris's retirement in March 1941. Hironimous retired from this position and from federal service in 1949. *See* Helen H. Hironimous Personnel file, National Personnel Records Center (St. Louis). (References to these records hereafter cited as HHH/NPRC.)

51. Sanford Bates to Mary Harris, 10 January 1936, MBH/NPRC and MBH/WWH. On the cost issue, *see also* W. T. Hammack to Sanford Bates, 7 February 1930, Box 658, National Archives.

52. Mary Harris, "Great Gawd Budjhut and his Consort Purrcapita," n.d., MBH/WWH.

53. Sanford Bates to Mary Harris, 10 January 1936, MBH/NPRC and MBH/WWH.

54. Hershberger, *Development*, p. 11. The 1934 Law is Public Law 73–461. Sanford Bates to Mary Harris, 16 March 1932, Box 658, National Archives.

55. Public Law 68–209, sec. 7. Details on the Alderson Advisory Board's activities in this period are in Boxes 658 and 659, Record Group 129, Department of Justice files, National Archives. On the membership through January 1975, *see* "Alderson Advisory Board File." Hammack warned that "A casual examination of the minutes [of 18 January 1930] would indicate the Superintendent of the institution is gradually bringing the board to function in practically the same manner a board of trustees would operate. Various questions of an administrative nature are brought to the attention of the Board, and the Superintendent thus secures the backing of an official body in connection with projects over which they really have no jurisdiction. . . ." *See* W. T. Hammack to Sanford Bates, 7 February 1930, Box 658, National Archives.

56. Bennett, *I Chose*, p. 13.

57. Adv. Bd. Mtg., 31 January 1931.

58. Ibid.

59. Ibid.

60. Ibid.

61. Ibid.

62. Mary Harris to Sanford Bates, 11 March 1932, Box 658, National Archives.

63. Lewellys Barker to Mabel Willebrandt, 14 March 1932, Box 658, National Archives.

64. Memorandum to the Attorney General from Sanford Bates, 16 May 1932, Box 658, National Archives.

65. Sanford Bates to Mary Harris, 10 January 1936, MBH/NPRC.

66. *The Work of the BOP* (Washington, DC: Bureau of Prisons, Department of Justice, November 1932), p. 4. The one-year extension of mandatory retirement came about through the intervention of Eleanor Roosevelt. *See* MBH/NPRC.

67. MBH/NPRC. There are about ten scrapbooks of news clippings in the MBH/WWH collection.

68. W. T. Hammack to Sanford Bates, 7 February 1930, Box 658, National Archives.

69. James Bennett to Sanford Bates, 4 November 1930, Box 658, National Archives.

70. Ibid.

71. Note the age difference among the leadership: Harris, born 1874; Bates, born 1884; Bennett, born 1894.

14

Women as Criminal Justice Professionals

A Challenge to Change Tradition

EDITH ELISABETH FLYNN

If the past is prologue, prediction requires an historical base. The history of the number of women employed in the American labor force clearly shows that women are headed for parity with men. However, one factor has remained largely unchanged throughout the decades: there are major earnings differentials between men and women that are not only enduring, but also surprisingly large.[1] Among the reasons for keeping women's compensation down, the literature identifies not only outright discrimination but also the sexual division of labor in American society.[2] Today, over 70 percent of all working women are found in traditionally female occupations: clerical work, sales, nursing, teaching, and service-related work.[3] While men become doctors, engineers, police officers, or judges, women become nurses, schoolteachers, telephone operators, waitresses, meter maids, or secretaries.

Edith Elisabeth Flynn

Surely, the most critical factor in the confinement of women to the "pink ghetto" is cultural in origin and firmly entwined with social attitudes about women and ingrained views about the "women's sphere" and the roles they have traditionally performed in society. Such roles have historically been linked to homemaking, supportive services, and woman's culturally defined role as helpmate to the dominant male in her life. Women seldom reach management positions in any field, a fact again attributable to a combination of long-standing historic, economic, social, and cultural factors. The discriminatory division of labor has been institutionalized in society and become self-perpetuating, since each young person is socialized, counseled, and trained for certain jobs and not for others. In this way, differential perceptions of job opportunities and differential utilization of women in the labor market reinforce one another and become self-fulfilling prophecies that tangibly restrict employment opportunities.

The status of women in the American labor market provides the necessary backdrop for the following in-depth examination of the status of women professionals in criminal justice. As will be seen in this chapter, women are one of the most underutilized and grievously misappropriated resources in criminal justice today. Every theme broached thus far—pervasive sexual segregation of occupation, earnings differentials, and outright discrimination on the basis of sex—is widespread within every component of the criminal justice system. Professionals working within the field of criminal justice hold positions that have historically and traditionally been deeply embedded in the male domain. Judges, lawyers, sheriffs, wardens, and police and corrections officers have almost exclusively been male. Women who do work in the criminal justice system do so mainly in the capacity of secretaries, file clerks, juvenile officers, nurses, dieticians, and personnel in matrimonial courts. But we rarely find them in the position of sheriff, warden, corrections commissioner, or trial judge. The scant literature on the subject of women professionals in criminal justice reveals clearly that despite gradually changing social attitudes and the development of new roles for women in society, women must overcome not only discriminatory hiring practices, but also pervasive organizational and attitudinal prejudices that dominate this traditionally male field.[4]

The purposes of this chapter are to examine the status of

women professionals in the criminal justice setting, to review prevailing employment practices and women's experiences within the different system components, and to analyze the barriers to equal employment opportunities they continue to face. The conclusion offers suggestions on how to overcome the many difficulties women job aspirants and incumbents encounter in their pursuit of equity in the criminal justice labor market. Since this nation prides itself for being governed by law, it is useful to begin the task at hand with an examination of what assistance, if any, women have received from the legislative, judicial, and executive branches of government in the area of fair employment practice.

LEGISLATIVE, JUDICIAL, AND ADMINISTRATIVE REMEDIES: THE STATE OF THE ART

The ensuing discussion will reveal a rich history of legislative pronouncements and case law on behalf of equal employment opportunity. Both are instances of using the law to direct social change, a practice that is time-honored and widespread in our society.[5] However, it is generally recognized that legislative and judicial decree is neither the most expeditious nor the most efficient means for bringing about social change. This is because most social change comes about incrementally, at a snail's pace, and largely as a result of multi-institutional and societal forces.

The basic guarantees of due process and equal treatment under the law are as old as the nation. But only in the last decade were major challenges launched by the federal and state governments to remedy the myriad problems associated with the equal employment opportunities of women and minorities in general and in criminal justice in particular.

The impetus for fair employment standards has its roots in long-extant civil rights legislation and in the due process clause of the Fifth Amendment, which states unequivocally that "No person shall . . . be deprived of life, liberty, or property without due process of law. . . ." Civil rights also traces its beginnings to the Thirteenth Amendment, which outlawed slavery, and the Fourteenth Amendment, which guaranteed due process and equal protection under law. Both have enabling clauses giving Congress the power of enforcement. The enabling legislation that followed—the Civil Rights Acts of 1866, 1870, and 1871—created enforcement laws that

Edith Elisabeth Flynn

became the foundation of the civil rights acts of the twentieth century.[6]

The most recent legislative efforts to ensure equal employment opportunity are rooted in the Civil Rights Act of 1964. This act is divided into a number of titles, each touching upon a particular area of potential discrimination, including voting rights, public education, public accommodation, and so on. Title VII represents the main body of federal legislation in the area of fair employment. Prior to 1972, Title VII was directed primarily toward private employment agencies, private employers, and labor organizations with twenty-five or more employees or members. In 1972, Congress expanded the coverage of Title VII with an amendment known as the Equal Employment Opportunity Act of 1972. This act expands coverage of Title VII to both public and private employers, including state and local governments, public and private educational institutions, labor organizations, and public and private employment agencies. Any organization within these areas with fifteen or more employees is affected. Under the authority of Title VII, the federal Equal Employment Opportunity Commission (EEOC) is empowered to act as a regulatory agency; its functions include setting standards, establishing guidelines for compliance with the requirements of the law, and enforcing Title VII as it applies to discrimination against women and minorities. The basic principle of Title VII is that all jobs must be open to both men and women unless it can be proven that sex is "a bona fide occupational qualification reasonably necessary to the normal operation of that particular business or enterprise. . . ."[7]

The Equal Employment Opportunity Act of 1972 and the Bona Fide Occupational Qualification (BFOQ) exception to Title VII are, without doubt, the two most important legislative provisions in relation to women's employment in criminal justice. Further, the legislative history of the BFOQ indicates that it is to be construed narrowly. When Congress passed an amendment to Title VII in 1972, it expressed grave concern about equal employment opportunities for women. In explaining the need for the amendment, the House Committee on Education and Labor wrote:

> *The situation of the working woman is no less serious than that of minorities. . . .*
>
> *Women are subject to economic deprivations as a class. Their self-fulfillment and development is frustrated*

Women as Criminal Justice Professionals

because of their sex. Numerous studies have shown that women are placed in the less remunerative positions on the basis of their sex alone.

Such blatantly disparate treatment is particularly objectionable in view of the fact that Title VII has specifically prohibited sex discrimination since its enactment in 1964. . . .

In recent years, the courts have done much to create a body of law clearly disapproving of sex discrimination in employment. Despite the efforts of the courts and the Commission (EEOC), discrimination against women continues to be widespread, and is regarded by many as either morally or physiologically justifiable.

This Committee believes that women's rights are not judicial divertissements. Discrimination against women is no less serious than other forms of prohibited employment practices and is to be accorded the same degree of social concern given to any type of unlawful discrimination.[8]

Since Congress left it to the EEOC to articulate with specificity the scope of the BFOQ exception, it is useful to examine the EEOC's position: it has stated that it will find a BFOQ exception warranted only "Where it is necessary for the purpose of authenticity or genuineness . . . e.g., an actor or actress." The following, however, are unwarranted:

(i) The refusal to hire a woman because of her sex based on the assumptions of the comparative employment characteristics of women in general. For example, the assumption that the turnover rate among women is higher than among men.

(ii) The refusal to hire an individual based on stereotyped characterizations of the sexes. Such stereotypes include, for example, that men are less capable of assembling intricate equipment; that women are less capable of aggressive salesmanship. The principle of nondiscrimination requires that individuals be considered on the basis of individual capacities and not on the basis of any characteristics generally attributed to the group.

Edith Elisabeth Flynn

> (iii) *The refusal to hire an individual because of the pref-*
> *erence of co-workers, the employer, clients or*
> *customers . . . .*[9]

Additional support for a strict and narrow interpretation of the BFOQ is offered by Cooksey: "If the exception is used simply to confirm the culturally accepted standards of what work a woman or man should be doing, the prohibition against discrimination on the basis of sex will be rendered meaningless.[10] Finally, case law provides that where a facial exclusion on the basis of sex is challenged, the burden of proof is on the employer to demonstrate that the position in question falls within the BFOQ exception.[11]

While neither law enforcement agencies nor court systems have managed to breach the tight provisions of the BFOQ, a corrections agency was able to obtain a favorable Supreme Court ruling to exclude women from working in a maximum security penitentiary for men. The case in question, *Dothard* v. *Rawlinson*, is examined in greater detail later in this chapter.[12]

In addition to the EEOC (whose activities and enforcement powers have been severely crippled by recent federal budget cuts), four other federal agencies are concerned with the enforcement of fair employment practices: (1) the United States Civil Service Commission, which has the responsibility to promulgate regulations ensuring that state and local jurisdictions participating in federal grant-in-aid programs adhere to merit system principles; (2) the United States Civil Rights Commission, located within the Department of Justice, which enforces federal statutes relating to civil rights through both criminal prosecutions and civil remedies; (3) the Office of Federal Contract Compliance (OFCC), housed within the Department of Labor, which coordinates enforcement of federal government policy prohibiting employment discrimination by contractors that do business with federal agencies or receive federal funds; and (4) the Law Enforcement Assistance Administration (LEAA), created in 1968 as a result of the Omnibus Crime Control and Safe Streets Act and located within the Department of Justice, which promulgated in 1973 equal employment opportunity guidelines prohibiting sex discrimination by any of its grant recipients. Since Congress has eliminated the budget authority for all LEAA criminal justice assistance programs in fiscal year 1981, that agency has now been rendered moot and is in the process of being phased out.

Women as Criminal Justice Professionals

In the judicial area, a landmark case was decided by the Supreme Court in 1971. In *Reed* v. *Reed*, the Court specifically applied the equal protection clause of the Fourteenth Amendment to prohibit discrimination on the basis of sex.[13] However, despite *Reed* and some other significant steps toward assuring equal rights for women, vacillations and divided opinions over the past eight years indicate that the Court's commitment to overcoming sex discrimination is less than total. The problem is that, in the absence of the Equal Rights Amendment, the Court is treading a delicate line between the Charybdis of constitutional interpretation and the Scylla of constitutional amendment or statutory enactment. Ginsburg, in analyzing the Supreme Court's record on sex discrimination in terms of the voting pattern of individual justices, notes a tenacious attachment by certain justices to stereotypes regarding the role and nature of women.[14] It is important to recognize that judges, like other decision makers, are creatures of the social environment in which they live. Their decisions reflect not only prevalent social values, but also their own values and life experiences—including their prejudices. While it is likely that Sandra Day O'Connor, the Supreme Court's first woman appointee, will raise the Court's sensitivity to women's issues, her effect on decisions remains to be seen.

DESPITE THESE RECENT legislative, judicial, and executive steps taken to guarantee equal employment opportunities, there has been no great increase in the employment of women across occupational categories, including criminal justice. While the gains in legislative guarantees are real enough, women are not entering the criminal justice system in equal numbers, nor, once employed, are they advancing in the various subsystems. According to the latest available statistics (1978), women make up 23 percent of the corrections work force, 3.2 percent of the law enforcement officers, 9 percent of lawyers, 5.8 percent of judges, and about 1 percent of administrators in each of these fields.[15] Thus, although limited gains have been made by professional women entering the criminal justice field, it is obvious that the goal of full equality is still far away. This sorry state of the art can be understood only by realizing that law is not the ideal vehicle for bringing about social change. While legislative and judicial dicta undoubtedly offer legal, moral, and symbolic support for a particular cause and may even provide tactical advantages to a specific contender, there is within the judicial bureaucracy a wide range of opportunities for noncompliance and evasion that can delay the implementation of a specific law or decree for decades. Further, even though laws are mainly directed at bringing about specific behavior changes (for example, the implementation of fair employment practices), they are not very effective at wholesale changes in people's attitudes and belief systems. And since a change in the latter is indispensable to permanent behavior change, it is easy to understand why legislative and judicial decrees have in fact been singularly ineffective in changing the norms and values of large segments of society.

Criminal justice is no exception. The field is ingrained with tradition; recalcitrant to change; and, most to the point, apathetic to legislative and judicial exhortations to alter its discriminatory employment practices. It is largely due to these characteristics that women continue to face major barriers to employment in law enforcement, the courts, and corrections—barriers that will now be analyzed through examination of the latest empirical evidence and the literature.

WOMEN IN LAW ENFORCEMENT

Although women professionals entered the field of law enforcement as early as 1891, when New York City hired its first matrons, police officials have one of the longer standing records of adamant resistance to the employment of women.[16] It was not until after World War I that women in law enforcement positions gained some ground, largely as a result of the feminist movement of that time.[17] Between the 1930s and late 1940s women made few, if any, advances in the field. But by 1969, a few large police departments had begun to experiment with the assignment of women officers to routine patrol. Predictably, major impetus did not come until the 1970s, with the passage of the previously discussed Title VII and other significant changes in federal policies. It was then that a few women began to be deployed by police as undercover operatives in drug and vice control. By 1971, there were approximately 3,700 women employed full-time in this nation's police departments.[18] Their employment, however, was closely linked to traditional stereotypes of women; they were assigned primarily to secretarial and clerical positions and to juvenile work, meter patrol, and other low-level administrative duties.[19]

According to the 1978 edition of the *Uniform Crime Reports*, sworn female police officers constitute only 3.2 percent of this country's police officer population at the local (municipal and county) level of government.[20] While a few women hold ranks as high as captain, inspector, or deputy chief, the vast majority can be found in the lower ranks.[21] Approximately half of the country's 25,000 police departments have no women officers at all.[22] It is not only the small- and medium-sized departments that shun women officers; many major cities also continue exclusionary practices.

However, these dismal statistics at the local level are overshadowed by the practices of state police departments, which have been most resistant to hiring women as police officers. A national study conducted in 1975 indicated that of the approximately 42,000 state police officers nationwide, only 135 (or .3 percent) were women.[23] At the federal level of law enforcement, it is estimated that about 2 percent of FBI agents are female, a figure that also seems to apply to the U.S. Secret Service.[24]

It is evident from these statistics that women continue to be vastly underrepresented in law enforcement. And when women are hired as police officers, they are disproportionately assigned to duties with female suspects, vice and sexual offense control, juvenile delinquency and child welfare cases, traffic, telecommunications, and clerical work.

Among the major barriers to equal employment of women in policing are: (1) the veterans' preference system; (2) physical requirements; and, most important, (3) sexual stereotyping of women officers by their male colleagues and superiors.

The Veterans' Preference System

One of the major barriers to the entrance of women into civil service law enforcement positions is the veterans' preference system. The underlying rationale for this system is the attempt to reward veterans for their military service and to assist them in the readjustment to civilian life. Since few women have military experience, they cannot receive veterans' preference points on hiring or promotional examinations.

While the majority of jurisdictions in the nation give preference points to veterans, Massachusetts and New Jersey are the only two states with a system of absolute veterans' preference. In June 1979 the U.S. Supreme Court upheld by a vote of seven to two a

Edith Elisabeth Flynn

challenge to the Massachusetts veterans' preference law; it decided that the law was not gender based because it put both men and women at a disadvantage as individuals, even though it did benefit men as a class.[25] The idea of assisting veterans is certainly laudable, but it remains an open question as to whether a system of absolute veterans' preference for civil service jobs is the most effective, fairest way to accomplish this objective. This question is particularly appropriate since the reward of some occurs at the expense of others.

Another ostensible reason for granting veterans' preference is the assumption that such a system identifies individuals with desirable qualifications for police employment, presumably in view of the "paramilitary" nature of police work. However, analysis of this rationale proves beyond doubt that prior military service is in no way predictive of effective police field performance.[26] Further, the military model is now considered out of place by many national organizations, including the Police Foundation, the Federal Bureau of Prisons, and the American Correctional Association.[27] There is also a particular "catch-22" for women in the fact that some police departments give additional points to disabled veterans; female veterans obviously do not qualify, because women are prohibited by law from membership in combat units.[28]

In summary, the veterans' preference system clearly negates the very purpose of civil service examinations, which is to identify persons best qualified for the position in question. While the extent of discrimination may well decrease if women continue to enter the military in growing numbers, discrimination even against a smaller proportion of qualified women is still discrimination.

Physical Requirements

Many women are excluded from law enforcement positions by rigid and arbitrary physical requirements. Many police departments tenaciously cling to restrictive standards in spite of the fact that every national advisory council and commission has deplored such practices.[29] For example, the President's Commission on Law Enforcement and Administration of Justice noted that requirements for physical stature and condition in many departments were unduly restrictive and resulted in many applicants (including women), who might otherwise have exceptional qualifications, being summarily rejected because of height, weight, or vision.[30] Such restrictions increase the odds against the selection of women even further. While many departments have begun to adopt different minimum height and weight requirements for men and women (usually 5'8" for men and 5'5" for women) largely as a result of legal challenges, others continue to adhere to the same standards for men and women unencumbered.[31]

Because physical standards have not been proven to be job related, they have been challenged by both the courts and regulatory agencies on a periodic basis.[32] For example, as early as 1971, the First Circuit Court of Appeals found that height and weight requirements were discriminatory because no evidence had been presented to substantiate their job relatedness. The Law Enforcement Assistance Administration followed suit by issuing guidelines forbidding discrimination through height and weight requirements.[33] Finally, in *Dothard* v. *Rawlinson* the Supreme Court upheld the District Court ruling that the Alabama statute requiring correctional officers to be at least 5' 2'' and to weigh 120 pounds was discriminatory because of its disparate effect upon women.[34]

In summary, even though most eligibility criteria and tests used for police recruit selection bear no relationship whatsoever to police performance on the job, such requirements continue to be used and thereby covertly help discriminate against women applicants. Continuation of such practices violates not only the spirit and the letter of Title VII, but also the need for a representative and democratic police force in this country.

Sexual Stereotyping

In 1873, the U.S. Supreme Court denied Myra Bradwell the right to practice law because of her sex. In doing so, the Court stated that:

> *The natural and proper timidity and delicacy which belongs to the female sex evidently unfits it for many of the occupations of civil life. The constitution of the family organization, which is founded in the divine ordinance, as well as in the nature of things, indicates the domestic sphere as that which properly belongs to the domain and function of womanhood.*[35]

While few contemporary police chiefs would have the temerity to express such an opinion in public, the Supreme Court's dictum expresses only too well the stereotyped image most police officers have of the female sex. It is for that reason that the previously discussed barriers to the employment of women, albeit real, are best seen as Potemkin's villages, erected to hide the real discriminatory motivations behind them.

Study after study on police perceptions of their work indicates their opinion that policing involves strength, action, danger, and male fellowship—that it is, in short, a masculine pursuit.[36] Similarly, many male police officers tend to believe that women are neither emotionally nor physically fit to handle dangerous situations. As a result, many police officials believe that women would be not only ineffective in police work, but also an outright hindrance and danger to the men in that they would require added protection. Women in uniform, wearing badges, riding in squad cars, carrying guns, arresting men, and so on, are bound to challenge deeply held cultural perceptions regarding the role and function of men and women in society.[37] We know that the law enforcement subculture has consistently stressed traditionalism, conservatism, and authoritarianism, and has placed an emphasis upon personal rather than general qualities. Such values abound in the working and lower middle classes.[38] And since the great majority of police officers are traditionally recruited from these particular social classes, it is easier to understand why women in blue continue to experience such persistent discrimination.

Whatever the effort on the part of some police departments to integrate women into the ranks, women continue to encounter deep-seated prejudice. For example, when permitted to grade anonymously, supervisory personnel in one study rated women officers as *less* competent in spite of the fact that objective ratings of the women consistently showed them to be *as* effective as men.[39]

A recent effort on the part of the U.S. Air Force to explore the feasibility of unlimited utilization of women in their law enforcement area (including antiterrorist forces) encountered prototypical prejudice: local policemen included in the study were found to be even more resistant to women police than were USAF security personnel! Respondents as a whole disapproved of women in the role of authority, in front-line policing involving dangerous confrontations, and in duties requiring strength. Women were also viewed as emotionally unfit for policing and useful only to the degree that they could deal with female victims of sexual crimes.[40] In a similar survey, the great majority of officers in an Ohio police department felt that women were incapable of executing patrol work and favored even more stringent enforcement of weight and fitness requirements to keep them out.[41]

The tenacious resistance of male officers to accept women into their ranks flies in the face of a veritable plethora of empirical studies, the vast majority of which point to the effectiveness of policewomen.[42] It has been found that women officers tend to improve the public image of a department; reduce police violence in general; use less violence in police–citizen encounters; and are more sensitive to victims of rape and other sex-related crimes.[43]

One of the most extensive and rigorous evaluations of the performance of women officers, conducted in Washington, DC, found that women and men performed patrol work in a similar manner. They responded to the same types of calls for police services while on patrol and encountered a similar proportion of citizens who were dangerous, angry, upset, or violent. When they responded to such disturbances, there was little difference between men and women in the way they handled the situations. Citizens were found to show respect for both male and female officers. New men and new women made approximately the same number of arrests and received comparable ratings in their general patrol skills. Even more to the point, the study included reports of some incidents in which individual women performed exceedingly well, even under the most difficult circumstances.[44]

Similar evaluation efforts launched in other cities have only added to the existing body of knowledge; there are no statistically significant differences between the sexes in the usual measures of police performance, including formal evaluations and amount of arrests, summonses, radio runs, and sick time.[45] Regardless of what data sources are used—field observations, citizen interviews to determine their satisfaction with police, performance ratings, records reviews, or supervisory personnel interviews—women perform police patrol duties as well as men.[46]

In summary, stereotyped images treat women as a class rather than as individuals. Such views deny women the opportunity to challenge the assumptions underlying these images and to demonstrate their individual capabilities. It is discouraging to have to note in 1982 that negative male attitudes toward women officers are the most impervious and critical factor hindering the advancement of women in policing. Legislative, judicial, and executive remedies are paving the way to some extent. National leadership by the Police Foundation and the National Sheriffs Association, and constructive attitudes of individual police chiefs, have made an impact. But women's hope for employment equality in law enforcement will not come until there has been a basic change in the attitudes of most of their male colleagues. And that kind of change is most notoriously slow in coming.

WOMEN IN THE COURT SYSTEM

As Judges

A 1977 analysis of equity in judicial representation revealed persistent exclusionary practices in both federal and state court systems.[47] In 1977 women held only 10 judgeships out of a total of 583 appointments to the federal bench. The latest available count shows that women now hold 44 out of the total 648 federal judgeships.[48] It took this country 200 years to see the first woman, Sandra Day O'Connor, appointed to the Supreme Court. Data from state courts also reveal low ratios of women judges. As of 1977, only nine women were reported to sit on the highest state appellate courts. Two women served on the appellate panel of the District of Columbia Courts of Appeals. Eighteen women sat on state intermediate appellate courts, while only 2.5 percent or 130 women could be found in major trial courts of the fifty state systems. Almost half of the states had no women on their major trial courts. The proportion of women on courts of limited and special jurisdiction was found to vary considerably, ranging from 0 to 36.8 percent. Of a total of 5,452 judges with limited jurisdiction, 317 or 5.8 percent were women, while the percentage of women on justice-of-the-peace courts ranged by state from 1 to 44 percent.[49] In her discussion of the "token" role of women in the courts, Cook notes that such tokenism is directly attributable to the restricted access of women to law schools and to the positions that prepare lawyers politically and professionally for the bench.[50]

Until the 1970s, women judges remained tokens and rare exceptions to the male monopoly of the bench. Looking at additional data, we find two separate information sources suggesting that the national proportion of women judges tends to match the national proportion of women law graduates on a time lag basis. In the 1960s, women constituted 1 to 2 percent of the legal profession, and women judges filled 1 to 2 percent of the bench. The 4 percent of the law school graduates who were women in the 1960s were reflected in the 4 percent of judges serving on the bench in the 1970s.[51] Given the current conservative trend spread across the country, these findings do provide a silver lining in an otherwise bleak situation. Conscious of past discriminations and prodded by the provisions of Title VII and federal financial assistance programs, law schools have rapidly expanded their admission of women. This impressive national increase in the percentage of women law students ranged in 1977 from a low of 6.7 percent in South Carolina to a high of 34.3 percent in New Mexico.[52] Since that time, these numbers have undoubtedly increased further. This trend, coupled with an anticipated reduction of discrimination in the recruitment of women to legal jobs on the one hand and a predicted growth of the judicial branch on the other, portends an eventual end of tokenism and a substantial increase in the number of female judges in the future. The appointment of the first woman to the Supreme Court is certainly the most significant step in this direction.

But in addition to their numerical underrepresentation, women judges face other problems of discrimination. For example, they tend to find themselves subjected to a pattern of specialization and isolation on the bench. They are assigned mostly to matrimonial and juvenile courts rather than trial courts, a reflection of stereotypical thinking about women in general. Additionally, Cook found that the presence of female judges in courts that handle estates and guardianships relates to the amount of money involved.[53] That is, more women tend to work in courts that process small amounts of money. There is also emerging evidence that women on the bench are more likely than men to be challenged at election time.[54] While there is currently not enough information to pinpoint the rationale for this pervasive phenomenon of discrimination, it may well be related to women's general lack of political power. No doubt the key to judicial selection lies in the political system. Since federal and state bar associations exert substantial influence over judicial appointments, it is significant that women are largely excluded from the boards of governors of bar associations and from executive positions within these organizations. Further, political party leaders who slate judicial candidates tend to follow value systems that invariably favor the selection of male candidates.

Edith Elisabeth Flynn

While the increasing number of women entering the political system on elective levels can be expected to rectify this situation, total rectification will not occur in the immediate future.

As Lawyers and Prosecutors

In the legal profession, women continue to confront tokenism and discrimination. In the not-too-distant past, women law students had almost no role models at law schools. While this situation is gradually changing, the current percentage of women law professors is still pegged at only 14 percent. Very few women are deans of the nation's 171 accredited law schools. Women lawyers are also making little headway in this country's more prestigious law firms; their rate of membership is estimated at 2 percent, and most of those who make it to this level are channeled (like women judges) into such legal doldrums as matrimonial law, trusts and estates, and tax law.[55]

The same general observation holds for the vast majority of women working as prosecutors at federal, state, and county levels. In contrast to the practices of such other nations as Japan and West Germany, the prosecutor's office in the United States has long been a major stepping-stone to either higher political office or the judiciary. As a result, women prosecutors are relegated mostly to domestic and juvenile matters, while highly visible criminal and civil cases are often reserved for men. Service as judges' clerks is yet another traditional stepping-stone for the judicial profession. At the U.S. Supreme Court—which has just recently been joined by its first woman associate justice—only three of the justices' thirty-two clerks in 1980 were women![56]

As Court Employees

Women have experienced some positive changes in their attempts to infiltrate the ranks of court employees; in fact, there is an increasing number of women in jobs previously dominated by men. For example, most jurisdictions now have roughly the same number of female and male court reporters.[57] While we have no precise statistics on the distribution by sex of clerks of courts, there is some evidence that women are being accepted in increasing numbers in such positions.[58] Women bailiffs are another relatively new addition to the American court system. Since bailiffs are furnished to the courts by law enforcement units, their proportional representation in the courtroom depends less on their acceptance by the judiciary than by the law enforcement officials in the various U.S. Marshal's offices or sheriffs' and police departments. One example of the entry of women into bailiff positions is provided by the Los Angeles Superior Court system, which reports that women bailiffs account for at least 25 percent of the total bailiff force.[59]

To summarize these findings, it is fair to state that court systems have embarked on the long road toward extending equal rights to women seeking employment. Yet, the principles of equal employment opportunity have been much more rigorously applied in the private sector and in public sectors other than the judiciary, where their application has been glacially slow. Findings of a 1978 survey by the National Center for State Courts[60] support this statement. Studying the status of Equal Employment Opportunity and Affirmative Action in state court systems, the authors note that few EEO programs were in operation in state courts at that time and that women and minorities continued to be vastly underrepresented in the judiciary as well as in the court system work force. But the most inauspicious finding of the report lies in a wide range of legal questions raised by some of the judges surveyed. Many questioned the applicability of Title VII to state courts in the light of the separation of powers doctrine, the Tenth and Eleventh Amendments to the Constitution, and the exception provisions contained in Title VII. Such questions clearly reflect serious judicial reservations concerning the concept of equal employment opportunity, reservations that become all the more ominous if we consider that the principle of equal employment opportunity does no more than establish the right of all persons to obtain work and to advance solely on the basis of merit, ability, and potential, without discrimination on the basis of race, sex, or other legally irrelevant criteria. When some of our judges cannot accept such a basic doctrine of fairness and equality in employment for their own courts, what do such views portend for the rest of the nation? Is not judicial unwillingness to apply standards of equality to the employment of women the epitomy of discrimination?

WOMEN IN CORRECTIONS

Employment Practices

In 1969, the Joint Commission on Correctional Manpower and Training noted that while women made up 40 percent of the national work force, they accounted for only 12 percent of the correctional work force.[61] More than a decade later, the great majority of women in corrections continue to be found in sexually segregated adult female and juvenile institutions. The few women employees who do work in state and federal institutions are, with rare exceptions, secretaries, clerks, and nurses. In spite of increasing pressure by legislative, judicial, and executive bodies, corrections has tenaciously resisted changing its traditional hiring practices. Such persistent discrimination against women as employees (particularly in institutions for male offenders) has had serious implications for women's career advancement in corrections, for there is a tradition to select managers and administrators from the ranks of institutional personnel. This practice, when combined with the fact that the number of institutions for males is much larger than the number of institutions for females, has meant that women are effectively excluded from management and administrative positions. It is no surprise, therefore, that the few women who are correctional administrators serve mostly as wardens of institutions for women.

However, women have recently begun to make inroads as corrections officers in male institutions. While a 1969 survey of state corrections agencies showed that only two out of thirty-eight agencies responding had hired women officers for their male facilities, another survey in 1977 revealed that twenty out of twenty-two agencies responding had hired women in such positions.[62] In addition, the California Department of Corrections, which has been so often in the forefront of innovation and progress in corrections, embarked in 1974 on a major effort to provide equal employment opportunities to women workers by means of a gradual and controlled increase in their numbers.[63] The program resulted in the employment of about one hundred female officers in such positions as safety coordinator, chief of inmate appeals, parole agent, and counselor. By 1975, all California institutions were employing female officers and some had opened all posts to women, including those requiring direct contact with inmates. Departmental evaluations found that women officers performed as well as their male counterparts. They were accepted by the inmates and appeared to have had a positive influence on the behavior of some of the prisoners as well.[64]

An important effort to improve corrections by setting national standards took place in 1973, when the National Advisory Commission on Criminal Justice Standards and Goals noted: "[T]he time is long overdue for a careful inspection of the assumptions and biases that have barred women from most positions in corrections."[65] Referring to Title VII and the EEOC guidelines, the commission made it quite clear that women should be hired for virtually any position in corrections. Undeterred by anticipated serious objections from the corrections community, the commission promulgated the most stringent standards yet for the hiring of women:

> *Correctional agencies immediately should develop policies and implement practices to recruit and hire more women for all types of positions in corrections, to include the following:*
> 1. *Change in correctional agency policy to eliminate discrimination against women for correctional work.*
> 2. *Provision for lateral entry to allow immediate placement of women in administrative positions.*
> 3. *Development of better criteria for selection of staff for correctional work, removing unreasonable obstacles to the employment of women.*
> 4. *Assumption by the personnel system of aggressive leadership in giving women a full role in corrections.*[66]

Similarly, in 1976, the American Correctional Association, the only national professional association representing all of corrections, adopted the following policy statement on the employment of women:

> *The American Correctional Association adopts affirmative action as a commitment to an on-going process which will ensure equal employment opportunity and employment conditions for minorities and women in correctional employment.*[67]

Since there are no data available on the subject of the employment of women in corrections other than the studies cited above, it would be exceedingly difficult to assess the impact, if any, of this impressive array of equal opportunity legislation and national policies, guidelines, and standards, were it not for Morton's recently completed national study on the employment of women as correctional officers in state-level adult male and female correctional institutions.[68] The following discussion summarizes the findings of this seminal study, which, for the first time in the history of corrections, provides the field with baseline data on the employment of women in state corrections systems.

With forty-five state systems (or 91.8 percent of the forty -nine surveyed) responding, Morton was able to document a significant increase in the employment of women in the overall corrections work force compared to only 12 percent found by the Joint Commission in 1969.[69] The increase amounts to a difference of 11 percent over the nine-year period involved, for a 91.7 percent overall increase in employment of women by correctional agencies. This finding compares most favorably to a 5 percent increase of women in the general labor force during the same time period.

Looking at the different jurisdictions, we find that with all systems surveyed responding (except Mississippi), only four states (Alaska, Pennsylvania, Texas, and Utah) reported that they did not employ women as correctional officers in male correctional institutions. It appears, therefore, that the hiring of women as correctional officers for men's prisons has become the norm rather than the exception. A rank order listing by state of the percentages of women employed in male institutions as of the target date (December 1978) reveals considerable variation.[70] In this respect the findings are comparable to police employment practices, which were also found to be devoid of patterns and highly variable. Nationally, women compose an average 6.6 percent of the correctional officer work force in state correctional institutions for men. Louisiana leads the responding states; its guard force in its male institutions is 18.2 percent female. Connecticut, New Jersey, and Arizona employed 1.7, 1.5, and 1.4 percent women respectively, while Montana weighed in with a fraction, .6 percent. Finally, while Rhode Island and Maine indicated that they hired women as correctional officers, they did not employ any in their male institutions at the target date of the survey.

An examination of overall staffing patterns across male and female institutions reveals both the expected and the unexpected. In most instances, women staff female institutions and men staff male facilities. Nationally, women accounted for 83 percent of the officers in correctional institutions for women, while men accounted for 17 percent.[71] One system, however, reported a majority of male officers (55 percent) in its women's prisons, and 18 percent of the systems reported their women's institutional correctional officer

Women as Criminal Justice Professionals

staff to be over 30 percent male! No relationship could be found between the percentage of male correctional officers employed in women's facilities and the percentage of women employed in men's facilities.

To analyze system motivations for the hiring of women, it is worth noting that a significant number of responding states (twenty-eight or 65 percent of forty-three systems) directly credited the requirements of the Equal Employment Opportunity Commission for their progressive employment practices.[72] This provides clear evidence of the impact of federal legislation on bringing about a significant social change in this area.

No consistent evidence of sexual stereotyping in the allocation of women officers within male institutions could be found in the study. Predictably, Morton found the proportion of women officers in minimum security institutions to be higher than in maximum and medium security facilities. However, a higher percentage of systems used women in maximum and medium security institutions than in minimum ones, which is an unexpected finding. As will be seen in the following discussion of barriers to the employment of women in corrections, the assignment of female officers to maximum security prisons is enlightening. For example, 17 percent of the systems surveyed by Morton reported using over 10 percent women in their maximum security institutions.[73] Only six systems (or 13.9 percent of forty-three reviewed) reported that they did not use any women at that security level. One system reported a surprisingly high 25 percent women officers as working in its maximum security male institution!

What better evidence can be presented against existing statutory, executive, or jurisprudential proscriptions of deploying women in maximum security institutions for men than the actual employment of women in such settings by such a significant number of state systems and with no apparent harmful effects? Granted, the Morton study does not offer details on the specific deployment of women within the surveyed correctional institutions. It was not designed to accomplish that. However, there is additional evidence in the literature that female correctional officers are assigned to positions involving contact with inmates and regularly serve on tiers in many facilities, including those in California's state system, the federal system, and many local systems; this evidence provides *prima facie* evidence as to their utility and effectiveness in such settings.[74]

Edith Elisabeth Flynn

Special Barriers in Corrections

Women professionals continue to face major barriers in corrections work, including: (1) the veterans' preference system; (2) physical requirements; (3) sexual stereotyping; (4) safety considerations for women in male correctional environments; (5) inmate "rights" to privacy; and (6) the issue of equality of assignment between the sexes. Since the barriers of veterans' preference, physical requirements, and sexual stereotyping are essentially the same in corrections as in law enforcement, they need not be reiterated here. Suffice it to say that their existence significantly impedes equal employment opportunities for women and should be discarded in favor of job-related performance criteria.

Safety of Women in Correctional Institutions. Can women be safe from attack while working in the closed environment of a prison with male felons, some of whom may have been incarcerated for violent sexual offenses? In my experience, this type of concern is usually expressed by corrections traditionalists who believe that women simply have no business in corrections.[75] Their opinion was recently reinforced by *Dothard*, the leading case in this disputed area.

In *Dothard*, the Alabama Department of Corrections claimed that the presence of female guards in an all-male maximum security prison not only exerted a disruptive influence on the institution, but also posed great physical danger to the women. The department suggested to the Supreme Court that sex be a bona fide occupational qualification whenever performance of duties entailed risk to a woman's physical safety. Unfortunately for the women seeking employment as corrections officers in Alabama maximum security facilities, the Supreme Court ruled in favor of the department, thus reinforcing the view that women must be protected from such settings.

> The likelihood that inmates would assault a woman because she was a woman would pose a real threat not only to the victim of the assault but also to the basic control of the penitentiary. . . . The Employee's very womanhood would thus directly undermine her capacity to provide security. . . .[76]

The Court ruled that being male was a bona fide occupational

Women as Criminal Justice Professionals

qualification for "contact" positions under "existing conditions in Alabama maximum security male penitentiaries."[77]

These findings, however, are contradicted by a growing body of expert opinion on prison administration as well as by significant empirical research in law enforcement, corrections, and mental health. For example, a policy statement by the Federal Bureau of Prisons reflects its commitment to integrating both sexes as officers in all of its institutions, including maximum security prisons; such integration would, the bureau argues, promote "the goals of normalization as part of improving the corrections facilities."[78] Similarly, Norval Morris, an eminent legal authority and criminologist, has urged staffing a model prison for repetitively violent male criminals with 40 to 50 percent women.

> That the injection of women into the prison at all levels, including that of the front-of-the-line guard, will tend to reduce violence is offered as a confident proposition. . . . As a matter of observation, men behave better in the presence of women. The social skills of many male offenders in dealing with women are distorted and undeveloped. Frequent and constructive association with women as staff members of the prison will have a positive impact upon the prisoners' later social relationships.[79]

Since these lines were written, the Federal Bureau of Prisons implemented the Morris prison reform model at the new Federal Correctional Institution at Butner, North Carolina. During a visit to that institution in October 1978, I obtained first-hand evidence as to the success of the facility's male and female staffing patterns in improving inmate behavior.

Additional evidence as to the effectiveness of sexually integrated prison staff comes from an early 1970s survey of correctional administrators, who conceded a significantly improved prison environment in such institutions.[80] Still further empirical evidence on the safety issue comes from the previously cited study of women police officers in Washington, DC. This study documents beyond doubt the equal competence of the sexes in dealing with dangerous and angry suspects.[81] Moreover, since sex is evidently not a bona fide occupational qualification for police patrol work, why should it be in corrections?

Morris's thesis on the positive effect of women in the correctional environment is corroborated not only at the new experimen-

Edith Elisabeth Flynn

tal prison at Butner, but also by several other law enforcement studies noting the tension reduction effect of women officers in potentially explosive and dangerous situations.[82] Further evidence comes from research conducted in mental hospitals, where it was found that integrated staffing patterns were most effective, and that female staff members seemed to have a calming effect on highly volatile, angry, and violent patients.[83] Finally, as noted previously, the California corrections system deploys women in contact positions with inmates at all security levels. An evaluation of women officers functioning in these positions found that male "inmates tend to behave better, use less profanity and care more for their personal hygiene when women officers are present."[84] Without doubt, the most persuasive statement on the issue of safety for women comes from a decision by California's highest court:

> *The desire to protect women from the general hazards inherent in many occupations cannot be a valid ground for excluding them from those occupations. . . . Women must be permitted to take their chances along with men when they are otherwise qualified and capable of meeting the requirements of their employment. . . . We can no more justify denial of the means of earning a livelihood on such a basis than we could deny all women drivers' licenses to protect them from risk of injury by drunk drivers. Such tender and chivalrous concern for the well-being of the female half of the adult population cannot be translated into legal restrictions on employment opportunities for women.*[85]

Inmate "Rights" to Privacy. Given the ignominious history of corrections, such concepts as "inmate rights" and "inmate privacy" are true anomalies.[86] Prisons are, almost by definition, places where inmates have lost their rights, their identities, and their privacy. Correctional administrators have long maintained that inmates duly sentenced for crimes to correctional facilities have forfeited most rights they might have under the Constitution. Even though the courts have in recent years remedied this situation by returning certain basic civil rights to inmates, the lack of any right to privacy from supervision necessary to maintain the state's interest in orderly and safe control of an institution has remained untouched.[87] Interestingly, with recent employment gains by women in male correctional institutions, a growing number of references have begun to dot the correctional literature, either asserting inmate "rights" to privacy or exhorting administrators to deploy females only in ways that will not violate inmate privacy.[88] Since corrections administrators have historically been loath to grant inmate rights in such areas as free communication and even access to the courts, it is all the more surprising that so many of them (joined by male correctional officers, who usually oppose them) have so vigorously picked up the theme and formed a veritable chorus line advocating the protection of inmates' privacy from the potential embarrassment of prying female eyes.[89] While this concern for inmate welfare is certainly refreshing, I agree with Chief Justice Marshall's description of this newly discovered protectiveness as "nothing but a feeble excuse for discrimination."[90]

In the absence of a final determination of this issue by the Supreme Court, it is useful to review relevant lower court decisions, current practices, and innovations impinging upon inmate rights to privacy. First, there has been some lower court action granting inmates' rights to privacy in California, Iowa, Pennsylvania, and New York.[91] Second, some jurisdictions have admirably managed to accommodate women's equal employment rights along with inmates' rights to privacy. For example, California does not have women officers perform skin searches of male inmates under ordinary circumstances. During emergencies, however, any officer is expected to perform this function. Women officers routinely pat-search inmates as their post orders dictate. (There is a bit of irony in the fact that such a policy has been in existence in California for many years whenever sexually integrated staff was present at women's institutions.) Of late, California has undertaken minor alterations in prison showers and toilets, installing modesty screening (which allows visibility of only the upper portion of the body) and fogging window areas so that just outlines of figures can be seen.[92] Minnesota has made similar accommodations for its new maximum security penitentiary, thus facilitating the employment of a sexually integrated staff.[93] Finally, under the auspices of LEAA, the National Clearinghouse on Criminal Justice Planning and Architecture developed a wealth of program options and architectural techniques for correctional facilities at state and local levels, to ensure more humane and physically safe environments.[94] These techniques included installation of safe but effective modesty screening in sanitary facilities and maximum security cells. Since most of the

Edith Elisabeth Flynn

recommended modifications could be installed in existing prisons and jails at little cost, the privacy issue is really moot unless its proponents wish to continue using it as a subterfuge for discrimination against the employment of women in maximum security institutions.

A final and related issue involves inmate preference for one sex or the other among staff. A preference for male guards by prisoners is occasionally alleged by administrators. However, reliance on such preference (even if it does exist) has clearly been banned by EEOC guidelines and case law. In *Diaz* v. *Pan American World Airways, Inc.*, the Fifth Circuit Court states:

> *While we recognize that the public's expectation of finding one sex in a particular role may cause some initial difficulty, it would be totally anomalous if we were to allow the preference and prejudices of the customer to determine whether the sex discrimination was valid. Indeed, it was, to a large extent these very prejudices the Act was meant to overcome.*[95]

It also appears that most (but not all) male prisoners either are indifferent to the sex of the correctional officer or welcome the presence of women in institutions.[96]

In summary, the evidence shows that the presence of women in male correctional facilities not only aids in the goal of normalization of prison life, but also seems to have a violence-defusing effect. Given the availability of feasible modifications of the prison environment to protect valid concerns for inmate privacy, and the positive experiences of maximum security prisons using women, the bona fide occupational qualification exception as to sex granted by the Supreme Court in *Dothard* would seem to have lost its validity.

Equality of Assignment. The final barrier to women's employment in corrections concerns the question of equality of assignment, an issue related to reverse discrimination. If implementation of the principle of equal employment opportunity leads to the assignment of women (or other minorities) to positions on the basis of physical characteristics (such as strength) or on the basis of other concerns (such as women's safety or inmate privacy) and thereby results in the preferential treatment of these persons, such actions would be vulnerable to charges of reverse discrimination. In California, for example, employee unions once charged that women officers, prohibited by policy from skin-searching male inmates, were not carrying work loads equal to those of male officers.[97] Similarly, Morton reports on an Iowa Department of Social Services case in which a state court found that a woman officer could not be promoted because her sex prevented her from being able to perform all of the functions of the higher position. The court found that such promotion would invade inmates' rights to privacy, subject the woman to the possibility of sexual assault, and be contrary to male inmates' "fixed ideas" about female roles—and would therefore lead to their resentment of women officers.[98] In response to such findings, however, it can be argued that men have been correctional officers, supervisors, and wardens in women's institutions throughout the history of modern corrections. How did they manage?

In conclusion, the record of the actual performance of women provides the best possible evidence that they can perform as well as men, if only given the opportunity to do so. Previously discussed evaluations of their performance in positions at every level in corrections and law enforcement corroborate this statement admirably. Therefore, achievement of equality of assignment is not impossible, unless a corrections system deliberately circumvents such assignments through prejudice or misguided notions of protectionism. Not only should qualified women be given the opportunity to work in any potentially dangerous situation if they want to, but their work assignments should not differ, to any degree, from the assignments of their male counterparts. Anything short of equality of assignment does constitute reverse discrimination.

CONFRONTING DISCRIMINATORY TRADITIONS

To deny equal opportunity, both law enforcement and corrections agencies have, then, traditionally tried to turn woman's comparative lack of physical strength into a bona fide occupational qualification issue. In recent times, corrections agencies have created out of the newly discovered issue of inmate privacy yet another barrier to the employment of women. Even so, experts in both fields have long insisted that brains are by far more important than brawn. Their opinion is confirmed by a major research effort designed to develop new methods for evaluating individuals for

positions in police work—an effort that resulted in an evaluation instrument known as the Police Career Index.[99] After analyzing the
performance of thousands of patrol officers and detectives, the study
concluded that it is not physical strength or athletic prowess that is
important to effective job performance, but rather the officer's ability to keep cool under pressure, maintain composure, and use tact
and skill in mediating disputes and settling conflicts.[100] Similarly,
in corrections superior physical strength on the part of an individual
officer has little meaning during actual confrontations. What does
count in such settings are tact, diplomacy, and plain competence, as
well as fairness and stability.[101]

It is not my intent here to deny the importance of either basic
physical conditioning or reasonable minimum physical standards
for law enforcement or corrections jobs. I only note that according
to the literature, such other criteria as psychological maturity and
responsibility take precedence. As long as physical requirements remain reasonable—as is the case in many progressive departments
today—they can be met by most job applicants, regardless of sex or
race. In addition, there is nothing to prevent departments particularly concerned with the physical prowess and self-defense
capabilities of their officers from developing training programs in
the martial arts (including jujitsu, judo, and karate). Just as the gun
is already the great equalizer between individuals of differing
strengths, the martial arts provide self-defense techniques in which
an opponent's strength and weight are effectively used *against* him.

Given the many options of low-cost and safe environmental
designs (or modifications) that exist today, the issue of inmate
privacy should be seen for what it really is, a proverbial red herring.
Practitioners and correctional officers who oppose extending job opportunities to women in their field simply use this issue to hide
their real motivations.

SUMMARY AND CONCLUSIONS

The introduction to this chapter briefly sketched the status of the
working woman in general, noting that she does not hold a place
equal to men in the American economy. Women have yet to escape
the stereotype of ''women's work,'' as can be seen from the fact that
the vast majority of all working women continue to be employed in
clerical, sales, service, and light industrial jobs. Moreover, wage dif-

ferentials persist. The earnings of the average woman worker in the twentieth century are still seemingly guided by the Old Testament rule that stated: "A male between twenty and sixty years old shall be valued at 50 silver shekels. . . . If it is a female, she shall be valued at 30 shekels."[102] Occupational segregation is the basic reason for the wage differentials: women tend to be relegated to lower paying jobs. Very few women have made it to the top as managers, professionals, or executives.

Given the experiences of working women in society as a whole, it is not surprising that the employment progress of women workers and professionals in the criminal justice system has been painfully slow and fraught with difficulties. Occupations within criminal justice have historically been off limits to women workers. While recent developments clearly indicate that the field has gradually become more sympathetic to the ambitions of women, it is evident that recent employment gains by women both in the lower echelon positions and as professionals have come largely as a result of persistent government prodding. In essence, criminal justice agencies have responded to government requirements banning sex and race discrimination rather than pursuing any "proactive" role in extending equal opportunity to women. The identification, therefore, of the critical role government has played as key change agent in the employment of women—in the general work force as a whole and in criminal justice in particular—is a major finding of this analysis. The review of heretofore unpublished research in corrections proves the point; over 90 percent of corrections agencies did not take the initiative to employ women as correctional officers in male institutions until Title VII of the Civil Rights Act of 1964 was expanded to cover state and local units of government.[103]

Sociological analysis of purposive social action has long noted manifest as well as latent functions of such actions.[104] *Manifest* functions include those objective consequences that are intended and recognized. While the manifest consequences of Title VII can be seen in the real (albeit slow) increase of women's employment in the justice system, we have just begun to identify some of the *latent* and unintended consequences of that legislation. In law enforcement, a latent consequence of the employment of women as police officers has been the introduction (or revision) by many departments of physical agility tests to insure that women will fail. The previous discussion has shown that physical characteristics have

Edith Elisabeth Flynn

yet to be positively correlated with more effective police performance. As a result, the latent consequences of more stringent physical requirements may well prove highly dysfunctional for police operations because more suitable (and potentially more effective) police candidates, including females, will be prevented from joining the profession.

In corrections, a significant latent consequence of the addition of women to the officer work force has been the recent "discovery" of the inmates' rights to privacy. While this development is certainly functional for the recent and growing movement to improve prisoners' rights, it is dysfunctional for women seeking equal employment in corrections. At least one author perceives this turn of events as a classic case of the collision of two constitutionally protected rights.[105] I disagree. The improvement of prisoners' rights, including the right to privacy, is a welcome development in an otherwise dismal field. But it has been shown here that none of these newly gained rights or concerns needs to be sacrificed at the altar of equal employment opportunity, as long as corrections systems respond with facility design modifications; some changes in scheduling or assignment; and related, acceptable variations that would enable prisons to function with male and female officers alike. Accordingly, this particular latent consequence can be seen as pragmatically unimportant to the corrections system; it need not be dysfunctional for either the inmates or the women in the system.

The road toward equality is fraught with problems and beset by continued stereotyping and often outright discrimination. The latter phenomenon is particularly acute when women occupy traditionally blue-collar occupations in law enforcement and corrections. However, despite these considerations and the additional fact that prediction of social change is notoriously difficult, I conclude with a note of cautious optimism by stating that progress will continue. This assessment is warranted for a number of important reasons. First, legislation, supported by moderate gains in case law, has laid the foundation for progress. Social change, as noted earlier, is by its very nature painfully slow. But it is almost impossible to turn back the clock. Second, women have successfully breached occupations that were heretofore culturally and traditionally reserved for men alone. The importance of this achievement should not be underestimated. To use an analogy, it takes only small amounts of snow to precipitate an avalanche. Third, as women move into top-echelon jobs, they open the way for others to follow. Stereotyping

Women as Criminal Justice Professionals

and prejudice are difficult to maintain in the face of effective performance. Thus, while legislative or judicial decree cannot change minds and hearts, performance and efficiency can become powerful persuaders and will gradually produce bona fide social change. Fourth, the increase in the number of women legislators and judges is bound to decrease current legislative and judicial attachment to sex stereotypes regarding women. And fifth, the combined progress of women working within criminal justice at all levels will generate the momentum needed to accelerate current trends. While full equality will probably not be realized in this generation, I do expect it to be achieved in the next.

NOTES

1. I. V. Sawhill, "Perspectives on Women and Work in America," in *Work and the Quality of Life*, ed. J. O'Toole (Cambridge, MA: Massachusetts Institute of Technology Press, 1974), p. 43; M. S. Cohen, "Sex Differences in Compensation," *Journal of Human Resources* (Fall 1971):19; V. Fuchs, "Differences in Hourly Earnings Between Men and Women," *Monthly Labor Review* (May 1971):23–24; H. Sanborn, "Pay Differences between Men and Women," *Industrial and Labor Relations Review* (July 1964):38.

2. V. K. Oppenheimer, *The Female Labor Force in the United States* (Berkeley, CA: University of California, Institute of International Studies, Population Monograph 5, 1970), p. 307; A. Seidman, ed., *Working Women: A Study of Women in Paid Jobs* (Boulder, CO: Westview Press, 1978), p. 24.

3. E. Ruina, *Women in Science and Technology* (Cambridge, MA: Massachusetts Institute of Technology Press, 1973).

4. D. L. Blazicek, "Women and the Administration of Justice," in *Fundamentals of Criminal Justice*, ed. D. H. Chang (Geneva, IL: Paladin House, 1977), p. 127; C. Feinman, *Women in the Criminal Justice System* (New York: Praeger, Holt, Rinehart and Winston, 1980); U.S. Department of Justice, Law Enforcement Assistance Administration, *Report of the Law Enforcement Assistance Administration Task Force on Women* (Washington, DC: Law Enforcement Assistance Administration, 1975).

5. J. S. Auerbach, *Unequal Justice* (London: Oxford University Press, 1976).

6. National Institute of Law Enforcement and Criminal Justice, *Affirmative Action in the Criminal Justice System* (Washington, DC: U.S. Government Printing Office, 1979).

7. Title VII, Civil Rights Act of 1964, amended in 1972, sect. 702 (e).

8. H. R. Rep. No. 92-238, 92 Cong., 1st sess. 5, 5 (1972).

9. 30 Fed. Reg. 14927 (2 December 1965).

10. A. Cooksey, 7 B. C. Ind. and Comm. Law Review 417, 429 (1965).

11. *Weeks* v. *Southern Bell Telephone Company*, 408 F.2d 228 (5th Cir. 1969).

12. *Dothard* v. *Rawlinson*, 97 U.S. Supreme Court 2720 (1977):2727.

13. *Reed* v. *Reed* 925 U.S. Supreme Court 251 (1971). In this decision, Chief

Justice Burger, speaking for a unanimous Court, stated that an Idaho statute giving men preference over women in administering estates denied would-be administrator Sally Reed equal protection of the law. At issue was a peculiar nineteenth-century directive that specified that between persons "equally entitled" to administer a decedent's estate, "males must be preferred to females."

14. R. B. Ginsburg, "Women, Men, and the Constitution: Key Supreme Court Rulings," in *Women in the Courts*, ed. W. L. Hepperly and L. Crites (Williamsburg, VA: National Center for State Courts, 1978), p. 36.

15. Feinman, *Women in the Criminal Justice System*; National Information and Research Center on Women in Policing, *General Information Packet* (Washington, DC: Police Foundation, 1980); B. B. Cook, "Women Judges: The End of Tokenism," in *Women in the Courts*, p. 88; J. B. Morton, "A Study of Employment of Women as Correctional Officers in State Level Adult Male Correctional Institutions" (Ph.D. diss., University of Georgia, 1980).

16. L. Acerra, "From Matron to Commanding Officer—Women's Changing Role in Law Enforcement," in *Law Enforcement Bible*, ed. R. A. Scanlon (Hackensack, NJ: Stoeger, 1978).

17. A. E. Simpson, "Changing the Role of Women in Policing," in *Readings in Criminal Justice*, ed. D. E. J. MacNamara (Guilford, CT: Dushkin, 1978).

18. C. G. Stuart, "Changing Status of Women in Police Professions," *Police Chief* 42, 4 (April 1975):61–62.

19. C. M. Breece, "Women in Policing—Changing Perspectives on the Role," in *Criminal Justice Planning*, ed.J. E. Scott and S. Dinitz (New York: Praeger, 1977).

20. Federal Bureau of Investigation, *Uniform Crime Reports for the United States—1978* (Washington, DC: U.S. Government Printing Office, 1979).

21. P. Murphy, *National Information and Research Center on Women in Policing* (Washington, DC: Police Foundation, 1980).

22. National Advisory Commission on Criminal Justice Standards and Goals, *Police* (Washington, DC: U.S. Government Printing Office, 1973), p. 101; P. Horne, *Women in Law Enforcement* (Springfield, IL: Charles C. Thomas, 1980), p. 48.

23. "Discrimination," *Crime and Delinquency* (April 1975):185.

24. U.S. Department of Justice and U.S. Bureau of Census, *Trends in Expenditure and Employment Data for the Criminal Justice System 1971–1977* (Washington, DC: U.S. Government Printing Office, 1978).

25. *New York Times* (10 June 1979), p. 20E.

26. B. Cohen and J. M. Chaiken, *Police Background Characteristics and Performance* (New York: The New York City Rand Institute, 1972), p. 1081.

27. E. Flynn, "The Police Role and Measures of Performance" (Special Report to the Equal Employment Opportunity Commission, Northeastern University, 1980). Copies available from the EEOC.

28. Horne, *Women in Law Enforcement*, p. 141.

29. Flynn, "The Police Role and Measures of Performance."

30. President's Commission on Law Enforcement and Administration of Justice, *The Challenge of Crime in a Free Society* (Washington, DC: U.S. Government Printing Office, 1967), p. 130.

31. Most law enforcement agencies select their recruits by administering written, general aptitude, and intelligence examinations that have no proven relationship to police work. It is interesting to note that many police departments require higher educational levels for women than for men! T. Eisenberg, D. Kent, and C. Wall,

Women as Criminal Justice Professionals

Police Personnel Practices in State and Local Governments (Washington, DC: Police Foundation, 1973), pp. 18–19.

32. B. E. Washington, *Deployment of Female Police Officers in the United States* (Gaithersburg, MD: International Association of Chiefs of Police, 1974), p. 45.

33. When LEAA revised its guidelines in 1977, it rejected the suggestion that the tests of "business necessity" should be retained and stated instead that height and weight minimum requirements would be a violation, unless they had been validated in accordance with the Justice Guidelines on Employee Selection Procedures. U.S. Department of Justice, Law Enforcement Assistance Administration, "Non-discrimination in Federally Assisted Crime Control and Juvenile Delinquency Programs," *Federal Register* 42, 32 (February 1977):9493.

34. *Dothard*, p. 2727.

35. *Bradwell* v. *Illinois*, 83 U.S. (16 Wall.) 130 (1872).

36. C. Dreifus, "People Are Always Asking Me What I'm Trying to Prove," *Police Magazine* 3, 2 (March 1980):18–25; P. Bloch and D. Anderson, *Policewomen on Patrol* (Washington, DC: Police Foundation, 1973).

37. B. Price, "Century of Women in Policing," in *Modern Police Administration*, ed. D. C. Schultz (Houston, TX: Gulf, 1979); C. A. Martin, "Women Police—A Survey of Education, Attitudes, Problems," *Journal of Studies in Technical Careers* 1, 3 (Spring 1979):220–227.

38. S. M. Miller and F. Riessman, "The Working Class Subculture, A New View," *Social Problems* 9 (Summer 1961):86–97; A. Cohen and H. Hodges, Jr., "Characteristics of the Lower-Blue-Collar Class," *Social Problems* 10 (Spring 1963):303–334; S. Lipset, "Democracy and Working-Class Authoritarianism," *American Sociological Review* 24 (August 1959):482–501; T. Adorno et al., *The Authoritarian Personality* (New York: Harper and Row, 1950).

39. Bloch and Anderson, *Policewomen on Patrol*.

40. K. E. Messik, "Policewomen in the United States Air Force Law Enforcement—An Opinion Survey," unpublished report (Wright-Patterson Air Force Base, OH: U.S. Department of the Air Force Institute of Technology, 1974). Copies available from the National Criminal Justice Reference Service, Box 6000, Rockville, MD 20850.

41. G. B. Aucoin and G. Baretine, *Evaluation of Physical Standards for Police Officers* (Columbus, OH: Columbus Police Department, 1973).

42. C. M. Rutland, *Comparative Analysis of the Relationship of Male and Female Security Specialists* (Springfield, VA: National Technical Information Service, 1978); Bloch and Anderson, *Policewomen on Patrol*; Horne, *Women in Law Enforcement*.

43. C. M. Breece, "Emerging Role of Women in Law Enforcement," in *Professionalization in America*, ed. J. Kinton (Aurora, IL: Social Science and Sociological Resources, 1975); L. J. Sherman, "Psychological View of Women in Policing," *Journal of Police Science and Administration* 1, 4 (December 1973):383–394.

44. Bloch and Anderson, *Policewomen on Patrol*; P. Bloch and D. Anderson, *Policewomen on Patrol: Final Report* (Washington, DC: Police Foundation, 1974); D. J. Anderson, *Evaluation of the Methodological and Policy Implications of the District of Columbia Policewomen on Patrol Study* (Ann Arbor: University Microfilms, 1976).

45. A. V. Bouza, "Women in Policing," *FBI Law Enforcement Bulletin* 44, 9 (September 1975):2–7.

46. L. J. Sherman, "Psychological View of Women in Policing," *Journal of Police Science and Administration* 1, 4 (December 1973):434–438; H. W. Bartlett, *Policewoman Effectiveness* (Denver: Denver Civil Service Commission, 1977); B. L. Garmire, "Female Officers in the Department," in *Police-Community Relations*, 2nd ed., ed. P. F. Cromwall, Jr., and G. Keeder (St. Paul: West, 1978).

47. S. Tolchin, "Exclusion of Women from the Judicial Process," *Signs* 2, 4 (Summer 1977):877–887.

48. *U.S. News and World Report* (20 October 1980):50.

49. Cook, "Women Judges: The End of Tokenism," pp. 87–88.

50. Ibid., p. 84.

51. M. Grossblat and B. Sikes, eds., *Women Lawyers: Supplementary Data to the Lawyer Statistical Report* 49 (1973); A. Parrish, "Women in Professional Training," *Monthly Review* 4 (1974):41–43.

52. Cook, "Women Judges: The End of Tokenism," p. 101.

53. Ibid., p. 90.

54. M. Oliver, "The Female in Trial Court," in *Women in the Courts*, pp. 1–20.

55. Hepperly and Crites, *Women in the Courts*, p. xiii.

56. *U.S. News and World Report* (20 October 1981):50.

57. Oliver, "The Female in Trial Court," p. 2.

58. Ibid., p. 4.

59. Ibid., p. 5.

60. F. L. Bremson and J. Mayson, "Equal Employment Opportunity in the Courts," *State Court Journal* 3, 3 (Summer 1979):11–18.

61. Joint Commission on Correctional Manpower and Training, *A Time to Act* (Washington, DC: Joint Commission on Correctional Manpower and Training, 1969), p. 14.

62. G. W. Paul, "Impact of Female Employees in Adult All-Male Correctional Institutions" (Master's thesis, University of Houston, 1972) (Ann Arbor: University Microfilms, 1972); A. Hill, *Corrections Compendium* (Lincoln, NB: CONtact, 1977), p. 27.

63. E. E. Flynn, "Standards and Goals: Implications for Facilities Planning," in *Correctional Facilities Planning*, ed. M. R. Montilla and N. Harlow (Lexington, MA: D. C. Heath, 1979), pp. 67–81; A. M. Becker, "Women in Corrections: A Process of Change," *Resolutions* 1 (Summer 1975):19–21.

64. Becker, "Women in Corrections," p. 20.

65. National Advisory Commission on Criminal Justice Standards and Goals, *Corrections* (Washington, DC: U.S. Government Printing Office, 1973), p. 466.

66. Ibid., p. 476. As a member of the Task Force on Corrections of the National Advisory Commission on Criminal Justice Standards and Goals, I had the opportunity to write the chapter "National Priorities and Implementation," which, reflecting the consensus of the Task Force, urges stringent pursuit of women and minorities for employment in corrections.

67. American Correctional Association, *Policy Statements Resolutions* (College Park, MD: American Correctional Association, 1979), p. 2.

68. Morton, "A Study of Employment."

69. Joint Commission on Correctional Manpower and Training, p. 4.

70. Morton, "A Study of Employment," p. 62.

71. Ibid., p. 66.

72. While forty-five state systems (of forty-nine agencies surveyed) responded in general, only forty-three systems chose to respond to this question.

73. Morton, "A Study of Employment," p. 69.

74. A. M. Becker, "California Department of Corrections—Utilization of Women Correctional Officers," unpublished report (Sacramento, CA: Department of Corrections, 1974).

75. As Associate Director of the National Clearinghouse for Criminal Justice Planning, I participated in the development of federal guidelines for the improvement of the nation's prisons and jails. In the process of rendering technical assistance to hundreds of institutions, my colleagues and I found that the issue of safety of women in correctional institutions emerged as a significant deterrent to women's employment in those facilities.

76. *Dothard*, p. 2730.

77. Ibid., pp. 2730–2731.

78. Federal Bureau of Prisons, Policy Statement No. 3713 (7 January 1976), p. 3713.

79. N. Morris, *The Future of Imprisonment* (Chicago: University of Chicago Press, 1974), pp. 108–109.

80. "The Sexual Segregation of American Prisons," *Yale Law Journal* 82 (1973):1229–1241.

81. Bloch and Anderson, *Policewomen on Patrol: Final Report*, pp. 2–3.

82. C. Milton, *Women in Policing* (Washington, DC: Police Foundation, 1972), p. 30; Breece, "Emerging Role of Women in Law Enforcement."

83. Milton, *Women in Policing*, p. 30.

84. Becker, "Women in Corrections," p. 21.

85. *Sail'er Inn, Inc.* v. *Kirby*, 5 Cal. 3d 1, 9–10, 485 P.2d 529, 534 (1971).

86. This observation does not apply, of course, to the prison's very beginnings. Under the famous Pennsylvania system of about 200 years ago, inmates went mad during their prolonged sequestration in single cells with nothing to do other than contemplate the Bible and labor at their workbenches.

87. I. P. Robbins, ed., *Prisoners' Rights Sourcebook* (New York: Clark Boardman, 1980); A. J. Bronstein, "Reform without Change: The Future of Prisoners' Rights," *The Civil Liberties Review* (September/October 1977):27–45.

88. Hill, *Corrections Compendium*.

89. Bronstein, "Reform without Change," pp. 27–45.

90. *Dothard*, p. 2735.

91. Morton, "A Study of Employment," p. 31; D. C. Tharnish, "Sex Discrimination in Prison Employment—The Bona Fide Occupational Qualification and Prisoners' Privacy Rights," *Iowa Law Review* 65, 2 (January 1980):418–445.

92. Becker, "California Department of Corrections," p. 21.

93. I served on an advisory committee to the Commissioner of Corrections in Minnesota in 1976. The purpose of the committee was to help design a high security facility at Stillwater that would incorporate the latest advanced practices, so that not only would inmates' rights be fully protected, but also that men and women on the staff would be able to serve under equal working conditions.

94. F. Moyer, E. E. Flynn, F. Powers, M. Plautz, *Guidelines for the Planning and Design of Regional and Community Correctional Centers for Adults*

Edith Elisabeth Flynn

(Washington, DC: U.S. Government Printing Office, 1970).

95. *Diaz* v. *Pan American World Airways, Inc.*, 404 U.S. 950 (1971) 442 F.2d 385–389.

96. M. Levi and N. Holt, "Attitudes of Male Inmates toward Female Correctional Staff," *California Department of Corrections Annual Research Review* (Sacramento: Department of Corrections, July 1976).

97. Becker, "California Department of Corrections," p. 21.

98. Morton, "A Study of Employment," p. 30.

99. M. D. Dunnette and S. J. Motowidlo, *Police Selection and Career Assessment* (Washington, DC: U.S. Government Printing Office, 1976).

100. Flynn, "The Police Role and Measures of Performance," p. 58.

101. E. E. Flynn, "From Conflict Theory to Conflict Resolution," *American Behavioral Scientist* 23, 5 (May/June 1980):745–773.

102. Leviticus 27:3–4.

103. Morton, "A Study of Employment," p. 74.

104. R. K. Merton, *Social Theory and Social Structure* (New York: The Free Press, 1957), p. 51.

105. Feinman, *Women in the Criminal Justice System*, p. 57.

15

Sex-Role Operations

Strategies for Women Working in the Criminal Justice System

PHYLLIS JO BAUNACH
NICOLE HAHN RAFTER

"WARDEN—and MOTHER OF 2," ran the headline in the *Phoenix Gazette* announcing the appointment, in October 1978, of Camille Graham as Deputy Director for adult institutions of the Arizona Department of Corrections. "New Corrections Official Diminutive in Size Only," the headline continued. Similarly, Boston's *Herald American*, in the spring of 1979, announced formation of " 'THE BROAD SQUAD'—Female Cop Team Uses Brains, not Bravado." Are Camille Graham and the two Boston policewomen part of a "rise of the new female professional" in criminal justice, counterpart to a "rise of the new female criminal" that is said to be carrying women into previously male-dominated territory? Or are Graham and the policewomen atypical and "the new female professional" in criminal justice a myth, just as the "new female criminal" is said to be more fantasy than reality?[1]

This chapter focuses on the employment of women in the criminal justice system. In particular, it seeks to identify: (1) problems common to women working in various parts of the system; and (2) strategies they have developed to cope with the difficulties of moving into predominantly male professions. The chapter is based on a symposium held in Boston in 1979, which brought together five women working in various criminal justice specialties to discuss sex-specific problems they encountered on the job and means they had devised to deal with them. To our knowledge, this was the first time women from disparate areas of the system were brought together to identify common job-related problems and cross-system coping strategies.

Before turning to the data of the symposium, we attempt to set the dilemmas of female criminal justice workers in historical and contemporary context. This preliminary discussion points to three conclusions. First, Camille Graham and Boston's "broad squad" are atypical indeed as criminal justice employees; far from representing a influx of women into criminal justice specialties, they and their female colleagues remain a small minority of workers in these fields. Second, their minority status is typical from an historical point of view, for criminal justice has a long tradition of denying entry to female would-be professionals and practitioners. Third, Graham and the Boston policewomen are typical in having to pay, for their professional gains, the price of attention to their physical or sexual (be it actual or imputed) status—through the "diminutive" and "mother" labels in the former case, that of "broads" in the latter. In contrast to men, whose entry into criminal justice is rarely accompanied by public attention to their physical characteristics or sexual status, women frequently experience sex-stereotyping when they move into such occupations.

WOMEN WORKING IN CRIMINAL JUSTICE: THE CONTEXT OF THE PROBLEM

For the purpose of our analysis, it is useful to divide criminal justice work into four areas: the three familiar subdivisions of police, courts, and corrections, plus the fourth of office support staff. Of the three traditional subdivisions, the courts have historically been most resistant to admitting women and corrections least resistant, with policing falling between the other two. In the fourth area of office support staff, women have been welcomed. These historical patterns continue to appear today.

Sex-Role Operations

That women have been most adamantly excluded from higher echelon court work is readily explained by the fact that the passport to such work is a law degree. Until recently, law schools rarely admitted women. The somewhat lesser degree of resistance to women in policing appears to be the result of two factors: the lower status of police work and the late nineteenth-century police matron movement. Scandals stemming from the handling of female arrestees (especially prostitutes) by male officers, in combination with late-nineteenth-century protective attitudes toward women and children, led to the hiring of police matrons. It is important to note, however, that sex-role stereotypes provided the rationale for allowing women to enter policing: matrons were added to staffs in big cities not because it was thought that they could handle work comparable to that of male officers, but because they could best protect arrested women and children from the indecencies and brutalities of men.[2]

Reinforcement of sex-role stereotypes was, similarly, the price paid for entrance of women into corrections. That women have been historically more successful here than in the other two traditional criminal justice areas was due to the nineteenth-century women's reformatory movement; adherents of this movement argued that the reformation of female prisoners was possible only if they were isolated from men, treated in sex-specific ways, and supervised by other women.[3] Finally, the relatively low resistance to women as clerical workers in criminal justice bureaucracies can also be explained by sex-role stereotyping. As male white-collar workers deserted secretarial jobs for better paid positions, the former were opened to women, who were considered temperamentally fitted for passive, low-status, service work in the office.

The historical lesson—that it is sex roles that have created the barriers to employment of women in criminal justice—continues to apply today. Because data on women's employment are thoroughly surveyed in Chapter 14, we shall summarize them only briefly here. Despite a few well-publicized exceptions, women continue to be excluded from high-level court positions.[4] Nationally, only 3 percent of sworn police officers are women.[5] As in earlier times, women fare better in corrections, where they constitute more than 25 percent of the professional work force.[6] However, few of the correctional jobs held by women are administrative, and it is difficult for women to find nonclerical positions in male penal institutions. As in the later nineteenth century, women who enter corrections tend to be isolated in institutions that hold juveniles or other women, or they are employed as clerical workers.[7] Indeed, it is still as office support staff that women receive their greatest contact with criminal justice agencies in general.[8] As in the past, they are relegated to positions based on sex roles.

THE CENTRAL ISSUE, of course, is how to increase the participation of female workers in nonclerical areas of criminal justice. But from the previous discussion, a second key issue also emerges: how can women who do gain entry to criminal justice positions cope with the difficulties presented by their minority status and by sex-role stereotyping? In an effort to address this second issue, women working in diverse criminal justice areas were brought together in a symposium held at Northeastern University in 1979. They were asked to identify common problems and the means they had developed to cope with these problems. The five participants included representatives from a local police department, the U.S. Marshal's office, court services, probation, and corrections. The remainder of this chapter summarizes the results of the symposium, discusses these results in relation to some of the literature on women as criminal justice professionals, and suggests directions for future research and policy development.

Four major problem areas common to women employed by criminal justice agencies were identified at the symposium: (1) "preferential" treatment; (2) higher expectations for women than men; (3) lack of access to the "old boys" network; and (4) sex stereotyping in job assignments. Although these problems are not peculiar to criminal justice, they are keenly felt among women in ·this area, perhaps because crime and crime control are so closely associated with traditionally "masculine" values.[9]

One of the Girls or One of the Boys?
The Issues of "Preferential" Treatment

Differential hiring practices, which route women into jobs associated with homemaking and record keeping and men into positions associated with power and strength, have long been defended on the basis of innate or learned differences between the sexes: women have special abilities for some kinds of work, it is argued, and men for others. Moreover, it is sometimes claimed that differential hiring of women actually means *preferential* hiring: women should be pleased to have reserved for them jobs that keep them out of the crossfire and off cellblock tiers. The problem is that some women aspire to rise above protectionism. Some perceive themselves—and actually are—as capable as men at catching criminals and controlling prisoners. Others, however, appreciate protective attitudes. Preferential treatment, then, raises a number of issues: To what extent, if any, is it necessary, is it useful to women, and is it acceptable? At what point does it become dysfunctional? As yet, there is no consensus on the answers to these questions.

Preferential treatment was identified as an area of particular concern by two symposium participants, one a detective working (by choice) in a juvenile unit, the other a prison worker (formerly a guard). Both had received preferential treatment from male colleagues, but their interpretations of this treatment differed sharply. The detective was pleased by preferential treatment, perhaps because she tended to see it as grounded in friendship rather than in sex roles:

> *The men in my department are very protective of me. . . . If I walk out of the office, they might say, "Make sure you have your radio" or "Are your batteries O.K.?" I appreciate that because it comes from us knowing each other. Some other women in the department don't get shown that kind of concern. I appreciate it [and] see it as a personal thing which happens because we get along.*

This participant interpreted assistance from male colleagues as peer concern for her welfare, rather than overprotectiveness. She was, however, wryly humorous about her willingness to use preferential treatment to her advantage in a professional capacity:

> *It's a funny thing, but if I go to Superior Court, I always wear a dress, probably something light blue, and the judges go crazy. Or, for example, when I worked in narcotics, and we would come up with peanuts, maybe an ounce of grass, I'd put it in a big cardboard box, so then it would look like something big, and the judge would say,*

"That's O.K., you just tell me whatever is in there, I'll take your word for it." The men have their tactics and we have our tactics too, I guess.

Previously, this participant had summarized her attitudes toward sex-role differences:

A man has certain qualities that he brings to police work by virtue of being a man that a woman doesn't have, and vice versa. Neither one is going to have those opposite qualities, but in a combination the different qualities can make an excellent police team.

This participant, then, felt it was natural that she be treated differently on the basis of sex.

The opposite was true of the prison worker, who expressed strong resentment at the protection forced on her by male peers:

I was the first woman who had ever worked on the tiers in my institution, which is a prison for men. But my presence proved to be more of a problem with the other officers than with the inmates. After two or three days on the tier, I was regarded by the inmates as a screw [guard] like any other screw, to be avoided and mistrusted. But my fellow officers wouldn't stop treating me like something special. They would team up when I went out on the tiers, one walking on either side of me, "for my own protection." I had to swallow my pride a lot.

Later the same prison worker remarked, "Even after three years at the prison, I still have to deal daily with [male] officers who don't want me out on the tiers." Through such comments, this participant registered her bitterness about preferential treatment, which constantly prevented her from performing her job adequately.

Recent studies of interactions between women and men in court situations suggest that preferential treatment continues to be the rule there. A Rhode Island study, for example, concluded that judges defer more to women than men in the courtroom. A study of women in trial courts found that judges act more politely to female lawyers and are reluctant to correct them if they make mistakes. These results indicate the simultaneous usefulness and dysfunctionality of preferential treatment. A recent observational study of interactions between female attorneys and judges in the course of trials found that judges chastise male and female attorneys differently: when singled out for errors in the courtroom, male attorneys receive "the full brunt of judicial wrath," while female attorneys are treated in a more "gentlemanly [*sic*] manner."[10] When asked how they reacted to this apparent paternalism, six of the ten female attorneys interviewed regarded it positively, given the courtroom setting. One interviewee noted:

> *The judge feels, and even I feel, that if they're [going to] scream at me, they should do it in a different way than they do it with a male lawyer. In other words, if they find something that I have done objectionable, they tend to handle it more softly, somewhat more tactfully than they do with a male lawyer . . . they want to seem like gentlemen in front of the jury. . . . It is different but I don't find it offensive.*[11]

The authors concluded that judges correct erring female attorneys differently from male counterparts in order to avoid endangering the appearance of impartiality!

These reports indicate considerable cultural disagreement as to whether women should be treated deferentially and, if so, in what circumstances and to what extent. Clearly, the issue is currently being confronted by women employed in criminal justice. These women should not be blocked by dogmatic opinions as they attempt to bring traditional role definitions into harmony with new employment realities. It is necessary, however, to observe that in a professional context, acceptance of preferential treatment may engender serious consequences for women in at least two respects. First, in some occupations preferential treatment may be dangerous. Consider, for example, the prison guard who, like one symposium participant, spends her first several months on the tier flanked by well-intentioned, protective male colleagues; if she does not develop her own sense of expertise, she will not know how to handle confidently an incident that may erupt when she is alone on the tiers. Second, seeking or accepting special treatment may, in the long run, foster an already flourishing double standard and merely augment the stereotype of women as incapable of making decisions in situations of power.

Phyllis Jo Baunach & Nicole Hahn Rafter

"Luckily, This Is Not Difficult"—The Importance of Superior Performance

One symposium participant described a poster she had seen recently, which read:

> **Whatever Women Do, They Must Do It Twice as Well as Men in Order to Be Thought Half as Good —Luckily, This Is Not Difficult**

The poster makes a point articulated by all participants: women must excel in order to gain acceptance from male colleagues. One member of the symposium advised:

> *When you are given something to do, you had better make sure you do it better than anyone else has ever done it before because they are going to look hard at everything you do and find a flaw in it. Even if you did it as well as anyone else, that's definitely not good enough if you are one of the first few women in the system.*

Other women in criminal justice professions have expressed similar views. For example, a policewoman in one study observed, "When you are first at anything you have to do it better, and I am afraid if one of the women is just average, it will reflect on all the rest of the women officers."[12] In response to questions about the advantages and disadvantages of being a female lawyer, a woman interviewed in another study indicated:

> *[B]y and large female attorneys are better prepared than their male counterparts and will spend more time preparing for the trial of a case because of their desire to do an effective job. If she does her job well, there will be very little discrimination because she is a female.*[13]

Superior performance is demanded not only of female line-level workers, but also of women in administrative positions. One symposium participant involved in directing research described how she was initially tested by her staff until they recognized her ability to handle the job:

> *I . . . had a couple of managerial crises almost immediately. I was being tested by my staff and colleagues: How*

much can she take? How is she going to handle this? They kept feeding me bizarre situations.

However, this same participant also reported that after about one year, she finally felt accepted as a competent professional:

> *They began to respect my work—that too reduced the initial pressure. Now that I've been in my position for nearly a year, I've built up a good record in terms of making research effective. For example, a study . . . I recently completed was written up in last Sunday's paper, and it has gotten a tremendous amount of publicity for my office. I've got an intimidation factor working for me. I'm no longer just a token woman but someone who is putting the department in the limelight.*

In *Women in Law Enforcement*, Peter Horne similarly points out that "women supervisors have had to work harder than male supervisors in order to prove themselves, but once they have shown that they know their jobs, the . . . subordinates usually accept their authority and position."[14]

These comments indicate that for female criminal justice professionals, competence establishes acceptance. They suggest that once a woman establishes her ability through superior performance, the testing and hostility will diminish. This view, if accurate, implies that acceptance of the first few women working in a new area will encourage the hiring of more women in that area in the future. One symposium participant made these assumptions explicit:

> *Be super—and then maybe in ten years . . . you will have changed attitudes. It may be easier for women then who are trying to get jobs because men who have worked with you will say to themselves, "I've worked with women and I know that they are just as capable."*

Discussing the importance of efficiency among female police officers, Horne similarly remarks, "Today's policewomen should perform their jobs with utmost efficiency so that they can pave the way for even more women to enter the policing profession in the future."[15]

Phyllis Jo Baunach & Nicole Hahn Rafter

This viewpoint, however, may be naive. The extent to which competent performance may reverse negative attitudes toward female professionals remains an empirical question. The symposium participants, the poster, and Horne's study of women in policing may all be overlooking complicating factors. For example, women who appear competent and efficient may be faulted for "mannishness." It is also important to recognize that some research on women in policing indicates that no matter what the performance level of female officers, male counterparts generally retain negative attitudes toward them. Some male officers, as Horne points out, may be reluctant to relinquish the "macho" image commonly associated with the police officer's role. Male officers who positively perceive themselves as "macho" and as totally different from women may be too threatened by female officers to accept the latter as equals.[16] Moreover, resistance among male criminal justice workers may flow from the quite realistic perception that women present a source of competition for jobs. With men who harbor this apprehension, competent women are in a double bind; the better they perform, the more resistance they will generate. In any case, it is crucial not to be too optimistic in anticipating the effects of competence on acceptance.

Effects of women's performance on the attitudes and subsequent behaviors of both male and female colleagues is a particularly important area of research. Especially needed are longitudinal studies of the relationship between women's performance levels in a variety of traditionally male criminal justice positions and acceptance among colleagues. These studies would help by identifying the dynamic processes underlying changes in acceptance. In addition, an important area of analysis is what effect male colleagues' age and duration of association with an agency has on their ability to change attitudes concerning female peers. A good deal of anecdotal evidence from women working in criminal justice areas indicates that acceptance of capable women comes relatively easily from male colleagues who are young and new in their positions. On the other hand, acceptance of women by older men and by those long associated with an organization appears to be much more difficult.

Penetrating the "Old Boys" Network

One of the greatest difficulties identified by women entering criminal justice positions lies in socializing comfortably with male colleagues. Being invited to "have a drink with the boys," for example, often presents a dilemma to a woman: if she accepts, her "morals" may be questioned; if she refuses, she may be considered aloof. As one symposium participant described the dilemma,

> *Being a woman makes it difficult to socialize with other workers. Everyone on the entire shift goes out for a drink on payday. If I don't go, I'm not one of the guys and if I do go I'm "asking for it." So I go, have one drink, and go home. Maybe they'll buy me three drinks, line them up, and assume that because they are there, I will drink them. But I leave them on the bar and go home. For a long time it was kind of a fight over things like that; and if I didn't have any social activity with them, I was considered snotty.*

According to another participant,

> *The area of socializing . . . is a particularly difficult one. . . . You can't go out and have a drink with a colleague on the way home from work because the stories will start. Christmas parties—I steer clear of them because I don't want to be accused of having one too many drinks or of sitting too close to somebody.*

A study of interactions between female attorneys and courtroom judges has pinpointed the related problems of access and acceptance. According to one female attorney who participated in this study,

> *[O]utside the courtroom . . . the judges are more friendly with the male attorneys and their attitudes with women attorneys are more obviously male-female types of encounters. . . . [T]hey're not quite willing to accept you as just a lawyer or just someone they can come in and chat with in their chambers.* [17]

Such comments suggest that neither male nor female professionals are as yet comfortable enough to be at ease together in informal settings. Yet informal socializing with colleagues is an important and satisfying aspect of most jobs. Women in criminal justice positions often have few other female colleagues, while men have the other "old boys"; therefore, women suffer most from the awkwardness between the sexes. Aside from their intrinsic values, informal interactions with colleagues may provide important job-related information. Exclusion from these interactions places women at a distinct disadvantage, as one symposium participant observed:

> *[I]f you don't sit down and talk with your colleagues, you miss an awful lot of information: What's going on? What bills are pending in the legislature? Who's going to be the new director of something or other? If you just go about your business, you'll be the only one who doesn't know that something critical is about to happen and you'll look foolish because you ask stupid questions. It's a big dilemma.*

As these remarks indicate, professional women face another double bind. If they are careful to be circumspect in their socializing, they may cut themselves off from valuable information. According to some authors, exclusion from informal social contacts may influence professional advancement. Horne, for example, refers to a British economic planning report that found that ease of socializing, along with drinking in the right places, works against the advancement of women as police professionals. The "old boys" network, Horne concludes, "will be difficult, if not impossible, for the female to crack."[18]

Penetration of the "old boys" network may become easier as more women enter key administrative roles, positions in which they themselves have access to information. Moreover, they may be more sympathetic than male administrators to the plight of other female professionals working for them. On the other hand women assuming power positions may be tempted to take on the attributes of men and thus perpetuate "old boyism" themselves. A vivid example of this danger was provided by a female police officer who, though not part of the panel, attended the Northeastern University symposium and contributed from the floor.

> *I've seen women in law enforcement whom you don't know after a couple of years on the police force because they want to act so much like one of the guys, one of the boys. I was at a conference of women police officers a*

couple of months ago and I listened to a discussion of six female police officers talking about all the people they've beaten up because that's cool, to beat people up. That's the truth. I was shocked myself. You know, how they put the handcuffs on and whacked them because it gave them a new sense of power or because it made them really accepted by their male counterparts. It was just like listening to a bunch of guys talk after roll call or after a shift. I was listening to the same garbage, only it was coming from women.

Women entering criminal justice professions, especially at the line level, may thus be absorbed and coopted by "old boyism."

An important area of inquiry, therefore, lies in discovering ways in which women can best cope with the difficulties engendered by informal social networks. How, for example, do women attempt to overcome the double bind encountered in socializing with male colleagues? To the extent that women have penetrated "old boys" networks, what strategies have they used? Perhaps most important of all, how can women begin to develop new networks that will bypass "old boyism" and circumvent the pitfalls of cooptation?

"Woman's Work" and Job Stereotyping

According to a traditional and widespread view of the employment of women, there are certain jobs that are "women's work." The flipside of this belief is that women have gender-specific traits that suit them for certain types of jobs. In the past, as we have seen, women in criminal justice were assigned to such specialized roles as matrons in jails or supervisors for juvenile delinquents, on the theory that they had unusual ability to handle women and children. Recently, there has been some expansion of task definition in criminal justice areas to make more room for the employment of women. However, as comments by symposium participants indicated, even women who have entered traditionally male preserves are still given assignments on the basis of sex role. For example, one woman noted:

I'm not the only police officer who has noticed that while many departments are very resistant to hiring a woman in

Phyllis Jo Baunach & Nicole Hahn Rafter

the first place, once they do get one they overload her with every woman-related thing that comes along.

The participant who had worked as a guard indicated that she had been asked to do a lot of "woman's work":

. . . filing, shaking down women who looked like they might have drugs, typing, sewing buttons. I was also asked to supervise the cooking of the meals at night. But if I worked through from the 4 to 12 shift to the 12 to 8 shift, they wanted me out of the kitchen in the morning. It was, "You know how men are in the morning; they don't want to have to look at a woman," and so I would be hustled out "for my own safety." Either in the kitchen at night or out of it in the morning, I was always being typecast as a woman.

A third participant reported that when she had first gone to work in a district attorney's office, she had been brought a lot of secretarial chores. However, partially due to the supportiveness of her (male) supervisor, she was able to refuse such requests:

At first cops gave us a lot of requests for typing; they thought stereotypically and decided that women in the DA's office must be secretaries. But now that attitude is becoming a thing of the past.

These observations indicate that women in criminal justice still tend to be given tasks congruent with stereotyped beliefs about their capabilities and interests.

Not all women find sex-role stereotyping objectionable; the police officer quoted earlier was convinced that "A man has certain qualities that he brings to police work by virtue of being a man that a woman doesn't have, and vice versa." Moreover, some authors argue that specialization of services is inevitable, given rising costs and the need for greater efficiency.[19] However, if specialization occurs, the danger exists that women may be "specialized" not because of their skills, abilities, or interests, but because of their sex.

One classic argument for allocating jobs according to sex roles has been presented by Anthony Vastola in *Police Chief.* Vastola delineates a theory of "social pluralism" as the basis for specialization according to traditional gender-specific characteristics. He believes that the employment of women in functions that socially support their ascribed cultural traits (crisis intervention, traffic enforcement) would minimize the role conflict that women feel in becoming police officers. Women would not be required to behave in a manner inconsistent with the way in which they were socialized. A second argument raised by Vastola in favor of specialization along sex-role lines is that women would then compete against other women, and men against other men, for positions. The net result would be greater acceptance of women on the police force by men, fewer role conflicts for women, and the development of separate but complementary police forces for men and women.[20]

The resulting "differentiated equality" would indeed set women apart from men, but it would probably not entail the "equality in status" or power that Vastola predicts. Ever since the *Brown v. Board of Education* decision in 1954, separate has been held to be inherently unequal. Thus, although Vastola's plan would curtail female police officers' competition with men, it would also curtail their opportunities. Further, many women (together with male supporters) strenuously object to any sort of sex stereotyping, because it is based not on ability but habit, and serves to keep women in dull, poorly paid positions.

CONCLUSION: A NEW BRAND OF JUSTICE

The points raised by the symposium participants and amplified by literature on women as criminal justice professionals show that a central issue for women revolves around gaining credibility with male colleagues and consequently being placed in positions of authority. The factors that militate against their success are "preferential" treatment, the superior performance required to prove themselves adequate, a seemingly impenetrable "old boys" network, and stereotypes about the suitability of women for specific types of jobs.

In attempting to overcome these obstacles, symposium participants uniformly agreed that the demonstration of competence is one of the primary ways in which to gain acceptance. However, if women are to demonstrate competence, they must be given the opportunity to do so; otherwise there is an inherent "catch-22" in the process of employing women in criminal justice positions. From the need for this opportunity flow several implications: (1) men must not offer special favors to "protect" female colleagues, nor should women accept them; (2) performance standards must be the same for both sexes—not higher for women; (3) men must welcome women to the inner circles of information sharing and decision making; and (4) both sexes must question assumptions about what work women can and cannot do. Only if these changes occur will a new breed of female criminal justice professionals truly begin to emerge.

There is also a great need for more informal information swapping of the type that occurred during the symposium, and for more research on strategies. Women have a lot to learn from each other about ways to cope with sex-role stereotyping—how, for example, to handle such derogatory terms of address as "honey" and "dear" effectively.[21] Research is badly needed on the stress effects of sexism and the means to deal with such stress.[22] More attention also needs to be given to the development of differential strategies: if women expect to constitute, at some point in the not-too-distant future, 40 or 50 percent of an agency's personnel, then they should perhaps concentrate on strategies different from those that would be most appropriate if they anticipate remaining a small minority.[23] Additionally, women in criminal justice could profit from applying strategies developed by women who have entered other traditionally male fields and by members of racial minorities who have entered predominantly white professions.[24]

Finally, it is incumbent upon women themselves to take an active role in their assimilation and, as Karen DeCrow has urged with respect to handling men in a courtroom, "to educate these men to a brand of justice and equality which includes women."[25]

NOTES

FOR THEIR HELP in generating this material, we wish to thank Irene Carpenter, Barbara di Natale, Rosemary Kelley, Marjorie E. Brown, and Darlene Therrien. We also thank Dean Robert Croatti of the College of Criminal Justice, Northeastern University; who made possible the transcription of the tape; Nicolette Parisi of Temple University, who commented extensively on an earlier draft; and Jean Magnotto and Kathy Sullivan for their efficient and thoughtful typing services. The views presented in this chapter are those of the authors and do not necessarily reflect the opinions of the National Institute of Justice or the U.S. Department of Justice.

1. *Phoenix Gazette*, 2 October 1978, p. A-1; *Boston Herald American*, 13 May 1979, p. B-1. The thesis that female offenders are penetrating previously all-male pre-

Sex-Role Operations

serves is set forth in Freda Adler, *Sisters in Crime: The Rise of the New Female Criminal* (New York: McGraw-Hill, 1975), and is critiqued by (among others) Joseph G. Weis in "Liberation and Crime: The Invention of the New Female Criminal," *Crime and Social Justice* 6(Fall/Winter 1976):17-27.

2. *See*, for example, Chloe Owings, *Women Police: A Study of the Development and Status of the Women Police Movement* (New York: Frederick H. Hitchcock, 1925); and Mary E. Hamilton, *The Policewoman: Her Service and Ideals* (New York: Frederick A. Stokes, 1924). Hamilton summarizes her view with these words: "In many ways the position of a women [sic] in a police department is not unlike that of a mother in a home" (p. 4).

3. Estelle B. Freedman, "Their Sisters' Keepers: An Historical Perspective on Female Correctional Institutions in the United States: 1870-1900," *Feminist Studies* 2, 1 (1974):77-95.

4. Beverly Blair Cook, "Women Judges: The End of Tokenism," in *Women in the Courts*, ed. Winifred L. Hepperle and Laura Crites (Williamsburg, VA: National Center for State Courts, 1978), pp. 84-105, esp. 100-101.

5. Timothy J. Flanagan, Michael J. Hindelang, and Michael R. Gottfredson, eds., *Sourcebook of Criminal Justice Statistics—1979* (Washington, DC: U.S. Government Printing Office, 1980), p. 52 (table based on 1977 data).

6. National Institute of Law Enforcement and Criminal Justice, LEAA, *The National Manpower Survey of the Criminal Justice System*, vol. III: *Corrections* (Washington, DC: U.S. Government Printing Office, 1978), p.53. Using 1974 data, Table IV-8 shows that 24.9 percent of "professionals" in correctional agencies were women in that year.

7. Ibid. According to Table IV-8, in 1974 only 11.8 percent of "officials/administrators" in correctional agencies were women, and according to Table IV-9, on the same page, in 1975 more of these women worked in juvenile corrections than in other types of correctional agencies. For a useful discussion of policy issues and legal problems connected with the development of sexually integrated guard forces, *see* James B. Jacobs, "The Sexual Integration of the Prison's Guard Force: A Few Comments on *Dothard v. Rawlinson*," *Toledo Law Review* 10, 2(Winter 1979):389-418.

8. According to Flanagan et al. (*Sourcebook 1979*, p. 52), when police employees are broken down into the categories of sworn officers and other police employees, women constitute 58.3 percent of the latter category, but only 2.7 percent of the former. According to the National Institute of Law Enforcement and Criminal Justice *Manpower Survey* (vol. III, p. 53, Table IV-8), of all women employed in correctional agencies in 1974, 41.6 percent were clerical workers.

9. Nor are these problems mutually exclusive. For the purposes of analysis they are dealt with separately, though of course they often do overlap.

10. Sophie Pfeiffer, "Women Lawyers in Rhode Island," *American Bar Association Journal* 61 (June 1975):743; Myrna Oliver, "The Female in the Trial Court," in *Women in the Courts*, p. 19; James Gilsinan, Lynn Obernyer, and Christine Gilsinan, "Women Attorneys and the Judiciary," *Denver Law Journal* 3, 4 (1975):901.

11. Gilsinan et al., "Women Attorneys and the Judiciary," p. 899.

12. Peter Horne, *Women in Law Enforcement* (Springfield, IL: Charles C. Thomas, 1980), p. 204

13. Shanna Kent, "The Female Lawyer," *Criminal Defense* 3 (May 1976):7.

14. Horne, *Women in Law Enforcement*, p. 122.

15. Ibid., p. 210.

16. Ibid., pp. 70-77.

17. Gilsinan et al., "Women Attorneys and the Judiciary," p. 899.

18. Horne, *Women in Law Enforcement*, p. 119.

19. Peter Horne, "Policewomen: 2,000 A.D." (Paper presented at the annual training seminar of the International Meeting of the Association of Women Police, St. Paul, Minnesota, 13 October 1978), pp. 13-18.

20. Anthony Vastola, "Women in Policing: An Alternative Ideology," *The Police Chief* 44, 1 (January 1977):62-69.

21. Airline stewardesses could prove to be a rich source of information along these lines. One of the authors of this chapter recently observed a stewardess deftly correct a passenger who was attempting to carry an overly large piece of luggage onto an airplane. "Aw, honey, it won't take up much room," argued the passenger, to which she replied: "It is too big and must be checked, *dear*."

22. The stress engendered by sex-role stereotyping was the focus of a conference held by the Massachusetts Association of Women Police in February 1981. Among other sources of such stress, the conference identified the alienation from other women, from husbands, and from parents that stemmed from entry into a "masculine" profession. Participants pinpointed paternalism as another primary source of stress. According to one officer, "I would rather have a sock in the stomach than the stress caused by the men trying to protect the women." See "They Talk about Stress in Their Job," *Boston Globe*, 22 February 1981, p. 23.

23. This astute observation by Diane Pike of Yale was passed on to us by Nicolette Parisi of Temple University.

24. Also useful are general analyses of sexism in the workplace. *See*, for example, Rosabeth Moss Kanter, *Men and Women of the Corporation* (New York: Basic Books, 1977).

25. Karen DeCrow, *Sexist Justice* (New York: Random House, 1974), p. 7.

16
Women in the Criminal Justice Professions

An Analysis of Status Conflict

NANCI KOSER WILSON

Nancy Drew, Miss Marple, and Charlie's Angels notwithstanding, the popular imagination still conceives of "crime fighters" as men. For women, the professional field of criminal justice remains one of the most difficult to enter. Whether as attorney, police officer, prison guard, or even researcher or teacher, the female criminal justice worker faces more barriers than does a woman entering any other previously male domain.[1] Why should this be so?

This chapter suggests that the problem women face entering criminal justice is one of status conflict: the "ideal" or stereotyped attributes for the status of "woman" and for the status of "criminal justice professional" are contradictory. In the following discussion, I use the term *status* to refer to "social position" and reserve the term *role* to describe behavior expected of an individual occupying a given status. Further distinctions are made between

Nanci Koser Wilson

ascribed status (one into which the individual is born or into which she/he matures) and *achieved status* (one that depends upon characteristics over which the individual exercises some control).

The two statuses analyzed here represent an *ascribed status*, sex, and an *achieved status*, occupation. Accompanying the ascribed status of sex is gender, which consists of culturally defined personality characteristics and attributes associated with an individual's expected behavior, or *role*, in a given sexual status.

Theoretically, in American culture achieved statuses are just that—those that can be attained by acquisition of certain skills, knowledge, or education; that is, they can be achieved by anyone. In spite of this egalitarian ethos, however, certain achieved statuses are sex-specific, *inherently linked* to an ascribed status. Only men or only women are allowed to occupy these statuses. In the case of occupations, this sexual specificity has resulted in an occupational segregation, with some jobs being defined as exclusively "male" and others "female." Legislation such as that creating the Equal Employment Opportunity Commission was fashioned with the aim of abolishing such segregation. To some extent, success in this enterprise has been achieved, but resistance to women is a hardy perennial; it continues to bloom year after year. The current problem is that many occupations, especially the criminal justice professions, are also gender-specific; that is, they are *circumstantially linked* to an ascribed status (in this case, sex) because it is assumed that only those individuals with certain gender-linked personal characteristics can perform these jobs.

The link between masculinity and criminal justice is so tightly bound that we may say it is true not merely that only men can be crime fighters, but even that to be a crime fighter means to be a man. Such a close connection between gender and occupation occurs in few other professions. It has recently been observed that "Today the ultimate in masculinity is the brutal cop whose work is the protection of a social order that is falling apart."[2] In criminal justice, occupational status affirms sexual status. Doubt concerning an individual's manhood may be erased simply with the information that he is a cop or prison official. Conversely, of course, women who cross gender stereotypes and enter such "masculine" fields are often considered unfeminine.

Just what are these occupational and gender stereotypes that color the expected roles of those who occupy the statuses of "woman" and of "criminal justice professional"? In what follows I shall describe these characteristics and note the fundamental way in which they conflict with one another, creating the most difficult problem women face as criminal justice professionals.

SEXUAL STATUS AND GENDER DIFFERENCES

Both sex (physiological characteristics) and gender (psychological and cultural characteristics) are occupationally relevant to the field of criminal justice. Sex continues to be relevant because in criminal justice physical strength is thought to be necessary for adequate job performance. Male status has been held to be a bona fide occupational qualification in recent affirmative action decisions.[3]

Although there is notable disagreement in the current scientific literature with regard to possible physiological differences between men and women, there seems to be general agreement that because of superior size, men are often stronger than women. Whether men or women of comparable size, physical training, and socialization are equally strong is debatable. Similarly, whereas there is consensus on the basic physiology of pregnancy and menstruation, there is little agreement on physiological and psychological consequences of woman's reproductive capacity. There is even less research that relates to physiologically based emotional cycles in men. Thus, the most that can be said at present is that many men are stronger than most women.[4]

The lack of evidence in regard to physiological differences between the sexes has not prevented most persons from assuming their existence. Cultural stereotypes continue to assume crucial differences in potential job performance based on purported degrees of strength, agility, and muscular development. These supposed differences are especially cogent in such occupations as police work that are thought to require physical force as a sine qua non.

In regard to gender, a host of characteristics are differentially attributed to men and women. There is disagreement in the literature as to the source of these differences; as to whether they stem from physiology or from differential socialization, treatment, and self-concept; and even as to whether they are either inborn or social constructs. Yet there is general agreement that gender differences do exist. Table 16-1 summarizes some commonly attributed gender differences.[5]

TABLE 16-1
Commonly Attributed Gender Differences

Category of Attribute	Male Characteristics	Female Characteristics
Degree of Activity	Active	Passive
	Self-reliant	Dependent
	Self-sufficient	Ineffectual
	Aggressive	Submissive
Social Relationships	Ego-centered	Other-centered
	Competitive	Cooperative
	Dominant	Compliant
	Assertive	Deferential
	Strong	Vulnerable
	Tough	Sensitive
Personal Style	Analytical	Empathetic
	Cool	Emotional
	Straightforward	Manipulative
	Critical	Compassionate

These differences suggest that the "male personality" is *active* (self-reliant, self-sufficient, aggressive) while the "female personality" is *passive* (dependent, ineffectual, submissive). They suggest that the male in social relationships is *ego-centered* (competitive, dominant, assertive) while the female is *other-centered* (cooperative, compliant, deferential). Whereas the male is analytical, cool, and straightforward in his personal style, the female is empathic, emotional, and manipulative.

These traits are differentially salient in opposite- and same-sex interactions. The male ego-centered traits of competitiveness and dominance mean that in opposite-sex interactions, males may feel the need to be dominant and females to be deferential. In same-sex interactions, however, it may well be that few of these "sex-linked" traits are evident. When men interact solely with other men or women with other women, aggressiveness, dominance, and empathy may be randomly distributed among the participants. While men may jockey among each other for dominance, so may women. Different degrees of aggressiveness may be observed within each sex, with some men acting much less aggressively than others. But the culture teaches us that men should *always* be dominant in relationships with women; therefore, when a male and female interact, even a usually submissive man may assert dominance and a usually assertive woman may become deferential.

Further, because these popularly attributed gender differences are more evident in opposite-sex interaction, women have a much more difficult time expressing such "male" traits as assertiveness or self-sufficiency when working in a sexually integrated environment. Concomitantly, men may suppress such traits as sensitivity, empathy, and compliance when they are working with women, although such behavior might otherwise be perfectly appropriate. Many of the difficulties that occur when a work environment is newly integrated arise from this suppression of normally appropriate traits in the interest of maintaining traditional gender distinctions.

OCCUPATIONAL STATUS

In addition to formal requisites and qualifications, certain occupations require a cluster of desired attributes in the potential employee. These informal desiderata are important because although they are difficult to measure, employers frequently see them as more crucial than formal criteria. Thus it is often said that a job requires employees with "good common sense" or the ability to "carry themselves appropriately." Police officers are thought to require "street sense," and correctional officers need to be "con-wise."

Women are at a disadvantage from the start in many professions because traditionally their sex status and occupational status are coextensive. The well-worn phrase "a woman's place is in the home" does not imply that a woman should not work, but that her work should be homemaking. In the minds of many, woman equals housewife equals mother. A number of assumptions underlie this equation, including the following: (1) homemaking is a full-time job; (2) women have the skills most appropriate to this job; (3) no family can operate effectively without a full-time homemaker; and (4) no woman is fulfilled unless she is a housewife/mother.

Thus, quite apart from the conflicts between occupational and sex statuses, which will be discussed below, there is a basic underlying conflict. Because the traditionally prescribed occupation for woman is housewife/mother, a woman who also works outside the home may be seen as merely a moonlighter. It is assumed that she is giving short shrift to one or the other of her full-time occupations. This issue is especially critical for the professions, in which it is assumed that workers give much of their time and an investment of personality to the job. The woman who is not a housewife/mother, but "only" a professional worker, is often considered (though perhaps not explicitly) to have personality problems and/or to be unfulfilled.

VARIATIONS IN STATUS CONFLICT

As noted above, each occupation carries with it a cluster of stereotypes or personal traits thought to be crucial to job performance. Within criminal justice, what are these traits and to what extent do gender traits conflict with occupational traits? In what follows, I will argue that the degree of conflict between occupational and sex status is a function of three variables within a given agency: (1) the organizational orientation or model; (2) the occupational subculture; and (3) the presence of occupational sub-statuses or job specialties.

Organizational Orientation

The various organizational models in the criminal justice system may be arranged along a broad continuum ranging from control to service. In general terms, the *control model* assumes that we are fighting a crime war against alien and vicious elements who must be suppressed or controlled for the safety of the rest of us.[6] The *service model* assumes that those in the criminal justice system provide services to clients who are unfortunate, misguided, undersocialized, disadvantaged, or otherwise in need of help.[7]

Relevant personal characteristics for individuals who operate within the crime control model are aggression, dominance, and strength—those commonly attributed to males. Relevant personal characteristics for the service model are cooperation, sensitivity, compassion, and empathy—those commonly attributed to women. The crime control model is seen as a hard-line approach and the service model as a soft-line approach. This neatly coalesces with the stereotypes of men as hard and women as soft.

TABLE 16-2
Organizational Models in Criminal Justice

Component	Competing Models	Characteristics of Agency's Work	Nomenclature of Participants
CJS: General	Control vs.	War on crime	Crime fighter
	Service	Service delivery	Public servant
Police	Crime control vs.	Danger, authority	Law enforcement officer
	Service	Community service and support Aid to citizenry	Peace officer
Courts	Adversarial vs.	Trial	Adversary
	Collaborative	Plea bargaining	Colleague
Corrections	Custody or punishment vs.	Security	Guard
	Rehabilitation	Therapy Vocational training Social work	Correctional officer

The competing models take on slightly different meanings within the context of each component—police, courts, corrections—of the criminal justice system. A police agency may orient itself toward the crime control model or the service model. In corrections, either the custody/punishment or the rehabilitation model may prevail. And in the court system, either the adversarial or the collaborative model is possible. These variations are displayed in Table 16-2. They indicate that even if crime itself is regarded as a male activity, the criminal justice worker may be conceived as either a hardcore crime fighter in a war against a vicious, dangerous enemy, or as a provider of services to underprivileged, disadvantaged victims of our social system.

Occupational Subculture

A second factor affecting the degree of conflict between occupational and sexual status is the occupational subculture within a particular agency. Sociologists generally agree that there is no single homogeneous culture in the United States; instead, there exists a

Nanci Koser Wilson

variety of subcultures, each with distinctive values, norms, perspectives, and lifestyles. Subcultures that derive from the working environment are thought to become increasingly important to a person's identity as other major institutions—religion, the family— weaken. Occupational environments that provide a total context for everyday life (such as a military base) or that require special lifestyles that isolate members from the rest of the community (such as a monastery) are most likely to develop subcultures.[8]

The subcultures that develop within criminal justice agencies are clearly male oriented. Lamber and Streib note that criminal justice agencies generally are "bastions of classical male chauvinism which operate in a variety of unspoken ways to effectively exclude women."[9] There are two ways in which subcultures that emerge in these agencies may foster antifemale attitudes. The first and more common way is through the notion that traditionally male characteristics—force, physical strength, toughness—are essential to the job. Police subcultures, as we shall see, frequently encourage such notions. Second, a subculture may arise that does not emphasize traditional male values or stereotyped traits but that is, nonetheless, an "all-male clubhouse." In such work environments, participants often value the exclusivity of totally male companionship as a desirable goal in itself.

Each of the three components of the criminal justice system produces its own distinctive occupational subculture with, of course, some variation in intensity and content from one particular agency to another. In other words, while the police subculture is identifiable across various police departments and differs substantially from that present in the court system or in corrections, there are also variations from one police department to another.

Police. The subculture to which police work gives rise has consistently been described in terms that stress its masculine orientation. Both Bittner and Rubinstein have emphasized physical strength as a characteristic of the police officer's role that helps to shape the nature of the police subculture. This is true even though the ordinary occupational routines of police work normally do not involve force; in fact, as Bittner observes,

> [T]he actual use of physical coercion and restraint is rare
> for all policemen. . . . What matters is that police proce-
> dure is defined by the feature that it may not be opposed
> in its course.[10]

Thus, police intervention means, above all, making use of the capacity and authority to overpower resistance. Similarly, Rubinstein argues:

> *The policeman's principal tool is his body. . . . For him a gun and a nightstick are not simply weapons . . . but extensions of himself whose use (and non-use) is linked to his notions about how he uses his body to do his work. . . . The moment he accepts the responsibility of being a policeman he assumes the risks of physical combat. . . . The essence of physical training is street fighting, and this . . . depends almost entirely on a person's willingness to hit and be hit.*[11]

This emphasis on physical prowess within the police subculture puts potential female recruits at a disadvantage. Some police forces that have recently recruited women have required that they prove their physical skills in competition with male officers. In Columbus, Ohio, for example, male and female cadets have been required to engage in boxing matches during training. The rationale for the fights echoes Rubinstein's theme: "We want to show the cadets they can get hit and survive." The negative reaction to this competition by the male officers redounds to the disadvantage of the women. One male combatant reported that "it was embarrassing and humiliating. I hit her a little to let her know what it feels like."[12] While this uneasiness at the prospect of physical combat with a female fellow officer, or with reliance upon her as a partner in physical confrontation with felons, is perhaps inevitable at the outset of sexual integration, it may become less stressful with custom. The point here is that the excessive emphasis on physical force as an element of police work is a major disadvantage to women. In spite of its actually minor role in police work, physical prowess becomes a central focus, thereby feeding into a markedly masculine subculture.

In his classic analysis of police work, Skolnick notes that, along with physical prowess, the twin elements of danger and authority also create a high degree of occupational solidarity. He argues that "The element of danger demands that the policeman be able to carry out efforts that are in their nature overtly masculine."[13] Physical fitness, agility, and toughness (characteristics that Skolnick sees as necessitated by the inherent danger of police work) patently are not limited to the male sex; however, it is important that they are *thought* to be so limited.

Gray describes police work as having "a subculture whose members share an acute sense of masculine identity, especially in a lack of squeamishness . . . , a willingness to accept personal risk, plus a high value on the exercise of authority, secrecy, and group solidarity." The subculture "encourages its participants to view the world as a hostile and potentially violent place." This sense of "masculine" identity is so important within the police subculture that it "becomes the cutting edge of selection when an applicant reaches the point of an oral interview." Gray specifically notes:

> *Women in their presentation of self are hard-pressed to overcome the impact of their physical makeup, regardless of their capacity to do the job. In short, women would, if hired for patrol, potentially undercut the basis of male solidarity.*[14]

Again, there is no evidence that lack of squeamishness and a willingness to accept risk are exclusively male traits or are central or exclusive to police work. The crucial point is that these traits are *thought* to belong solely to the male sex and to be definitive of police officers.

The Courts. Similar male-oriented subcultures arise within the judicial component of the criminal justice system. The valued characteristics of courtroom personnel do not seem, at first glance, to be necessarily masculine; cooperativeness and persuasiveness are emphasized. Skolnick suggests that court professionals "see greater advantage in cooperativeness than in conflict." He also cites administrative efficiency and a public relations orientation as desirable attributes. The courts, he notes, constitute a "system of decision making that is predominantly pre-trial in character."[15] This factor implies that the emphasis is less on the adversarial character of trial proceedings and more on good-faith bargaining out of court. Friedman, too, observes that "the center of gravity of law has moved from the courtroom to the office," where the lawyer's job is to "persuade, . . . to strike a good bargain."[16] Finally, Blumberg sees the practice of law as a "confidence game" in which lawyers serve as "agent mediators" and in which stage management and the manipulation of the client are extremely important.[17]

Women in the Criminal Justice Professions

The subculture that these job imperatives produce is not "necessarily masculine" in the same sense that the emphasis on force produces a masculine subculture in police work. Yet researchers have demonstrated that there exists a general belief that "women are not tough enough or analytical enough to be successful as attorneys."[18] Gilsinan, Obernyer, and Gilsinan report that judges, when faced with female attorneys, can "turn the situation into male–female types of encounters. . . . They're not quite willing to accept you as just . . . a lawyer."[19] The same researchers also suggest that the task of being accepted in such informal work settings as judges' chambers is more difficult for women "because there is an atmosphere of male camaraderie that is threatened by female intrusion."[20]

In sum, the nature of court work does not lend itself as readily to a masculine subculture as does police work; it lacks the emphasis on physical strength and brute force. However, the sense of an "all-male club" persists in court work and is difficult for female professionals to overcome.

Corrections. Within the corrections component of the criminal justice system, the major emphasis rests with the institution's requirements for security. Fogel emphasizes that guards are strictly controlled by a military style of work, regulation uniforms, and the mandate to follow orders unquestioningly. They have frequent off-duty contact and appear to develop a social subculture based on their work life.[21] The military model of correctional work lends itself to a masculine type of subculture. Further, the stereotype of the typical correctional administrator is also a masculine one; he is described as "tough-talking, cigar-smoking, hard-hitting."[22] Even the probation officer must be "aggressive, have strength, and be willing to take risks."[23] Hartinger, Eldefonson, and Coffey describe traits that may disqualify a person as a correctional officer in California; one of these is "homosexual or effeminate habits."[24]

THE OCCUPATIONAL SUBCULTURES that arise within each of the three major components of the criminal justice system are, if not overtly antifemale in values and attitudes, at least distinctly male oriented. However, each agency possesses its own distinctive version of the occupational subculture, and hence the extent to which a *particular* agency—a particular police department, municipal court, or prison —will be an unfavorable work environment for women is an empirical question.

Nanci Koser Wilson

Occupational Specialties

A third variable likely to affect the degree of conflict between occupational and sexual statuses is the presence of a variety of occupational "sub-statuses" or specialties within an organization. To the extent that an agency is large enough to be bureaucratically organized, it is likely to develop such specialties. For example, in a police agency, such specialties include homicide, vice, and juvenile "details"; in correctional agencies, specialized roles include officers, administrators, counselors, and educators. The proliferation of specialties opens the door for certain of these occupational sub-statuses to be defined as "women's" or "men's" jobs.

Because women generally are an anomaly in criminal justice fields, the tendency has been to admit them as *women*, not as professionals per se. They tend to be employed in three kinds of capacities: (1) handling female clients (victims, legal clients, and prisoners); (2) performing administrative tasks traditionally handled by women in other occupational areas (for example, secretarial work); and (3) performing tasks considered suitable to their "unique" qualifications as women. For example, in all-male maximum security prisons women are considered to be uniquely qualified to work as tower guards because of their supposed tolerance for boring, "detail" work, and to be qualified as secretaries or clerks because "a pretty face" may encourage male inmates to act in a socially approved manner.

In agencies that organize work along hierarchical lines so that career development demands movement "up through the ranks," women are at a disadvantage; they tend to be employed as supplementary professional staff rather than in line positions. Such staff as teachers, researchers, or planners often are completely outside the lines of authority and advancement, and are thus effectively excluded from normal promotional ladders.

Some of the clearest examples of occupational gender stereotyping come from police work, where separate job lines, pay scales, and promotion lines have traditionally been the lot of the female police officer.[25] The tendency to give them cases involving only female clients often limits them to dealing with female complainants and questioning rape victims; the "women's traditional work" line of reasoning relegates many to secretarial and clerical work. The "special skills" argument limits their work to juvenile and domestic cases; community relations; and aid to the sick, aged, lost, and stranded.

Women in the Criminal Justice Professions

Female lawyers who specialize in criminal law are rare, but specialized functions for women in this area do exist. For example, female prosecutors are seen as appropriate for "cases involving crimes against women, particularly rape."[26]

The development of "women only" jobs—job segregation—serves a special function: it allows alleviation of conflict between gender and occupational statuses because men and women are not directly competing with each other. Further, since women often do not interact directly with male colleagues under such circumstances, the pressure of an antifemale subculture may not be as difficult for them on a daily basis.

Is occupational specialization based on sex a useful strategy for women who wish to be employed in the criminal justice professions? Many women desire traditional female jobs within male-dominated fields. Further, it has been noted that insistence on the hiring of women in all job categories may reinforce resistance to women in any role.[27] And the notion of creating special "women only" jobs within the field is appealing to some female workers as an interim measure. However, this strategy is likely to produce only short-term gains; long-term losses include continued discrimination, in which the double standard is reinforced and made justifiable.

I argued earlier that women are more likely to be accepted in a job category if it is seen as having essentially a service rather than a crime control function. Yet female officers who have taken advantage of the fact that a service model uniquely "fits" certain specialized police jobs have found that in terms of advancement, the crime control model prevails, with advancement dependent upon patrol functions and arrests. Therefore, although female officers assigned to juvenile work may do an important job, they find it ridiculed as the "diaper detail"; as such, it does not help them to advance to the higher ranks.[28] Sexual job specialization appears to be a dangerous compromise that is counterproductive in the long run. Certainly women should be encouraged to make use of gender-specific skills they already possess, adapting them to such new assignments as defusing disputes. But they should not allow their jobs to be defined *solely* in terms of such skills.

CONCLUSION

The barrier facing women who wish to enter the criminal justice professions goes beyond the simple exclusion of "the fair sex" encountered in many other occupations. The lack of equal opportunity in criminal justice is a severe problem, one less amenable to legislative reform and more resistant to change than it is in many other occupations because it cuts to the core of important gender stereotypes. Cultural stereotypes defining what it means to be a man are deeply embedded in images of what it means to be a crime fighter. On an analytical level, the problem of women's entry into criminal justice can be seen in terms of a status conflict between the two statuses of "woman" and "criminal justice professional." Traditionally ideal attributes for these two statuses simply do not match. Until we can substantially alter the cultural stereotypes that insist that crime fighting is man's work and homemaking is woman's, the severity of these problems will not lessen.

The degree of conflict between the two statuses does vary, however. If an agency follows an organizational model of *service* rather than *crime control*, women are likely to be less disadvantaged. If the occupational subculture within an agency is male-oriented only in the sense of the exclusivity of an all-male club (rather than being fashioned from such occupational imperatives as physical force), women will find themselves more accepted by their coworkers. And finally, if occupational specialties labeled as "men only" or "women only" jobs are allowed to develop within an agency, women will have achieved a short-run gain at the expense of long-term loss.

Future research should be directed toward: measuring the relative importance of the three variables suggested as crucial; discovering the extent to which resistance to women may be changing as integration is achieved; and describing the personal adjustments that individual female pioneers in criminal justice are forced to make. Such research would inform us in regard to the progress of women and the effects of status incongruity. Perhaps most important, it would provide guidance for those whose hope is the ultimate sexual integration of all fields of work.

NOTES

1. With the possible exception of the military. The use of force and its accompanying personality stereotype—aggressiveness—marks police work and the military

Women in the Criminal Justice Professions

as inherently masculine to an extent that is not present even in such heavily male fields as construction work, fire fighting, and coal mining.

2. In a review of books on male sexuality: Judith Adler Hennessee, "What Do Men Really Want?" *Psychology Today* 11, 9 (February 1978):113-118.

3. *See Chapter 14* for a summary of these cases.

4. Shirley Weitz, "The Biological Maintenance System," in *Sex Roles: Biological, Psychological and Social Foundations* (New York: Oxford University Press, 1977).

5. Helen S. Astin, Allison Parelman, and Anne Fisher, *Sex Roles: A Research Bibliography* (Rockville, MD: National Institute of Mental Health, 1975).

6. Herbert L. Packer, *The Limits of the Criminal Sanction* (Stanford: Stanford University Press, 1968); Donald Cressey, *Theft of the Nation* (New York: Harper and Row, 1969).

7. E. Eugene Miller and M. Robert Montilla, *Corrections in the Community* (Reston, VA: Reston Books, 1977).

8. Leonard Broom and Philip Selznick, *Principles of Sociology* (New York: Harper and Row, 1970).

9. J. S. Lamber and V. L. Streib, "Woman Executives, Managers, and Professionals in the Indiana Criminal Justice System," *Indiana Law Review* 8 (1974):353.

10. Egon Bittner, *The Functions of the Police in Modern Society* (Rockville, MD: National Institute of Mental Health, 1970), p. 41.

11. Jonathan Rubinstein, *City Police* (New York: Farrar, Straus and Giroux, 1973); cited in *Police in America*, ed. Jerome Skolnick and Thomas Gray (Boston: Little, Brown, 1975), p. 48.

12. *Mount Vernon* (Ohio) *News*, 20 January 1978.

13. Jerome H. Skolnick, "Why Police Behave the Way They Do," in *Police in America*, pp. 31-37.

14. Thomas Gray, "Selecting for a Police Subculture," in *Police in America*, p. 48.

15. Jerome Skolnick, "Social Control in the Adversary System," *Journal of Conflict Resolution* 11 (1967):52.

16. Lawrence M. Friedman, *Law and Society* (Englewood Cliffs, NJ: Prentice-Hall, 1977), pp. 25-26.

17. Abraham S. Blumberg, "The Practice of Law As Confidence Game," *Law and Society Review* 1 (June 1967):15-39; Abraham S. Blumberg, *Criminal Justice* (Chicago: Quadrangle Books, 1967).

18. Lamber and Streib, "Woman Executives," p. 307.

19. J. F. Gilsinan, Lynn Obernyer, and Christine Gilsinan, "Woman Attorneys and the Judiciary," *Denver Law Journal* 52 (1975):899.

20. Ibid., pp. 902-903.

21. David Fogel, *We Are the Living Proof* (Carbondale, IL: Center for the Study of Crime, Delinquency and Corrections, 1975), p. 25.

22. Larry Bennett, personal communication, 1977. Dr. Bennett, currently Director of Program Evaluation for the National Institute of Justice, has had lengthy correctional experience as Director of Research for the California Department of Corrections.

23. Walter Hartinger, Edward Eldefonson, and Alan Coffey, *Corrections* (Santa Monica, CA: Goodyear, 1973), pp. 125-126.

24. Ibid., p. 139.

25. Theresa M. Melchionne, "The Changing Role of Policewoman," *The Police Journal* 47 (1974):340–358.

26. Lamber and Streib, "Woman Executives," p. 320.

27. Joseph S. Coughlin, personal communication, 1979. Professor Coughlin, currently with the Center for the Study of Crime, Delinquency, and Corrections, Southern Illinois University, is a correctional administrator with over thirty years of experience.

28. Melchionne, "The Changing Role."

Index

Index

Index

Index

Index

Prisoners, male, privacy rights of, 328–330, 334

Prisoners, women as: gender stereotyping and, 11–13, 243–244, 246, 254, 256, 266–267; data on differential periods of incarceration of, 214; medical profession and, generally, 261–262, 269–271; general medical needs of, 263–264; emotional problems of, 264; use of drugs on, 264–265; general treatment of, 265–266; gender-based discrimination and, 266–267; race-based discrimination and, 267; class-based discrimination and, 276–268; legal status of, 268; as patient, social role of, 268–269. *See also* Defendants, women as; Federal Industrial Institution for Women in Alderson, W.V.; New York State Prison for Women at Auburn; Offenders, women as; Parole; Probation; Sentencing procedures

Prisoners' Rights Project, Legal Aid Society (New York City), 270–271

Prison employees, women as. *See* Corrections, women in

Prisons, women's: training programs in, 12–13; studies of murderers in, 158; custodial and reformatory, early, 237–238, 278, 298–299; health care in, 261–273; male employees in, 324–325. *See also* Federal Industrial Institution for Women in Alderson, W.V.; New York State Prison for Women at Auburn; Offenders, women as; Prisoners, women as

Probation: preferential treatment of women on, 207, 211; punitive treatment of women on, 209; of juveniles, 226, 232

Probation officers: juvenile, 65; characteristics of, 369

Professionals, criminal justice, women as: gender stereotyping and, 7–8, 13–14, 306, 309, 315–318, 332–335, 341, 342, 353–355, 356, 359–361, 372; and employment differentials, generally, 305–306; remedies for discrimination against, 307–312, 318, percentages of, 311; historical perspective of discrimination against, 342–344; "preferential" treatment of, 344–347; superior performance and, 348–350; "old boys" networks and, 350–353; occupational stereotypes and, 359–361; and sexual status and gender differences, generally,

Professionals (cont'd)
361–363; occupational status and, 363–364; and conflict between occupational status and sexual status, 364–371. *See also specific occupations*

Project on Legal and Ethical Issues in the Delivery of Health Care within Detention and Correctional Institutions, 270

Prosecutor Information System (PROMIS), 112, 117, 118, 119, 213

Prosecutors: questioning of rape victims by, 9; chivalrous treatment of women by, 12, 173, 207–208; treatment of rape victims by, 52, 53; responsibilities of, generally, 63–64; organizational context of decision making by, 64–66; early case screening by, 66–67, 70–78, 206; and domestic violence, 88; preferential treatment of female defendants by, 207–208; juveniles and, 231; female, 354, 371. *See also* Victims, women as; Witnesses, women as

Prostitutes, 116, 131–132, 200; images of, 3, 143–144, 148–149; as witnesses, credibility of, 71–72; reasons for and modes of becoming, 132–137, 141–142; work patterns of, 137–142; status stratification of, 142–146; self-images of, 147–148, 149; sentences for, 213

Quarterly Cumulated Index Medicus, 31

Race: discrimination based on, 99, 206, 267; and victim–offender relationship, 119, 167–170; and status stratification of prostitutes, 142–143; as predictor of homicide victimization, 152, 165–166

Rape: victim-precipitated, theory of, 4–5, 9, 29–30; complaints, male responses to, 9; medical literature on, 30–53; and stereotype of women as liars, 30, 33–37, 38, 41–42, 44, 46, 47, 48, 52; of children, 37–42, 48–49; common law of, 42–43, 49; and force and absence of consent, 44–46, 49, 50–51, 73; and attitudes since 1960, 46–48, 52–53; crisis and response units, 48, 51; and relationship of victim and offender, 69, 73–74; in marriage, 96, 98. *See also*

Index